THE HIDDEN

PLACES OF

SCOTLAND

CONTENTS

1.	The Borders	1
2.	Dumfries and Galloway	57
3.	Ayr, Arran and Bute	99
4.	Glasgow and Lanarkshire	133
5.	Edinburgh and the Lothians	157
6.	Kingdom of Fife	199
7.	Central Region	237
8.	Tayside	269
9.	The Grampians	305
10.	Highlands and Islands	341
11.	Argyll	391
	Tourist Information Centres	436
	Town Index	439

CHAPTER ONE

The Borders.

Hermitage Castle

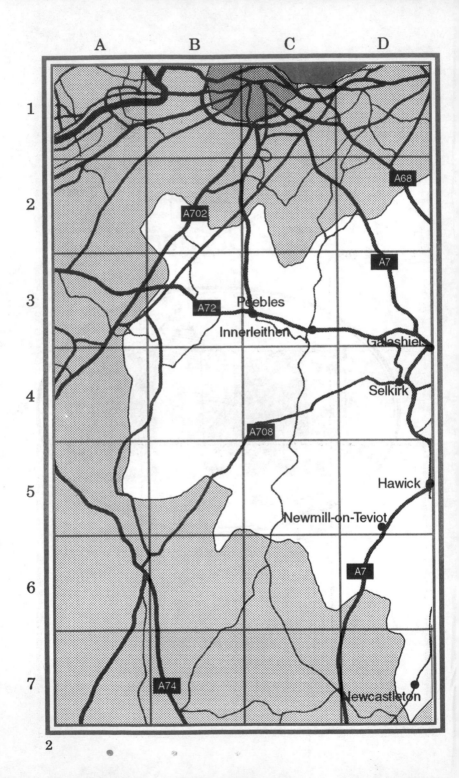

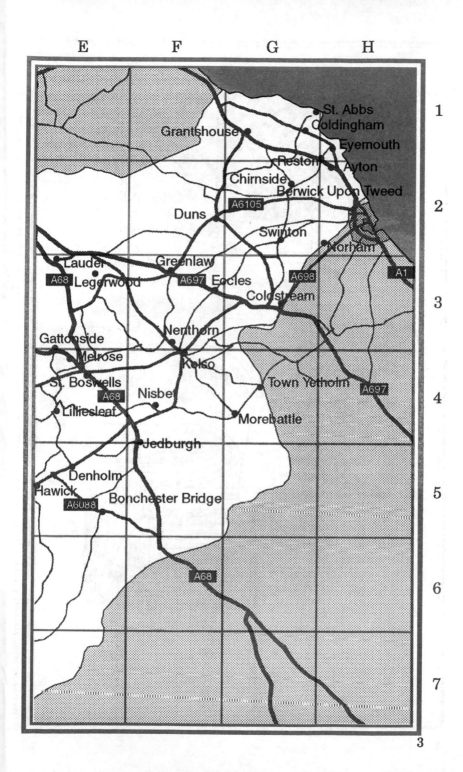

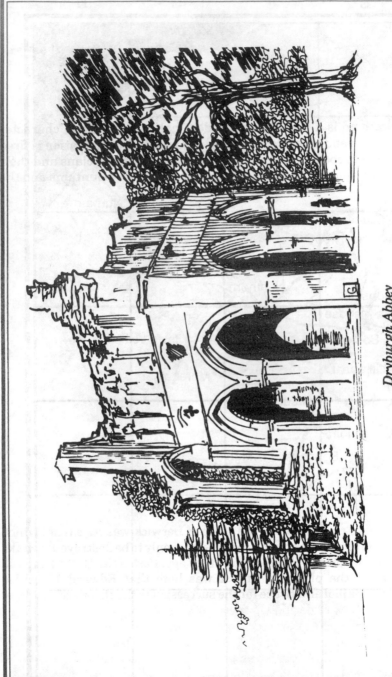

Dryburgh Abbey

CHAPTER ONE

The Borders.

Scotland is a fiercely independent nation, majestic in character with a rich and often bloody history. The visitor's imagination is fired by tales of rebellion and struggle, heroic legends, the clans and their castles, remote islands and strange tongues, high mountains and the taste of fiery malt spirit.

It's a pleasure to have a chance to travel in this beautiful land abundant with hidden places.

Our journey through Scotland begins in the Borders, with its noble heritage and often turbulent past, alive today with the names of the people and places that have played a vital role in the shaping of this proud and ancient area.

There can be no more fitting place to begin a journey than **Berwick Upon Tweed**, ideally situated on the edge of the border with a history stretching back to Roman times. There are beautiful and awesome medieval fortifications here and even today the Elizabethan walls are regarded as the best preserved in Europe.

Although, strictly speaking, Berwick now lies in England, the history books tell us that it changed hands no less than fourteen times in the continual tug of war that existed between the English and the Scots. Today the old and the new mingle in this lovely town and you are sure to be delighted in its many contrasts of customs and buildings, where Elizabethan architecture is joined by elegant Georgian buildings.

If you follow the old walls, you will have a fascinating journey. For nearly two miles they wind and twist around the narrow streets of pretty houses and small alleyways.

In more restless times the pride of Berwick was its castle, which managed to withstand centuries of sieges only to be destroyed to make way for the railway just over a century ago. Part of the Great Hall still stands by the platform, and it was here that Edward I decided between Balliol and Bruce for the succession to the throne of Scotland in 1291. Edward decided in favour of Balliol, only to seize the throne himself in 1296. You can almost imagine the ghost of Edward Plantagenet stalking the remains of the Great Hall after dark.

Although at first glance **Scotsgate Restaurant** on Castlegate looks rather small don't be put off, for the delight of wonderful food in fine surroundings awaits you within. Friendly proprietor Ian Longstaff has many years catering experience and provides an extensive and very reasonably priced menu which caters to every taste, with tempting daily specials listed on a blackboard. A popular venue with visitors and locals alike, Scotsgate seats up to 48 people, but due to its popularity, booking is advisable for Sunday lunches. Above the restaurant, Ian also provides luxurious accommodation in a well-equipped holiday flat which he lets at various times during the year on a bed and breakfast basis.

Scotsgate, 6 Castlegate, Berwick. 0289-308028 Map Ref: H2

Berwick shouldn't just be considered a 'museum town'. It has lovely parks and gardens to walk in, plus wide sandy beaches in the resort of Spittal , a stone's throw away across the Tweed.

With its independent character it comes as no surprise that it was once customary in Acts of Parliament for Berwick to be mentioned separately after Wales, as it was considered to be a territory of its own, the borders of which were known as the Berwick Bounds'. The symbolic marking of this area is a custom that is still carried out each year, accompanied by festivities on the first of May.

There is much to do and see in Berwick. The Barracks, which are the oldest purpose-built in the country, now house a fascinating museum complex and art gallery. The town itself has many interesting shops and its narrow streets come alive on market day, which is traditionally held each Wednesday and Saturday.

If you have a sweet tooth then you might try Berwick's cockles, not as you might expect a shellfish, but a peppermint sweet in the shape of a cockle.

Berwick is dominated by the sea and the magnificent River Tweed that sweeps through the town. The livelihood of the town was based on the sea, and Berwick's most famous industries were in salmon and sea fishing, which have survived here despite the decline suffered in many coastal towns.

The River Tweed is spanned at no less than three points by historic bridges: Berwick Bridge, which dates from the 17th century, The Royal Tweed Bridge, built in 1928 and The Royal Border Railway Bridge, which was designed by Robert Stephenson and has twenty eight arches, this was opened by Queen Victoria in 1850.

From a point nearly four miles above Berwick Bridge, the Tweed follows the border for some eighteen miles. The Tweed is really one of the most enchanting and distinctive border rivers, and if you are feeling up to a walk it is well worth taking the time to explore it by way of a bankside path that starts from Tweedmouth.

For an excellent family day out, make your way to **Paxton House,** which lies on the B6460 just outside Berwick-upon-Tweed. Built in 1758, this magnificent Neo-Palladian mansion houses a stunning collection of paintings and beautiful antique furniture. The Picture Gallery, which is now an outstation of the National Galleries of Scotland, has been carefully restored to a late 19th century decorative scheme, thus providing the ideal setting for these wonderful works of art. However, Paxton House offers many other attractions, to complete your day out. The surrounding 70 acres of gardens, parkland and woodland border the River Tweed and provide a wealth of walks, whilst the adventure playground allows younger family members to run off some energy, before enjoying some refreshment in the excellent tearoom.

Paxton House, Berwick. 0289-386291 Map Ref: H2

From Berwick we join the northbound A1 and keep with the coast on the A1107, which takes you into **Eyemouth**. It's a picturesque fishing town, which retains not only its cobbled streets but also a distinct old world charm.

The harbour has a breakwater that dates from 1770, and is protected by the 'Hurkars' rocks. Overlooking the harbour is Gunsgreen House, an 18th century mansion, and an old haunt of smugglers. The coast here is rich in smuggling legend, with numerous cliffs hiding caves and passages. Eyemouth harbour is still a busy place, and a fascinating time can be had watching the fish being landed and auctioned here. The fishing is mainly for white fish, prawns, lobster and crab. And it is possible for you to charter a boat and do some sea fishing of your own - if you're feeling adventurous.

The **Ship Hotel** stands right on the quayside in Eyemouth and has been offering fishermen and travellers refreshment and accommodation for over 200 years. Today that welcome hospitality is supplied by Andy and Kate Anderson who have created a nautical theme throughout. The bar, with its barrelled seating and open fire provides a warm, friendly atmosphere where locals and visitors mix easily, swapping tales over a pint of excellent Real Ale. A selection of tasty bar meals is available both lunchtime and evening at surprisingly reasonable prices and a substantial breakfast is provided for those staying overnight. There are seven attractively furnished guest rooms and being so close to the quay, guests can watch local fishermen coming and going with their daily catches.

The Ship Hotel, Harbour Rd, Eyemouth. 08907-50224 Map Ref: H1

During a great storm in 1881, Eyemouth endured a terrible tragedy when half of the fishing fleet was sunk and over one hundred men lost. A marvellous tapestry depicting the disaster was sewn by local women in 1981 to mark the centenary. It is fifteen feet long, containing one million stitches, and all of the women involved in the work were descendants of the men who were drowned. The tapestry can be seen in the Eyemouth Museum, together with the story of the storm and other exhibits, which show how both fishing and Eyemouth have changed over the years.

On the B6355 road, midway between Eyemouth and **Ayton**, non-smokers will discover a peaceful, relaxing haven at **Ayton Mains farmhouse**. A former working farm, it lies in five acres of land belonging to the Ayton Castle Estate which is situated nearby. Built in 1846, this charming Victorian house, with its high ceilings and lovely decoration and furnishings, is a credit to Mr. and Mrs. Riach who are warm, welcoming hosts. Awarded a Listed and Commended grading by the Scottish Tourist Board, accommodation is provided in four comfortable bedrooms and there are two bathrooms for guests' use. After a day exploring the lovely surrounding countryside or visiting local places of interest, you can relax in the comfortable lounge, with an open log fire to toast your toes by.

Ayton Mains Farmhouse, Ayton. 08907-81336 MapRef: H2

Back on the nearby coast a scenic clifftop walk takes you from Eyemouth to St. Abbs via Coldingham. **Coldingham** itself is an 18th century town, though the priory here dates back to 1098 and now serves as a chapel. There are a wide range of activities available in Coldingham and, apart from numerous walks, there is a small art studio in the village where classes are held each summer. If you like diving, then this is just the place to put it into practice. The waters here are ideal and there are facilities for this very popular sport. Both sailing and sea angling are also available.

Set within 150 acres of magnificent countryside with cliffs, woodland, lakes, grass paddocks and a 22 acre loch, **West Loch**, at

Coldingham, offers a taste of paradise for lovers of self-catering holidays. Here in this very special, secluded location you will find three cottages and six chalets, offering full facilities for between two and six people. Lochside Cottage is particularly special, being built over a boathouse and with power supplied only by calor gas, therefore no television, which makes it ideal for those really seeking to 'get away from it all'. There is stabling available for horses and residents can fish for brown and rainbow trout in the Loch. With beautiful walks on all sides and even its own Iron and Bronze Age ruins, West Loch is a very special place indeed.

West Loch House, Coldingham. 08907-71270 Map Ref: G1

Those of you seeking bed & breakfast accommodation in Coldingham should take the A1107 towards Edinburgh. If you continue for half a mile beyond the village and turn right at the signpost, you will find **The Loan**.

The Loan, Coldingham, Eyemouth. 08907-71667 Map Ref: H1

A small friendly bed and breakfast establishment, standing in six acres, it is run by Jim and Margaret Manderson, with pony trekking run by their daughter Lyn. The Loan boasts wonderful, panoramic views of the surrounding countryside which visitors can explore on horseback at their leisure, with fully supervised rides of varying lengths, catering for all ages and abilities. Should you wish to stay, very comfortable overnight accommodation is provided in the attractive converted outbuildings and Margaret will set you up well for a day's riding, with a breakfast fit for a king!

Set within its own grounds overlooking the sea at Coldingham Bay, The **St. Abbs Haven Hotel** is a true haven of peace, tranquility and luxurious comfort. To reach it, take the St. Abbs road out of Coldingham and after about half a mile, turn right at the hotel sign and follow this road to the end.

The St. Abbs Haven Hotel, Coldingham Bay. 08907-71491
Map Ref: G1

Beautifully furnished throughout, the hotel has fifteen superb en-suite guest rooms, ranging from singles to the wonderful Elizabethan, Victorian and McGregor Suites. You can't help but relax and unwind in the comfortable guest lounge with its magnificent Minstrel's Gallery and the hotel's Coffee Shop boasts breathtaking views and provides a lovely setting for a mid-morning cuppa. Dining is a delight, with a superior bar menu and a mouthwatering selection provided in the elegant restaurant. Within easy reach of many local attractions it is hard to imagine a nicer holiday base.

There is much to see on this beautiful coast, and it is always rewarding to take a closer look at **St. Abbs**, a picturesque fishing village which nestles around a tiny harbour. The harbour is still used by a small fleet of crab and lobster boats. Here you can see a row of tiny buildings which were apparently used by the fishermen to store their gear.

Just yards from the harbours edge is **Springbank Cottage**, a delightful fisherman's cottage. Gwyneth and Philip Linley are warm welcoming hosts who provide very comfortable accommodation for non-smokers in three well-furnished guest rooms, each with washbasin, colour TV, hot drinks facilities and best of all, a sea view. Gwyneth is a fine cook who offers a wide choice at breakfast to suit everyone's tastes, including diabetic preserves if needed. You can sample more of her expert homecooking in the cottage Tea-Garden, where you can sit out and enjoy the view whilst savouring a slice of homemade cake or a light snack.

Springbank Cottage, The Harbour, St. Abbs.
08907-71477 Map Ref: G1

If you are feeling fit, do walk on further towards **St. Abb's Head**, the view of the three hundred feet high red sandstone cliffs is truly spectacular. There are superb opportunities for the painters and sketchers amongst you, with the landscapes and seabirds of the National Nature Reserve here. It is an important area for seabirds; many species can be seen here, especially between April and July, and these include guillemots, razorbills, kittiwakes, fulmars and even puffins. Birds on land include wheatears, meadow pipits and stonechats. The nature reserve is an ideal stopping-off place for the birds travelling south from the Arctic winter. It's enthralling to watch the artists trying to capture the entrancing scenes on paper.

On your way to or from St. Abbs, it is well worth calling in at **Northfield Farm** which is signposted on the B6438. This 550 acre mixed working farm is owned and run by Anne and Peter Gordon who work the land, with the emphasis on natural farming, and in addition to the acres they own, rent St. Abb's Head. Within some former outbuildings you will find an art gallery and picture framers, coffee shop, weaving workshop, wooden toy maker and National Trust information room. After browsing and choosing a suitable memento, you are sure to be kept lingering in The Head Start Coffee Shop, which offers a tempting selection of homemade cakes, snacks and light meals.

The Head Start Coffee Shop, Northfield Farm, St. Abbs.
08907-71707 Map Ref: G1

Three miles to the west of St. Abb's Head, off the A1107, is one of the most extraordinary ruined castles that you could hope to discover. **Fast Castle** is perched precariously on a stack of rock; barely accessible by steep cliff footpath it's best viewed from above by those unsure of their feet. Fast Castle was used by Sir Walter Scott as the model for Wolf's Crag in 'The Bride of Lammermuir'. Fourteen year old princess, Margaret Tudor, used the castle as a resting place on her way to marry James IV of Scotland, Flodden's tragic monarch.

With magnificent views across to the sea and lying just five minutes away from lovely beaches, **Townhead Farm** makes an excellent holiday base.

Situated on the A1107 coastal route between Cockburnspath and Eyemouth, this is a working farm set in 440 acres of rolling countryside. Mrs. Russell is a welcoming hostess who provides comfortable bed and breakfast accommodation in two guest rooms within the main farmhouse as well as excellent self-catering accommodation in three cottages. Built over 200 years ago, these former farm workers' cottages have been completely refurbished and are equipped with all household essentials. Both Berwick and Dunbar are within easy reach by car, making Townhead Farm a peaceful yet convenient touring base.

Townhead Farm, Cockburnspath. 03683-465 Map Ref: F1

On reaching the A1 just outside Cocksburnspath our journey turns southwards and not before long comes to **The Grantshouse Inn**, a delightful roadside tavern which makes an ideal stopping-off point. Parts of the building date back to the mid-1830s when there was a railway station opposite and beer barrels would be brought from Edinburgh by train and ferried across the road in wheelbarrows! This is a place full of character and atmosphere, much of which is down to David and Kay Gauld who are super hosts who provide first class refreshment and can even offer you a bed for the night in one of two very comfortable guest rooms. You can sample various Real Ales and savour fine homecooking and on fine days, relax outside where there are two feature Romany caravans.

The Grantshouse Inn, Grantshouse. 03615-233 Map Ref: G1

Just off the A1 in the village of **Grantshouse** is **Harelawside**, a delightful 200 year old farmhouse set within a 550 acre mixed working farm. Ideally situated for touring the beautiful Scottish Borders, Harelawside offers very comfortable and peaceful accommodation for non-smoking guests in three lovely bedrooms all with that extra personal touch and one with en-suite bathroom. Maureen and John Burton are warm, welcoming hosts who enjoy sharing their charming home with their many guests and in addition to a full breakfast, Maureen provides her speciality of homemade wholemeal and granary bread. If you are lucky, John may entertain you with his superb organ playing which has earned him the job of organist at the village church.

Harelawside, Grantshouse. 03615-209 Map Ref: G1

Our journey continues down to **Reston**, just off the A1. Situated on the Main Street in the village, **The Red Lion** makes a super stopping-off point in any journey.

The Red Lion, Main Street, Reston. 08907-61266 Map Ref: H1

Built just over 100 years ago it was originally a cottage that sold ale, but today, it is a popular, family orientated pub run by a friendly couple, John and Maggie Sparham. There is a fine choice of ale and the menu is excellent, ranging from baked potatoes to full steak dishes, with a wide selection of ice cream sundaes among the tempting desserts. It makes a refreshing change too, to find somewhere that offers a complete children's menu with appropriate portions at an appealing price. On a fine day, the rear patio area with its small putting green and feature aviary provides the perfect setting for a relaxing family lunch.

From Reston we wend our way inland towards Duns, passing through the villages of Auchencrow and Chirnside. **Chirnside Hall Hotel** lies on the A6105 Duns to Berwick road on the east side of the lovely village of **Chirnside** and is ideal for a quiet break away. The village was the home of famous racing driver Jim Clark, who lies buried at Chirnside Church. Carrying a 3-Crown Commended rating, Chirnside Hall is set in magnificent grounds which include an original walled garden. The Pine and Parker families are friendly hosts who successfully combine first class facilities and professional service, with a relaxed, country house atmosphere. The ten guest rooms, are all superbly decorated and furnished, as is the hotel throughout. Dining is a pleasure, with a menu which caters for every taste, and after dinner you can unwind with a game of snooker.

Chirnside Hall Country House Hotel, Chirnside. 0890-818219
Map Ref: G2

A mile or so to the east of Duns is **Manderston House**. This is one of the finest examples of Edwardian country houses in Britain. There is much to see here, the 'downstairs' domestic quarters, which have been preserved, give visitors a real flavour of life in such a house

16

eighty or ninety years ago. The house itself is a wonderful example of extravagance, and has a staircase which is a replica of the Petite Trianon at Versailles, the rails being plated in silver!

Duns itself is situated right in the heart of Berwickshire. The name is a strange one, and derives from an old word for hill fort, the original settlement being situated on the slopes of Duns Law, a word for hill. In Newton Street take a look at the Jim Clark Memorial Room , which is a rather unusual museum. It commemorates the life and career of the Berwickshire farmer and racing driver who lived in Duns and was world champion in 1963 and again in 1965, before his tragic death at Hockenheim, Germany in 1968. The museum is open from Easter to October and contains many of the trophies and memorabilia of a driver held to be the finest of all time by his peers.

Lovers of pottery in all its forms will discover a real haven when they visit **Swinton Pottery**, which is situated on the Main Street in **Swinton**, south of Duns on the A6117. John and Sandra Day are highly experienced potters who are making an extensive collection of fantasy figures, inspired by the myths and legends of Scotland, and large viewing windows into the workshop enable the visitor to see the potters at work. They also stock a vast range of items produced by the finest artists throughout Scotland and England. Situated opposite the village green, this wonderful pottery studio will have browsers lingering for hours, as they follow the fascinating history behind The Celtic Legend story and painstakingly choose a memento of their visit, which is no easy task. Back home you can be kept up to date and add to your collection through their personal mail order service. Whatever else you do and wherever else you go, if you are anywhere near Swinton, make sure you call in at this delightful pottery centre.

Swinton Pottery, 25/27 Main Street, Swinton. 0890-860283
Map Ref: G2

Enjoying the views of the Lammermuir Hills, and Dirrington Great Law to the north, our next destination, the ancient town of **Greenlaw**, originated in 1147. Set against wooded country, and on the Blackadder Water, the present town dates from the 17th century, replacing the older village that stood on a nearby hill. The church here was built in 1675 and has an interesting tower that adjoins it, originally used as a prison.

Greenlaw was of importance for two main reasons. It was the market town of Berwickshire for over one hundred and fifty years until Duns took over this role, as a larger and more important town. Secondly, Greenlaw became a convenient stopping place for weary stage coach travellers between Edinburgh and Newcastle in the days of horse-drawn transport. A fire in 1545 destroyed much of the village, although it was subsequently rebuilt, and by 1698 had become the chief burgh of the shire.

You could have been forgiven for thinking that Blackadder was the invention of Rowan Atkinson and his team of merry men. But if you are keen on fishing you will not be disappointed with the trout fishing on the Blackadder from March to early October. Permits are available from the post office or from hotels in Greenlaw.

A little south of Greenlaw, situated on the B6461 Kelso to Berwick road is **Eccles** village. On the outskirts is the magnificent country mansion **Eccles House**, owned by Nick and Nicki Heliker. Set in 28 acres of scenic countryside and woodlands with the ruins of a 12th century nunnery within its grounds, it was built at the end of the 19th century by an affluent landowner as a wedding present for his daughter.

Eccles House, Eccles, By Kelso. 0890-840205 Fax: 0890 840367
Map Ref: F3

Full of character and warmth, the splendour of Eccles House has to be seen to be believed, with its magnificent staircase and snooker room just two of its many features. The dining room, lounge and seven beautifully furnished guest rooms are all a picture and combined with the breathtaking views, first class hospitality and very special atmosphere make staying here a sheer delight.

Inland along the Tweed from Berwick, and due east of Greenlaw, at **Norham** you will come across **Norham Castle**, which was apparently the inspiration for several landscapes by Turner, and certainly worthy of your attention, set as it has been for some three hundred years in this lovely setting.

Norham village itself thoroughly charmed us. It's a very pleasant place, with its cottages lining each side of a lovely green. The church dates from 830AD, and surprisingly it had more than once been occupied as a base from which to besiege the castle.

Coldstream, upstream, gave its name to that most famous regiment The Coldstream Guards, founded here in 1639 by General Monk, a supporter of Charles II. A plaque on the Guards' House, rebuilt in 1865, at the east end of the market place, indicates their original headquarters. Coldstream is also family home to Alec Douglas Home, Lord Home of the Hirsel. Widely held as one of Britain's finest Prime Ministers, who gave up his Earldom in order to become PM only to be deposed by his party because he did not come over well on television. You can't help but wonder what would have happened to many other famous PMs if there had been TV in their day.

A few miles from Coldstream lies the site of the Battle of **Flodden**, 1513, where ten thousand Scotsmen, including their King, James IV, perished at the hands of the English, despite outnumbering the enemy. It was one of the most fearful days in Scottish history, where the flower of nobility was slain. The disastrous defeat was a result of some bad tactical decisions by the King, who at one stage dismounted his horse and fought hand to hand surrounded by his soldiers in a valiant attempt to turn the tide. This great loss is still remembered each year in Coldstream.

Like Gretna Green, Coldstream, being on the border, has had its fair share of runaway marriages. Although not as well known as Gretna, eloping couples used to cross at Smeaton's Bridge and make for the old marriage house that can still be seen.

Once described by the writer, Sir Walter Scott, as "the most beautiful town in the land", **Kelso**, set majestically at the junction of two rivers, the Tweed and the Teviot, must certainly be a contender for this coveted title. A busy market town with a population of just five thousand, Kelso has a lovely elegant square which is surrounded by fine buildings. The roofs, pinnacles and small streets of the town look strangely continental, with shop windows peering through arches, and grey and brown houses fronting the market square.

There was once a bullring in the centre of the square, the point where bulls were once tethered during markets. Today markets and shows are no longer held here, but in Springwood Park, which is across the river. The arched bridge spanning the river was built in 1800, and was in fact the model for the old Waterloo Bridge across the Thames. There are two lamp posts here which were retrieved from London Bridge when it was demolished in 1930. During World War II, Polish troops were stationed in Kelso, and there is a plaque in the town which was presented by the visitors in gratitude for their stay. They must surely have enjoyed being here. The surrounding countryside is very beautiful, and there is so much to be explored.

The magnificent **Kelso Abbey** was built on the instructions of King David I, and was started around 1128. Vatican records show that it was one of the largest of the Border abbeys. In 1545 it was used as a stronghold against the English invasion and sadly the defendants, including the monks, were ruthlessly slaughtered.

One place that always proves a popular attraction for visitors to Kelso, is **The Kelso Pottery** which lies 100 metres behind the historic Abbey, alongside the free car park at The Knowes. Since 1970, Ian and Elizabeth Hird have been creating beautiful and original pieces of pottery which have been exhibited all over the world.

The Kelso Pottery, The Knowes, Kelso. 0573-224027 Map Ref: F4

Both are experienced potters and Ian concentrates on developing hard-wearing, but attractive domestic ware featuring the ever changing colours and patterns of the Border landscape, whilst Elizabeth produces beautiful animals, birds and figures as well as exquisite models of buildings. The stunning display in the showroom leaves you mesmerised and spoilt for choice, but the price range means there is something to suit every pocket.

For peace and tranquility in these stunning rural surroundings, look no further than **Whitehill Farm**, a 455 acre mixed working farm in **Nenthorn**. Home of David and Betty Smith, this charming early Victorian farmhouse can be found by taking the A6089 out of Kelso to Nenthorn village and the farm lies a short distance further on the right. Awarded a Two Crown Highly Commended rating by the Scottish Tourist Board, there are four spacious and attractively furnished guest rooms, one with en-suite shower room, plus a fine dining room and comfortable lounge to relax in. The atmosphere here is one of friendly hospitality and should you wish, in addition to a farmhouse style breakfast, Betty will prepare an excellent homecooked evening meal by prior arrangement.

Whitehill Farm, Nenthorn, Kelso. 0573-470203 Map Ref: F4

If ever there was a jewel in the crown, then **Floors Castle** must be a prime example. This magnificent mansion overlooking the River Tweed and the town of Kelso is the home of the tenth Duke of Roxburghe.

Built in 1721 by the builder/architect William Adam, Floors Castle became the Scottish seat of the First Duke of Roxburghe, an eminent gentleman who was bestowed with many titles by Queen Anne and became the first Secretary of State for Scotland following the Union of 1707.

The castle occupies the site of the previous home of the Earls of Roxburghe, 'Auld Floors', which had been their home since 1650 when they abandoned the now ruined Cessford Castle, which had been the principal seat of the Kers for four centuries. It is interesting to note

21

that 'Auld Floors' was sometimes known as 'Floris' which in Scots tongue means 'Flowers'.

Floors Castle is rich in history, for 'Auld Floors' was known to be a refuge for the Royalists in the days of 'Habbie' Ker, the first Earl. Another story tells us of the present castle being used as a temporary lodging for Prince Charles' men during the 1745 rebellion. At this time however, the castle was still under construction.

Romance is not far away either; romance connected with drama, a drama that interrupted the family line. The third Duke of Roxburghe, a man known for his great intellect, became deeply attached to Christina, the elder daughter of the Duke of Mecklenberg-Strelitze. Unfortunately for him, her younger sister, Charlotte, became George IV's Queen and court etiquette decreed that an elder sister could not become a subject of a younger sister. Their love was thwarted and in their despair both undertook a life of celibacy.

The Duke sublimated his affections by becoming the most discerning book collector of his century. Amongst his collection are such books as Caxton's 'Recuyell of the History of Troy' and a first edition of 'Decameron'.

The hiccough in the family line in the early 1800s, caused partly through Duke John's lack of issue, was the subject of a lengthy lawsuit which continued for seven years. As the fifth Duke took his rightful place, the lawsuit had to be funded from the sale of the Roxburghe library. Irony, but not total disaster, for the main components of the library were saved by a handful of peers who founded the Roxburghe Club. They each held originals and undertook to produce a number of facsimilies until they each had a complete collection.

Floors Castle

Part of Scotland's heritage lies in the grounds. There are the mounds of the old city of Roxburgh and of Roxburgh Castle; in its day one of Scotland's principal fortresses and home to many monarchs. Alas, all that remains now are the ruins of a postern gate. Much later, in 1460, King James II was killed when one of his own cannons exploded; a holly tree marks the spot in the parkland before the Castle.

Following your wander through the castle you may well require a cup of tea, or perhaps a meal. You can enjoy either in the castle's restaurant which offers food from the estate and river cooked in the castle kitchen. Within the courtyard you will find a pleasant little gift shop, And if you have the time to spare, there is a regular minibus from the castle to the Garden Centre, which is enclosed within the Walled Garden.

There are many places to stay and relax in the countryside around Kelso. Set within 1200 acres of rolling farmland, stretching from the valley floor to a mountain peak, **Morebattle Tofts** is the lovely 18th century farmhouse home of Debbie and James Playfair who provide first class overnight accommodation carrying a Two Crown Commended rating.

Morebattle Tofts, Kelso. 0573-440364 Map Ref: G4

Somewhat 'hidden', the farm can be reached by taking the Morebattle road (B6401) off the A698 and following it through the village after which you turn left onto the A6346. Immediately after crossing a hump-backed bridge, Morebattle Tofts is the first house on the left set in lovely grounds. The beautiful decor is enhanced by a wealth of period furniture and a major feature is the magnificent spiral staircase. The three guest rooms are all named after flowers, one with en-suite facilities, but to ensure availability, advanced telephone bookings are preferred. Debbie is an excellent cook using Scottish produce to its full potential and she readily provides evening meals and picnic lunches by arrangement. The area is excellent for walking and fishing can be arranged.

Set right in the heart of **Morebattle** village you will find the **Templehall Hotel**, a first class hostelry run by friendly couple Ron and Jill Bowers. Formerly a group of 19th century houses set within ten acres of land, the pub itself was created in 1960. Ron and Jill's hard efforts have turned the Templehall Hotel into a very welcoming place for locals and tourists alike, with traditional furnishings enhancing a warm, relaxed atmosphere. There is a tasty and varied bar menu available both lunchtime and evening with a fine wine list to accompany your meal. For those wishing to stay, very comfortable accommodation is provided in three spacious guest rooms and those staying for five nights or more can obtain a permit for fishing if they wish.

Templehall Hotel, Morebattle, Nr Kelso. 0573-440249 Map Ref: G4

The Plough Hotel, Town Yetholm., Kelso 0573-420215 Map Ref: G4

In the nearby village of **Town Yetholm**, along side the Bowmont River and famous for its gypsies, you will find a warm welcome awaits you when you call in at **The Plough Hotel**. Built in the early 19th century, it became a coaching inn during the 1860's and since then has continued to provide travellers with fine ale, good food and comfortable accommodation. Ian and Isabel Angus are caring, friendly hosts who immediately make you feel at home. In a warm, cosy atmosphere you can relax with a pint of well-kept ale and sample the extensive menu which is available every lunchtime and evening and includes children's portions. At the end of the evening you can retire to one of the four comfortably furnished guest rooms for a refreshing night's sleep.

On Main Street in this unusually named conservation village you will discover a lovely place to stay, named **Paramount**. This elegant town house is the charming home of Marilyn and John Mackenzie and is part 18th and part 19th century. Although attractive from the outside, the inside has to be seen to be believed, with beautiful decor, furnishings and furniture lending a stately yet welcoming air, which in turn makes this a simply wonderful country guest house. The three guest rooms are fully equipped and have en-suite bathrooms for complete comfort and Marilyn's cooking makes dining a treat. With magnificent views of the Cheviot Hills to the rear, this really is a place to be recommended.

Paramount, Main Street, Town Yetholm, Kelso. 0573-420505 Map Ref: G4

The road from Kelso to Melrose runs along the southern banks of the Tweed and is one of the loveliest routes in Scotland. It passes through the village of **St. Boswells**, which is situated on a common, with the main part of the village built mainly in the local red sandstone. It's hard to believe that in the 18th and early 19th

25

centuries, this common was the setting of the largest annual fair in the south of Scotland, with lambs, cattle, horses and wool all being sold.

Nearby is Dryburgh Abbey. Attacked by the English in 1322, 1358 and 1544 the ruins are still an impressive sight, the cloister buildings being some of the most intact of any monastery in Scotland. Sir Walter Scott and his biographer J.G. Lockhart are buried in the grounds, as well as Field Marshal Earl Haig, Commander-in-Chief of the British Army during most of The Great War.

Lying on the B6404, just 400 yards off the A68, **The Clachan** is an ideal base for visitors touring this scenic part of Southern Scotland and is the charming home of Nina and A.J. Johnstone. The main part of the house was built by monks and dates back to the 16th century, although it has been added to a couple of times over the past 400 years. It is a very impressive building, both inside and out and you will find very comfortable accommodation provided in four attractively furnished guest rooms. The atmosphere is homely and relaxed, just what you need after a day's exploring and if you wish, Nina will provide your evening meal, with advance notice.

The Clachan, Mains Street, St.Boswells. 0835-22266 Map Ref: E4

Merton House, just two miles to the east of St. Boswells, is well worth your attention. Designed by Sir William Bruce in 1703, It became the home of the sixth Duke of Sutherland, and boasts twenty acres of beautiful grounds, with lovely walks and views of the river Tweed.

Those of you with a taste for fine country houses may like to take the A68 north from St. Boswells to the town of **Lauder** . Here you will find **Thirlstane Castle**. It's possibly Scotland's finest grand

Thirlstane Castle

symmetrical design and certainly has one of the most imposing frontages.

What the visitor sees today was started in 1670 by the first - and last - Duke of Lauderdale around the original castle. The Duke supported Charles II's attempts to foist his religious values on the Scots and he became the virtual 'uncrowned king' of the country. The castle features some very impressive Baroque plaster ceilings, as well as a huge historic toy collection and a Border life exhibition.

Situated four miles out of Lauder towards Edinburgh and just a mile off the A68, **The Tower Hotel** is an attractive establishment with its 'tower' giving the impression of great age, although the hotel was in fact built in 1903. With a commanding view overlooking the valley of Lauderdale, this lovely country hotel is run by friendly hosts Meg and George White who in their relatively short time here have created a very special place indeed. The public bar is cosy and welcoming with old pictures and prints on the walls adding to its character and charm. Accommodation is provided in three spacious, individually decorated guest rooms and there is a comfortable residents' lounge to relax in before enjoying fine homecooked fare in the pleasant restaurant, which has a menu to appeal to the whole family.

The Tower Hotel, Main Street, Oxton, By Lauder. 0578-750235
Map Ref: D2

It would be hard to imagine a more picturesque or tranquil setting for a relaxing holiday than that of **The Smithy**, the beautifully converted 18th century home of Betty and George Pope, whose careful refurbishment of the property has retained many features as a reminder of its working life. This gem of a place can be found in the midst of rolling farmland in the village of **Legerwood** which lies between the A68 and the A6089. Packed lunches can be provided and having tasted Betty's breakfast, the optional four course evening meal is sure to tempt you. There are four lovely guest rooms all beautifully decorated and situated on the ground floor provide easy access whilst equally comfortable alternative accommodation is available in the adjacent self-catering cottage which sleeps up to four.

The Smithy, Legerwood, Earlston. 0896-84 518 Map Ref: E3

Returning south to the A6091 takes you to the beautiful ruins of **Melrose Abbey**. Impressive by day they are best viewed, according to Sir Walter Scott, by moonlight. Although badly damaged, some of the surviving parts are considered to be amongst the most splendid and detailed work of the time, and include the famous jolly figure of a pig playing the bagpipes on the roof. The heart of Robert the Bruce is also reputedly buried near the high altar.

Melrose itself is a beautiful and intriguing border town, steeped in history and with lots to offer. One of special note is the railway station. Once described as the "handsomest provincial station in Scotland", Melrose Station lay derelict from 1969 when the Waverley Route from Edinburgh to Carlisle was axed.

Now the only town station still standing in the Borders region, Melrose Station was saved from the same fate as its sister stations by the foresight of architect Dennis Rodwell, who purchased the building in 1985. He recognised that the station had the potential to house a craft centre which would be the focal point for skilled craftsmen and women throughout the Borders to display their skills and products.

After two years of hard work and sympathetic restoration, this fine Jacobean style building now houses not only the craft centre itself, but also workshops where visitors can see hand crafted articles during manufacture. There is also an art gallery which provides a changing

29

programme of art and craft exhibitions, mainly featuring the work of Borders artists and craftspeople.

For railway enthusiasts, The Waverley Route Heritage Centre and Model Railway provides a fascinating reminder of the old Waverley Route and Borders branch lines. The Heritage Centre displays a wide variety of photos, posters, signs, lamps, documents and tickets. There is also a large working model railway and you can purchase general and specialist books, posters, cards and railway souvenirs.

Additionally there is an exhibition mounted by The Trimontium Trust which offers those interested in archaeology colourful and informative displays related to the Roman fort at Newstead. Melrose Station should certainly be on your itinerary.

In the centre of Melrose you will find **Burts Hotel**, without doubt one of the finest hotel and restaurants for miles around. Owned and personally run by Graham and Anne Henderson with their son Nicholas, this superb establishment is featured in many recognised publications including Egon Ronay, the Michelin Guide, Les Routiers and STB Taste of Scotland. Awarded three stars by the RAC and AA, the hotel also carries a Four Crown Commended rating by the Scottish Tourist Board although after staying here, you will probably rate it higher. Accommodation is provided in 21 superior en-suite guest rooms, each equipped and furnished to the highest standards. However, Burts is as much a restaurant as a hotel, and is renowned throughout the area. The quality and diversity of the menu caters for every taste and includes fresh local game and fish when in season, all imaginatively prepared and beautifully presented, which makes dining as well as staying here a memorable treat.

Burts Hotel, Melrose. 0896-822285 Map Ref: E4

Nearby is **Abbotsford**, the home of Sir Walter Scott, whose fame has ensured that Melrose is now a busy tourist centre. There are many tributes to this man throughout the whole of this area; he was a well-loved figure who, through his writings, is credited with the preserving of the stories and ballads of the Borders.

Although Sir Walter Scott was actually born in Edinburgh, the area which has always been most associated with the poet and story-teller is the Scottish Borderlands where he made his home.

His family history is not without its own characters and tales. One of Scott's ancestors was captured by a rival hostile clan, and offered a choice between marriage or hanging. He apparently took one look at the bride, who was the daughter of the clan's chief and not the most fortunate looking girl, and chose hanging! He was, though, persuaded to change his mind at a later date.

As Walter grew up and went to school, he became well-known as a teller of tales and a voracious reader of books, all the time developing the love of the beautiful countryside that surrounded him. He went to university in Edinburgh and on to practise law. He made good progress in his position and was appointed Sheriff of Selkirk in 1799.

With a good income and a stable position, he was able to work on his collection of ballads and poetry. Scott became well respected and among his admirers were the Wordsworths, who visited him at his home in the Borders.

In 1812 Scott bought the farm that was later to develop into the extravagance of Abbotsford. The farm as it was then was unimpressive and was in fact known as 'Clartyhole', meaning 'dirty hole'. The place was renamed 'Abbotsford' by Scott.

By 1825, Abbotsford was vastly expanded, taking in many surrounding farms and estates and it became Scott's pride and joy. However, the renovation severely drained Scott's finances and he was forced to work harder to pay the bills. His pace of work is said to have contributed to his death and on the twenty first of September, 1832, he died at the age of sixty-one.

Today the house is much as it was in Scott's day, with its remarkable collection of armour and historical relics, such as Rob Roy's sporran, Napoleon's cloak clasp, a lock of Bonnie Prince Charlie's hair and even a silver urn from Lord Byron. The library and study where Scott worked are fascinating to look at. Abbotsford gives you a vivid picture of one of the Borders' greatest characters.

It is only a short distance from Abbotsford to **Gattonside** on the B6360 8Coming from the A68 if you take the first left in the village and you will find **Hoebridge Inn** on your left at the end of the road. Originally built during the 1850's as a Pirn Mill, it later became a farmhouse and today exposed oak beams and bygone memorabilia enhance the warm, welcoming ambience.

Owned and personally run by Joy and Carlo Campari, this delightful establishment has a well-deserved reputation and has been included in 'Best of Britain' by Richard Binns. The menu is both extensive and mouthwatering, catering for every palate in substantial portions at surprisingly reasonable prices, all of which makes this a very special place.

Hoebridge Inn, Gattonside, Melrose. 0896-823082 Map Ref: E3

Manufacturing has been going on since 1622 in our next destination, **Galashiels.** The name is an interesting one and it does have its roots in an associated trade, as it actually comes from the words 'gala' and 'sheiling' which mean 'huts of the shepherds'.

The town is now famous for its woollens and textiles, and the Scottish College of Textiles, which was founded here in 1909. If you are interested in finding out more about the industry then head for the **Woollen Museum at Waverley Mills** where, at Peter Andersons, there are guided tours showing the process of tartan weaving.

Galashiels is able to offer the visitor a superb choice of golf courses, both at Torwoodlee and at Ladhope. Fishing is also available on the Tweed and Gala waters, whilst horses can be hired for pony-trekking, if desired.

Every year in July, the town hosts the Braw Lads' gathering which, amongst other things, celebrates the marriage in 1503 between James IV and Margaret Tudor, sister of Henry VIII. This union is commemorated by a symbolic mingling of a bouquet of red and white roses.

During the spring and summer months visitors can delight in the wonderful amount of flowers that seemed to abound in the town centre, the fragrance and splendour of Bank Street Gardens in full bloom are wonderful. It's an ideal place for the traveller to stop and catch their breath, there is always the temptation to press on and see as much as possible, in the end missing so much.

But we must away, travelling along the A72 to **Innerleithen**, which sits neatly between Peebles and Galashiels. The rivers Tweed and Leithen meet in this charming mill town which has a famous watering place known as St. Ronan's Well. This was found in 1777 by local inhabitants who were drawn to it by the large number of pigeons sampling its benefits. The fame of the spa spread, and visitors are still able to sample the waters that are supposedly health giving.

Another interesting visit to make in the town is to 'Robert Smail's Printing Works', in the High Street. This is a vintage printing press and printworks, formerly driven by water wheels and now owned and displayed by the National Trust for Scotland as a museum.

In the heart of Innerleithen on the High Street, stands **The Tweedside Hotel**, ideally situated as a touring base for this lovely area of the Scottish Borders. Built almost 150 years ago, this former coaching inn still has the old stables and is full of character and charm. A small hotel, it is tastefully decorated throughout and in the warm, welcoming atmosphere of the bar you can choose from a wide range of fine ales and a selection of tasty bar meals. For those wishing to stay, very comfortable accommodation is provided in three spacious and well furnished guest rooms, two with en-suite bathroom and there is private parking available to the rear of the hotel.

The Tweedside Hotel, 58 High Street, Innerleithen. 0896-830386
Map Ref: C3

Another excellent place to stay in the town is the **Corner House Hotel** on Chapel Street. Completely refurbished by the new owners, this cosy, welcoming establishment offers superb accommodation in six beautifully furnished en-suite guest rooms, one with four poster bed and all equipped with hot drinks facilities and colour TV. Dining in the attractive restaurant is a real treat, with an extensive and reasonably priced menu providing excellent homecooked food all day and in the large comfortable lounge bar you can savour a wide range of real ales. All these factors combined with friendly, attentive staff, make Corner House Hotel a super place to stay.

Corner House Hotel, 1 Chapel Street, Innerleithen. 0896-831181
Fax: 0896-831182 Map Ref: C3

There is so much to do in Innerleithen, from country sporting pursuits to hill walking or visits to the nearby Border Abbeys. There is also ample opportunity for fishing on the river Tweed and permits can be obtained locally. Out of town on the B709 towards Heriot you will find **The Ley.** As you wend your way up the tree-lined drive towards the house, you realise you have discovered one of those rare 'hidden places' which combine the ideals of superior accommodation, outstanding cuisine and a tranquil, secluded setting.

The Ley is the magnificent mid-19th century home of Doreen and Willie McVicar and can be found by taking the B709 out of Innerleithen towards Heriot for 2 miles and after passing through the golf course turning left at the sign for The Ley, crossing over a small bridge. Set in 30 acres of wooded and lawned grounds, this splendid building with its lovely turreted tower is well deserving of its Three Crown Deluxe rating from the Scottish Tourist Board. The house is beautifully furnished throughout with lovely antique furniture and the three en-suite guest rooms are all equipped to the highest standards. Doreen's love of cooking is immediately apparent when you sample one of her mouthwatering four course dinners which is probably the high point of The Ley experience and leaves you eager to return.

The Ley, Innerleithen. Tel/Fax: 0896-830240 Map Ref: C3

Just outside the town you will find **Traquair House**. Formerly known as Traquair Castle, this famous house has played host to twenty-seven kings.

The house as we see it has been virtually unchanged since the 17th century, and there is a fascinating story concerning the 'Steekit Yetts' or Bear Gates, which were formerly the main entrance to the house. The gates were last closed after the departure of Bonnie Prince Charlie (Stuart), who had called on his cousins to enlist support for his march on England in 1745. They have remained unopened since then, and, according to legend, must remain so until a Stuart sits once again on the throne.

Traquair Gates

The current laird is a very industrious person, as he brews and sells his own brand of bottled ale, and, be warned, it is to be savoured in small amounts, such is its strength. A visit will always prove worthwhile, there is much to see in the house, and in its outbuildings are housed a number of craftworkers, including potters, weavers and woodworkers.

There are many woodland and riverside walks to choose from, and afterwards you may be refreshed with a cup of tea in the cottage, which is in the garden dating from 1745. Before you leave this fascinating place, why not take a look around the maze?

It is all together too easy to become addicted to the glorious countryside in this area of the Borders known as Tweedale. Its green hills and twisting country lanes, with glimpses of the river from time to time, are really quite beautiful. You may find yourself in an area of forest, and if you decide to walk you may well be lucky enough to catch a fleeting glance of a deer.

.There are times when you come across a place that stays with you for many years, and **Peebles** has all the right ingredients to do just that. It epitomises everything that you can enjoy in the Border country; being picturesque and historical, and yet with a thriving sense of its own character.

The Tweed, one of the most famous salmon rivers, runs through its centre. Peebles gives the impression of a place that was built for leisurely strolling, with its fine buildings and open parklands going down to the banks of the river. It has a wide shop-filled High Street, where you can browse at your leisure in the many small craft shops and cafes, here in the cobbled streets.

The Oven D'Or, 24 High Street, Peebles, 0721-723456 Map Ref: C3

Tucked down an alley off the High Street in Peebles, The **Oven D'Or** is one place well worth seeking out. This excellent restaurant is housed within a building which dates back to the mid-19th century and as its name suggests is a veritable pot of gold.

Owned and run by Keith and Jo Hitchcock, the appearance and atmosphere here changes throughout the day, as they cater for mid-morning coffee, lunches, high teas and finally evening meals, with soft furnishings and an intimate atmosphere creating an almost continental air.. The menus are extensive, varied and of the highest quality, with all dishes freshly prepared from the finest produce, which is why The Oven D'Or proves such a popular venue when eating out.

Do you play scrabble? Or have you ever become frustrated at a crossword puzzle? The chances are that if you have done either of these things then you have at some time reached for your faithful dictionary. You might be interested to know that the Chamber brothers were born in Peebles. They were of course famous for their publications of encyclopaedias and dictionaries.

William Chambers donated the Chambers Institute to Peebles, and it is now a museum and civic centre. Thriller fans amongst you will be intrigued to know that a writer associated with Peebles was John Buchan, who was the author of, amongst other things, 'The Thirty Nine Steps', made into a celebrated film by Alfred Hitchcock.

Kingsmuir Hotel, Springhill Road, Peebles. 0721-720151 Fax: 0721-721795 Map Ref: C3

Just five minutes from the town centre, you will find a charming place to stay at **Kingsmuir Hotel**. This family-run establishment welcomes families and offers first class accommodation in ten en-suite guest rooms, recently refurbished to a very high standard for maximum comfort. The emphasis here is on a warm welcome and discreet but friendly service. Award winner in The Best Eating Place competition of 1992, dining here is a treat and the restaurant is open to non-residents. The menu is extensive and offers a superb selection of homecooked food including fresh local fish and game when in season, plus a wide range of vegetarian dishes, which is reason enough to stay here!

Depending on when you visit Peebles, you may be able to see the agricultural show which is held each year in August, and if you go in September there are not only the Highland Games to look forward to, but also Peebles Arts Festival. It has been running for some seven years, and is proving to be a wonderful myriad of drama, music, dance and exhibitions.

Walking along the Tweed, following the river upstream out of town, leads to **Neidpath Castle**. This fortress of a palace reputedly has walls that are as thick as ten feet. Cromwell was at considerable pains to destroy it on account of this, though it is now fortunately restored.

If you think that the surrounding area is not as thickly wooded as it might be you'd be right. The Queensbury family, who once owned the castle, incurred the wrath of the poet Wordsworth as a result of cutting down every tree on the estate to pay off their gambling debts in 1795.

Crossburn Caravan Park, Edinburgh Road, Peebles. 0721-720501
Map Ref: C3

Situated just outside Peebles on the A703 in the most beautiful surroundings, **Crossburn Caravan Park** makes an ideal holiday base. Personally owned and run by David and Marie Chisholm, you will find they take every care to provide everything you need to make your stay at Crossburn comfortable. All the static caravans are furnished and equipped to the highest standards and are connected to the mains services. There is a separate area for touring caravans, campers and tents, with hardstanding and electric hook-ups provided. The excellent park facilities include a nine hole putting green, a play area, a laundry room, and a shop which stocks all essential grocery items as well as a wide range of camping accessories. You can even buy new and second hand caravans!

A short drive south from Peebles along the B709 and you will find yourselves on the shores of **St. Mary's Loch** at the edge of the Ettrick Forest.

This truly is a beautiful spot, set amongst some of the smoothest rolling green hills that you'll ever have the pleasure to experience. The loch is three miles long and these days it is commonly used for sailing, with a popular sailing club on the western end. The atmosphere is wonderfully peaceful here, and it's great to just linger by the shores, skimming stones and generally letting time just pass by.

Curiousity was also satisfied at St. Mary's loch. 'Tibbie Shiel' is a legendary name in these parts and if you travel to the neck of land that separates St. Mary's Loch from the smaller Loch of the Lowes, you will find an inn with a tale to tell. The A708 from Moffat passes the door, as does the Southern Upland Way, and any traveller should visit the **Tibbie Shiels Inn**, if only to discover its historical past. The inn was originally a cottage owned by Lord Napier and rented by Tibbie and Robert Richardson, a mole catcher. It was St. Mary's Cottage then, but, on the death of her husband, Tibbie reverted to her maiden name of Shiel and started to take in lodgers to support herself and her six children. Until her death in 1878, in her ninety sixth year, Tibbie played host to such famous names as Sir Walter Scott, Professor Wilson, alias Christopher North, the publisher Robert Chambers and local poet James Hogg, the Ettrick Shepherd.

Tibbie Shiels conjures up images of days gone by and of James Hogg penning his verse in the candlelit inn with only the log fires for company. There are certainly many references to Tibbie Shiels in his poetry and his literature. He obviously felt, as you may too, that the Tibbie Shiels Inn is worth writing home about.

There's no point in hurrying a journey along the A708 towards Selkirk, catching brief glimpses of the Yarrow Water that runs beside. Some four miles before reaching Selkirk, you will come across **Bowhill**. Set a whole day aside for exploring this magnificent mansion and home of the Scotts of Buccleuch.

Erected by the third Duke of Buccleuch in 1795, it is open to the public during the summer months. The house contains many fine works of art, including paintings by Van Dyck, Reynolds, Raeburn and Claude Lorraine, and has the privilege of having the 'Madonna and the Yarnwinder' which is the only painting by Leonardo da Vinci still in private hands in this country.

There are also many fine examples of 17th and 18th century furniture and clocks. One clock especially appeals, as it is able to play eight different Scottish airs, or tunes, though the mechanism was so set that the clock actually observes the Sabbath by not striking from twelve o' clock on Saturday until midnight on Sunday.

In the grounds there are some fine gardens, with nature trails and lovely woodland walks. For the children you will find that the adventure playground is ideal. If, after your walk, you have built up a thirst, then you can stay awhile and have a drink or a snack in the tea rooms.

From the delights of Bowhill it is a short distance to the town of **Selkirk** which, like so many of these Border towns, has a history linked to those fateful conflicts with the English. The town itself was actually destroyed by the English after the Battle of Flodden in 1513. Selkirk sent eighty men to fight in the battle for James IV, but only one of them survived to come back to this saddened and decimated community.

The story goes that he returned, however, bearing a captured English flag and, unable to speak of his sorrow and of the loss of his countrymen, he simply waved the flag down towards the ground. This act is symbolically re-enacted each year in the Common Riding, in remembrance of all those who have fallen in battle.

Sir Walter Scott was sheriff of the county in the early 18th century and his statue stands in the market place, near to the courthouse where he dispensed his justice. Another visit to make in Selkirk is to the Halliwells House Museum and Gallery. Located on the west side of the main square, it consists of a row of 18th century dwelling houses renovated to make a museum of Selkirk's colourful history. The buildings have links with the ironmongery trade and these have been renovated, providing a fascinating insight into the world of Edwardian shopping with a wonderful collection of domestic hardware from the period. In the adjoining Robson Gallery there is a range of touring exhibitions. Nearby to the museum and next to the post office is Robert Douglas' Bakery , where the baker made the original Selkirk 'bannock', a fruit loaf which is said to have been much favoured by Queen Victoria.

The town has a long association with shoemaking, Selkirk natives were once known as 'souters' and on one famous occasion supplied Bonnie Prince Charlie and his army with two thousand pairs of shoes for their ill-fated march to Derby in 1745.

Selkirk is still very much alive as a centre for tweed and woollen goods, and some of the mills are open to visitors. Another extremely interesting visit to make is to 'Selkirk Glass'. Here you are able to get a birds-eye view of the glass- making process, as everyone is made welcome to watch the craft in progress, producing the lovely glass products such as paperweights and perfume bottles that are exported all over the world.

Selkirk is a fine and effective example of the blending of old and new crafts, which is never an easy task. This Borders area excels in producing one of Scotland's most famous products; tweed. Did you know that 'tweed' is actually a misnomer? The weave's name does not originate from the river Tweed at all, but is in fact the result of a misspelling of the word 'tweel' by, of course, an English clerk.

For a peaceful, relaxing break in the heart of the beautiful Scottish Borders, head for **Philipburn House Hotel** which lies off the A707 in Philipburn village, close to Selkirk. Jim and Anne Hill are warm, welcoming hosts who offer first class hospitality in a refreshing, 'Alpine' atmosphere.

Winner of various awards, Philipburn House carries a Four Crown Highly Commended rating by the Scottish Tourist Board and provides first class accommodation in sixteen individually styled en-suite rooms or suites, attractively furnished and equipped to the highest standards. Dining is a treat, with a choice of the candlelit Poolside and Zum Zee Restaurants offering superb cuisine complemented by an award-winning wine list. Various leisure activities are readily available and many local historic attractions are within easy reach, making Philipburn an excellent all year round holiday base.

Philipburn House Hotel, Philipburn, Selkirk. 0750-20747
Map Ref: D4

To the south-east of Selkirk on the B6400 at **Lilliesleaf** you will discover **The Plough Inn**. A superb establishment it is ideally situated as a touring base and as an en-route stopping-off point.

Built around 1725, careful refurbishment has provided modern comforts, whilst not detracting from the original character of the building. Douglas Hannah is a welcoming host who offers friendly Scottish hospitality, well-kept ales and excellent food and accommodation. All the rooms from the bars to the bedrooms are beautifully furnished and outside, the rear garden is a wonderful sight, thanks to the green fingers of Douglas's father. The menu offers superior 'pub' fare and for those wishing to stay, the three guest rooms provide very comfortable accommodation, two with en-suite facilities and one with private bathroom.

The Plough Inn, Lilliesleaf, Nr Selkirk. 0835-870271 Map Ref: E4

Being surrounded by so much beautiful countryside we should always be keen to learn more about our habitat. And by taking the B6453 and B6400 from Selkirk you'll find the perfect place for gaining a greater understanding of the woods that are so important to us.

Harestanes Countryside Visitor Centre is about three miles out of Jedburgh, near **Nisbet**, on the B6400.

The centre is housed within beautifully converted farm buildings and offers various attractions including the fascinating Wooden Games Room, which contains a selection of unusual games all of which are made from wood.

There are regularly changing countryside exhibitions, a stunning audio visual display and if the children get restless, they can run off some energy in the adventure playground. In addition there is a Wildlife Garden, Countryside Discovery Room, an attractive millpond and a variety of Ranger-led activities which are available all year round. With a tearoom to relax in, a shop full of countryside mementos, not to mention beautiful walks in the surrounding estate land, you have all you need for a wonderful family day out.

Harestanes Countryside Visitor Centre, By Ancrum, Jedburgh.
08353-281/306 Map Ref: F4

And so to **Jedburgh**, just down the A68, only ten miles from the border and presenting a pleasant and striking blend of the old and the new. The town is perhaps best known for its Abbey; which was once rich and powerful but suffered the wrath of Henry VIII and his Reformation, along with the Borders other abbeys. Its majestic ruins stand just outside the town.

In the middle of the High Street, now dressed in up to date modern garb, lies what is reputedly the oldest hotel in Scotland, and fourth oldest in the British Isles; The Spread Eagle. In October 1566, Mary Queen of Scots, travelled to Jedburgh to hold a Justice Ayres, or Circuit Court, in the Tolbooth that stood in Canongate, and as the Spread Eagle Hotel had already been established, she naturally sought lodging there. She remained until driven out by a fire next door, when she moved to 'Mary Queen of Scots' House, which has been excellently preserved since its complete renovation in 1928, a hundred yards away. Another distinguished guest at the hotel was Sir Walter Scott, who lodged there when engaged in the local circuit court, where he made his first appearance as an advocate. Robert Burns also lived, for a short time, some hundred yards away and one can safely assume that he also had a knowledge of the 'Spread', as it is known locally, and of the fiery fluid purveyed therein.

In the town centre, adjacent to the Tourist Information Centre, you find **The Carters' Rest**, a super restaurant run by Michael Wares. Made from ancient Abbey Stones, the original building has a long history and was at one time the local grammar school, until 1887 when it became a popular refreshment stop for local carters, hence its name. Sympathetic refurbishment has retained all its character and charm, and outside the lower floor restaurant, there is a delightful restored hill cart.

The former hayloft and stables is now the lounge and steak bar, where you can relax with a drink and choose from a superb menu. Restaurant opening hours are 12-2pm Monday - Saturday, 6-9pm Monday - Thursday, and 6-10pm Friday/Saturday, plus Easter - October, Sunday opening from 12.30-2pm and 6-9pm.

The Carters, Jedburgh. 0835-863414 Map Ref: F4

Bridgehouse, 5 Bridge Street, Jedburgh. 0835-62906 Map Ref: F4

The weary traveller visiting Jedburgh will find delightful accommodation at **Bridgehouse**, the impressive home of Sandra and James Scott. Enjoying a lovely location beside the Jed Water River and only minutes walk from the town centre, Bridgehouse can be

Jedburgh Abbey

found by following the High Street away from the Abbey, turning left by the Pheasant Inn and then first right and it stands on the right.

Built in 1817, it was used as a toll-house for over 25 years and is listed as a building of historic interest. Totally refurbished by Sandra and James, it now boasts three beautifully appointed and well-equipped bedrooms, each with a television and a breakfast room where guests are superbly fed each morning. As a peaceful yet central touring base, it really is ideal.

If you don't feel like cooking or you just want a treat, you will find an excellent place to eat at **The Wayfarer Restaurant** on Jedburgh's Main Street. Winner of the Scottish Borders Tourist Board 'Best Evening Meal' award, this lovely family-run licensed establishment offers a cosy and intimate setting whether for lunch or dinner, with superior crockery and glassware on the tables adding that extra touch of class.

Originally built around 1898, the building has quite a history, having variously been a government building, a Post Office, an Italian ice cream parlour for forty years, then left derelict until the current owners Ralph and Mary Jonentz acquired and totally refurbished it, running it with their son Dieter as Head waiter. There are separate lunch and dinner menus, offering a wide selection to tempt every palate. Ralph has over thirty years experience in Hotel Management and as a chef and his experience shows in the rich variety of dishes available. You might be attracted by Curried Scampi with Rice, Ox-Tongue with Red Wine or a simple Mixed Grill, but whatever you choose, Ralph will do his best to make sure it is just as you like it. Open daily from 11.30am-2pm and 6-10pm, it is a popular venue for locals and visitors alike, so booking is advisable on weekend evenings.

The Wayfarer Restaurant, 51, High Street, Jedburgh. 0835-8635
Map Ref: F4

Just outside the town centre, enjoying an elevated position in a quiet residential area, **Froylehurst Guest House** is an impressive Grade B listed detached house. Following Exchange Street out of the Market Place, take the first right into Friars and Froylehurst lies approximately 1000 yards up on the left, at the end of a long sweeping drive.

Froylehurst, Friars, Jedburgh. 0835-62477 Map Ref: F4

Set within beautiful gardens, the house has ample private parking, which is a must here. The front door features lovely stained glass windows as does the landing on the stairs, and you are immediately struck by an air of elegance created by the beautiful decor and period furniture. The five guest rooms are furnished to an equally high standard, well deserving of the Two Crown Highly Commended award by the Scottish Tourist Board.

Hundalee House, Jedburgh. 0835-863011 Map Ref: F4

A mile south of the town set in 10 acres of lovely wooded grounds and gardens, **Hundalee House** is an impressive 18th century manor house fit for royalty and guests here are treated as such. Lying a short distance off the A68, the house is easy to find, being clearly signposted from the main road.

The gardens are simply delightful and once inside, you immediately understand why this charming establishment boasts a Deluxe rating from the Scottish Tourist Board, the highest award for quality that such a property can receive. The five guest rooms are all individually furnished and fully equipped, three with en-suite bathroom, and the dining room provides an elegant setting for the excellent breakfast which awaits you each morning.

Leaving Jedburgh, following the B6357, which is a lovely scenic route leading through the Wauchope Forest, you will eventually find yourself in the village of **Bonchester Bridge**.

In the heart of Bonchester is **Hobsburn House** who have joined with the Scottish Academy of Falconry to provide unique country pursuits holidays. Leonard and Diana Durman-Walters at the Academy are falconry experts and leaders in their field, whilst Bruce and Louise Graham-Cameron at Hobsburn House have a lifetime's equestrian experience.

Their shared knowledge has revived the ancient sport of falconry and hawking by horseback, and in the beautiful countryside of the Scottish Borders guests too can enjoy this stimulating sport. There are numerous other exciting activities available, and whether you stay at Hobsburn or the Academy, you will be royally looked after, in a relaxed and friendly 'house party' atmosphere, with superb food, fine wine and first class hosts.

Hobsburn House, Bonchester Bridge. 0450-86642 Map Ref: E5

It is now only a brief drive up the A6088 to **Hawick**; the largest of the Border burghs, with a population of around seventeen thousand. It has a thriving reputation for the manufacture of quality knitwear, clothing and carpets. The town is the home of such names as Pringle of Scotland, Lyle and Scott, Peter Scott and many other smaller firms producing fully fashioned knitwear in cashmere, lambswool and Shetland yarns.

The centre of a vibrant farming community, Hawick has an interest in animals both alive and dead, as it is the centre for the longest established auction mart in the whole of Britain. It also boasts a number of butchers producing that Scots delicacy the Haggis, each to their own closely guarded recipe.

The Scottish Borders was for centuries an area of turmoil and intrigue. To the English, it was the area of first and last encounter with a traditional enemy and the target for quick and often bloody retribution. All of the Border towns were destroyed many times by raiders from England. Hawick was burned down no fewer than six times by the mid 1600's.

On one occasion the natives of Hawick burned the town themselves to prevent the English from having the pleasure of extracting their vengeance. Traffic in marauding was by no means confined to the Scottish side - many English towns suffered a similar fate when the 'Rievers' of the Borders, on their small ponies, appeared from nowhere to burn, kill and rob.

Perhaps it is because Hawick was not 'stable' enough that few ancient buildings exist - no abbey or castle or magnificent building has survived. The Black Tower of Drumlanrig - perhaps the oldest building - has suffered partial destruction on numerous occasions (the latest being dry-rot and vermin). Needle Street, in the town's West End, is the oldest remaining street.

A dearth of ancient buildings does not mean a lack of ancient tradition and ceremony however. Each year the town holds its colourful Common Riding Celebrations on the first and second weekends of June, a legacy of the aftermath of Flodden in 1513. The Horse Monument in the High Street also commemorates the battle, a disaster for the town when nearly all the menfolk were killed.

Riders visiting Hawick at the time of the festivities, or indeed at any other time of year, might like to try the 'Hawick Circular', which is a twenty seven mile ride running along minor roads, tracks and cross country sections. Surely an ideal way to take in this glorious countryside.

There are many fine places to stay and visit in the hills and dales around Hawick. Enjoying a picturesque and sheltered valley location, overlooking hills and fields **Wiltonburn Farm** makes a peaceful and

The Horse Monument, Hawick

relaxing holiday base. John and Sheila Shell are warm, welcoming hosts who provide very comfortable bed and breakfast accommodation within their charming 250 year old farmhouse home. Listed and Commended by the Scottish Tourist Board, the house is attractively furnished throughout and there are three spacious guest rooms, one of which is en-suite. Set within 400 acres of land, this mixed working farm also offers accommodation for the self-catering enthusiast, with two fully equipped cottages, one sleeping 3/4 and the other 4/5, each carrying a Three Crown rating by the Scottish Tourist Board, making Wiltonburn Farm an ideal holiday base, whatever your needs.

Wiltonburn Farm, Hawick. 0450-72414 / 78000 Map Ref: D5

Situated a mile out of the town on the A7 road to Galashiels and set in an acre of land beside Howdenburn stream, **Brenlands** is a splendid licensed guest house. Here you are assured of comfortable accommodation and fine food in an atmosphere of friendly hospitality, easily accessible and an ideal touring base for the Scottish Borders.

Brenlands, Howdenburn, Hawick. 0450-75481 Map Ref: D5

Some 200 years ago, this dry stone granite house started life as a lodge cottage built into the hillside and somewhat recently further floors were added to it, creating the impressive building you see today. Accommodation is provided in five well-furnished, spacious guest rooms, each with en-suite facilities for maximum comfort. In addition to a full breakfast, excellent homecooked evening meals are available accompanied by a choice of wines, making your stay here complete.

While you are out exploring the area one place well worth calling in at is **Auld Cross Keys Inn** at **Denholm** on the A698, birthplace of Dr. John Leydon. The inn is run by a lovely couple, Peter and Heather Ferguson and won the Scottish Borders Tourist Board Best Eating Place 1992 competition, in the Afternoon/ High Tea category.

This is understandable when you see the extensive, mouthwatering menu. High Teas are served on Sundays from 4.00pm - 7.00pm, but you can savour Heather's excellent homecooking throughout the week at lunchtime and evenings. Situated opposite the village green, Auld Cross Keys is a very old building, full of character, and offers a warm, friendly atmosphere in which to enjoy a pint of fine local cask ale and a tasty meal.

Auld Cross Keys Inn, Main Street, Denholm, by Hawick..
0450-87305 Map Ref: E5

To the south of the town **Teviotdale Lodge** enjoys a secluded location in two and a half acres of beautiful wooded gardens. Overlooking the River Teviot at Commonside, it provides non-smokers with a restful haven, where they can escape the stresses of modern living. To find this super country residence, turn off the A7 two miles prior to **Newmill-on-Teviot**, down the No Through Road after the bridge, where you will see Teviotdale Lodge signposted.

Built in 1930 as a shooting and fishing lodge, Teviotdale is a picture, with ivy climbing up its pale pink exterior walls. Inside, it is equally impressive with beautiful furnishings throughout. Jan and Donald Macdonald are friendly hosts, who succeed in providing their guests with the best of service in a warm, relaxed atmosphere.

Teviotdale Lodge, Commonside, Hawick. 0450-85232 Map Ref: D5

The seven guest rooms are spacious and well-equipped, with prettily co-ordinated fabrics and most providing en-suite bath or shower. The cosy sitting room with its small bar offers the opportunity to relax with a pre-dinner drink, whilst the lovely breakfast/dining area with its views across the garden, provides the perfect setting for both the substantial breakfast and excellent two-course set dinner. Children are welcome and cots, highchairs and a playpen are available if required and the laundry room for guests use is an invaluable asset, as any parents of young children will know!

Anyone staying in or around Newmill-on-Teviot would be foolish to miss out on a meal at **The Old Forge**.

The Old Forge, Newmill-on-Teviot, Hawick. 0450-85298 Ref: D5

Situated on the A7, this delightful licensed restaurant is housed within a group of 19th century buildings which, until 8 years ago, formed the local Smiddy or blacksmith's. A cosy and characterful establishment, exposed brick walls, beamed ceilings and genuine working bellows add to its charm. Friendly hosts Simon and Judith Findlay have earned a wide reputation for superb cuisine, which makes booking almost essential, but then the table is yours for the evening. In addition to an excellent lunch menu, there is a set 3-course dinner from Tuesday to Thursday and a 4-course dinner Friday and Saturday, plus Sunday lunches, all featuring the finest food, imaginatively prepared and beautifully presented. Children are welcome and the restaurant is accessible to wheelchair users.

Rather than taking the A7 towards Langholm and our next chapter, it's preferable to take the B6399 from Hawick towards Newcastleton. The road roughly follows the old Edinburgh - Carlisle 'Waverley' route and there are often reminders of the long closed railway, like the huge and forlorn viaduct near Stobs. Another mark of the railways passage is the delightfully named nearby village of Steele Road.

This road takes us to one of the Borders most famous castles, the **Hermitage**. Aptly named stood quite alone, grim and oppressive, in the wild remote Liddesdale hills its history is vivid and often bloody. Built in the 13th century it is still one of the most impressive medieval castles in Scotland.In October 1566 the fourth Earl of Bothwell badly wounded in a skirmish with border rievers, was paid a surprise visit by Mary Queen of Scots. She had been presiding over a Royal Court at Jedburgh, but on hearing of her lover's plight the Queen rode twenty furious miles to the castle and two hours later back again, a feat that cost her a fever and nearly her life. Even on the sunniest day the castle's brooding presence makes the Queen's adventure all to easy to imagine and admire.

Nearby **Newcastleton** is one of few planned villages in the Borders. Built in 1793, it consists of a single long 'high' street astride the main road and a regular pattern street plan.

We started this chapter in England and we finish just back over the border. Situated close by ,off the B6318, in the delightful area of Bailey, **Bailey Mill** offers everything you could possibly need for a perfect holiday. This beautifully converted 18th century Grain Mill provides superb accommodation in five characterful apartments which sleep between four and nine people. Each is fully equipped for maximum comfort and the standard of decor and facilities is well-deserving of the 3-Key Commended rating awarded by the Cumbria Tourist Board.

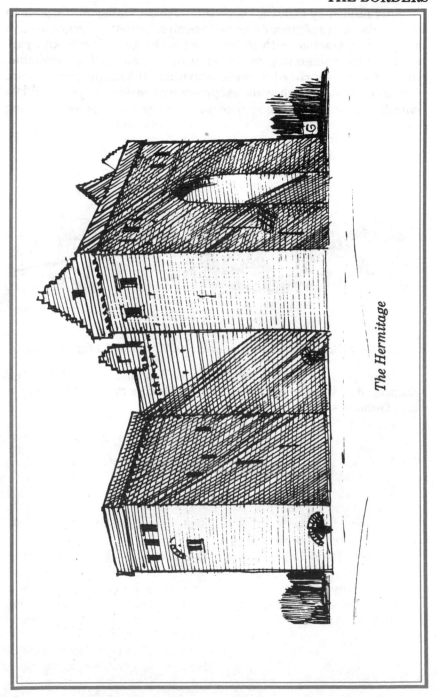

The Hermitage

Surrounded by beautiful open countryside, Bailey Mill stands in its own five acres of grounds, home to ponies, lambs, and goats, always a popular attraction with children, as is the games room and play area. For the energetic, pony trekking, fishing and golf are available, whilst for those inclined towards relaxation, the sauna, gymnasium, jacuzzi and solarium provide an opportunity to pamper yourself. The laundry room and farm kitchen meal service makes self-catering easy.

Bailey Mill, Bailey, Newcastleton. 0697-748617 Map Ref: D7

Bailey is very close to the border with England and with our next chapter. And it is the last village we visit before our journey takes us into Dumfries and Galloway.

CHAPTER TWO

Dumfries and Galloway.

Caerlaverlock Castle

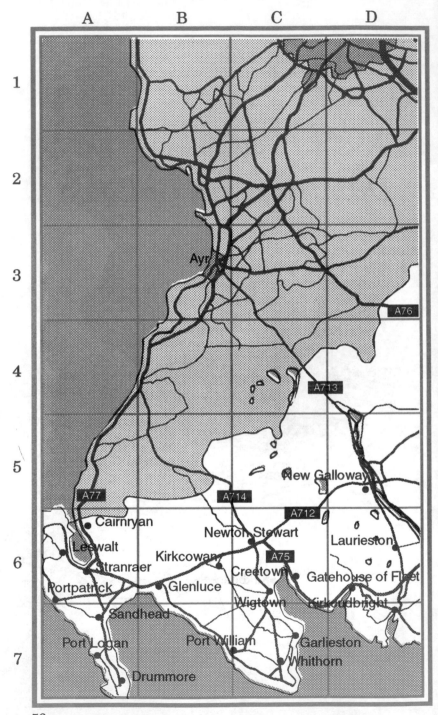

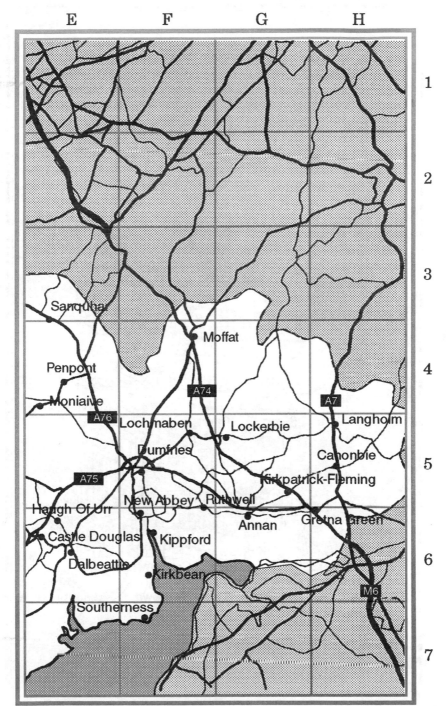

Dumfries Mid Steeple

CHAPTER TWO

Dumfries and Galloway.

Our journey through this chapter begins just across the Scottish border in that place renowned for its runaway couples and hasty marriages, **Gretna Green**. It's strange to think that marriages by declaration could in fact take place at any house or shop, provided there were two witnesses available.

In 1856, after much indignation from the church and even local people, who were not too happy with what they saw as 'immoral practices', the law was changed. The new legislation demanded a residential qualification of three weeks for one of the runaway couple, which we would imagine was not quite so helpful to those in a hurry. Even when the couples had been married their problems were not always over, and there have been several cases of bridegrooms being arrested on their return to England.

In one particular case, where a music master was wed to his twelve year old pupil, he was sentenced to nine months in jail for abduction. In 1940 marriage by declaration became illegal, although the age of consent was still lower than that in England, and therefore the attraction of Gretna Green continued to lure young couples. This attraction only really declined when the age of marriage without parental consent was lowered in England from twenty one to eighteen years, in 1970.

It's worth spending some time looking around this most famous place. The blacksmith's shop today has a range of curiosities and souvenirs from the marriage trade and you could even find yourself involved in a mock ceremony.

Travelling out of Gretna on The Old Annan Road (B721), **Newhouse Farm** is the welcoming home of Alice Blackwell. Here you will discover a hidden treasure trove called Alice's Wonderland, a museum collection of over 1000 doll's from all over the world, dating from the 18th century to the present day. Among these are some rare oriental dolls, the most notable collection being the Hina Festival Set. There are also teddy bears, golliwogs and popular TV and book characters to meet, all of which makes this a place that will appeal to adults and children alike. After marvelling at the many exhibits, you can enjoy refreshments in the café and should you wish to stay, Alice provides bed and breakfast accommodation in three guest rooms within her house.

Newhouse Bed and Breakfast, Annan Road, Gretna. 0461-337711
Map Ref: H6

Gretna itself is situated on the River Sark, which flows into the Solway Firth, and we are staying with the coastline following the A75 westwards to the town of Annan . It's a shame that so many visitors to Scotland these days rush through the border spurred on by the thought of reaching their next destination. They are the unlucky ones who will miss out on some of the most delightful towns and scenery to be found in this country.

The small red stone town of **Annan** sits overlooking the Solway Firth and the mountains of the Lake District. This ancient burgh was in fact founded by the family of King Robert the Bruce, and displays the Bruce coat of arms as its own.

Standing close to the border as it does, Annan has many times been subject to the unwelcome attentions of the English, and was destroyed repeatedly between 1298 and 1660. It was, however, the waters of the river Annan which brought about the first of many tragedies for this burgh. A curse was put on the town by the renowned mystic Saint Malachy, who was angered by the decision of one of the lords of Annan to execute a robber on whose behalf he had interceded. The site of the castle, which was formerly in the churchyard, still bears the scars of river erosion. The town today, however, bears little sign of those turbulent years and you should find it pleasant and peaceful in this lovely riverside setting. Annan, once an important shipbuilding and trading centre, now offers the visitor strolls around the attractive riverside park. There are many walks nearby around Hoddom Castle, and there is a golf course with lovely views over the Solway.

In nearby **Ruthwell** village you'll find the Duncan Savings Bank Museum, site of the first savings bank in Britain. Also worth a visit is Ruthwell Church , where you can see the famous and impressive Runic Cross, covered with the ancient writing of the Norse. A short drive away is **Comlongon Castle**. Exceptionally well preserved, it contains many original features including the great hall, kitchens, dungeons and bed chambers, with their 'privies'. A real opportunity to see how life was in a 15th century castle.

Crossing back over the picturesque River Annan once more, take the B6357 towards the village of **Kirkpatrick-Fleming**. There you'll discover The Station Inn, a perfect example of the sort of charming country inn you can find in Scotland, if you take the trouble to get away from the main roads. The Station Inn is over two hundred years old. Inside, the theme is, not surprisingly, railway based, and there is plenty of fascinating memorabilia.

Some of this relates to Quintinshill Signal Box, scene of Britain's worst rail disaster. One busy morning in May 1915 a train carrying a regiment of the 7th Royal Scots struck a standing local train and the wreckage was run into by a north bound express. The following conflagration took an estimated 226 lives, the final number never being known as the regiments records were destroyed in the train. Another 200 were badly injured. As the disaster involved troops during wartime it didn't receive the publicity which usually attends such catastrophes, few people have heard of Quintinshill.

With the whole of Dumfries before you it is not easy to decide where to head next, so, in keeping with our main intention to avoid the main routes, we're taking the B6357 to **Canonbie**, which proved to be a welcome discovery. Standing on the left bank of the river Esk, it is set in a particularly picturesque valley. The parish church here dates from 1822 and is situated on the opposite side of the river, which emerges dramatically from between the red sandstone cliffs. Interestingly it was designed by William Atkinson, the architect of Sir Walter Scott's Abbotsford.

The A7 follows the river from Canonbie back towards its source, and we followed this road upwards to **Langholm**, a typical border town in appearance, situated on the river with its narrow streets. Like Edinburgh, Langholm is divided into a new and old town. It is hard to believe that three rivers join here, and not surprisingly there are three bridges. As the famous engineer Thomas Telford was born nearby, you can't help but wonder if he had a hand in the building of any of these bridges.

Being a true Border town, Langholm has an annual Common Riding which takes place on the last Friday in June. A feature of this day is that the colours worn by the Cornet for his ride are the same colours of the winner of the Epsom Derby each year. An unusual custom that is over one hundred years old and must have a reason, now seemingly lost. If you are lucky enough to be here for this special event you will be treated to a day full of the most exciting spectacles, including horse racing, foot races, wrestling and Highland dancing. In the evening, if you have any energy left, you can take part in the open air dancing. Be warned though; the celebrations of the day start at five o'clock in the morning.

In the Market Place, you will find an excellent holiday base at **The Eskdale Hotel**. Run by Norman Gormley and his friendly team of staff, this former coaching house dates back several hundred years and has been tastefully refurbished to provide every modern comfort in an atmosphere of warm hospitality. The seventeen guest rooms are all attractively furnished and well-equipped, ten with en-suite facilities. The restaurant provides both an à la carte and table d'hôte menu, offering an extensive choice to suit every palate and the cosy bar is ideal to relax in after a busy day exploring or enjoying your favourite leisure pursuit.

The Eskdale Hotel, Market Place, Langholm. 03873-80357/81178
Fax: 03873-80357 Map Ref: H5

Langholm is an excellent centre for exploring the quiet valleys and hill country on foot, but, if you prefer, there are marvellous opportunities for cycling, or even driving. There is also excellent fishing nearby. To the north of Langholm, and in the heart of some of most magical forests and scenery, you will discover the village of **Eskdalemuir**. In 1905 an observatory was built on the moors, and there is also a weather station here. Some of the lowest temperatures in the winter are recorded at this station.

In this remote setting is the Kagyu Samye Ling Tibetan Centre, which, you may not be surprised to learn, is a Buddhist centre. This is a thriving international community, and holds pottery, woodcarving and carpet-weaving workshops. There is also an art studio and a printing press. If you are of a mind, then you can take the chance to learn some relaxation here. Meditation, healing and Buddhism are also taught. The centre is a highly unusual place, and promises an enjoyable visit.

The B7068 from Langholm passes through some spectacular scenery, as it winds its way towards **Lockerbie**. The origins of the town go back to the 16th century, when it grew as a market town in this largely agricultural area. The character of the town has been retained, and there are many interesting shops and fine buildings dating from the 17th and 18th centuries.

If you wish to sample some period delights and relax in style, then just off the B723 and half a mile from the bustling town centre you will find the **Lockerbie Manor Country Hotel**.

The hotel is housed in an imposing, magnificent building dating back to the 18th century, and was originally built by Dame Grace Johnstone and Sir William Douglas, Marquisses of Queensberry. It was in this very building that the Queensberry rules of boxing are said to have been formulated; a direct result of the 8th Marquis' passion for boxing, among other things.

Lockerbie Manor Country Hotel, Boreland Road, Lockerbie.
0576-202610/203939 Map Ref: G5

Today, the Lockerbie Manor Country Hotel still retains most of its period charm, enhanced by original wall panelling and a superb collection of artwork. There are 30 rooms all prettily furnished in antique style, with en-suite facilities and all the modern conveniences you would expect in a top class hotel. These include a courtesy tray, tea and coffee making facilities, central heating, colour television, trouser press, hairdryer, direct dial telephones and room service. All VIP rooms contain traditional four poster beds.

The restaurant enjoys wonderful views over the surrounding lawns and woodlands and, with its subtle lighting and magnificent wood panelling, provides the perfect atmosphere in which to relax and enjoy the superb cuisine. There is a delicious selection of new classical dishes, as well as traditional English and Scottish food. An extensive wine list ensures that there is something here to suit all tastes and complement every dish.

Lockerbie Manor is ideally placed for touring the Borders and Solway Firth. The hotel offers golf at Lockerbie and Moffat and seven other golf courses, salmon and trout fishing, stalking and clay pigeon shooting by prior arrangement. Tuition in all of these pursuits is available.

A special service offered by the hotel is a two day break offering table d'hôte dinner, bed and full Scottish breakfast. These breaks are available any two days throughout the year. Conferences for up to 150 can also be arranged.

However long your visit, whether for a couple of days or a couple of weeks, proprietor Joan Yuen-Walther is always on hand to ensure your stay is a pleasant one.

Near to Lockerbie is **Lochmaben** and here you'll find the ruined castle of Robert the Bruce. It's a delightful place to 'take five' on the shores of the castle loch watching the sailing boats and the fishermen trying their luck. The loch is also an ideal place for bird watching.

It is only a short distance to our next stop, **Moffat**. It has a reputation as a picturesque town, and you won't be disappointed. Its wide main streets, with attractive shops and hotels, make for pleasant strolling. The fabulous gardens and parks have helped earn Moffat the title of the 'Best Kept Village in Scotland' award twice in recent years.

In the centre of the town is a handsome square with the Colvin Fountain, surmounted by a ram. This statue proclaims the importance of sheep in this area and the role played by Moffat as a sheep and wool trading centre.

Those of you with a taste for traditional home cooking will find that Moffat has a rich heritage of food. Why not search out some traditional Moffat toffee, or even try the famous Scottish haggis? You can still find a traditional bakehouse in the old part of the town, in which the Moffat Museum is situated. The Scotch oven, an old furnace used for baking bread, is an interesting feature on the ground floor. The museum also has an exhibition, tracing local history which follows Moffat's rise as a health resort in the mid-eighteenth century due to the discovery here of mineral springs. As a result of this, Moffat became famous as one of the few spa towns in Scotland. The Old Well and Hartfell Spa have both been restored, and make fascinating visits.

Just a few minutes walk from the town centre of Moffat, **Rockhill** is the charming home of Phyl and Barry Fosket who enjoy sharing it with their many guests. The first impression on your arrival is of flowers everywhere and it comes as no surprise to learn that the Foskets have won horticultural awards. This elegant mid-Victorian house provides very comfortable accommodation in ten spacious and attractively furnished guest rooms, some with en-suite facilities. As with the outside, the interior is filled with flowers and plants and the atmosphere is one of relaxed informality. A hearty Scottish breakfast sets you up for a day's exploring and if you wish, you can enjoy a freshly prepared homecooked evening meal on your return.

Rockhill, 14 Beechgrove, Moffat. 0683-20283 Map Ref: F4

Apart from fishing, Moffat can offer a wide variety of activities for the visitor. There are many beautiful walks around the surrounding countryside, and. Horse riding, pony-trekking, cycle-hire, sailing and swimming are all available locally. And the annual South of Scotland Tennis Tournament held here actually pre-dates Wimbledon?

Whether you intend to take in the whole of Southern Scotland or explore more local phenomena, such as the intriguingly named Devil's Beeftub and the Grey Mare's Tail waterfall, Moffat is an ideal centre for touring not only the borders but also the south and west. It is also handy, being close to the main A74, for forays into the exciting cities of Edinburgh and Glasgow.

Our route now takes us along the A701 southwards past the unusually named Forest of Ae. Take your time and make the most of the wonderful scenery in this beautiful area, which truly is the heart of Dumfriesshire.

Cross the Ae Water and you're only a small distance from the royal burgh of Dumfries, which lies in the heart of the district of Nithsdale. This area takes its name from the river Nith, which winds its way southwards from the Lowther Hills to the Solway. It is truly a picturesque river, running through such a variety of countryside that the area is sometimes referred to as "Scotland in miniature". The river reaches the Solway at Dumfries.

If the Borders are associated with the tales and legends of Walter Scott, then Dumfries and Galloway are forever associated with the poet Robert Burns. He lived in **Dumfries** and worked as an exciseman here until his death in 1796. There is a statue in the High Street commemorating this town's most famous citizen. Many people come to Dumfries each year to visit the monuments and places associated with the poet, and this period in his life is widely considered to be one of his most productive. Whilst the French Revolution and the Napoleonic Wars were going on, and the country was alive with rumours and alarms, there were food shortages and riots in Dumfries.

It was during this time that Burns produced some of his best work, despite being heavily in debt and suffering from a serious illness. He first came to Dumfries in 1787, though did not eventually settle here until some four years later, after finding his farm, Ellisand, to be uneconomical. He first lived in Bank Street, and the building can still be seen. In 1793 Burns moved to a larger house in what is now called Burns Street. Here he worked until his death three years later. The two storey house where he spent his last years is now a museum, with many items associated with the poet on display. Burns is buried in the graveyard of nearby St. Michael's church.

While Burns was in Dumfries he was no stranger to the taverns of the town, and one with special Burns links is the Globe Inn just off the High Street. In the small panelled rooms it is fascinating to think of the poet sharing a glass of port or a tankard of ale with his friends. His favourite armchair is still there, but before you try it out for size be warned, as anyone who sits in the chair can be called upon to buy a round of drinks for everyone present.

In 1790 Burns had an affair with a young barmaid and she bore him a child, which his wife later took in and cared for as one of her own. For a full explanation of the poet's links with this town, why not take a look at the Robbie Burns Centre situated on the banks of the Nith. This building houses a permanent exhibition and an audio-visual presentation on the poet.

The most familiar landmark in Dumfries is the Midsteeple, and this has been witness to some famous characters from the past. Bonnie Prince Charlie would have passed it on his way through Dumfries with the bedraggled remains of his army.

Apparently they needed some more shoes on their return journey, the ones from Selkirk being worn out, only this time the folk of Dumfries were not as forthcoming. A request for one thousand pairs of shoes only resulted in two hundred and twenty five being offered, whereupon, according to legend, the soldiers began to stop people in the street and take their shoes from them.

If you look at the Midsteeple you might notice something odd about it. Well you'd be right, as it now leans over, although not so far as to risk of toppling. Walking around the streets give you the opportunity to look at many interesting buildings, from the elegant Trades Hall to the quaint Queensberry Square with its old-fashioned closes.

It comes as a surprise to learn that Dumfries was the inspiration for the story of Peter Pan. The young James M Barrie was a pupil at the predecessor of Dumfries Academy. In 1860 Barrie came to Dumfries, and was at one time in the school's amateur dramatic club. He even wrote one of its earliest productions. When he returned to Dumfries, some years later as Sir James Barrie, he revealed that it was while playing in the gardens on the banks of the river Nith that he conceived the original basis for Peter Pan.

The house in which he stayed whilst at the Academy is in Victoria Place, and is marked with a plaque. A short journey down the river takes you us down towards the Solway by the B725, to find **Caerlaverock Castle.**

Unique in Scotland with its triangular layout and moat it proved a formidable fortress for the Maxwell family. In 1330 King Edward the laid siege and in 1638 it capitulated to the Covenanters after a siege of some 13 weeks.

Caerlaverock Castle.

Nearby is the Caerlaverock Nature Reserve, covering some 13,594 acres of saltmarsh and sand along the coastline of the Solway Firth. The marshes and mudflats stretch for six miles along the coastline, and in winter the reserve is home to great flocks of barnacle geese and other wildfowl. It also provides a breeding ground for the rare Natterjack toad. The wildfowl reserve is open from mid-summer until the end of April.

If you have time, it is well worth paying a visit to nearby **Ruthwell**. In the parish church you will find the Ruthwell Cross. This seventeen foot high cross is a testament to the faith of the early Christians, and has survived many attempts to destroy it. Dating from the early 8th century, it features intricate and beautiful carvings, illustrating episodes from the Gospels.

The next leg of our journey follows the river Nith towards its source. Following the A76 northwards passing **Ellisland**, where Burns had his farm. This is now open to the public, and the Burns relics, including the old farmhouse kitchen, are fascinating.

Make a small detour and branch left at the B729, which leads to Glenkiln Reservoir, and discover an unexpected surprise. For here on the hillsides surrounding the loch is a wonderful collection of sculptures by Henry Moore and other artists. It's a strange experience watching these figures, though you are not allowed to approach them since they are on private land.

From the loch it is an easy drive back towards Dunscore, and then the A76. We took the left turning off at Auldgirth and drove towards **Penpont**. This is a very relaxing and scenic route, and enabled us to see a particularly interesting example of a fortified house now being run as a hotel.

The south west of Scotland is particularly richly endowed with historic castles, peel towers and fortified houses. Many of these date from the late 16th and early 17th centuries when a side effect of the reformation was to release a great deal of land from the hands of the church.

At this time the area was wild, and torn by feuding and violence. In a none too successful effort to subdue this problem, King James VI gave parcels of the released land to his supporters, making it a condition of each grant that the new owner build a fortified house on the land. His idea was that these houses would provide a safe refuge for the population in times of strife, but in practice their owners seem to have found them more useful as a base from which to attack their enemies.

Be that as it may, future generations inherited a wealth of architectural diversity as the buildings developed from the original square towers to L-shaped and, subsequently, to Z-shaped towers decorated with gables, balustrades, corbels and other features.

There is a strong French influence in many of the designs, as the Auld Alliance brought to Scotland courtiers and architectural advisors who adapted the pepper-pot turrets of their own chateaux to the rigours of the local climate.

A handsome and uncompromising example of the L-shaped version is **Barjarg Tower**, which forms the north east corner of a mansion house lying on the west side of the River Nith some four miles south of Penpont and twelve miles north of Dumfries. Approaching from the south, turn left off the A76 at Auldgrith and then, three-quarters of a mile up the hill, turned right on the road signposted to Penpont. 'Barjarg' by the way means 'the red hill top'.

The original tower dates from the late 16th century when it was built by one of the Earls of Morton and gifted by him to Thomas Grierson. A later owner, a Mr Erskine, planted the magnificent Wellingtonia trees that have stood guard behind the house since the beginning of the 18th century. In 1740, the property passed to a Reverend Hunter, a Doctor of Divinity from Edinburgh, who was related to the Hunters of Hunterston in Ayrshire, the remains of whose castle is now a near neighbour of a nuclear power station. Dr Hunter was the founder of the Hunter Arundell family who have owned the property and its surrounding estate for some two hundred and fifty years.

Early in the 18th century the main part of the house was built with a symmetrical frontage and a matching tower at the west end. However the old tower is well preserved and visitors can see the original iron gate and many other features.

Taking the A702 at nearby Penpont west takes you to the small village of **Moniaive**. Set between Craigdarroch and Dalwhat Waters, the streets are small and narrow with brightly painted houses. Moniaive is a village renowned for its peaceful atmosphere and beautiful surroundings.

There are many references to the Covenanters in these parts, and the curious might wish to learn a little more about them. They were Presbyterians who were persecuted for refusing to renounce their faith during the reigns of Charles II and James II. They were often cruelly put to death without trial, and due to this the 1680s later became known as the 'Killing Time'.

Rejoining the A76 at **Thorburn**, which features wide streets lined with the lime trees planted by the Duke of Buccleuch in 1861. The monument at the end of the street was erected by the Duke of Queensbury in 1714, the Pegasus being his winged emblem. The town

Queensbury Monument, Thorburn

is dominated by the magnificent Queensbury mountain which stands at 2,285 feet.

Our next stop is the romantic **Drumlanrig Castle**, which is a beautiful stately mansion and is open to the public. The mansion was built by the first Duke of Queensbury between 1679 and 1690. It was indeed a departure from the style of most Scottish castles, and reminded us somewhat of a fairy tale castle with its superb, pink sandstone walls and enchanting roof. You may like to spend some time within its walls, as there is the finest collection of furniture, paintings, silver and china in Scotland. Bonnie Prince Charlie slept here on his retreat northwards from Dumfries in 1745. His bedroom can still be seen as can a few of his mementoes and personal relics.

The castle has a magnificent setting and there are lovely views of the surrounding countryside. There are forty acres of garden, and you may be interested to have a look at the craft shops while the children take advantage of the adventure playground. Drumlanrig is a stop worth making, and we are sure you will enjoy a day spent here.

Rather than taking the A76 its worth taking the parallel unclassified road to the west that leads from Drumlanrig northwards, and find yourselves before long in a town with the beautiful name of **Sanquhar**. This name, which conjures up any number of exotic images, apparently means simply, 'old fort'. The post office here is the oldest in Britain, and still retains some of its old world charm.

It's saddening to discover that at one time workers in the mines here were subject to laws of bondage, which meant that miners and their whole families could be bought and sold as slaves. They could only avoid this iniquitous system by escaping and staying free for a whole year and a day. Capture, however, would result in brutal punishment. It was not until the end of the 18th century that the final traces of this custom were removed by an Act of Parliament. There is an interesting local museum in the old tolbooth of 1735, which is now a visitor and information centre.

We've come as far as intended in this area and now must retrace our steps to Dumfries, and on into neighbouring Galloway.

Travelling west from Dumfries, you find yourselves with a choice of three roads leading into Galloway - one of Scotland's most beautiful areas, with its mild climate warmed by the Gulf Stream, enabling even palm trees to grow in some of the gardens. As a result, this part of the country is particularly mild in both spring and autumn, making an out of season visit well worthwhile.

The roads are a pleasure to drive along, as there are no busy motorways or huge traffic jams, only lovely country roads that crisscross the open countryside, enabling the explorer to drive from loch to glen to forest with the minimum of fuss.

For this venture into Galloway we start by leaving Dumfries on the A710 which takes you once again towards the Solway Firth. This road follows the Solway Coast Heritage Trail, a recommended route of particular interest. Seven miles south of Dumfries is the picturesque village of **New Abbey**. A thoroughly charming and unspoilt haven with the impressive ruin of Sweetheart Abbey nearby.

Enjoying a prominent location in the village square, **The Abbey Arms Hotel** is an ideal holiday base, with ready access to many places of interest and a variety of leisure activities to suit the needs of every guest. Within the hotel, the public bar provides a comfortable setting for a quiet drink and offers a wide selection of hand drawn ales, wines, spirits and liqueurs with light bar meals available both lunchtime and evening. The restaurant has a deserved reputation for the variety and quality of food it serves, always freshly prepared using local produce whenever possible. The ten guest rooms ensure a good night's sleep, each equipped with en-suite bathroom and colour TV for maximum privacy and comfort.

The Abbey Arms Hotel, New Abbey. 0387-85215 Map Ref: F6

Right at the bottom of Criffel Hill, the Abbey was built in the thirteenth and fourteenth centuries by Lady Devorgilla in memory of her husband John de Balliol. You may remember that their son was the King of Scotland for a short while, chosen by Edward I.

There is a popular story that after her husband's death Lady Devorgilla carried his embalmed heart in an ivory casket wherever she went. When she eventually died, some twenty-one years later, the casket was buried with her in front of the high altar. The name of the

Sweetheart Abbey, New Abbey

Abbey comes from the Cistercians who, as a tribute to this lady, called it 'Dulce Cor' or Sweetheart.

No visit to New Abbey would be complete without calling in at **Abbey Cottage Coffees and Crafts** which stands right beside the Abbey ruins. A non-smoking establishment, this is the perfect place to relax with a drink and a snack before purchasing a memento or gift. The combined efforts of Morag McKie and Jacqui Wilson ensure that all the food is freshly prepared and of the highest quality, which has earned them an entry into various prestigious guides. In addition to tea, coffee and soft drinks, you can enjoy a glass of wine or beer with your meal. After sampling the excellent food, the adjoining craft shop leaves you faced with the dilemma of what to choose from the wide range of locally produced high quality arts and crafts.

Abbey Cottage Coffees and Crafts, New Abbey. 0387-85377
Map Ref: F6

After looking around the Abbey it is well worth paying a visit to the delightful **Shambellie House Museum of Costume**, which is just a quarter of a mile to the north of the village. The building itself is notable for having been designed by the architect David Bryce in 1854 and the house reflects the rich characteristics of Bryce's style, referred to as "Scottish Baronial,". Particularly fascinating are the crow-stepped gables, towers and turrets. The Scottish heritage is uniquely reflected in the appearance of the building with its suggestion of battlements, a reminder of the many castles seen in this part of the country.

Inside the building houses the most fascinating exhibition of clothes, mainly from the eighteenth and nineteenth centuries, which were collected by Charles Stuart of Shambellie, an illustrator who developed this collection over a period of years starting before the Second World War.

If you are feeling energetic, then why not attempt a climb up nearby Criffel Hill? This hill is one thousand eight hundred and sixty eight feet high, so it is not really for the faint-hearted. The granite can be quite steep and rough in parts, making the wearing of a good pair of stout walking shoes advisable. Take it on good authority that the views at the summit are spectacular.

We continue on the A710 past Overton on the coast and down towards the little village of **Kirkbean**.

Just off the A710 at Kirkbean, **Cavens House Hotel** makes an excellent touring base from which to explore the local area. This charming establishment was originally built during the 18th century by Richard Oswald, a wealthy merchant who as a friend of Benjamin Franklin, had strong links with the government and was one of the signatories for the Treaty of Independence which ended the Seven Years War. Today Cavens House is a welcoming hotel with flowers everywhere adding a colourful touch and tea and scones awaiting you on your arrival. Accommodation is provided in six lovely guest rooms, all en-suite and dining is a treat, with a mouthwatering five-course dinner menu freshly prepared using the finest local produce.

Cavens House Hotel, Kirkbean, By Dumfries. 0387-88234 Ref: F5

At nearby **Arbigland** there is a fascinating house and gardens which are open in the summer. John Paul Jones was born in one of the cottages in 1747. He was to become one of the area's most famous sons and later became known as the "father of the American Navy". The story of John Paul Jones is very interesting and definitely worth a mention here, as he was not solely regarded as a hero. Indeed some people, including the British, branded him a pirate.

77

When he was only thirteen he boarded a boat at nearby Carsethorn and began an apprenticeship that was to last for seven years in the Merchant Navy. His travels took him around the world visiting such beautiful places as Barbados and Virginia, and eventually he assumed command of his own ship.

In Tobago however, he killed a man in self defence whom he claimed had been a mutineer, and as a result was forced to leave the navy, spending a year in America. When he discovered that officers were needed for the Congress' new navy he signed on as a first lieutenant. His most notable involvement in the colonial conflicts came when he staged raids against the port of Whitehaven and across the Solway at Kirkcudbright Bay.

Legend has it that he planned to seize the Earl of Selkirk as a hostage, but upon finding that the Laird was away from home he gave his men permission to loot the family plate. After the conflicts were over, however, Jones apparently purchased the plate and returned it to the family.

John Paul Jones continued his exploits throughout America and Europe where his feats brought him recognition as a war hero. He was awarded a gold medal in recognition of his services by the US Congress, and in France a dance was named in his honour. He was even invited to Russia where he helped the navy of the Empress Catherine defeat the Turks.

In 1953, the US Naval Historical Foundation and the Daughters of the American Revolution presented a plaque to be erected at his birthplace. At Carsethorn, where the Steam Packet Inn still stands, there are the remains of the old wooden jetty where John Paul Jones left to start his adventures.

Interestingly, once upon a time, a regular steam ship service left from here to go to Whitehaven and Liverpool. In addition although these old ports on the Solway seem to be relatively sheltered, they suffer from unusually high tides and strong currents, making them extremely difficult to navigate.

It's worth paying a visit to the lighthouse at **Southerness** which was built in 1748 and has the distinction of being the second oldest purpose built lighthouse in the country. The lighthouse is no longer in use, though many people come to Southerness today for it is a delightful holiday village with many attractions, including a famous golf course with nineteen holes. With its many creeks and tidal rivers, it's not surprising to learn that the Solway was at one time notorious for smugglers.

This was especially true since, until 1876, the Isle of Man lay outside British Customs regulations, encouraging regular dealings in contraband goods. Sir Walter Scott wrote a vivid account of smuggling in this area in his book 'Guy Mannering'.

A little further round the coast and set high on the hillside, with wonderful views over the Colvend Valley, **Thorniehills** is the perfect place to relax and unwind. This delightful whitewashed cottage is the home of Peter and Hazel Donkin who provide very comfortable accommodation in three well furnished guest rooms. Dating back to at least 1750, the character of this lovely cottage is enhanced by country style furnishings, interesting prints and artefacts and an abundance of books, some of which are antique. The dining room provides a comfortable setting in which to savour Hazel's excellent cooking and an evening meal is available by arrangement. The nearby fields and woodland are a haven for deer and red squirrels and with the beach just a short walk away, this the perfect country lover's retreat.

Thorniehills, Colvend, Nr Dalbeattie. 0556-63295 Map Ref: E6

Taking a side road from the A710 brings you to **Kippford** on the estuary of the River Urr. Kippford, or as it used to be known "Scaur", is a fascinating place and at one time ships would set sail from here for the industrial areas of Northern England and Central Scotland with cargoes of barley, meal and potatoes. Kippford has a delightful setting and, with its old inn and jetty, is today one of the foremost yachting and sailing centres in the south-west.

Situated by the waters edge **The Mariner** enjoys the most fabulous views across Urr Water to the hills beyond. In this lovely setting, friendly host David Georgeson offers a selection of hand pumped Real Ale accompanied by tasty, homecooked food. From the comfort of the split level bar area, with its lovely views, you can admire the pub's many nautical artefacts, including various model ships and an unusual lamp made from a genuine diving helmet. You may well feel tempted to linger and David offers excellent accommodation in four en-suite guest rooms, all offering the same wonderful views. Alternatively, you can choose to stay in the self-catering flat on the top floor, which sleeps six.

The Mariner, Kippford. 0556-62206 Map Ref: F6

Close to the Urr and a couple of miles inland is the town of **Dalbeattie** . You may notice that this distinctive town has mostly been built in the same colour granite. This is the grey granite that was quarried in the area and was a very useful source of income for the town, making it famous throughout the world. This striking material was shipped to many places and was used to construct London's Embankment. Four miles to the south-west on the A711 is Orchardston Tower which is a unique circular tower house built in the 15th century.

Rascarrel Cottage, Auchencairn, Castle Douglas. 0556-64214
Map Ref: E6

Further south is Auchencairn and a couple of miles south of here you will discover a peaceful, relaxing holiday base at **Rascarrel Cottage**, the delightful home of Ellice and Jim Hendry.

Set within a 400 acre working farm, the cottage boasts lovely panoramic views over rolling farmland across the Solway Firth towards the Cumbrian Hills. Awarded a Two Crown Highly Commended rating by the Scottish Tourist Board, very comfortable accommodation is provided in three spacious guest rooms, two on the ground floor and two with en-suite facilities. Breakfast is taken in the attractive conservatory/dining room with views of the sea and the surrounding countryside which may well inspire you to wander the 500 yards to the beach for a stroll.

Travelling north out of Dalbeattie on the B794 brings you to the **Motte of Urr**. This is an impressive site and is the most extensive motte-and-bailey castle in Scotland. It's siting here is something of a mystery as there does not seem much to commend the position. It is possible however, that the river once surrounded it, making it an island. The circular mound here is eighty feet high.

In the nearby village of **Haugh Of Urr** there is a bridge over the River Urr, built in 1760, and anglers amongst you may be of a mind to take advantage of some of the pleasures available to you on this small salmon river, which also has a good run of sea trout in high summer. The village is ideally placed for plethora of country pursuits such as fishing and shooting and of course walking. There is an abundance of forest, coastal and cliff walks to enjoy, with many fascinating Heritage Trails amidst the Galloway Hills and the Colvend Coast.

Our route now joins the A75 on the other side of Haugh of Urr and takes us towards **Castle Douglas**. The market town is only ten miles from the Solway Coast and its sandy beaches. The surrounding area excels in natural beauty and fishing; sailing and riding are all available either locally or within easy motoring distance.

Enjoying a central location at the corner of St. Andrew Street and Queen Street, the **Kings Arms Hotel** is an ideal base from which to explore the beauty of southern Scotland and the Borders. This splendid hotel has been offering refreshment and accommodation to weary travellers for over 200 years, and although modern improvements have been made over the years, the original charm and character still remain. The guest rooms are all comfortably furnished and equipped for comfort, most with en-suite bathroom and the cosy bar provides a relaxing setting for a quiet pint or 'wee dram'. With beautiful walks on your doorstep and many local attractions within easy reach, the Kings Arms Hotel makes an excellent holiday base.

Kings Arms Hotel, St. Andrew Street, Castle Douglas.
0556-2626/2097 Map Ref: E6

The streets of Castle Douglas have a certain planned elegance about them as a result of the town being developed by an enterprising landowner named William Douglas, who had made his fortune in America. He encouraged the development of the town as a cattle market and today it is still a focal point for the local farming community.

Overlooking the Market Hill with its lovely floral display, **The Market Inn Hotel** in Castle Douglas is a welcome stopping-off point in your journey.

Please Don't Forget...

To tell people that you read about them in

The Hidden Places

The Market Inn Hotel, 6/7 Queen Street, Castle Douglas.
0556-2105 Map Ref: E6

There is a comfortable wood panelled lounge bar at the front of the

Threave Castle, Castle Douglas

inn and a public bar to the rear, where on Mondays and Tuesdays, local farmers coming to market call in to swap tales over a pint. Both bars are open all day, offering a selection fine Scottish ales and homecooked bar meals at lunchtime and in the evening on weekdays and throughout the day at weekends. The cosy atmosphere and the friendliness of everyone here ensures that any visitors immediately feel welcome at The Market Inn Hotel.

Threave Castle makes an impressive sight stood on island in the River Dee here and is accessible by a short boat trip. This castle was once the stronghold of the Douglas' and is built on an island in the River Dee. From here, the family oppressed the local population, defying even the authority of the king himself. On one infamous occasion, a Douglas captured the sheriff of Galloway. On being ordered to return him, he had the sheriff beheaded in Threave, afterwards sending the body to the awaiting king's messengers, with the insolent remark that he was "somewhat wanting in the heid!"

Not far away is the lovely **Carlingwark Loch**, where you can row out in a small boat to look at the swans and be rewarded with the bonus of a wonderful view of nearby Screel Mill. There was once an ancient causeway that led to a dwelling on an artificial island at the centre of this loch. A stones throw away, are the delightful **Threave Gardens**, which you will find approximately a mile from the Loch.

These gardens and the visitor centre stand majestically in sixty acres surrounding a Victorian mansion. The house is used by the National Trust of Scotland for their School of Gardening. There is much to see here including rock gardens, heathers, herbaceous and rose beds and in the spring time nearly two hundred varieties of daffodil provide a dazzling display. On the River Dee there are many species of wild geese and duck.

For a relaxing break away in an atmosphere of quiet luxury and elegance, you need look no further than **Airieland House**, the charming home of John and Josephine Herbertson which lies south of the loch, just a short distance out of Gelston on the B727. Built in 1895 as the mansion house for the Airieland Estate, sympathetic restoration has provided every modern comfort without detracting from the building's original character.

Awarded a 3-Crown Deluxe rating by the Scottish Tourist Board, this beautiful house offers non-smokers lovely accommodation in two well-equipped guest rooms, one en-suite and one with private bathroom. The comfortable guest lounge, like all the rooms, boasts super views of the surrounding countryside, and, out of consideration to other guests, no children under the age of twelve or pets are allowed.

Airieland House, Gelston, Near Castle Douglas.
0556-680375 Map Ref: E6

We leave Castle Douglas by the A75, again travelling southwards, towards Kircudbright. When crossing the River Dee at Tongland Bridge it's worth taking time to look closely at this structure. Although it is shrouded by trees and not immediately obvious to the traveller, this handsome bridge is a fine piece of engineering.

It was designed by Thomas Telford in collaboration with the famous Edinburgh architect and painter, Alexander Nasmyth. It is interesting to note that the single span bridge had to be built to cope with the tide which would rise six metres or more. The difficulty of this was brought home to the builders when the original foundations were washed away on the first attempt. The three small arches to either side are designed to help cope with the flow of water at high tides.

From here it does not take long to get to the county town of **Kirkcudbright**. This beautiful town and harbour proved to be a welcome discovery with much to recommend it. Take a look around the streets here and you will find many examples of seventeenth and eighteenth century buildings. Particularly striking is the fabulous colour used throughout the town with reds, blues and blacks producing an effect that is almost continental.

Kirkcudbright is an ancient place with quite a history. As far back as the 8th century the Vikings established the church of St. Cuthbert near the town. The town seal today still reflects the rather bloody times of old with a picture of St. Cuthbert with the head of the martyred St. Oswald, king of Northumbria, in his lap. Facing England across the Solway meant that the conflicts between the two countries were reflected in the fortifications and defences around the town. These included a water filled ditch and wall enclosing the town.

The ruins of **Maclellans Castle** date from a period when building reflected a combination of the need for safety and a certain amount of comfort. It was built in the sixteenth century by Sir Thomas Maclellan who benefitted from the dissolution of the monasteries by acquiring the lands and buildings of the Greyfriar's convent on this site. He even built his castle with the stone from the dismantled buildings.

If you have a look around the ruin, take a close look at the fireplace. It's some ten feet wide and would have had a fire burning continuously throughout the winter months. A closer inspection reveals a small hole in the back of the fireplace, which puzzled us. Apparently, this was a spy hole located in a small room reached from the stair. Here, Maclellan could watch and listen to what was being said, without fear of discovery.

Besides Maclellans Castle, the Tolbooth is another interesting building dating from the same period. Overlooking the market square, the Tolbooth was the point where taxes were paid and prisoners incarcerated. Pronouncements would have been made from its steps and it is fascinating to see the original manacles that were used to hold the prisoners during their punishment. The area was caught up in the persecution of both witches, and later, Covenanters. The case against witches usually began with a series of events or disasters occurring within the community, until eventually someone came to be suspected of causing them. The case of Elspeth McEwen is a typical local example. She was accused of making her neighbours' hens stop laying and of having a moveable wooden pin at her command that was capable of drawing milk from their cows. The unfortunate woman was imprisoned and tortured in Kirkcudbright Tolbooth until she confessed and was subsequently found guilty "of a compact and correspondence with the devil and of charms and accession to malefices". She was executed in 1698.

Later in the 17th and 18th centuries the town developed along more civilized lines with smart new dwellings arising for the merchants and lawyers. A walk along Castle Street or Old High Street gives a clear indication of the elegance of Georgian Kirkcudbright. It was an important town for shipping, trade went as far as the West Indies and the North American Colonies. As a result it became a centre for Customs and Excise Officers engaged in the capture of the smugglers who were operating from France, Ireland and the Isle of Man, running contraband along the shores of the Solway.

In the late 19th century there was an artists colony established here and the town has become associated with many fine painters and craftsmen. One famous resident was E.A. Hornel (1864-1930) and his house in the High Street contains a display of his paintings and furniture. Close by, is the house of the artist Jessie M. King (1875-1949) and examples of her work can be seen at the Stewartry Museum in St Mary Street. There is also a host of articles and information on this pleasant town. Visitors during the mid July to August period will be in luck as there is an annual Summer Festival, which provides an extensive programme of entertainment.

Situated on the old High Street, the **Selkirk Arms Hotel** makes a delightful base from which to explore the beauty of Galloway. Originally built in 1770, it is said that Robert Burns wrote 'The Selkirk Grace' whilst staying here in 1794. Today, proprietors John and Sue Morris successfully combine first class facilities, fine food and warm hospitality to create a relaxing haven. The fifteen attractively furnished guest rooms are all en-suite and the restaurant is justly renowned for its extensive and imaginative menu of mouthwatering dishes, freshly prepared using local meat and fish. With many places of historical interest within easy reach, the Selkirk Arms is an ideal holiday base.

Selkirk Arms Hotel, High Street, Kirkcudbright.
0557-30402 Map Ref: D7

South west of the town is the small village of Borgue and the 'Cow Palace', a model dairy farm built at the turn of the century. Design and built at great expense in a Gothic style it's grandest feature is the central water tower, which ironically failed as a means of water supply. Still a private farm it is visable from the road and a must for the folly spotter or those with a taste for the unusual.

Our next destination of interest is **Gatehouse of Fleet,** a few miles along the A755. A fascinating place with its brightly coloured buildings and scenic setting. It doesn't immediately spring to mind that this town was once at the forefront of Scotland's Industrial Revolution. However, a closer look reveals that many of these bright buildings were at one time working mills in a town that was built to rival the centres of industry in the North of England. The town was planned and built in the late 18th century as a centre for cotton manufacturing and other industries. It once boasted six cotton mills employing a workforce of more than five hundred people. The industries did eventually decline in response to better transport related businesses elsewhere.

There is a visitors centre in one of the former mills. The town also features one of the counties few follies, if indeed the Jubilee clock tower can be so described, surmounted by improbable castellations it is an impressive time teller never the less. Those of you with an interest in the haunts of the poet Burns, will be interested to find that the Murray Arms Hotel is reputedly the place where he wrote 'Scots Wha Hae'.

Just a mile to the south west of the town is **Cardoness Castle**, once the home of the McCullochs of Galloway. An unruly family who feuded with and plundered those around them. The family line ended in 1690 when Sir Gordon McCulloch was executed in Edinburgh for murder. Tall and gaunt with its four stories standing on a rocky mound, it must have seen much of the bloody troubles that beset the area for centuries.

We leaving the main routes behind once again and head north on a small road that leads into the countryside by the Forest of Glengap and deep into the Laurieston Forest. The road finally emerges at the village of **Laurieston** and into one of the most renowned beauty spots and activity centres in this part of the country, Loch Ken.

Starting at the south end of the Loch in Townhead of Greenlaw means you're able to join the A713 which follows the shore of the loch up to New Galloway.

Whether you are a birdwatcher, water skier, rambler, sailor or fisherman you will find that there is something to cater for you on Loch Ken. There are a large number of tracks and footpaths for either more experienced walkers or novices. Fishermen amongst you might like to know that apart from salmon and sea trout, Loch Ken has become famous for the size of pike that have been caught. If you enjoy pony trekking then you are sure to enjoy the facilities on offer here as the surrounds are ideal for this activity.

The A713 takes you right to the top of the loch where it reaches New Galloway. The road is notable for its lovely scenic views of the waters and more than once tempts you to stop and take a deep breath.

New Galloway is itself a very attractive little town which is actually the smallest Royal Burgh in Scotland and, standing on the River Ken, it is a popular base for anglers. Those of you who like to spend time browsing in craft shops will find much to look at in the surrounding area, especially in nearby Balmaclellan and St John's Town of Dalry . The latter town derives its name from a stone on which St John the Baptist is reputed to have rested.

Crossing the River Ken at New Galloway and travelling on the A712 brings you to **Clatteringshaws Loch** and the Galloway Forest. The loch is surely one of the most scenic spots in Galloway with transfixing views over the waters to the hills beyond. This road takes you through the Galloway Forest Park and the route was officially opened as 'The Queens Way' in commemoration of the Silver Jubilee of Queen Elizabeth II in 1977.

The park takes in a huge area and the road gives splendid views of mountains, lochs, and waterfalls. If you are lucky you may well spot red deer or even wild goats. To get thoroughly clued up on the park and its wildlife visit the Galloway Deer Museum at Clatteringshaws. Here there is a display on the history of the area and the wildlife in the park.

Opposite Clatteringshaws Loch is the famous 'Raiders Road' which is a trail following an old cattle rustler's route alongside the Black water at Dee.

From the nearby Newton Stewart the River Cree flows down towards the sea and we follow its path on the A75 southeast towards **Creetown**, six miles from Newton Stewart at the head of Wigtown Bay. This thoroughly charming friendly village features as 'Port- an- Ferry' in Scott's 'Guy Mannering' and has a history steeped in smuggling legend.

The village is built in the distinct and attractive local 'silver' granite, which most attractive. You can discover all about rocks, minerals and gems at the **Gem Rock Museum**. This beautiful collection comes from all over the world and took over 50 years to amass. Recognised as one of the most comprehensive of its kind in the world, as well as precious stones it contains many startling examples of the mineral forms created by nature.

Enjoying a central location in Creetown, **Marclaysean Guest House** and **Ferrytoon Gifts** on St. John Street is a real gem of a place, run by friendly hostess Irene Seal-Spiers. Over 100 years old, this delightful granite fronted house is Listed and Commended by the Scottish Tourist Board and offers immaculate accommodation in three bright and airy guest rooms, each equipped with colour TV and hot drinks facilities. There is a private guest lounge and outside the attractive garden comes complete with patio and pet ducks! The adjoining gift shop, also owned and run by Irene, offers a wonderful range of cards, souvenirs and toys, including beautiful dried flower arrangements made to order - perfect for that special gift or holiday memento.

Marclaysean Guest House, 51 St. John Street, Creetown.
0671-82319 Map Ref: C6

There is much to do in this lovely village and you may be surprised by the amount of facilities on offer to the visitor. There are many walks, from along the Minnipool Burn with its pleasant surroundings, to the slightly more ambitious Cairnsmore of Fleet which, at 2,329 feet, is one of the highest hills in Galloway. The views are stunning and take in the Isle of Man, England and the Mountains of Mourne in Ireland.

It was said to Queen Victoria that the road from Creetown to Gatehouse of Fleet is 'the finest in the kingdom', the next finest being the road from Gatehouse of Fleet to Creetown. Whatever you decide, you will surely agree that Galloway is a truly beautiful place.

Once more crossing the River Cree back at **Newton Stewart** we enter a fascinating corner of Galloway. Recently voted 'The Friendliest Town in the U.K.' it lies in the shadow of the Galloway Hills and it is here that you will discover **Lynwood Guest House**, the welcoming home of Jenny Gustafson and her family. Winner of the Galloway Preservation Society Small House Improvement Competition in 1989, Lynwood has the high ceilings and ornate cornices so characteristic of Victorian houses. Awarded a One Crown Commended rating by the Scottish Tourist Board, very comfortable accommodation is provided in three spacious and individually named guest rooms, all with views over the lovely garden which has excellent play facilities for children.

Smoking is restricted to the guest lounge, and the separate dining room provides the setting for both breakfast and an optional evening meal.

Lynwood Guest House, Corvisel Road, Newton Stewart. 0671-2074
Map Ref: C6

On the outskirts of the town, you will find **Bruce Hotel**, an excellent touring base with a character and appeal all of its own. This Category B Listed Building is a 200 year old coaching house which offers a combination of comfortable en-suite accommodation, fine ale and first class food in a warm, friendly atmosphere. The lounge bar with its small library provides a cosy setting for pre-dinner drinks and the 'Red Bar' has the unusual feature of a metal sculpture of a spider's web on the wall! It makes a refreshing change to find a guest lounge where you can relax without a TV to disturb you and in the split level restaurant with its panoramic views over Cairnsmore, there is a fine selection of fresh, homecooked local produce to tempt the palate.

Bruce Hotel, 88 Queen St, Newton Stewart. 0671-2294 Map Ref: C6

Heading south on the A714 coming out of Newton Stewart the road take our journey to the little town of **Wigtown,** that overlooks Wigtown Bay and the mouth of the River Cree. The feeling of calmness in the town today belies its previously fierce competitive spirit as the former county town of Wigtownshire, fighting for the royal burgh's trading 'freedoms' (which mean monopolies) over Whithorn and Stranraer.

The site of the ancient town reputedly lay more than a mile to the east which, if you look at a map, would have placed it firmly within the grasp of the sea! There is a small church on the east side of the town that was erected next to a ruined church dedicated to St Machitis.

There are some solemn reminders of the fate of the Covenanters here. For example you will find a headstone, located in the burial ground. This was erected in memory of the sad fate of eighteen year old Margaret Wilson, who with Margaret Lachlan, aged sixty three, was drowned for her religious beliefs tied to a stake in the sea. A stone post now within dry land marks the site of the drowning.

Take the B733 from Wigtown, and you'll come across the **Torhouse Stone Circle**, which is a captivating sight of nineteen boulders on the edge of a low mound dating from the Bronze Age.

A short drive on is the delightful village of **Kirkcowan.** which is just of the A75. Situated next to the parish church, **Church End** is a charming white-painted house where you will find first class accommodation.

Church End, 6 Main Street, Kirkcowan. 0671-83246 Map Ref: B6

The charming home of Sue and Gary Pope, Church End was originally two 18th century workmen's cottages which were later made into one house. There are three very comfortable en-suite guest rooms which like the rest of the house are attractively furnished in country cottage style, enhancing the character of the house. To the rear is an acre of garden complete with ducks who produce fresh eggs which Sue uses in her cooking. As well as a substantial breakfast each morning, you can take advantage of the optional evening meal which often incorporates homegrown vegetables from the garden.

Rejoining the A714 just south of Wigtown gives you the opportunity to visit the distillery at Bladnoch should you have a taste for the malt. There are tours available at the distillery, which is open all year round.

Leaving the distillery we take the B7004 which leads down to the village of **Garlieston** overlooking the bay. The small port was founded in the 18th century by Lord Garlies. His father, the 6th Earl, built nearby Galloway House. The house is not open to the public, although you can enjoy a quiet afternoon in the gardens which cover nearly thirty acres with superb displays of daffodils, rhododendrons and azaleas. There are lovely old trees here and the position of the garden, which leads down to a sandy beach by the sea, is delightful.

Whithorn is a few miles further south on the B7063 and the fact that this ancient town is on the very tail end of Scotland did not diminish its importance, for it existed as far back as the second century. It was here, in AD 397, that St Ninian established the first Christian centre in Scotland. The site of the chapel which he founded is thought to have been a few miles further south, close to the Isle of Whithorn and the area has long since been the focus of pilgrimages.

Robert the Bruce came here in the last months of his life, severely weakened by years of hard campaigning and suffering from leprosy. He had, apparently, to be carried in a horse-litter as he was too weak to support himself. Another noted visitor had no such problem. He was James IV who came here many times reputedly walking on foot from Edinburgh. Mary Queen of Scots also made this journey in 1563. Indeed, such was the influence of this place that, after the Reformation, an Act of Parliament was passed to make the practice illegal.

The Isle of Whithorn was, as the name implies, originally an island, although this charming seaside village is now joined to the mainland and is a popular spot for yachting. The area is rich in religious interest with a wealth of crosses and the Priory , itself the focus of attention for pilgrims. There are also a number of notable sites for the budding archaeologist, with a team digging here throughout the summer. The excavations are fascinating and you cannot help but admire the patience of these dedicated people, who are painstakingly revealing the history of this ancient area, and the folk who have lived here throughout the centuries. There is a "Dig" shop that will provide you with a wide range of souvenirs and local crafts. There is also a visitor centre and museum providing much detailed information, with a guided tour of the site available.

From here it is only a short drive to **Port William,** a small and attractive fishing port on the eastern side of Luce Bay. At nearby Monrieth Bay you may notice a small statue of an otter overlooking the water. It is a tribute to the author Gavin Maxwell, who wrote lovingly about the area in his book, "The House at Elrig".

Close to this sleepy and attractive harbour village is Monrieth House. Built in 1799, it has charming gardens and a park. The White Loch is here also and apparently even in the coldest of winters it never entirely freezes over.

The area boasts an abundance of prehistoric sites and in particular the Drumtrodden Standing Stones which were three upright stones (though one has now fallen), and also nearby the fascinating "cup and ring" markings, which were probably carved during the Bronze Age. Theories abound as to the meaning of the cup and ring markings which can be found in many places in Scotland. One source lists a remarkable one hundred and four theories that have been put forward to explain their meaning and usage. The most likely explanations are either that they had some connection with metal prospecting and smelting activities, or that they had some religious meaning perhaps related to sun worship or astronomical observation.

You'll be rewarded with refreshing views of Luce Bay as you make your way north along the A747 to **Glenluce.** This village sits on the edge of the Water of Luce and close to Luce Bay. It is fascinating to think that there has been a settlement in this area from as early as 6,000BC.

A mile to the north is Glenluce Abbey which was founded in 1190 and was visited by King Robert I, King James IV and Mary Queen of Scots on their pilgrimages to Whithorn.

The abbey is said to have associations with a 13th century wizard named Michael Scott. Legend has it that he managed to persuade some witches, who were paying him too much close attention, to spend their time spinning ropes from the sands of Luce bay. The results of their task can supposedly be seen at very low tides. Another interesting story was that of poor Gilbert Cambell, who was apparently haunted by the devil of Glenluce for four years from 1654 to 1658. Fortunately the local Presbytery was able to eventually rid him of his unfortunate possession.

Glenluce Motor Museum houses a splendid display of vintage cars, motorbikes and memorabilia. A great place for the fan of wheeled transport to while away an afternoon.

It's well worth exploring the southern peninsular of Galloway and journeying down the A715 from Glenluce you come to the charming little town of **Sandhead**. Here the town's Main Street overlooks nine square miles of sandy beach, voted the cleanest, safest and warmest in the area. The local Logan Botanical Gardens are held in great respect and are to be found just off the B7065. Here, practically surrounded by the sea, there is the most amazing collection of exotic plants. Although usually associated with the southern hemisphere, they are thriving due to the mildness of the climate warmed by the Gulf stream. The famous cabbage palms and tree ferns were especially interesting, though you may also enjoy the walled gardens and many varieties of flora on show.

From the gardens, our journey takes us to **Drummore** which is the most southerly village in Scotland. The people of this village are said to have visited the well of the "Co'" which is near St Medan's Cove on the Mull of Galloway. Supposedly on the first Sunday in May, they would come down to bathe in the waters which were widely accredited with having healing properties. Coins have been found in the well which date as far back as the reign of Charles I.

There is a lighthouse situated beyond the "Double Dykes" which was built in 1828, and from here on a clear day you will be able to see both the Isle of Man and Ireland, some twenty six miles away.

Rumour has it that the Picts brewed a drink from heather that was sweeter than honey and stronger than wine, and when the Scots invaded from Ireland, they were most keen to learn the secret of this renowned brew. It was here at The Double Dykes that the secret is said to have died with the final defence of the Picts against the invaders. The story goes that a treacherous Druid betrayed the chief and his two sons, to whom only the secret of the drink was known. One son promised to reveal the secret, if his father and brother were first thrown off the cliffs, to prevent them witnessing his treachery. This request was duly obliged and then the remaining son flung himself off, shouting that the secret would die with him.

At **Port Logan** on the western side of the peninsula, sits a small fishing village where there is a tidal pool on the bay. This was built in 1800 by a McDougall laird as an artificial sea- water larder to keep himself supplied with cod. The pool is thirty feet deep and fifty three feet in circumference. The cod today however, have no worse fate than being fed by hand and are so tame that they rise to the surface whenever a bell is rung. On the road back up towards Sandhead you pass Ardwell House. Here there are more lovely gardens and you are able to enjoy walking around the two attractive ponds which look out to sea.

From Sandhead, taking the B7042 brings you to the popular

holiday village of **Portpatrick**. This is the largest village on the west coast and is dominated by the impressive Victorian hotel on the cliff top. The village has the feeling of an amphitheatre about it and is in fact quite exposed to the winds and sea. There was an artificial harbour built here due to its proximity to Donaghadee, which is a mere twenty one miles over the Irish Sea. Unfortunately the harbour was constantly damaged by the elements, so trade was eventually moved to the safer haven of Stranraer. Children, young and old, will love Little Wheels, a huge model railway, toy and transport exhibition in the village. The railway tracks extend for over 100 metres and would be train drivers can have ago.

This picturesque village has something to offer everyone, with golf, bowling and tennis among the many sports available or for the more leisurely visitor, walks along the unspoilt harbour with its beautiful views across the Irish Channel. For visitors to this delightful fishing village **Braefield House**, home of Anne and John Moffat, provides an excellent holiday base. The house was built around 1880 for a spinster who only came here on a visit, wanting to take the waters and who then stayed here and lived to be 102 years old! Accommodation is provided in seven lovely guest rooms, four with en-suite bathroom, and the house is set in wonderful gardens with the added attraction of a dovecote.

Braefield House, Braefield Road, Portpatrick. 0776-81255
Map Ref: A6

Enjoying an elevated position in the village, **Mount Stewart Hotel** offers superb views across the harbour which on a clear day reach as far as Ireland. Originally a Victorian house, Mount Stewart was converted into a hotel during the early 1900's and retains a homely family-run atmosphere whilst offering very comfortable accommodation, fine food and friendly hospitality. The restaurant has a well-deserved reputation in the area for its imaginative and mouthwatering menu which incorporates local fresh seafood according to season. For a less formal meal you can relax with a drink in the bar and choose from a wide selection of very reasonably priced bar meals. With the unspoilt harbour just a stroll away and a range of sporting activities available nearby, you have all you need for an idyllic holiday.

Mount Stewart Hotel, Portpatrick. 0776-81291 Map Ref: A6

Leaving Portpatrick on the B738 takes you up to **Lochnaw Castle**, Lochnaw dates back to 1426 and is one of the few 15th century castles still in existence. This charming and historic country residence was for centuries the ancestral home of the Agnew family, hereditary Sheriffs of Galloway. Built along simple Norman lines, the castle stands at the very edge of the loch, unspoilt and undisturbed.

Do not miss the small charming village of **Leswalt** which is close by, and why not follow the coast road up towards Kircolm, on the banks of Loch Ryan? There's a legend of a ghost that at one time was said to haunt Caldenoch Tower on the west shore. This ghost had the rather nasty habit of seizing old women and flinging them into the water, and also would drown the voices of ministers who tried to stop its anti-social behaviour. Eventually one particularly long-winded minister proved to be too much for the ghost, causing it to utter, "Roar awa, McGregor. I can roar nae mair!"

At the head of Loch Ryan, **Stranraer** is a busy seaport which attracts many visitors each year. It is, of course, the port which operates a regular ferry service to Ireland having taken over from Portpatrick. While the destroyed harbour in Portpatrick is a fitting testament to the power of the sea, there is a more solemn tribute in

Stranraer's, Agnew Park , which commemorates the loss of one hundred and thirty three lives in the sinking of the ferry in 1953. Before the ferry came to Stranraer, the local people, in the 18th century, made a living from the seasonal shoals of herring in Loch Ryan, until the fish began to die out in the early 19th century. There is a castle here and parts of it remained in use as prison cells until 1907. It was also used by John Graham of Calverhouse during his persecution of the Covenanters in the 17th century. The earliest surviving municipal building is the former town hall of 1776. There was a guide book published in 1877 which referred to the town hall as "like some ladies - not Stranraer ladies, however - very much indebted to paint for its good looks". The Old Town Hall is now an interesting museum with plenty of information on local history as well as changing exhibitions.

To the east of Stranraer you can visit the gardens of **Castle Kennedy** which are open to the public and are famous for their displays of rhododendrons, azaleas, magnolias and embothriums. We travelled to the north east along the A77 and passed the 16th century Craigcaffie Tower, originally the home of the Neilsons who held it from the 1470's until 1791 when it came into the possession of the Earl of Stair. Unoccupied for some years it has recently been sold by the Stairs with the intention that it is restored.

The small coastal village of **Cairnryan** was a base in the Second World War for handling transatlantic traffic. Here too were made the parts for the Mulberry Harbour which was vital to the success of the Normandy landings in 1944. It is fascinating to think that those massive Sunderland flying-boats also used Wig Bay as a base, the remains of which can still be seen.

With that we leave Dumfries and Galloway, still heading along the coast into Ayrshire, our next chapter.

CHAPTER THREE
Ayrshire, Arran & Bute.

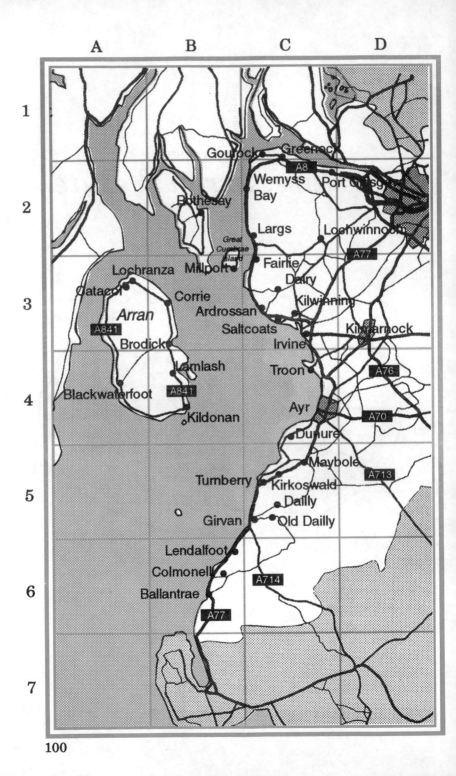

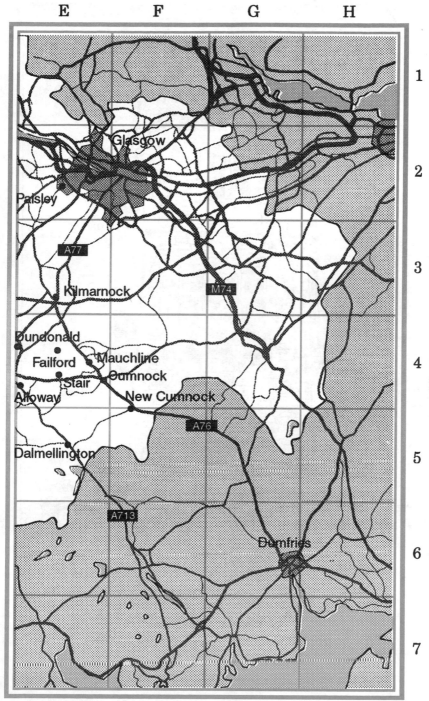

Burns Memorial Tower, Mauchline

CHAPTER THREE

Ayrshire, Arran and Bute.

Those of you familiar with Robert Louis Stevenson might recall the novel 'The Master of Ballantrae'. Although **Ballantrae** was not the setting that he used for the plot, it is a pretty seaside town popular with visitors. It is also, the starting point for our visit into Ayrshire, where the river Stinchar, well known for its trout and salmon fishing, runs into the sea. It has a delightful harbour filled with both fishing and pleasure boats, whilst, above the river and the old bridge, stands the ruins of Ardstinchar Castle.

For a taste of luxury in tranquil, secluded surroundings, you would be well advised to seek out **Balkissock Lodge** near the village. This splendid 200 year old country house is the charming home of Janet and Adrian Beale, whose previous restaurant experience has earned them reputation for the superb cuisine they offer to non-residents as well as their many guests. Attractively furnished throughout, there are three en-suite guest rooms within the guest house and excellent self-catering accommodation is provided in Balrazzie cottage. The breakfast and dinner menus are extensive and varied, with considerable choice for vegetarians and special 'gastronomic breaks' can be arranged. With beautiful fell walks to the rear, this really is the place for that quiet break away from it all.

Balkissock Lodge, Ballantrae. 0465 83537 Map Ref: B6

The small churchyard at Ballantrae bears witness to a vicious local

103

feud that once took place between members of the Kennedy family. The Bargany Aisle in the kirkyard is a memorial to Gilbert Kennedy of Bargany who was killed in a fight with his near relative, the Earl of Cassillis, in 1601. Theirs was a family torn by conflict for over forty years, beginning when the fourth Earl of Cassillis kidnapped and roasted one Allen Stuart until the unfortunate man signed over his lands. On a later occasion, the wicked earl was only just persuaded not to blow up the castle at Ardstinchar, which was the home of the Bargany branch of the family, on the grounds that it might displease the king. The feud was ended in the High Court in Edinburgh in 1611, leaving the Earl a little chastised although still the supreme ruler in the family.

Just to the north of Ballantrae lies Bennane Head and it was here, so the tale goes, lived a rather nasty piece of work by the name of Sawney Bean. Apparently he and his family were cannibals and preyed on travellers passing their cave. The cave can still be visited by more intrepid visitors without, it should be added, the fear of being eaten.

Further along the coast, between the shore and the rising hills, is **Lendalfoot**; which was once the haunt of smugglers and is overlooked by the ruins of Carleton Castle. One of a series of Kennedy watchtowers along the coast, it achieved minor notoriety in a ballad, as the seat of a Baron who rid himself of no less than seven wives by pushing them over the cliffs. His eighth wife, May, returned the gesture.

Following the unclassified road past the castle, our journey ventures away from the coast into the hills. The hill on which the village of **Colmonell** sits is known as 'Knockdolian' which derives from the Gaelic words for hill, 'cnoc', and 'dall', meaning 'to mislead'. It seems that in times past the hill was mistaken by mariners, in bad weather, for Ailsa Craig which lies off the coast. This pretty village takes its name from Saint Colmonella who died in AD 611 and the village has many old castles of interest.

Nearby, there is the one time hiding place of Robert the Bruce, Craignell,. and marvellous views of the surrounding countryside and the river Stinchar laid out below. The road follows roughly the passage of these waters, and we take the A714 northwards for a mile and then turned off at the B734 which, still following the course of the river, leading to the village of Barr.

Barr is a charming little conservation village nestling on the banks of the River Stinchar, seven miles south of the fishing port of Girvan. This parish is the largest in the Scottish lowlands and around sixty years ago was said to have been populated by the most sheep and fewest people! Looking around the churchyard, you may notice two headstones in memory of Covenanters who were put to death. There is also, a richly sculptured stone showing one Reverend John Campbell, whose unfortunate demise occurred in his pulpit.

At Barr, the road winds northwards and we follow it up toward the strangely named villages of **Old Dailly** and **Dailly**. The latter village grew up with the mining industry though there seems to be little evidence of this in the surrounding landscape.

A good place to get some idea of the history of a place is in the churchyard. And you'll not be disappointed on this occasion with evidence of the industry here. There is a headstone to the memory of one John Brown, a sixty six year old collier who became trapped underground by a roof fall in the pit in 1835. He was eventually brought out alive, 'having been twenty three days in utter seclusion from the world and without a particle of food'. Ultimately however, John Brown only managed to survive for three days after being set free. You can't help but notice the large mausoleum of the Bargany family in the churchyard - it is as high as the church.

At Old Dailly, you will notice two large stones inside the churchyard. These were known as the Charter Stones and were used in local contests of strength to see who could lift them.

Not far away is **Girvan**. The town can boast one and a half miles of safe sandy beach, which stretches southwards from the harbour, which is a hive of activity and a bustling centre for the fishing fleet.

No-one looking out to sea will fail to notice the large island that is some ten miles offshore. This is **Ailsa Craig** which is the plug of an extinct volcano. The isle was once known as 'Paddy's Milestone' as it is thought to be located halfway between Glasgow and Belfast. A number of boatmen operate trips out to the island from the harbour and it makes for an interesting excursion. If you go, you will have a chance to see where the fine grained granite was mined to make some of the highest quality curling stones. There was even a castle perched high on the island, which was once the subject of an invasion by Hew Barclay of Ladyland, who attempted to seize the island for Philip of Spain.

Today the Ailsa is home to one of the largest colonies of gannets in the British Isles. If your visit coincides with low tide, you will be able to walk around the island and look up at the breeding colonies.

Although the necessary town charter was granted by Charles I in 1668, Girvan is known to have been occupied since at least 5,000 BC. As late as 1961, archaeologists have been discovering more and more about Girvan's past, including a site of Bronze Age urnfields located off Coalpots Lane, east of the town.

The A719 north from Girvan follows a delightful coast route up

Culzean Castle Gatehouse

towards **Turnberry** where there are a few remains of a castle that was the main seat of the ancient earldom of Carrick. This was inherited by Robert the Bruce and indeed, it is believed to have been the place of this great man's birth. It is also where Bruce landed to begin his return to Scotland in 1307. The lighthouse now commands the most prominent position.

Most of us are however familiar with Turnberry for another reason, as it is here that the famous Open Championship golf course lies. It is not far from the course to one of the most famous and best examples of Scottish 'strongholds', situated in a magnificent country setting. **Culzean Castle and Country Park** is the most visited National Trust property in Britain and with the range of interests and activities it offers, it is easy to see why. The castle itself was built by Robert Adam between 1772 and 1792, and is noted for its magnificent oval staircase and round drawing room, which are now considered to be among Adam's most outstanding achievements.

Of course, there are many other permanent visitor attractions at Culzean, including the exhibition, shops and Visitor Centre. A visit to the fully licensed restaurant is a must, especially if you've made your way round the deer park, swan pond, adventure playground and walled garden!

One of Scotland's more unusual attractions is just a few miles north of Culzean on the A719. Croy Brae, also known as **Electric Brae**, gives the optical illusion that cars are travelling up hill when in fact they are going down! Park in the lay-by take off the handbrake and watch as you roll up hill - Seeing is believing. Just a short drive from Electric Brae is the delightful coastal village of **Dunure**, overlooked by the dramatic jagged ruins of its castle.

Dunduff Farm, Dunure. 0292 50225 or 0850 688033 Map Ref: C4

107

Just outside the village you will find a delightful place to stay at **Dunduff Farm**. The charming home of Agnes Gemmell, Dunduff stands in 600 acres surrounded by beautiful views over the sea and mountains. Agnes has three light and spacious guest rooms all offering panoramic coastal views and each with colour TV, hot drinks facilities and en-suite or private bathroom. There is a guest TV lounge and the cosy dining room provides the setting for a wide choice of breakfasts. For those who prefer, Dunduff Farm Bothy offers self-catering accommodation of an equally high standard. With beautiful walks nearby and a trout pond to fish from, your tranquil country break away is complete.

It simply is not possible to come to this part of Scotland without hearing the name of **Robbie Burns**, and it is, of course, fitting for us to mention here Scotland's most cherished poet. In this area of his birth and upbringing there are many places that associate themselves with the man and the country, which has become known as Burn's Country.

Robert Burns died at the age of thirty seven and his life story is one of both tragedy and romance, and yet full of colourful character. It is his honesty and ability to express himself that people find endearing the world over. He has come to represent the vitality and spirit of this corner of Scotland, and is an important part of its living history.

Our journey now comes inland from Culzean to the village of **Kirkoswald**, stood on the A77. Burns studied surveying here for a short period. You may still visit **Souter Johnnie's Cottage** which was built in 1785, and occupied by John Davidson the shoemaker. Robert Burns took the real man and turned him into an immortal character of fiction in his celebrated poem 'Tam O'Shanter'. Douglas Graham, the actual model for Tam O'Shanter lies buried, as does John Davidson, in the old parish churchyard. The ancient font, discovered at Chapel Donan and now in the kirkyard at Kirkoswald, is rumoured to have been used for the baptism of Robert the Bruce. Almost two hundred years ago Burns himself wrote about the Kirkoswald hostelry, Kirkton Jean's , in his poem Tam O'Shanter. Since then Kirkoswald has been put firmly on the Burns heritage trail, and Kirkton Jean's today is a popular watering hole for those exploring and living in Burns country.

The A77 takes us out of Kirkoswald and towards the town of Maybole. We passed the fine ruins of **Crossraguel Abbey** on the way and we were impressed by the state of preservation which gives an interesting insight into life in this 13th century settlement. The abbots who lived here apparently made the most of the plentiful seabirds who nested on Ailsa Craig, as they were often served here on the dinner table. It was the unfortunate owner of the lands of Crossraguel after the Reformation, Allen Stuart, who was himself basted and roasted by the Kennedys. An interesting note about the monks who lived here was that they actually minted their own pennies and farthings. Not surprisingly, these coins are much sought after by collectors.

Maybole Castle, in the town itself, was the stronghold of the Kennedy's and their descendants now occupy Cassillis House which is situated four miles north east of Maybole, high above the River Doon.

The position of **Maybole** is somewhat lofty, set two hundred to three hundred feet above sea level. The town is the fifth largest in Ayrshire and commands a wonderful view of the area. Apart from visiting the castle, the town offers splendid opportunities for walks as well as a golf course and an indoor heated swimming pool.

We were now not far from Ayr; however you may like to take in a little more of this wonderful countryside. The B7023 from Maybole leads on to the B741, taking us down towards Dalmellington. It's worth taking your time, so as to look at the pretty villages of Crosshill and then Straiton.

Dalmellington makes an excellent base for exploring the River Doon, immortalised by Burns in verse. Its source is at **Loch Doon** and an enjoyable day is to be had with a picnic on its shores. The road actually follows the shoreline of the loch and provides ample opportunity to just stretch your legs, or perhaps take up the challenge of a more invigorating walk. The castle here dates from the early fourteenth century, though it has actually been removed from its original site on an island in the middle of the loch.

This ambitious scheme was undertaken as the waters of the loch were raised in the 1930's, and the castle was removed to the west bank to prevent it being lost forever. This must have been quite a task, since the walls are seven to nine feet thick. The island can still be seen from time to time as the water level tends to fluctuate.

The loch has been the base for a number of schemes, one of which was the siting of a gunnery school during the First World War. You can still see the remains of the concrete blocks which carried the monorail target for the school. More recently, in 1978, the area was targeted by the nuclear industry for the deposition of nuclear waste. It is thanks to the vigilance of the locals, who fought tooth and nail, that the scheme was abandoned to let us enjoy the peace and calm of this beautiful place today.

Back in the town, **Cathcartson Interpretation Centre** contains an interesting display of weaving, mining and other aspects of the area's industry, and the town is full of fascinating buildings from the eighteenth and nineteenth centuries.

The B741 continues through the area of Kyle Forest and give some lovely views as you make your way towards the A76 and the village of **New Cumnock**.

Only recently, thanks to a prolonged dry weather spell, was it realised that the Romans used this road on their way to the Clyde from Hadrian's Wall, nearly two thousand years ago. Aerial photographs revealed a hitherto unknown batch of forts along the road.

Underneath this area ran rich coal seams that provided much of these towns with their industry for many years. Turning left at New Cumnock, we travel for six miles on the A76 to the village of **Cumnock**, once famous for the manufacture of snuff boxes. James Kier Hardy, regarded as the founder of the Labour Party, lived here and built himself a house nearby.

A little further north on the A76 is **Mauchline**, immortalised by the Burns, the tall and rather grand Burns Memorial Tower celebrating the fact. It was near here that the family moved after his father's death and to which Burns returned to live with his new wife, Jean Armour, who came from the town. You can pay a visit to the room where the couple first abided, as the house on Castle Street is now the Burns House Museum. There is a wonderful collection of memorabilia here. There is the sad sight of the graves of four of Burns' daughters in Mauchline churchyard.

Across the road is Poosie Nansie's ale house , which inspired 'The Jolly Beggars' and is still in use today. At one time Mauchline was a centre for the manufacture of curling stones. You can find out about this unusual sport and other local industries in the museum.

While you are here don't miss one of Scotland's most magnificent river scenes. Follow the A76 south to where the road crosses the river Ayr. Use the old, two arched bridge to make a descent which will take you on a path to the river along the rim of the **Ballochmyle Gorge** and under the railway viaduct. The view of sweeping woodlands and the river far below is breathtaking. The viaduct itself is of interest as a great feat of engineering, being the highest railway bridge in Britain, at 51 metres, and the main span being the widest masonry arch railway bridge in Britain, at 55 metres in length.

Following the road back to Mauchline, we turn west onto the A758 passing through the hamlet of **Failford** where there is a monument commemorating the last meeting between Burns and his lover, 'Highland Mary', who died the following autumn. There is a path from Failford that leads you to **Stair** through some charming countryside in the Ayr Gorge Woodlands Wildlife Reserve.

Whether you make the trip on foot or drive via the B730, it's well worth taking time to discover this pretty little village. Here, standing on the banks of the river Ayr, is The Stair Inn. A listed building of considerable character and dating back to around 1670, this is a traditional country hostelry situated in a beautiful conservation area. Pictures of Robert Burns adorn the walls reminding you that this inn was frequented by the poet in his lifetime. Neighbouring the inn are the farmlands and woodlands of the Earl of Stair, and just across the river is the only hone stone mine works remaining in Britain. This still produces the celebrated Tam O'Shanter and Water of Ayr hone stones.

In the past the inn was used for church services when the local church roof leaked. After the service, every member of the congregation received a jar of ale and it's been said that these were the best attended services ever!

Rejoining the A758 we make our way slowly to the principal town in Burns country - **Ayr**. This busy resort is one of the most popular and beautiful on the west coast of Scotland. The town developed from settlements in Roman times, and has always retained an attraction due to its extensive sandy beaches, golf courses and many recreational activities. You may choose to enjoy some of the traditional seaside entertainments or perhaps walk around the many colourful parks in the town. Here, of course, is the famous racecourse which hosts meetings throughout the year.

Ayr has a history of trading and markets, and there is a busy fish market at the South Harbour which makes an interesting visit. Today the Ayrshire Agricultural Show takes place every year in April. Around 1900, the cattle market in Ayr was relocated to its present site in the town's Castlehill Road. Here you will find the aptly named Market Inn, a well known watering hole for Ayrshire landowners and farmers seeking refreshment after a hard morning's bargaining.

There are two bridges that cross the river. The Auld Brig and New Bridge were written about by Burns in 'The Brigs of Ayr' where he correctly forecasted that the old bridge would outlast the new. In the poem, the Old Brig says to the New; "I'll be a brig when ye're a shapeless cairn". Indeed, the New bridge fell down in a storm in 1870. The connections between Ayr and Burns are very strong, especially as Alloway, where the poet was born, is now a suburb of the town, though it was once separated by two miles of countryside.

Visitors to **Alloway** are able to go to another Burns Interpretation Centre, this permanent exhibition, like the other mentioned before, displays events, characters and memories of the life of the poet. Nearby you will be able to see the cottage where he was born, on the

25th of January 1759, and spent the first five years of his life. Just a few minutes walk away is the Auld Brig O'Doon where the chase in the epic poem 'Tam O'Shanter' took place, and The Burns Monument.

It is only a little way up the coast to our next destination. As far back as the beginning of the 18th century the attractions of coastal towns like **Troon** were becoming clear to those who lived in the cities and industrial areas. Indeed, Troon was considered at the time to possess "an excellent situation for sea bathing". Happily on this count Troon is unchanged, and this small fishing town is still a popular holiday resort that can boast two miles of soft, sandy beaches stretching from either side of the harbour.

Enjoying an enviable location on the sea road which runs from the centre of Troon, **South Beach Hotel** is an impressive family-run establishment which has everything you need for a perfect holiday. The sun lounge at the front of the hotel boasts wonderful views across the Firth of Clyde and is the perfect place to relax after a busy day exploring. The 27 en-suite guest rooms are spacious and attractively furnished and equipped with every modern facility for maximum comfort. In the large elegant dining room you can savour an extensive à la carte menu and if you are worried about the calories, South Beach has its own fully equipped health club where you can tone up in the gymnasium.

South Beach Hotel, South Beach, Troon. 0292-312033 Map Ref: C4

The harbour itself is a fascinating place with much going on; the yachts arriving and berthing, anglers trying their luck and children exploring all the nooks and crannies of the many rock pools.

The towns biggest association must of course be with golf. Royal Troon Golf Club was formed in 1878 and its course has hosted the Open Championship on several occasions.

The main route out of Troon to the east is the A759, through Loans and crossing the Dundonald Hills. The road passes through the village of **Dundonald** which developed beside the site of the castle, dating from 1390. The street of houses near this castle are quite picturesque and there is a beautiful 19th century church. At Gatehead, the road crosses the railway line and we turn towards Kilmarnock. There's an excellent example of an old railway viaduct, and in fact one of the first railway bridges to be built in Scotland.

It's well worth taking the opportunity to see this splendid example of railway architecture, since bridges like these are certainly disappearing rapidly in Britain today. It is not far from here into **Kilmarnock**. The first edition of Burns' poetry was printed here and became known as the 'Kilmarnock' edition. In Burns' day the town was full of handloom weavers who lived and worked in their cottages. The industrial heritage has continued throughout the years, and today Kilmarnock is a busy producer of many goods.

Just off the Kilmarnock bypass, north of the town centre, is **Dean Castle Country Park**. This is the sort of place where the whole family can spend a super day out. Apart from an adventure playground woodland walks, children's corner and riding school, there is Dean Castle itself with its dungeons and museum. The stronghold dates back to around 1360 when the main keep was built to defend the lands of the Boyd family, lords of Kilmarnock. The castle then expanded along with the fortunes of the Boyds, until fire destroyed all but the shell of this once powerful family seat.

Now run by Kilmarnock and Loudon District Council, Dean castle was superbly restored to its original grandeur by the 8th Howard de Walden, and houses his collection of European arms, armour and tapestries. There is also the Van Raalte collection of early musical instruments. There is, furthermore, exhibits and displays of medieval life, plus, of course, various artefacts from the life and works of none other than, Robert Burns.

Travelling to London Road we came across the **Dick Institute**. This contains Kilmarnock's main library with a museum and art collection that has many fine paintings, including work by Constable, Corot, Turner and members of the Glasgow School, as well as housing a variety of exhibitions throughout the year.

We now take the A71 from Kilmarnock which lead us to the town of **Irvine** , close to the coast. Many of Irvine's activities are based around the attractions of the sea, and one of the most popular is the Magnum Leisure Complex . This dominates the harbour area and its features are too many for a complete list but include swimming pools, an ice rink, bowls hall, theatre, cinema, sauna and solarium, plus many other activities inside and outside in the two hundred and fifty acre beach park.

A covered shopping mall spans the river connecting the town to the harbour area. In the latter is the Scottish Maritime Museum, which includes a shipyard worker's flat, which has been restored to its original 1910 decor. There are many fine historic ships moored in the harbour, which visitors are encouraged to board. Nearby is the enchanting 'Sea World' which creates an underwater environment for observing marine life, housed in special tanks, ranging from sea anemones and starfish to lobsters and even giant conger eels.

Back in the town there are fascinating walks along the narrow cobbled streets of old Irvine, taking in the fine examples of 18th and 19th century buildings. Nearby Glasgow Vennel was once the main route to Glasgow, though now is traffic free, and was recently the winner of an award for its restoration.

Being in the heart of Burns country, you will not be surprised to learn that the Poet came here in 1781, not to pen his verse though but to learn the flax dressing trade. The buildings where he worked, and stayed for two years, are now some two hundred year later, home to the Ayrshire Writers and Artists Society. You can take a look at his attic bedroom which is open to visitors and located at number four.

On the opposite side of the house is the **Buchanite Meeting House** which was once occupied by an infamous religious sect, led by one Elizabeth Buchan. The agricultural revolution in the late 18th century brought many country folk in to the towns in a desperate search for work. This led to an increase in the general instability and a result of this was the flourishing of religious cults. The most unusual of these were the Buchanites who set up their sect in Irvine. Elizabeth Buchan talked of the second coming of the Messiah when she and her followers would be taken up to heaven. The townspeople of Irvine were rather taken aback by all this and promptly ran the lady and her followers out of town.

Coming out of Irvine, the road take us north to nearby **Kilwinning** , where there's the strange ancient custom of 'shooting the papingo'. A papingo, or wooden bird on a pole, is set up as a target from the clock tower of the Abbey Church for the Ancient Society of Kilwinning Archers to test their skills. This annual shoot is re-enacted each year, and the table gravestones beside the church have been chipped by the arrows that presumably have missed the papingo! There is a magnificent Silver Arrow Trophy dating back to 1724 that is displayed in the town's library.

From Kilwinning we drive to **Saltcoats** and neighbouring

Ardrossan, on the coast. Saltcoats, as its name suggests, developed a salt panning industry established here by James V in the 16th century. The harbour was built in the 17th century and coal would come here via a canal for export to Ireland. Since the development of the harbour at Ardrossan however, the use of Saltcoats as a working port declined and only small boats are seen here today, although the place is very popular with holiday makers. Keep an eye open at low tide in the harbour for you will see the fossilized remains of tree trunks here. The tower above the school is a Martello Tower . There are examples all around the coast of Britain, gun positions to protect us from French warships during the Napoleonic Wars.

Saltcoats and **Ardrossan** are divided by the Stanley Burn and crossing it brings you into the 19th century town. There has in fact been a castle here since the 12th century, though, despite its seemingly strong position it was captured by Cromwell, who used its stones to build his castle in Ayr.

There was a very ambitious plan to connect the port and harbour at Ardrossan with Glasgow by linking the two with a canal. Both Telford and Rennie were engaged on the construction. Unfortunately their funding ran out in 1815 and the plan was abandoned. Had it gone ahead the town of Ardrossan might have been a very different place. Ardrossan has instead became important for its ferry crossings to the Isle of Arran and to Belfast, and developed into a popular resort boasting sandy beaches to rival the best of the west coast. You will notice Horse Island just off the coast and not surprisingly this is a bird sanctuary.

Taking the crossing to **Arran** lands our journey on the first of the many and very different islands of Scotland. The Isle of Arran is a fascinating 10 by 20 mile island that is perhaps with some justification referred to as Scotland in miniature.

It unfolds dramatically, from mountains in the north capped by Goat Fell at 2868ft to the farmlands and rolling moors of the south. Its history is turbulent, being held not only by the Dalriada Scots from Northern Ireland but also by the Vikings, whose links with the Isle are still celebrated, and finally by the Scottish Crown. Robert the Bruce stayed here in 1307 before leaving for the mainland to continue his struggle for Scottish Independence, which he finally achieved at Bannockburn after some seven years.

A regular services link the Isle with the Mainland and the ferry unloads the visitor at **Brodick**, after a journey time of about an hour. The name Brodick has Viking associations, as do many of the names of the Isle, it is Norse for 'Broad Bay'. Brodick is the largest village on

Arran, and lies to one side of Brodick Bay. From here you are treated to a fine view of the mountains to the north.

Visitors will find a lovely holiday base at **Carrick Lodge**, the charming home of Eric and Mairi Thompson. Built from local red sandstone, this splendid Victorian manse enjoys a super hillside location just 300 yards from Brodick Pier and boasts fabulous views across the bay. Awarded a Two Crown Commended rating by the Scottish Tourist Board, very comfortable accommodation is provided in six attractively furnished guest rooms, five en-suite and each with colour TV and hot drinks facilities, two rooms on the ground floor being suitable for the partially disabled. In addition to a full breakfast, there is the option of an excellent home-cooked evening meal, which guests can complement with a bottle of wine if they wish. Alternative accommodation of an equally high standard is provided in a self-catering property situated in the garden of Carrick Lodge.

Carrick Lodge, Brodick, Arran. 0770-302550 Map Ref: B3

At **Kilmichael Country House Hotel** in Glen Cloy you will discover a true taste of paradise for here in beautiful and historic surroundings, you will find the perfect blend of luxurious accommodation and superb cuisine in an atmosphere of friendly hospitality. To find this tranquil haven, turn left opposite Brodick Golf Club and continue for almost a mile. Believed to be the oldest house on the island, Kilmichael is steeped in history and Grizel's Room, one of the ten exquisite character bedrooms, features a 17th century plaque pronouncing a declaration of love. The abundance of porcelain and antique furniture throughout enhances the peaceful, intimate ambience while in the elegant restaurant a mouthwatering menu incorporates both traditional and more exotic dishes to tempt the most discerning palate. All these factors ensure a holiday here is one you will treasure.

Kilmichael Country House Hotel, Glen Cloy, Brodick, Arran. 0770-302219 Map Ref: B3

A mile and a half from the Brodick Pier is **Brodick Castle**, another fine Trust property. The castle is the former seat of the Dukes of Hamilton and dates in part from the 13th Century. Over the many following decades, additions to the Castle have included a gun battery erected in 1652 by Oliver Cromwell's troops, who occupied the Castle at that time.

1844 was also a busy year for the masons who carried out work in traditional Scottish Baronial style. Inside, there are many fine paintings, a large number of which depict sporting scenes and reflect the sporting nature of the Hamiltons. An indicator of the hunting skills of the family are the stag heads which line the walls of the grand staircase. For those of you, however, who favour less energetic pastimes, there is a fine collection of silver and porcelain to enjoy, as well as the valuable art collection.

The last owner of Brodick Castle was the Duchess of Montrose, daughter of the 12th Duke of Hamilton. It was she who created the magnificent rhododendron collection, now regarded as one of the finest in Europe. The Castle gardens these days form part of Brodick Country Park, and as well as the Woodland Garden which houses the rhododendrons, there is a Walled Garden which dates back to 1810.

Also in the Park is the mountain of Goat Fell, and part of Glen Rosa and Cir Mhor, 2618ft. A thoughtful touch is the Nature Trail designed especially for wheelchair users, and for everyone, a Ranger Service is provided to answer the many questions posed by curious trekkers.

Young visitors will love the Adventure Playground, and a visit to the Castle shop and tearoom rounds the day off perfectly.

Visitors to the castle will notice a strong Bruce connection as this stronghold has a room known as 'Bruce's Room'. The story goes that in 1307 Bruce, and his small band of colleagues, waited in hiding for a signal that it was safe to cross to the mainland. However, the King and his followers saw an unrelated light and set forth, across the waters. Luckily the misunderstanding did not hamper Bruce's arrival.

There is another version of the story which claims that the room, from which Bruce watched for the light, was in the now ruined Kildonan Castle, some nine miles to the south. Brodick at the time was the headquarters of King Edward's governor, and possibly the last place that Bruce would find refuge, while Kildonan Castle was owned by a branch of the Clan Donald of the Isle, who were a friends and supporters of Bruce. Whomever is right, it's a fascinating piece of history.

To get a real feel for life on the island before 1020 it's recommended that you pay a visit to the **Isle of Arran Heritage Museum** which is located between the castle and the village. Here there are accurate representations of life on Arran, including a Smiddy and an Arran cottage.

The museum also features a plaque in memory of the 112th Scottish Commando. The Isle was the training ground for the officers and men during the last war. It was this Commando Unit which was responsible for a daring raid on General Rommel's headquarters in the North African desert in November 1941.

Going back even further in time, the importance of Arran as an archaeological centre cannot be forgotten. There have been recently excavated sites, which have been dated back to 2500 BC, and are considered to be some of the most important remaining examples of Bronze and Iron Age finds in Europe. There are many sites to see if you are interested in these ancient monuments, and the Isle can boast a rich choice of tombs from the Neolithic period and circles of standing stones from the Bronze Age.

The same must be said for Arran's importance as a geological centre. The local rock is Permian desert sandstone which is 250 million years old. James Hutton, who is regarded as the father of modern geology, made discoveries at Lochranza, which was the first certain proof of the great age of the Earth. The Douglas Hotel in the town often plays host to trainee submarine captains who come to Arran, twice a year, for simulated deep sea dives, and attack manoeuvres around the island.

For visitors to the Isle of Arran, one treat not to be missed is a trip to **Creelers**, a superb seafood restaurant and shop situated a mile north of Brodick. Tim and Fran James are friendly proprietors who pride themselves on using only locally caught fish. Housed within a converted barn the restaurant has a lovely 'bistro' feel, and on fine days you can enjoy your meal outside.

Creelers, The Home Farm, Brodick, Arran. 0770-302810
Map Ref: B3

Although principally a seafood restaurant, Creelers caters for all tastes and the mouthwatering menu includes a selection of daily changing blackboard specials, with a wide range of starters, accompanied by a carefully selected wine list. Tim, a fisherman for many years sells his day's catch from the adjoining shop as well as their own 'Arran Smoked Products' which are also available through a highly popular mail order service.

Gillian Langley, The Byre, High Glen Cloy, Brodick, Arran.
0770-302505 Map Ref: B3

The beautiful Isle of Arran has much to offer the holiday maker, with splendid mountain scenery to the north and gently rolling farmland to the south, interspersed with little towns and villages providing a wealth of places to eat and shop. Lovers of self-catering will be spoilt for choice when they call Gillian Langley, for she manages no less than thirteen properties across the island. One of these is **Derneneach Farmhouse** which enjoys a central location, five miles outside Brodick. This traditional Scottish farmhouse carries a Four Crown, Highly Commended rating by the Scottish Tourist Board and provides accommodation of the highest standard, ensuring a restful holiday for all. All thirteen properties enjoy a quiet location and are fully equipped, two being suitable for disabled guests.

The one main road that circles the Isle is the A841, and we decided to follow this road southwards towards the village of **Lamlash**, which nestles on the shores of Lamlash Bay. It is here in 1263 that a naval battle was fought between the Norwegians and the Scots. Prior to the battle, the Viking King Haakon's fleet was anchored off the shore, and every year the village of Corrie, which in fact is to the north of Brodick, holds the 'Corrie Capers' to remember this time by burning the replica of a Viking long ship.

The small island off the shore of Lamlash is called Holy Isle, and is a paradise for bird lovers. You can visit the Island, which is only a short boat trip away, and catch sight not only of the birds but also a herd of wild goats which roam around its rocky crags. Holy Isle also contains St. Molio's cave to the west of the island, along with St. Molio's Well and the Judgement Stone which is a 7ft sandstone table. The island takes its name from the 7th century St. Molaise, who is said to have lived to be 120. Perhaps this is a testament to the healthy life here in the Isles. If you pay a visit to his cave you may notice some 'graffiti' on the walls in runic, the old Norse alphabet, which was carved by Norwegian sailors who were here before the battle in 1263. The Vikings lost the battle to Alexander III of Scotland, who effectively ended centuries of Norse control of the Western Isles.

In 1829 the brig, 'Caledonian', stopped here at Lamlash Bay. It's purpose was to pick up 86 emigres who had lost their places on the land as a result of the clearances, when they were forced to leave their homes to make way for the more profitable sheep, whom the landowners were bringing in. There is a monument here to these unfortunate people.

Visitors to Lamlash will also find a lively marina here, and if you are of a mind, you will be able to hire a boat for a spot of sea fishing. Those of you with a taste for the underwater world may like to hire some diving equipment, and you will be able to get excellent advice on the best places to drive locally.

The cottages along Hamilton Terrace were originally built for estate workers, who would move to the backs of their houses each summer in order to let the main front house to visitors. Another interesting shop in Lamlash is the Arran Provisions factory which produces a world famous range of jams, jellies, chutneys and mustards.

The road continues south through Whiting Bay , which is a truly lovely spot and close to the Glenashdale Falls , a picturesque place of sparkling waters which makes a pleasant excursion on foot from the other side of Whiting Bay.

The Burlington Hotel in Whiting Bay enjoys a peaceful location and makes a relaxing base from which to explore this lovely island. Awarded a Three Crowns Commended grading and listed in Les Routiers and Logis of Great Britain, this small privately owned hotel provides very comfortable accommodation in ten individually styled guest rooms, half with private shower/w.c. Renowned for its imaginative use of fresh local produce, the licensed restaurant is open to non-residents. The guest sitting room boasts wonderful views across the bay and to complete your stay, hillwalking, ponytrekking, golf and guided tours of the island are readily organised.

Burlington Hotel, Whiting Bay, Arran. 0770-700255 Map Ref: B4

There is a rich abundance of sea-life around the Isle, and were told that it has been quite common in the earlier part of the summer for sightings to be made of basking sharks in the waters. These huge plankton eating fish can grow up to 40ft in length, and swim around for six to eight weeks before taking their leave. It is amazing to think that little is known about the habits of these creatures, which are harmless. Another visitor to the Isle is the whale, and both killer and bottlenosed have been sighted around the shores. There can be few more stirring sights.

Lovers of self-catering will discover a superior holiday base at **Dippin Lodge,** a splendid Victorian Hunting Lodge once owned by the Duke of Montrose. Lying ten miles south of Brodick and set within 80 acres of gardens and wooded countryside, this is a very special place indeed, offering privacy and seclusion, whilst still being within easy reach of all the attractions the Isle of Arran has to offer. Sympathetic restoration and modernisation over the years has incorporated every modern facility for maximum comfort without detracting from the history and character of this delightful establishment and size of the property, with seven beautifully furnished bedrooms, makes it ideal for large parties or families sharing a holiday. An atmosphere of elegant luxury pervades throughout and ensures you leave Dippin Lodge feeling relaxed and refreshed, yet eager for a return visit.

Dippin Lodge, Dippin, Arran. 0770-870255/213 Map Ref: B4

Kildonan and its castle are situated at the southern tip of the island, and the harbour is another centre for diving as well as having opportunities for boat hire. Around Bennan Head at Kilmory is the creamery that manufactures the prize winning Arran cheddar cheese, all three hundred tons of it each year!

At **Blackwaterfoot** there's a choice of pony trekking and riding centres, with much of the island open country horse back is an ideal way to explore. Not far from here you will be able to visit the legendary cave occupied by Robert the Bruce. Legend has it he watched a spider attempt to make his web. Inspired by this one little spider he left vowing to try again.

The approach to **Machrie Bay** is features some fine examples of

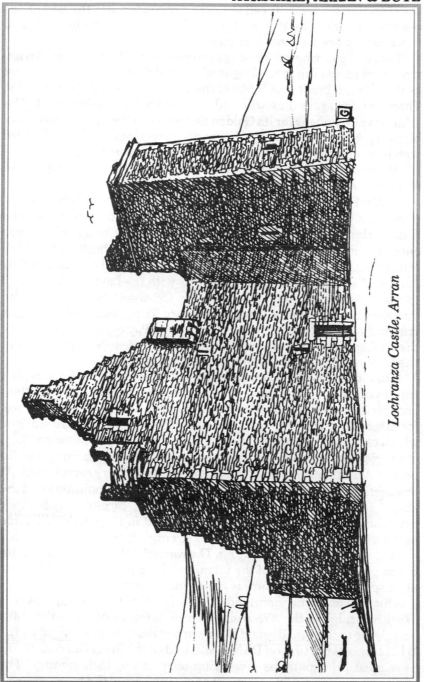

Lochranza Castle, Arran

the standing stones. 15ft tall they are a reminder that the island has been settled since the Bronze Age. The bay itself has lovely sands and is an ideal place for a walk or picnic.

Those of you who take the opportunity to walk around on Arran, may come across the special sight of wild red deer. This is not unusual as the Isle can boast over 2,000 of the species in the wild hill country. They wander around at will and are a most impressive sight. The Island is also famous for its Golden Eagles, as well as a wealth of other birds of prey including hawks, buzzards, peregrines and kestrels. Bird watchers amongst you will enjoy a rewarding time here.

Along the coast at **Catacol** there is a rather intriguing row of identical terraced cottages know locally as 'the Twelve Apostles'.

A little further north on the northern tip of the island is **Lochranza**, which is a delightful community situated around the shores of Loch Ranza. Here you will find the ruins of Lochranza Castle , which was once the hunting seat of Scottish kings, and was built in the 16th century. It stands on a sand spit in the middle of the loch. Used by James VI as a base during his struggles with the Lords of the Isles in the early 1600's and later garrisoned by Cromwell the castle fell into disuse by the end of the eighteenth century. Today there are many fine craft industries based here, visitors to Arran Pottery are able to watch the craftsmen at work and the Gold and Silver jewellery produced at the Castle Workshop is both intricate and beautiful.

Corrie, previously mentioned for holding the 'Corrie Capers', is a small village of closely packed white cottages. It makes an excellent base for hill walking and climbing in the area. It is ideal, for instance, for attempting the majestic challenge of Goat Fell, or Glen Sannox which can be seen from the village. The old fishing and mining village of Corrie has seen much in its historical past, although this peaceful part of Arran has now been purely residential since around 1945. At the northern end of the village, sitting between the mountains and the shore, is a layer of black basalt lava. This, together with other interesting geological features, has resulted in the whole shoreline being designated as a site of special scientific interest.

A stay on Arran is enchanting. The warmth of the people, the sense of the past, the majesty of the terrain and the peace of the place, are all inspirational. Departure is often tinged with regret.

Once more on the mainland our journey slowly heads up towards West Kilbride on the A78 and there can be few coast roads that take you closer to the sea. Beyond the town our route heads inland on the B781 towards the town of **Dalry**. Situated on the River Garnock it was developed principally as a weaving town in the 18th century. The grounds of nearby Blair estate, to the south east of the town, are well

AYRSHIRE, ARRAN & BUTE

worth exploring. The house here is quite interesting. Standing on the bank of the River Bambo, it is based around an ancient tower and later developed into a T-shaped plan with three and four storeys. The Blair family can trace their antecedence back to 1165 and the house, started in the 1500's, is still in their hands. The estate is surrounded by a wall, and there are attractive lodges and an interesting smithy worth looking at.

The Dusk Water flows through the estate and for those of you interested in caves, we suggest a trip to Cleaves Cove on the south bank of the water. Excavations here in 1883 show that the caves were inhabited in prehistoric times! These are a series of limestone caves and contain some well known stalactites. Those of you entranced by the beauty of waterfalls should go to the Caaf Water to the south-west of Dalry. Here a path alongside the stream lead to another fine waterfall and the remains of a mill.

The road up towards Largs is extremely picturesque, drive slowly, and you'll have the opportunity to absorbing the beauty of both Camphill and Muirhead Reservoirs which are next to the A760.

Largs faces directly onto the sea and it was here in 1263 that the Scots defeated an invasion force of Norsemen; and in 1912 the "Pencil", a distinctive monument on the coast of the Southern end of Largs, was erected to commemorate the victory. In September each year, a Viking festival is held where, strange though it may seem, many Scandinavian entertainers return to celebrate the Vikings only defeat on mainland Scotland.

Drive south and you'll arrive at the historic estate of Kelburn, located on the A78 between Largs and Fairlie. **Kelburn Castle** makes an impressive background here and there is much to do in the lovely grounds for all of the family.

Fencebay Fisheries, Fairlie. Fish Farm 0475-568918 Restaurant 0475-568989 Fax: 0475-568921 Map Ref: C3

A little further is **Fairlie**, and **Fencebay Fisheries**. Here, in pools filled with spring water from the mountains, trout are reared for sale and you can even have a go at fishing for some yourself. In the fish hatchery there are lobsters, crabs, oysters and various other shellfish and the smokehouse uses traditional methods to create that distinctive flavour for a variety of smoked fish, all of which can be bought in the farm shop.

In the comfortable surroundings of a converted barn, the aptly named Fins Restaurant-Café offers a diverse menu of mouthwatering fish dishes and after enjoying your meal, you can take a stroll to the beautiful waterfalls which lie half a mile to the rear of the farm.

Largs is an ideal centre for the touring of North Ayrshire and it is also the place to cross the water to visit **Great Cumbrae Island**, which lies between the Isle of Bute and the mainland. Small though the island is - just ten miles in circumference - a vehicle ferry service is available. It take just ten minutes cross to this fascinating place, where you can witness some superb views of Scotland from the highest point, the Glaidstane.

Millport, on the south side of the island, is a friendly town There are good pubs here, and you can gaze awhile at the smallest cathedral in Europe. The Garrison House is now the Museum of the Cumbraes, which is packed with photos, memorabilia and articles telling the story of the island and its much smaller sister, not surprisingly called Little Cumbrae. Garrison House, and was originally built by Captain Crauford, of the famous cutter, 'The Royal George', as a barracks for his crew in 1745.

Those of you who enjoy a taste for more active pastimes might like to take advantage of the National Watersports Centre . You can opt for wide choice of tuition courses in a variety of watersports for beginners and enthusiasts alike.

The island is a haven for research, and the Marine Biological Station and Museum is located at **Keppel**, where it has been involved in research since it was opened in 1887. It is open to the public who are able to enjoy looking at the fine aquarium here. It is a reluctant return to the mainland after the peace and tranquility of Cumbrae.

The A78 threads its way north from Largs along the coast, passing the castle of **Skelmorlie**. It was built in 1502 and very nearly destroyed in 1959 by a huge fire. Now restored, with the Victorian additions of 1852 removed, it is a private family home.

In order to visit the Isle of Bute we need to travel on up to **Wemyss Bay**, from where the ferry sails. The crossing takes about half an hour and it is not long before you are docking at **Rothesay**.

Though the island is only about fifteen miles long and just over a mile wide, it has an amazing wealth of scenery. The land at the northern end of the island has a wild feeling about it while the southern end is altogether more soft and gentle. Rothesay itself is a popular holiday resort with an ample choice of activities and entertainments, so in high season it can get busy. The burgh was first granted a royal charter in 1401. In 1398 King Robert III created his eldest son 'Duke of Rothesay', and the title still exists today being held by none other than Prince Charles. Opposite Mansion House is The Bute Museum , which has a fascinating exhibition covering all aspects of the Isle. The islands unusually mild climate is a result of the effect of the warm Gulf stream. This reaches the west coast, allowing the magnificent palm trees and azaleas to thrive here.

Rothesay castle was in existence as early as 1203. In 1230 the Norse, led by Uspak, laid seige and having failed to storm the castle hacked their way through the wall. The breach and subsequent repairs are still visible today. Retaken in 1263, when the Norsemen were finally cleared from Scotland, the castle was substantially strengthened with higher walls and four round towers. These improvements enabled it to withstand a seige in 1527 that saw most of the Royal Burgh destroyed. It finally succumbed to the English in 1544 and was used by both Charles I and Cromwell as a garrison. The Roundheads partially dismantled it when they left and what remained was put to the torch during the rebellion of 1685. In Victorian times the Bute family, appointed hereditary keepers in 1498, had the remains cleared and repaired.

Half a mile south of the town is the remains of St. Mary's Chapel. A late medieval church, it contains two fine examples of recessed and canopied tombs, with effigies of a knight in full armour and lady and child.

In nearby **Ardencraig** are Ardencraig Gardens. These were bought by the Royal Burgh in 1968 they now supply flowers for the colourful floral displays all over the island. Visitors will also enjoy the aviary and ornamental ponds, which contain many unusual species of birds and fish, as well as a fresh brew in the tearoom.

To the north of Rothesay are the two castles of **Kames** and **Wester Kames**. Neither have any great historical significance but both are in a good state of repair. Kames is now part of a holiday home for the Scottish Council for the Care of Spastics and Wester Kames was restored in 1900 for the Third Marquess of Bute, after remaining a derelict for many years.

Depending on your next destination it is possible to cross back to the mainland at **Rhubodach** in the north, landing you at Colintraive.

This is an ideal starting point to explore Argyll but that is another chapter in our journey, so we must head back to Wemyss Bay and on into Renfrew.

Just a short journey from Inverkip, the next village up the coast, into the hills is **Cornalees Bridge Centre**. Part of the Clyde Muirisheil Regional Park it offers a series of delightful walks and trails along the banks of Loch Thom, as well as one that utilises the Greenock Cut a historic aqueduct that once supplied the houses and factories of the town.

Back on the coast, north of Lunderston Bay, is Cloch Lighthouse, standing on Cloch Point. This white painted lighthouse was built in 1797, and whilst not open to the public it offers magnificent views of the Firth of Clyde and the hills of Argyll beyond.

Our travels turn a corner at Cloch heading along the banks of the mighty Clyde, famous the world over. There are several towns caught between the river and the Inverclyde hills. The Clyde has long been the life blood of the area. For over two hundred years ships from up the river have sailed the world and now with shipbuilding almost at an end these waters offer excellent leisure sailing, with many international yachting and watersports events held each year.

Back on dry land all these towns have vivid reminders that the sea is not far from peoples minds. The Kempock Stone at the Castle Mansions of **Gourock** is also know as Granny Kempock's Stone. It stands over six feet high and was undoubtedly of great significance in prehistoric times. More recently it was used in fair weather rites ceremonies by local fishermen, and couples intending to marry would encircle the stone to gain Granny's blessing. Gourock also offers the traveller ferry services to Dunoon, ideal if you are keen to get into Argyll.

In the nearby town of **Greenock** is Maclean Museum and Art Gallery. Pride of place in the museum is taken by a collection of model ships. These were often built at the same time as the real thing and either kept on display at the shipyard offices or presented to the ships owners. There are also items relating to James Watt, born in Greenock, who pioneered the basic steam engine and gave his name to the measurement of Power.

To discover more about the towns entrepreneurs of the past it is well worth visiting the Smugglers Museum, housed rather ironically in the Custom House.

From Princess Pier there are regular sailings on the Upper Firth of Clyde to Helensburgh, Kilcreggan, Dunoon, Rothesay, Largs and Millport, **Clyde Marine Cruises** provide the perfect way to admire the scenic coast of Scotland in leisurely comfort. Popular destinations

Cloch Lighthouse

include Millport and Tighnabruaich (Kyles of Bute), although you can plan your cruise to suit your own requirements, whether you are bringing a school party on an educational trip or having a special family celebration or party. All Clyde Marine's vessels have toilets on board and The Second Snark and Kenilworth both have a licensed bar. Tea, coffee and light refreshments are also available, ensuring maximum comfort during your cruise. The wonderful panoramic views will soon have you using up a reel of film in your camera providing you with perfect mementos of your trip.

Clyde Marine Cruises, Princes Pier, Greenock. 0475-721281
Map Ref: C1

Newark Castle (one of three in Scotland) is just off the A8 at **Port Glasgow**. Despite being surrounded by shipyards and their attendant industries the castle remains an impressive example of the fortified baronial residence. Though not complete this former home of the Maxwells is well worth a visit, stood four square on a spit of land jutting out into the river.

Port Glasgow was originally called Newark until Sir Patrick Maxwell sold the land and village to the magistrates of Glasgow in 1668. They built a port to facilitate the transfer of goods from ocean going vessels to those which could navigate the then shallow Clyde.

A few miles from Port Glasgow at Langbank is the home of Clan MacMillan - **Finlaystone**. The estate has beautiful formal gardens and woodland walks, picnic sites and children's play areas. The visitors centre also offers a ranger service as well as a Celtic art exhibition. The House, which has historical connections with 16th century preacher John Knox and poet Robert Burns, has a large doll collection and display of Victoriana. Enchanting and relaxing the estate offers the visitor a break from the hurley burley of the outside world.

Another ideal place to escape the 20th century for just few hours is **Formakin Estate** along the riverside at **Bishopston**. The 150 acre estate was designed by Sir Robert Lorimer between 1903-1913. The Mansion house is incomplete internally and set in landscaped gardens and grounds overgrown but being restored. There is plenty to explore: the estate workers bothy and stable block with courtyard, craft workshops, towerhouse, gatelodges and a derelict mealmill. The estate also runs a rare breeds farm and if all the exploring makes you peckish there is restaurant.

Exploring inland from Bishopston taking the B-Roads through Bridge of Weir brings us to **Lochwinnoch Nature Reserve**. Run by the RSPB there are great views from the observation tower and a wealth of information on the local wildlife in the Nature Centre. For the twitchers amongst you there are hides within a short walk, two overlook the marshes and a third gives excellent views over Loch Barr. As with so many lochs Barr has its castle, if a some what dilapidated one.

In the village of **Lochwinnoch** is the community museum. It features a series of changing exhibitions reflecting the life and times of the village and its surrounding area. Off the B786 north of the village is **Muirsheil Country Park**. You may recall that we have already touched on the park at Cornalees Bridge Centre. The park covers several square miles and offers a huge choice of trails and walks. There's something for everyone, from the afternoon stroller to the committed hikers, and peace and tranquillity just a half hours drive from Glasgow. And it is back in that direction we head to Renfrewshire's city, **Paisley**.

There's a wealth of architectural gems in the city, from an impressive selection of Victorian churches to the restored Sma'Shot cottages, where once local artisans plied their trade. These are in George Place and consist of a traditional 19th century millworkers' two-storey, with back of the house iron staircase, and an 18th century Weavers's Cottage. They give us a valuable insight into the lives and living conditions of Paisley's working community over a hundred years ago.

The town has benefited from its commercial past, not least in the outstanding architectural legacies of the Coats and Clark families, whose names are synonymous with the textile industry. The striking Renaissance-style Town Hall is a lasting testament to the Clarks, while the stunning gothic spire of Thomas Coats Memorial Church marks it out as one of the finest Baptist Churches in Europe.

Those interested in the world famous Paisley cloth can discover much more at **Paisley Museum and Art Gallery** in the High Street. It houses the world-famous collections of Paisley shawls. as well as displays that trace the history of the Paisley pattern; the development of weaving techniques and the social aspects of what was a tightly-knit weaving community. There are also fine collections of local history, natural history, ceramics and Scottish painting.

Paisley also boasts a fine Cluniac Abbey Church founded in 1163 and the birthplace of the Stuart dynasty. In 1307 Edward I of England ordered its destruction. After victory at Bannockburn it was rebuilt and restored in the century following. The choir has a fine stone-vaulted roof and features some beautiful stained glass, as well as the tombs of Princess Marjory Bruce and King Robert III. Outside there is an impressive Norman doorway, cloisters and Place of Paisley. The Barochan Cross, a weathered Celtic cross, 11ft high and attributed to 10th century is also in the Abbey.

Nearby is **Coats Observatory** on Oakshaw Street. Since it opened in 1882 there has been continuous astronomical observation and meteorological recording. The recent addition of the latest seismology equipment and a satellite weather picture receiver has made it one of the best equipped observatories in the country.

Those tired by all this exploring may like to pay a visit to the Lagoon Leisure Centre, off Mill Street. This modern swimming pool complex has saunas, steam room and jacuzzi as well as bar and cafeteria. The ideal place to relax before we go on to the next chapter and the great city of Glasgow.

CHAPTER FOUR

Glasgow and Lanarkshire

S.S. Waverley

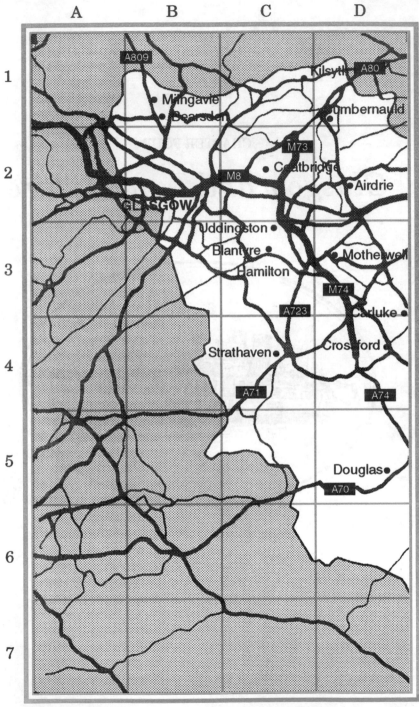

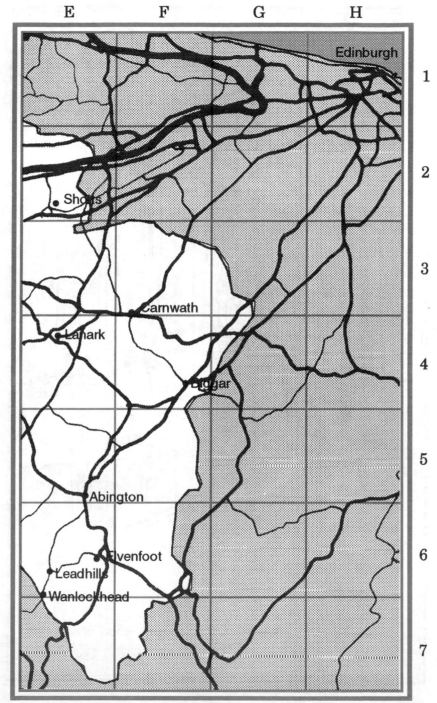

E　　F　　G　　H

Edinburgh

Shotts

Carnwath

Lanark

Biggar

Abington

Elvenfoot
Leadhills
Wanlockhead

1

2

3

4

5

6

7

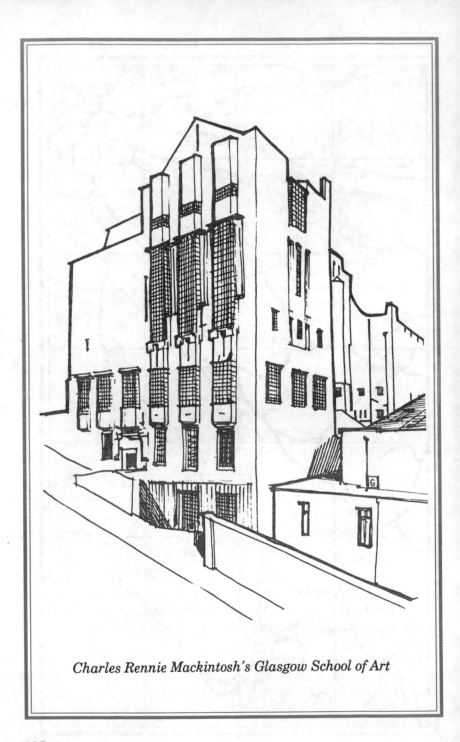

Charles Rennie Mackintosh's Glasgow School of Art

CHAPTER FOUR

Glasgow and Lanarkshire.

It would be difficult for a book of this size to do little more than scratch the surface of this great city. However we can certainly highlight some of the hidden places well worth seeking out, as well as suggest the places that no visitor should leave unexplored.

Glasgow has a character and flavour all of its own. It is full of opulent 19th Century architecture, and wonderful museums and galleries. Charles Rennie Mackintosh designed the Glasgow School of Art in Renfrew Street and in the famous Sauchiehall Street, much beloved by that famous old variety artist Harry Lauder, is his Willow Tea Room. If you enjoy seeing those buildings then take a look at his church at Queen's Cross which has recently been restored and the Hunterian Art Gallery, Hillhead Street, where you will have the opportunity to see reconstructions of his Glasgow home's interiors. Another opportunity to see his work can be found in Bellahouston Park where his domestic house design for a competition in Darmstadt in 1900 has been recreated. In Glasgow particularly but throughout Scotland you will notice his influence and his designs are copied on everything from furniture to restaurant menus.

Charles Rennie Mackintosh was the leading spirit of what became known as the 'Glasgow Style', whch earned the city a place in the world of Art Nouveau comparablc with Paris. Comparison with the French capital is only natural. We tend to forget that since the days of Mary Queen of Scots, it has been the French and not the English who have been the dominant influence in Scottish cultural life.

If towards the end of the last century you had wanted to buy Impressionist paintings without crossing the Channel, it is to Glasgow that you would have come, not London or Edinburgh, in order to meet several distinguished and highly respected dealers. The greatest of whom was Alexander Reid, a personal friend of many of the Impressionists.

The most famous collection in Glasgow is the **Burrell Collection**. On his death in 1944, a Clyde ship-owner, Sir William Burrell bequeathed to the city his magnificent collection of 8000 items of the ancient world, paintings and oriental art. He was quite specific in his will about how the collection should be housed and this resulted in a

Henry Moore Sculpture, Burrell Collection

superb gallery being built in Polloch Country Park. There is no question that this is a must for anyone visiting Glasgow. Leave plenty of time as it is easy to spend a day here.

The **Glasgow Art Gallery and Museum** in Kelvingrove Park has one of the finest municipal collections in Britain, ranging from Rembrandt to Dali. There are also impressive collections of ceramics, glass and silver, clocks, snuff boxes, pewter, Egyptian antiquities and rare arms and armour. More unusual is **The Tenement House** on Buccleuch St. A Victorian flat, it has remained unchanged since 1892, right down to the smallest detail. If you like oddities, especially of the gothic variety, Glasgow is full of them but perhaps the most memorable is the Necropolis, a hill crowned with obelisks, monuments, statues, columns and miniature temples. In Victorian Glasgow unless you were buried here you were a nobody!

Alongside the Necropolis is **St Mungo's Cathedral**, which has a long history. It was around the little church founded here in the 6th century by St. Mungo which the city of Glasgow grew. Take a look at the Lower Church which has what is considered to be one of the very best vaulted crypts of Gothic Europe. It is of beautiful proportions and very graceful. In the centre is the simple tomb of St Mungo who was buried on the site beside an ancient well in 603. The Cathedral now has a museum that celebrates the world's religions, the only one of its kind in Britain.

So many people just expect Glasgow to be an industrial city but it wasn't picked as a European City of culture on a whim. Its University for example was founded by Pope Nicholas V in 1451, which makes it the fourth oldest in Britain, after Oxford, Cambridge and St. Andrews. It is also home to Scottish Opera, Scottish Ballet and the Royal Scottish Orchestra.

Glasgow is a city of fun as well as culture, there are good theatres, concert halls, good eating houses and hotels, and there is even an underground system to help you get around.

Of course the city will be forever associated with the mighty River Clyde, yet the river was for centuries shallow and unnavigable. The city had to rely on the harbours at Greenock and Dumbarton both over twenty miles away; a short journey today but then heavy goods could take several days to cover it. After the union of England and Scotland in 1707 the city was able to trade freely with the Americas and it was clear to the city fathers that fortunes could be made. However, unless the ships could bring their cargos into the heart of Glasgow, those fortunes would come no nearor than the other ports.

So an ambitious project to deepen the Clyde was begun. After many false starts in 1781 an engineer, John Golborne, discovered that by narrowing the river the water could be made to flow faster, and 'scour' out its own channel. He achieved this by building a series of dykes into the river. His work was continued later by famous engineer Thomas Telford; who joined the ends of of Golbourne's dykes to contain the Clyde within stone banks, rather like a canal. During the 19th century dredgers took over the task of deepening the river. By the 1930's some of the world's largest vessels were being launched from Clydebank and over 40ft of water flowed where people had once walked across the river at low tide.

It was this feat of engineering that made Glasgow the greatest ship-building centre in the world. One of the most famous yards was that of John Brown & Co at Clydebank. Established in 1871, opposite the mouth of the River Cart, it had the extra room to launch larger ships. The Lusitania, whose sinking drew the United States into the First World War, was launched here in 1906, and in 1934 they needed every inch for the launch of the Queen Mary, over 1000ft long and with a draft of over 35ft. Her sister-ship the Queen Elizabeth and her famous successor QE2 also came from the yard.

The world's first steam ferry started on the Clyde between the city and Greenock on the 14th of August 1812. The ship (the Comet) was wrecked in 1820, but you can see a replica of her at Port Glasgow. Things have almost come full circle on the Clyde, where once it was said you could walk across the river on the dense mass of shipping it is now quiet and much cleaner.

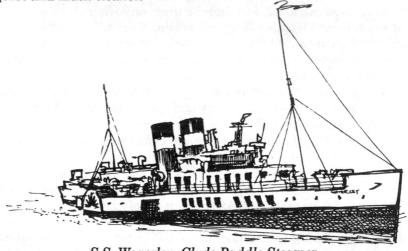

S.S. Waverley, Clyde Paddle Steamer

Today it is well worth taking a trip down to the Firth of Clyde, and what better way than on the **Waverley**, the world's last sea-going paddle steamer. Built in 1946 to replace her 1899 predecessor lost at Dunkirk and retired in 1973, she now spends the summer months cruising the Clyde and the islands of the Firth. Just along the waterfront from Anderston Quay where the Waverley docks is the impressive Finnieston Crane, erected in 1932 and still in use, it is Glasgow's largest ever dockside crane and can lift 175 tons.

Glasgow's rich transport history reaches far beyond the river. The **Museum of Transport** at Kelvin Hall has a wonderful collection of vintage cars, old locomotives and trams; the city once having one of the finest tram networks in the world. And its factories built locomotives that not only pulled trains the length and breadth of the country but move passengers and goods on every continent. Springburn Museum, on Ayr Street, preserves the heritage of the locomotive builders of the Springburn plant by recording the memories of the local people at work and at home.

Those of you with more organic interests should take the short journey from the city centre to the **Botanic Gardens**. They feature over 40 acres of woodlands and open lawns, crossed by the River Kelvin. Here you'll also discover the magnificent **Kibble Palace**, a great cast iron glasshouse that could only be Victorian. Inside amongst the tropical ferns keep your eyes open for the white marble statues. A gem of a different kind is the Barras Street market which has stalls heaving with collectables and bric-a- brac, full of local colour, and not to be missed.

If you choose to stay in Glasgow there are plenty of things to see and do in the surrounding area. **Bearsden**, to the north west of the city, has the country's finest example of a visible Roman building in its bath house; built around AD140 for the troops manning the Antonine Wall. Its all too often forgotten that the influence of Rome progressed a lot further north than Hadrian's Wall.

Nearby **Milngavie** is home to the purpose built **Lillie Art Gallery**. The gallery features an impressive collection of 20th century paintings, sculptures and ceramics, as well as hosting exhibitions of contemporary art.

Travelling a little further east takes us into the **Strathkelvin** district. Full of rural charm set amongst the southern Campsie Fells its picturesque towns and villages have a rich heritage that stretches back to Roman times. The **Antonine Wall** runs through the area. This turf and ditch rampart stretches between the Clyde at Old Kilpatrick and Bo'ness on the Forth. At Bar Hill near Twechar you can still view the remains of one of the walls forts. If you'd like to learn more about the areas past Kirkintilloch's Barony Chambers museum has many absorbing exhibitions depicting the area's social and industrial history. It's also possible to step back in time at the Clachan of Campsie conservation area, a small arts and crafts community that nestles at the foot of Campsie Glen.

Those of you with a taste for fine Victorian mansions will find **Colzium House** near **Kilsyth** a delight. Set in 68 acres of attractive woodlands and lawns, which feature a walled garden and arboretum, curling pond and Children's zoo. The house contains a museum of local history as well as function rooms.

If your tastes are a little more thespian then the diminutive **Cumbernauld Theatre** provides a great evenings entertainment. One of Scotland's most renown venues, it hosts a wide variety of concerts and productions throughout the year. Call them on 0236- 737235 to find out what's on.

For somewhere to stay in the area and awarded a Two Crown Highly Commended rating by the Scottish Tourist Board, **Easter Glentore** is a 245 acre stockrearing farm lying between the villages of Greengairs and Slamannan. Situated approximately six miles north of Airdrie on the B803 Greengairs road, Easter Glentore makes a peaceful and relaxing touring base from which to explore the beautiful surrounding countryside. The home of Alastair and Elsie Hunter, this welcoming establishment offers very comfortable accommodation in three attractive guest rooms, one with en-suite bathroom. Elsie is an excellent cook and guests will find themselves tempted by the lovely aroma of homecooked cakes and biscuits as well as the full breakfast prepared each morning. She will also prepare an evening meal by prior arrangement.

Easter Glentore Farm, Greengairs, Airdrie. 0236-830243
Map Ref: D2

Monklands District was once hailed as the 'Workshop of the

Traction Engine Rally, Summerlee Heritage Trust, Coatbridge

World', and while Manchester's Trafford Park may disagree with that, the area with its iron and coal industries was certainly at the forefront of the revolution. Monklands' pride in its heritage is celebrated at the award winning **Summerlee Heritage Trust** in **Coatbridge**. Once an ironworks and now one of Greater Glasgow's most exciting museums, it covers every aspect of social and industrial history, with an emphasis on working exhibits. The massive exhibition hall is filled with sounds and sights of heavy industrial machinery at work. Whilst outside there is a preserved electric tramway, the first in Scotland, as well as a restored canal wharf. The newest addition is a reconstruction of a 19th century shallow coal mine, where you go underground to experience mining in the late 1800's. A row of period miners' cottages completes the picture. There are many other authentically reconstructed buildings on the site and throughout the year the museum plays host to a whole range of festivals and shows.

The Monklands of earlier years can be glimpsed at the **Weaver's Cottage Museum** in **Airdrie** town centre, just along the A89 from Coatbridge. Here, in two 'n'Ben' cottages of 1780 have been restored, one as a master weavers house the other for displaying artifacts and exhibitions. Visitors get a fascinating insight into one of the area's oldest traditions, as well the daily lives of the weavers.

For the more energetic Coatbridge has plenty to offer the visitor. **The Time Capsule** is Scotland's largest leisure centre. Half ice and half water it has a choice of ice skating, tropical wave pool, curling, a thrilling rubber ring ride and high speed glacier run. If all that sounds a little to cold or wet then nearby **Drumpellier Country Park** has golf, fishing and a superb tropical Butterfly House. It is also an outdoor pursuits centre with orienteering courses available.

Blairmains Farm, Harthill. 0501-51278 Map Ref: D2

Adjacent to junction 5 of the nearby M8, with entry on the slip road towards Edinburgh, **Blairmains Farm** is an ideal touring base for all the main attractions of the region. In an hour or less you can travel as far afield as Glasgow or the Trossachs, Fife or the Borders and numerous other places of interest. The welcoming home of Moira Ireland, Blairmains is a 200 year old farmhouse with a lovely view to the rear over Forrestburn Reservoir. Accommodation is provided in seven comfortably furnished guest rooms and there is also a separate guest lounge to relax in. A farmhouse style breakfast sets you up for a day's exploring and on your return, Moira will readily provide a wholesome evening meal.

Picking up our journey once more, southwards out of Monklands on the A73, we head toward **Motherwell**. The name of this town is an interesting one, and comes from an old healing well which was situated on Ladywell road. The skyline south of Motherwell was, from the beginning of the century, dominated by the massive steel works at Ravenscraig, now no more.

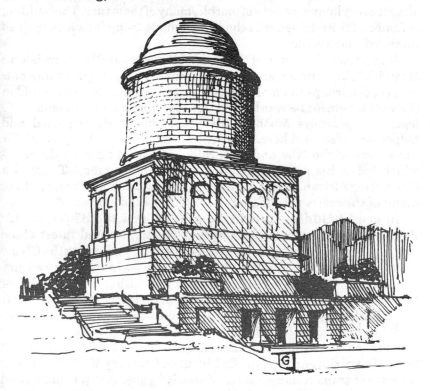

Hamilton Mausoleum, Strathclyde Country Park

The short drive toward **Hamilton** brings us to **Strathclyde Country Park**, which lies on both sides of the Clyde. It features a man-made loch complete with sandy beaches and a nature reserve, as well as wide open spaces. There once stood here one of the largest palaces ever to have been built in Scotland. Hamilton Palace was originally started in 1591 and substantially added to throughout the centuries, but not however to everyone's taste. Dorothy Wordsworth called it a "heavy lumpish mass". However she need not have worried, as underground mineworks caused the foundations to start sinking and it was eventually demolished in 1927. The **Hamilton Mausoleum**, which can be clearly seen from the M74, was built by the tenth Duke of Hamilton, who was considered to be an eccentric. The building dates back to the mid-19th century and took four years to complete, costing over one hundred and fifty thousand pounds. A large portion of this sum was spent on the floor alone, a wheel mosaic containing almost every known variety of marble, many of them rare. The building is famous for its 15 second echo, which made using it as a chapel, as intended, impossible.

Just a few miles north of the park on the A724 at **Blantyre** is **The David Livingstone Centre**, which offers a very different day out. Subject of perhaps the most famous quote ever, his life story is told in the very tenement he was born in. An adventurer and missionary his legendary journeys amongst the people he loved, respected and helped are described here. His battles with slave traders, search for the source of the Nile and, naturally, that meeting with Stanley - which led to his name becoming part of our language. There is a fascinating African Pavilion; which features a Zambian Bazaar, where many of the crafts are for sale.

In nearby **Uddingston** on the old A74, now the B7071, stands **Bothwell Castle**. Once acclaimed as the largest and finest stone castle in Scotland, it stands on a rock promontory guarding the Clyde. Built in the 1200's and rebuilt by the Douglases in the 15th century the castle was constructed on a massive scale and has walls fifteen feet thick, the central donjon or keep is 65 ft in diameter and stands 90 ft tall. The name donjon interestingly comes from the latin dominus, lord; hence the dwelling of the lord.

From here it is but a short distance south on the A723 to the small town of **Strathaven**, and the **Calderglen Country Park**. This park consists of three hundred acres of wooded gorge and parkland, and makes for a very enjoyable day's outing. There are many lovely marked routes around the park, as well as the woodlands and river

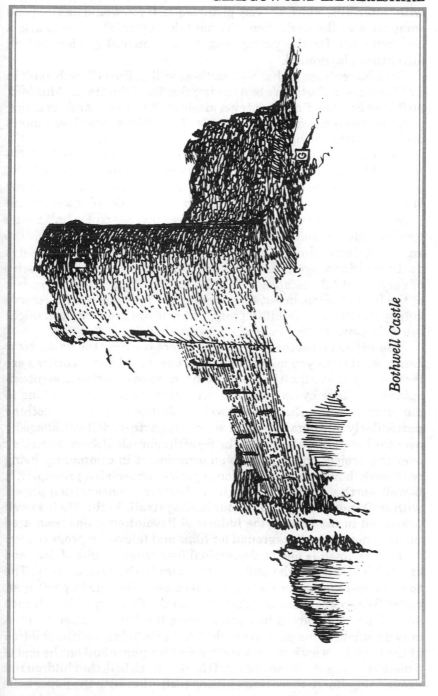

Bothwell Castle

with waterfalls, which are very picturesque. If you would like to spend some time in the park then why not take a picnic? There is also a children's zoo for the young ones, an ornamental garden and an adventure playground.

Strathaven's centre has own castle as well as East Church, built in 1777 and one of the town's best landmarks. The John Hastie Museum, on Three Staines Road, contains displays of weaving and ceramics, once the areas main industries; as well as relics of the Covenanters and the radical rising of 1820.

Our next destination, **Lanark**, is arrived at by following the A726 to the M74 and then the A744. Here are the famous **Falls of Clyde**, which start where the river becomes swollen with the waters of the Douglas. There are three falls, the first being Bonnington which surges over a drop of thirty feet. The river presses on for half a mile further before coming to Corra Linn, the middle fall.Although the waters of Corra Linn fall ninety feet they do not seem as impressive as those of Bonnington, as the drop is not quite so sheer, but is a series of very beautiful cascades. Two miles further down are the broadest of the falls at Stonebryes. Surrounding the falls is a nature reserve run by the Scottish Wildlife Trust, where if you are lucky you might see red squirrels, kingfishers, otters and badgers.

You will not be in the area for long before you hear the name **New Lanark**. It is, as you might suppose, a 'new town', but its origins are fascinating. It was built in the 18th century as an experimental cotton-spinning village by an entrepreneur called David Dale, working in partnership with Richard Arkwright. Although there is nothing particularly uncommon in this, when the partners fell out allegedly over the hanging of a bell on the belfry of the church, Robert Owen took over the project and it became an experiment in community living with work, housing and education organized on socialist principles. It is well worth visiting today, as it has become a conservation project with craft industries and a famous heritage trail. As the site is so well preserved in the style of the Industrial Revolution it has been used many times as the background for films and television programmes.

Lanark itself is one of the original four royal burghs of Scotland created by David I, who built a castle here in the 12th century. The town is well known for its traditional ceremonies, one in particular, called 'Whuppity Scoorie', takes place on the first day of March each year. This ceremony is believed to drive the harsh winter away. A crowd gathers at the parish church of Saint Nicholas, and the children of the crowd are each given a tightly wadded paper ball on the end of a piece of string. At the sounding of the six o'clock bell, the children run around the church three times hitting each other with the paper balls on the way. Five miles to the north west of Lanark on the A72 is **Crossford**, and here you will find **Craignethan Castle**, a Hamilton stronghold of the 16th century. It was once a refuge of Mary Queen of Scots and is said to be haunted by the Queen, minus her head, of course.

Craignethan Castle, Crossford

A drive along the B7056 will take you to **Carluke**, now, thanks to recent housing developments, the largest town in Clydesdale. It is famous for is jam, made from fruit grown in the area. The town also has what is claimed to be the most complete windmill in Scotland. Highland House was built in 1795 and became a steam powered mill in 1895. Now privately owned it hasn't worked since the 1930's.

About 100 yards past the main traffic lights in the town, you will discover a superb restaurant and wine bar called **The Chardonnay**.

The Chardonnay, 17 Kirkton Street, Carluke. 0555-751006
Map Ref: D3

Run by three sisters, Mari, Isobel and Eleanor Hamilton, the emphasis here is on using the finest local produce freshly prepared and beautifully presented, whether you are just calling in for a mid-morning coffee, a light snack or an intimate dinner for two. Coffees and snacks are served throughout the day and in the separate 'bistro' style restaurant you can choose from a mouthwatering dinner menu, accompanied by an extensive wine list which not surprisingly includes five Chardonnays. To finish your meal, try the rich, sweet homemade tablet and a cup of frothy cappucino - rated the best in the area!

Once a small community Carluke has the distinction of having three of its citizens receive the Victoria Cross. And just outside the town, at Miltonhead, a plaque commemorates a man dear to all seekers of hidden places. General William Roy was born here in 1729 and went on the become the 'father' of the Ordnance Survey.

It is now back south along the A/M74 that our travels take us, turning off at the A70 to take us to the village of **Douglas**. Taking its name from one of Scotland's most prominent families. The castle here was destroyed in the 1940s because mining works were found to have damaged its foundations. The chapel however can still be seen, and it contains the tombs of the famous Douglas chiefs including Good Sir James, 'the Black Douglas', who took King Robert the Bruce's heart on the Crusade against the Moors in Spain. Sir James' story is an interesting one, as he was Bruce's friend and the greatest of his lieutenants, much feared by the English. Apparently, on his death bed Bruce charged him with the task of removing his heart from his dead body and taking it on the crusade. Sir James obeyed his king's command and got as far as Spain before being killed. His body and the king's heart were retrieved and the heart, as you may remember, is reputedly buried in Melrose Abbey. Since that time the Douglas coat of arms has carried a red heart beneath the three stars on blue.

There is also a memorial in the town to the Earl of Angus, son of the Marquis of Douglas, who founded the Angus, or Covenanters, Regiment. Later renamed the Cameronians the regiment earned many battle honours before being disbanded in the town in 1968, the spot being marked by a monument. Coalmining dominated the local economy from before the First World War until 1967, when the last mine closed.

You will discover a lovely touring base for the area at **Gilkerscleugh Mains Farm** which can be found by leaving the M74 at junction 13, following the two roundabouts to Crawfordjohn, staying on the B7078 for about half a mile and then turning left and following this road for about two and a half miles. The home of Mrs. Audrey Hodge this is a 150 year old mixed working farm set in 250 acres and surrounded by lovely views. This is a very quiet, peaceful area where you can really relax and unwind. The two bright and airy guest rooms are both en-suite with attractively co-ordinated fabrics and furnishings enhancing the country farmhouse atmosphere. A hearty breakfast sets you up for a day's walking or exploring and on your return, by prior arrangement, you can enjoy a fine homecooked evening meal.

Gilkercleugh Mains Farm, Abington. 08642-388 Map Ref: E5

Our travels now take us south once more, along the B797, and into the Lowther Hills to discover about a different mining from that of Douglas. Not only gold but both silver and lead were first discovered in Wanlockhead and the aptly named Leadhills as far back as Roman times. Gold from the area was used to make parts of the crown of Scotland, which is kept of course in Edinburgh Castle.

Wanlockhead Lead Mining Museum

Wanlockhead is in fact the highest village in the Lowlands of Scotland, standing at 1,500 feet above sea level, and is almost completely isolated in its setting amongst the Lowther Hills. The mines were closed in the 1930s, after some four hundred years of production. The **Museum of Scottish Lead Mining** depicts how lead was mined and smelted, as well as displaying local gold, silver and rare minerals. Every half hour a guide takes visitors to explore the Loch Nell Mine. Worked between the 1700's and 1860 this walk-in mine really gives you an idea of conditions underground. The picture of life in the village is completed at the Miner's Cottages, where you can step back in time and contrast a miner's home in 1740 and 1890. The village also has a unique water powered beam engine, which was used to drain the Straitsteps Mine in the 19th century.

Leadhills, which unsurprisingly is the second highest village, is the birthplace of Allan Ramsay, 1686-1758, who was an important poet in the eighteenth century revival. Leadhills also has the Allan Ramsey Library; founded by miners in 1741 it is the oldest subscription library in Britain, probably Europe. It also holds many rare books and detailed records of mining in the area.

Following the B7040 take us to **Elvanfoot**, which is close to the source of two of Scotland's greatest rivers, the Forth and the Clyde, standing in some of the wildest lowland country in Scotland. There is a lovely red sandstone church here, with a stained glass window commemorating the actor-manager Wilton Barrat, whose drama productions achieved fame before the advent of television. Rejoining the A/M74 once again our journey takes us back north turning on to the A73/702 travelling through the Tinto Hills towards Biggar. The name 'Tinto' derives from the Gaelic 'tienteach' or 'place of fire' and there are ancient rhymes and stories which connect this place with fire raising powers. Tinto Hill itself is, at 2320ft, the highest in Lanarkshire.

The town of **Biggar**, with its broad main street, can trace its history back to Roman times. It is a colourful town with brightly painted shops and hotels and is well known for its markets and fairs. Every Hogmanay on the main street the townsfolk gather around a huge bonfire to 'Burn out the old year' and welcome the new. The town is also rightly proud for its many fascinating museums. The family of the British prime minister Gladstone came from Biggar, and the **Gladstone Court Museum**, open from Easter to October, features an interesting 19th century town with shops, a library and a schoolroom. Behind the museum is the **Albion Archive**. Albion Motors started on a local farm in 1899 and went on the become the largest truck manufacturer in the British Empire before being absorbed into Leyland Trucks. There are plans to build a motor museum but in the meantime every August the town plays host to a multitude of vintage and classic cars, motorcycles, commercial and military vehicles at a commemorative rally. Almost next door is Biggar Kirk built by Mary Queen of Scots' Uncle, Lord Fleming. Finished in 1546 it was the last pre-reformation church in Scotland.

Across Kirkstyle is **Moat Park Heritage Centre**, which depicts life in the Clyde Valley over the past 6000 years. As well as figures from its turbulent past there are many splendid models and a magnificent Victorian patchwork, with some eighty colourful figures stitched into place by a rather eccentric local tailor during the Crimean War. The Moat Park is open everyday between Easter and the end of October.

By heading up Kirkstyle you will discover **Greenhill Covenanters House**. The house take visitors back to the 17th century and the 'killing times'. The signing of the National Covenent forced many to worship in open fields rather than attend state controlled churches. These 'covenanters' were hunted down and many put to death for their beliefs. The house, which was moved to its present site to save it from dereliction, contains many relics of this bloody period in Scotland's history. Visitors will find the house open between 2pm and 5pm everyday from Easter through to late October.

If the industrial revolution fascinates you you're in for a treat at **Biggar Gas Works**. The last rural gasworks in Britain were built in 1839 and rebuilt in 1914, closing in 1973 with the arrival of North Sea gas. Fortunately the works were saved from the fate of every other town gasworks and are now open to the public. Here you can watch the hot and filthy work of turning coal into the gas that kept Biggar's (and Britain's) kettles boiling for over a century. The works are open daily between Easter and October and on Sundays in July and August. For full details of the admission costs and opening times of Biggars excellent museums call Biggar Museum Trust on 0899-21050.

Not finished yet the town also boasts a beautiful Victorian Puppet Theatre, a must for the children and a relaxing respite after all the museums. A last curiosity about this small town is the occasional and ancient contest for the Biggar Jug; which is open only to the Queen's bodyguard in Scotland, the Royal Company of Archers.

We leave this chapter by taking the B7106 to Carnwath. Carnwath House, where Bonnie Prince Charlie supposedly slept at one time, is now the golf course clubhouse. Nearby **Couthally Castle** was originally the stronghold of the Sommerville family, and it is known for providing James V with a mistress, Katherine Carmicheal, whom he first met at a wedding party here.

Situated about two miles from the village on the A721 at Newbigging, **Nestlers Hotel** is a small, family-run business where personal attention and friendly hospitality are the order of the day. Awarded a Three Crown Commended grading, the hotel has an intimate, homely ambience in which you can't fail to relax. The 'Harvest Nest' Restaurant provides a cosy setting in which to savour a variety of homecooked Scottish recipes, including home baked ham with local honey and fresh game when in season. Alternatively, a selection of country snacks are available throughout the day in the comfortable lounge bar. After a refreshing night's sleep in one of the three lovely guest rooms, you can explore the surrounding countryside or venture further afield to Lanark or Edinburgh.

Nestlers Hotel, Newbigging. 0555-840680 Map Ref: F3

From Carnwath we take the A70 setting out across the Pentland Hills and across the border into The Lothians.

Lanarkshire provides some of Scotland's biggest contrasts; from the hurly burly of metropolitan Glasgow to the wild isolation of the Lowther hills and their quiet unspoilt hamlets. Most people pass through the region in a flat-out dash up the M74 but there is much to gained from taking your time.

Finnieston Crane, Glasgow Waterfront

CHAPTER FIVE

Edinburgh and the Lothians.

Forth Bridge

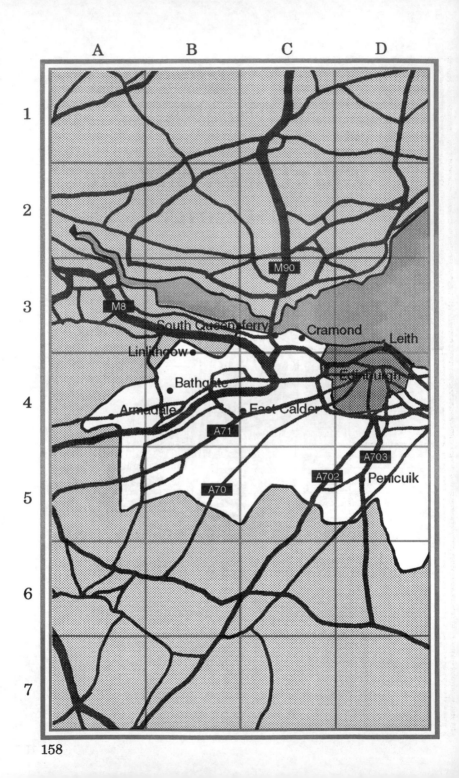

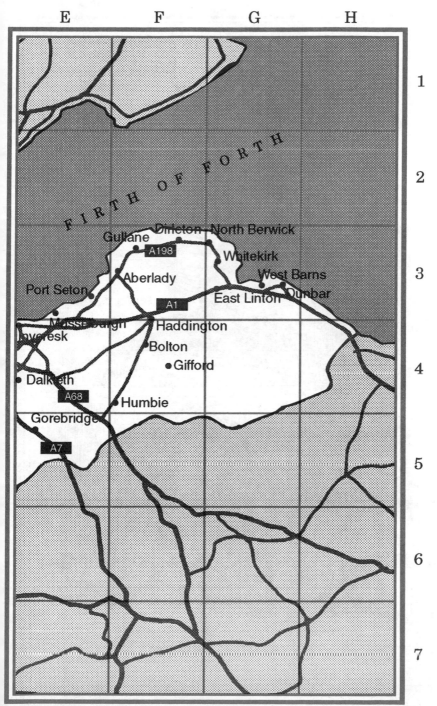

St. Giles Kirk, Edinburgh

Edinburgh and the Lothians

The start of this chapter is, uncharacteristically, a long high speed run along the A70 and into the great city of **Edinburgh**. The story of Edinburgh is almost the story of Scotland itself, and on every corner there is a tale to be told. Edinburgh is a truly lovely city, full of beauty and character, and there is so much pleasure to be gained from its vast range of attractions which draw visitors each year from all around the world.

It would be difficult to do Scotland's capital city justice in a few pages, instead we aim to guide you to some of its hidden places and to tell you a few of the stories that lie behind this dramatic place.

Edinburgh, like Rome, is built on seven hills and at the centre of these is the Castle Rock. This, together with the other main promontory, Arthur's Seat, helps to give a unique and splendid skyscape which has acted as a backdrop for some of the most poignant events in history.

At the centre of the city lie the Royal Mile, running from the castle at one end to Holyrood Palace at the other, and Princes Street, which divides the city into the Old Town and the New. The most dominant feature in Edinburgh is of course the famous castle. Perched high as it is, this great defender of the city features in every view. There has been a castle here for over a thousand years, and its dominance and important position has never been lost.

The name 'Edinburgh' stems from an encampment created by a former King of Northumbria called Edwin, whose building on top of the rock became known as Edwin's Burgh. In the years that followed, the town developed, clinging at first to the Castle Rock and stretching to the site of the palace and former abbey at Holyrood.

The **Castle** is an ideal place to begin our look at Edinburgh. It was here that Mary Queen of Scots gave birth to her young son, James VI of Scotland, who was eventually to become James I of England. There were many who were not happy at the birth of a Catholic king and stories abound of his early life. One tells that the infant James did in fact die when he was on a tour of the Borders with his mother and that the Countess of Mar, who had charge of the young prince, substituted her own child in his place.

Some say that if you look at a portrait of James he bears little resemblance to the facial characteristics of the Stuarts, but shows a startling likeness to the Earl of Mar. This theory was revived in 1830 when rumour has it that a small oak coffin was found in the wall of Mary's apartments in the castle. It contained the body of a small infant, wrapped in an embroidered silk covering bearing the initial 'J'.

Queen Mary's apartments can be seen in the castle, and her story is one that is linked vividly to the castles and abbeys of Edinburgh and the Borders. Indeed she seems to have been an unfortunate victim of circumstances and events who led a life doomed to be tragic. At seventeen Mary Stuart was Queen of France. A year later however her husband died and she was taken home to Edinburgh as the 'Queen of Scots', taking up residence in Holyrood Palace.

She was reputedly a great beauty, and with all the power of Scotland in her hand, she was victim to the struggles and scheming of all those who meant to take advantage of her position. She met and fell in love with Lord Darnley and they married in 1565. This proved to be a disastrous mistake, as Darnley was a callous and vain person. Mary was vulnerable and fell in love again, this time with the Earl of Bothwell. Again, tragedy struck when Darnley was killed in Kirk o'Field in 1567. Bothwell was blamed for the death of Darnley, and although he married Mary in secret in her own council chamber, he had many enemies who were powerful people. Mary was taken prisoner, forced to abdicate, and held on a tiny island on the shores of Loch Leven. In 1568 she escaped only to eventually run into the hands of the English, where she was to face nineteen years of captivity and finally death at the hands of the axeman.

In the crown room of the castle you will be able to see the 'Honours of Scotland' which are the equivalent of the crown jewels and include the Crown worn by Robert the Bruce, the Sceptre and the Sword of State. Many attempts have been made to have these precious items removed to London. Even a request by Charles I was turned down and he was forced to come to Edinburgh to be crowned King of Scotland. Cromwell was determined to get his hands on these symbols of royalty, but they were smuggled away from him to Dunnotter Castle for safe-keeping. After being buried in a churchyard they were eventually returned to Edinburgh Castle and sealed up in a room until Sir Walter Scott made a search and rediscovered them in 1818.

Of the large iron cannons that sit in the castle, the most famous was 'Mons Meg' and, though it now sits indoors, this cannon was renowned for its use at the siege of Norham, and it could blast a five hundredweight stone at a target more than a mile away. Today on the high ramparts a slightly newer 25 pounder gun is fired at one o'clock everyday.

The broad esplanade fronting the castle has always been used as a drilling ground. Today the Edinburgh Military Tattoo revives some of its former glories for three weeks in the autumn. This military spectacle is world famous, the massed pipes and drums conjuring up memories of the campaigns and heroism of centuries gone by. A wonderous spectacle of military precision not to be missed.

The streets and narrow alleys, or closes, off the Royal Mile, contains some of the most fascinating tales and the character of the old town. Across the street is Cannonball House with its two cannonballs lodged in the wall. These were supposedly fired from the castle at the time of the 1745 uprising, when Prince Charles Stuart was about to enter the city.

Castlehill has many tales to tell, some quite chilling. A bronze plaque fixed to the wall tells us that between 1479 and 1722 more than three hundred terrified women were branded as witches and cruelly put to death on this spot. One unique way to view the city from here is the Camera Obscura. Built in Victorian times this optical device projects an amazing live view of the city on to a table placed at the top of an outlook tower.

In the early days the supply of water to Edinburgh had serious problems. Most families owned a pair of 'stoups' for collecting water. These were two wooden vessels about two feet high which narrowed towards the top. They were popular wedding presents at the time. Queues would form around the various wells in the city at around six in the evening and the wait for water might last until as late as three in the morning, with the possibility of nothing to show for it if the wells ran dry.

If you had been in the Lawnmarket area two hundred years ago you might have been privileged enough to watch the local gentry and nobility displaying their finery whilst taking the air. To get a flavour of those times visit Gladstone's Land at 477B, built in 1620 this six-storey has fine painted ceiling and has been refurbished as a typical house of the period.

Nearby, Brodies Close was the home of a real life 'Jekyll and Hyde' character. Deacon William Brodie was a respected member of the town council by day, and an extremely clever house burglar by night. However, unfortunately for him, he ventured out once too often and was recognised, arrested and hung. If his ghost ever passes he may well be amused to see that an inn bearing his name stands by the site of the gallows where he was executed.

In nearby Tanners Close there once lived two rogues, much loved by the makers of horror films. They were Burke and Hare, and these two enterprising gentlemen found that there was a trade in the supply of dead bodies for the purposes of medical research. Then, as now, the city had a reputation for medical research and bodies for disection fetched a high price. The infamous duo took to grave robbing and then ultimately murder to meet the demand. They murdered and sold 18 victims before being caught and hanged in 1828. The kirkyard at **Greyfriars** has many elaborate graves enclosed in heavy iron cages, known as mort-safes and intended to prevent bodysnatchers going about their work. The kirkyard also provided the venue for the signing of the National Covenant in 1638, during the persecution that followed over 1400 covenanters were held in the yard.

Perhaps the best known grave in the yard is that of John Gray. When he died in 1848 his faithful Skye terrier, Bobby, watched over his master's grave for 14 years. Just outside the yard is a statue of Greyfriars Bobby, a small monument to the little dogs loyalty, opposite the pub of the same name.

As you pass through Lawnmarket into High Street you will come to the High Kirk of Saint Giles. In the early days of Edinburgh there was little room for shops, so traders would set up stalls wherever they could find room around Saint Giles. This is where both rich and poor would do their shopping for meat, bread, fish and other groceries. When the congestion reached the point of chaos the magistrates decided to act, allocating various places where the traders could do business. Today you can spot the old places of these traders with such names as Grassmarket, Lawnmarket, Flesher's Close, Candlemaker Row etc.

The Royal Mile is rich with history, full of stories about kings and queens and dramatic turns of events. It eventually leads us to **Holyrood Palace**, and the ruins of the abbey. Across the road at intervals the letter "S" can be seen. This marks the sanctuary line of Holyrood Abbey, a line that many a debtor has been chased across by pursuing bailiffs.

The abbey was destroyed by the English under orders from Henry VIII when his demand for the return of the infant Mary Queen of Scots was refused. Also destroyed were the palace and the abbeys of Melrose, Kelso and Jedburgh on the Borders. The palace was eventually restored and you can visit the chambers lived in by Mary here. Queen Victoria visited here in 1842, and today the Queen stays here when she visits Edinburgh. The palace and abbey remains sit in the perfect setting of Holyrood Park, dominated by Arthur's Seat, rising up to some eight hundred and twenty two feet at the summit and providing views across the city roofs.

Greyfriars Churchyard

The exposed rocks on the west side are known as 'Samson's Ribs', and below this point is a road that runs to **Duddingston**, a pretty village on a loch in the shadow of Arthur's Seat. Here you'll find **The Sheep Heid Inn.** The inn is the oldest and most historic in Edinburgh's dating back to 1360. Patronised by Bonnie Prince Charlie when he lodged in Duddingston village, you can still see the house where he stayed. Mary Queen of Scots, is another of the Sheep Heid's historical customers, known to have stopped here for refreshments on her way to Craigmillar Castle. The inn's present name comes from an ornate snuff box in the shape of a ram's head, which was presented to the pub by James VI in 1580. He considered the Sheep Heid to be one of his favourite hostelries, and although the snuff box was proudly displayed in the bar for many years, its whereabouts are now unknown.

Our exploration of the city now takes us into the New Town of Edinburgh. In 1752 steps were taken to oversee the development of Edinburgh in a style in keeping with the city's status. Designers and architects were employed to ensure the quality of the work and they began to construct the spacious and elegant streets that make Edinburgh famous throughout the world today. It is without doubt one of the finest Georgian urban landscapes in the country, an opulent mixture of classical, gothic and baroque architecture in the grand style. Craiglieth stone, used extensively in the New Town, is particularly attractive, and much of it was sent south to provide building materials for Buckingham Palace and the British Museum. The area was planned and laid out by a young architect, the winner of a competition for the submission of the best design. Remarkably James Craig was only twenty three at the time.

Princes Street is of course one of the most famous shopping streets anywhere in Britain and, with its buildings on just one side of the street, it must surely rank as one of the most picturesque.

Another feature of Princes Street is the Scott monument which began in 1840, eight years after the death of Edinburgh's most famous son. Surprisingly it was designed by an untrained joiner called George Kemp, who was unfortunately drowned before he had a chance to see the finished result. If you are feeling fit you might like to attempt the two hundred and eighty seven steps climbing to the top. You will be rewarded with lovely views over Princes Street and the Castle. The monument itself has much of interest to look at, including over sixty small statues of the figures in Scott's books.

Princes Street Gardens offer pleasant walks and a respite from the teeming shops. Here you will find fine floral displays, as well as what is reputed to be the oldest floral clock in the world, dating from 1903.

Calton Hill

There are more than twenty thousand plants used in the display on the clock, which are changed several times a year.

Just ten minutes walk from Princess Street is **Stuart House,** a delightful 150 year old Georgian-style town house. Run by Gloria Stuart, this superior Guest House is situated in a quiet residential district of the city and has six comfortable bedrooms, all with en-suite facilities. Highly Commended by the Scottish Tourist Board and with recommendations from the RAC and AA, and ourselves at the Hidden Places, Stuart House offers quality Scottish hospitality on the doorstep of the city.

Stuart House, 12 East Claremont Street, Edinburgh. 031 557-9030

There is of course so much more to see and do there are a great many fine churches and historical houses to explore, art lovers will enjoy the profusion of galleries and theatres and there are fine parks to explore. Those with a love of animals are sure to enjoy the Zoo, with its world famous penguin colony. Of course no visit to Edinburgh would be complete without reference to the spectacular Edinburgh Arts Festival that takes place every summer. What can we say about one of the most renowned and famous arts events staged anywhere in the world? The festival includes music, opera, ballet, theatre, dance, poetry and of course the fringe events that take place on every corner. All in all Edinburgh is a wonderful melting pot, rich in character and charm. The city is an experience not to be missed, but accommodation around Festival time, the last three weeks in August, can be difficult to find.

Newington Guest House, 18 Newington Road, Edinburgh.
031-667-3356 Map Ref: D4

Just ten minutes by bus from the centre of Edinburgh, situated on

Newington Road, **Newington Guest House** is a super holiday base for visitors to this beautiful, historic city. Having parked in the guest car park, a lovely floral display catches your eye as you approach the front door of this splendid town house and a warm welcome awaits you from friendly hosts Ray and Jeanne Bouchet. Lovely period furnishings enhance the charm of this spacious Victorian house and very comfortable accommodation is provided in eight well-equipped guest rooms, five with en-suite facilities. The city and all its attractions, are within easy reach, making Newington Guest House ideal base to explore from.

It's easy to forget that Edinburgh is beside the sea, much of its history and wealth being landbound but follow Leith Walk from Princes Street and you will eventually arrive in **Leith**. Here there was a village that marked the point where the waters of Leith entered the Firth of Forth. Leith is also home to the **Clan Tartan Centre** on Bangor Road. If there's Scots in your blood here's the place to discover it, as well as all about the Clans themselves. And if you fancy your very own unique tartan they can create one here for you. The dock area has undergone some refurbishment and now features a couple of very good seafood bistros and a fine Indian, making it well worth the detour.

Travelling eastwards from the port of Leith and you'll come across the once famous resort of **Portobello**, and if you are seeking the sort of activities you would not normally associate with a capital city then you need look no further. If you prefer something a little more adventurous, however, then why not try a little water and jet skiing, or even parascending, all activities available on the waterfront.

Almost adjoining Portobello is the small town of **Musselburgh**, which was once known as Eskmouth, and is situated on the mouth of the River Esk. The modern name derives from a profitable mussel-bank in the river's estuary. Musselburgh is a place of very independent character. The tolbooth dates from 1590 and has an interesting story behind it, as it was built from the ruins of the Chapel of our Lady of Loretto which was destroyed by the English in 1544. Unfortunately the act of building the tolbooth from the sacred ruins was considered to be a sacrilege and brought the citizens under sentence of Papal excommunication for two hundred years.

There is a race course and golf course here, on which King James IV is said to have played in 1504. The actual golf club was founded in 1774 and used to offer a prize for the best fish-wife golfer. If it was unusual to find women on a golf course in the eighteenth century, it was not considered so in Musselburgh as the womenfolk had a tough reputation. One such woman who was hanged at the Grassmarket in Edinburgh in 1728, only to be taken down to be buried in Musselburgh.

The jolting of the wagon on her last journey however revived the spirit of this indomitable woman and we are told that she lived to get married and produce many children.

To the south east of Musselburgh is a rather charming village called **Inveresk** and you will find here a fine selection of buildings and houses dating from the seventeenth and eighteenth centuries.

Back along the coast road our journey passes **Prestonpans** and the Prestongrange site of the **Scottish Mining Museum** (more of which later), The site has a beam pumping engine that kept the mine from flooding as the miners dug out under the sea, as well as a colliery winding engine and steam engines. The 'Cutting the Coal' exhibition tells the story of mechanical coal extraction from the mid-1800's. Prestonpans provided the setting for one of Bonnie Prince Charlie's victories during the '45 Jacobite rising. The market place also features an impressive cross, one of few that survives as built and in its original position. Probably dating from around 1617, when the Hamiltons of Preston obtained the right to hold a fair.

Just a few miles further along the B1348 is the picture postcard harbour of **Port Seton**, complete with colourful fishing smacks and lobster pots. The village also has an interesting late 15th century church which features a fine vaulted chancel and apse.

Overlooking the Firth of Forth estuary at Port Seton, **The Olde Ship Inn Hotel** was originally built at the turn of the century as a clubhouse for the golf course and since then has developed into a popular venue for locals and visitors alike.

The Olde Ship Inn Hotel, 40, Links Road, Port Seton.
0875-811725 Map Ref: E31

There is a lovely beer garden and children's play area for those warmer days and inside, the hotel successfully combines the old with the new. The cosy atmosphere of the bar is enhanced by traditional wood panelling and exposed oak beams while the modern function suite is ideal for those special celebrations. The excellent homecooked food is freshly prepared and served in ample portions, with a separate children's menu catering for younger family members. Surrounded by a warm, friendly atmosphere and with five very comfortable guest rooms to choose from, The Olde Ship Inn is an excellent place to stay.

Just a little inland on the A198 is the village of **Longniddry** and **Gosford House**. Overlooking the Firth of Forth this impressive house features a central section by Robert Adam built in 1800 and north and south wings completed in 1890 by William Young. The south wing has a celebrated marble hall and the grounds ornamental waters have nesting wild geese. The house is open in June and July on Wednesday, Saturday and Sunday between 2pm and 5pm.

At Longniddry our journey joins the A198 following the coast through **Aberlady**. One of Scotland's real 'hidden gems', **Greencraigs** is a superb restaurant and hotel situated just outside the village. Built in 1926 as a private residence it stands on the banks of the Firth of Forth, with wonderful views across the water to Edinburgh and Fife. The hotel stands off the A198 on the Edinburgh side of Aberlady, just before the village, on the left. Surrounded by wonderful scenery, Greencraigs really is a picture both inside and out, with lovely furniture and furnishings enhancing a warm, relaxed atmosphere.

Greencraigs, Aberlady. 08757-301 Fax: 08757-440 Map Ref: F3

Friendly owners Ray and Olly Craig offer their many guests first class accommodation in five en-suite guest rooms and one master suite, all equipped to the highest standards with the nice added touch of fresh fruit, mineral water and other goodies. However, the highlight of staying here is the outstanding mouthwatering cuisine offered in both à la carte and table d'hôte menus which guests can savour in the intimate ambience of the restaurant overlooking the sea. All these factors combine to ensure a holiday at Greencraigs will leave you with memories to treasure.

Just east of the village is **Luffness Castle**, standing at the head of Aberlady Bay. With origins in the 13th century it was built to defend nearby Haddington. Bought by the Earl of Hopetoun in 1739 for £8350, it remains the Hope family home. For those of you weary of travel and who simply enjoy a day on the beach both Aberlady Bay and Gullane both have beautiful stretches of golden sand to relax on.

For visitors to **Gullane** looking for somewhere to stay, **Faussetthill House** on Main Street is ideal. This elegant Edwardian house is the charming home of welcoming hosts George and Dorothy Nisbet who have a knack of making you feel like old friends. Awarded a Two Crown Commended rating by the Scottish Tourist Board, this lovely 100 year old house is set in delightful gardens and provides very comfortable accommodation in three spacious, attractively furnished guest rooms, two with en-suite bathroom. Dorothy was the winner of the 1991 Scottish Dairy Cook competition, no mean feat when you consider there were over 12,000 entrants. The only problem you may have once you are here, is tearing yourself away from your lovely hosts and Dorothy's excellent homecooking!

Faussetthill House, Main Street, Gullane. 0620-842396
Map Ref: F3

On the main street of Gullane on the A198 you will find a simply wonderful place to eat at **The Rosebery**, a restaurant of class owned and run by brothers Robert and John Burns and their wives Amanda and Anne. Well known throughout the area, this is a place where the finest Scottish produce is prepared with imagination and flair and served in an atmosphere of friendly hospitality. This is accompanied by an extensive, quality wine list. A cosy, intimate ambience is immediately apparent, making this the ideal place for that quiet dinner for two. Closed on Mondays, The Rosebery is open six days a week from 12.00pm - 2.00pm for lunch and 6.30pm - 10.00pm for dinner, but booking is advisable for weekend evenings.

The Rosebery, 3, Rosebery Place, Gullane. 0620-842233
Map Ref: F3

The A198 now by-passes the village of **Dirleton** but if you follow sign to the village you'll find the very pretty village green and its impressive ruined castle. The castle dates back to 1225 and was destroyed in 1650. The gardens enclose a 17th Century Yew lined bowling green. Refreshment can be had and the view enjoyed admirably from the Castle Inn on the other side of the green.

North Berwick is a popular yachting resort and centre for tourism. Offshore is the fascinating **Bass Rock,** rising some three hundred and twelve feet from the sea, now a famous bird sanctuary, providing one of the few nesting colonies for the gannet, a bird with legendary diving abilities and, surprisingly, once a sought after dish. Many other birds nest on the rocky cliffs and slopes. Boat trips can be made by arrangement from North Berwick, and you are guaranteed an amazing view of the sights and sounds of the birds on this spectacular rock, the third largest gannetry in the world.

Visitors to this delightful coastal town will receive a warm welcome when they stay at **Seabank**, the charming home of Sandy Gray. Originally built in the 1840's, Seabank and the adjoining property were all one building, the whole being run as a private hotel. Eighteen years ago, the building was divided in half and since then, Seabank has been both a private residence and a bed and breakfast establishment. Comfortable accommodation is provided in five guest rooms and there is a lovely homely atmosphere. Outside, to the rear, there is a large open area ideal for children's games, with the town's six hardcourt tennis courts and two superb putting greens alongside. With ample off-street parking for guests, a golden beach just across the road and packed lunches available on request, you have everything you need for a relaxing break by the sea.

Seabank, 12, Marine Parade, North Berwick. 0620-2884
Map Ref: G3

Lovers of art in all its various forms will delight when they discover **Westgate Gallery**, situated on the main street of North Berwick. Stewart Muirhead, the gallery owner is a well-informed host who has created a wonderful place with a special atmosphere all of its own.

Westgate Gallery, 39-41 Westgate, North Berwick. 0620-4976
Map Ref: G3

There is a vast array of many differing crafts on display, ranging

174

from paintings and ornaments to furniture and pottery, as well as gifts of every description. To the rear of the shop there is always a beautifully laid out exhibition of fine works of art, many by internationally renowned artists. The works displayed change regularly, with about ten such exhibitions throughout the year. With so many arts and crafts of such high quality, it is difficult to know where to look and you find yourself in a dilemma when trying to choose a memento or special gift. The gallery's layout makes browsing easy, but if you feel like resting, you can enjoy excellent tea or coffee with biscuits in the cosy seating area at the front of the shop.

Nestling between shops on Station Hill, North Berwick you will find an outstanding pottery workshop called **Shape Scape Ceramics**. Elaine Dick is the highly skilled proprietor of this 'hidden' gem and her creative talents are immediately apparent when you see the stunning and unusual display of clocks, pots, lamps and gifts of every description within her studio shop. Having gained a BA Honours degree in Art and Design followed by a Master Degree in Ceramics with distinction at North Staffordshire Polytechnic, Elaine decided to set up her pottery studio here in 1982 and since then has displayed her work at numerous exhibitions throughout the UK, including the British Craft Centre and the Design Council in London. In addition, selected pieces of Elaine's Design have been commissioned by Glasgow Art Galleries, The Scottish Craft Collection and The Fremantle Arts Centre, Western Australia, all of which has enhanced her growing national and international reputation.

Shape Scape Ceramics, The Pottery, Station Hill, North Berwick.
0620-3157 Map Ref: G3

Inland from the town, the country rises to North Berwick Law which is six hundred and thirteen feet above sea level and can be seen from as far away as Edinburgh and Fife. On the top of this ancient volcano are the jaw bones of a whale, a watch tower dating from Napoleonic times and stunning vistas on a clear day.

General Monk, who destroyed Dirleton Castle, also severly damaged **Tantallon** at the same time. A few miles east of the town, the castle, built by the Douglases, is a curtain wall that blocks off a promontory from cliff to cliff. Once considered impregnable it is now, with The Hermitage and Bothwell, one of the most striking castle ruins in Scotland.

Our path now turns briefly inland to the village of **Whitekirk** and its rather special parish church, St. Mary's. Dating back to the 6th century and with a Norman high square tower this large red sandstone place of worship was in medieval times a place of pilgrimage, with a healing well. The tithe barn to the rear of the church is one of the oldest still standing in Britain.

We are once more drawn back towards the sea, heading for Dunbar. Just a couple of miles before the town, situated on the edge of **West Barns**, you will find the perfect stopping-off point in your journey when you come to **West Barns Inn**, a real family pub. Housed within what were originally two 17th century cottages, when the inn was re-roofed some years ago, an old musket was found hidden within the eaves. Roy and Caroline Knox are friendly hosts who have created a very special place where visitors mix easily with locals in a cheerful, lively atmosphere. Caroline's cooking is excellent and the varied menu includes a wide selection for children, all at very reasonable prices. An added attraction for visitors calling in on a Sunday evening is live traditional Scottish music which always proves popular.

West Barns Inn, 5 Duke Street, West Barns. 0368-62314 Ref: G3

And so to **Dunbar**. Here is a town which boasts more sunshine hours than any other location in Scotland. It is also a popular holiday resort, with Belhaven Beach to the west and White Sands to the east. Dunbar has a history of brewing which goes back to the Middle Ages, and today boasts a number of brewing firms renowned for their real ales, still brewed in the original manner.

Dunbar was at one time a prosperous fishing centre, and in 1879 could boast a fishing fleet of over three hundred boats. The wide high street and big solid sandstone buildings are evidence of the prosperity that was brought to the town through the industry. Indeed, a walk around Dunbar will be a rewarding experience.

Enjoying a wonderful hilltop location with marvellous views over the Firth of Forth, **Redheugh Hotel** is a first class place to stay where you will find superior accommodation and cuisine combined with a homely, relaxed atmosphere. Janette Young and her super team of staff have created a very special place here, which is no doubt why it is so popular. All ten en-suite guest rooms are equipped to the high standards you would expect of a Four Crown Commended hotel. The guest lounge has a small bar which is only available to residents, ensuring you of personal attention and an element of privacy and the elegant restaurant offers a varied table d'hôte menu of superb homecooked food, freshly prepared using local produce wherever possible. To find this wonderful 'hidden' gem, head towards the town centre. At the bottom of the High Street turn left into Bayswell Road and the hotel lies a little further up on the right.

Redheugh Hotel, Bayswell Park, Dunbar. Tel/Fax: 0368 62793
Map Ref: G3

Dunbar Castle overlooks one of the town's two harbours. It was here that Mary Queen of Scots was brought by the Earl of Bothwell in

April 1567, and where they remained for ten days prior to their marriage.

To the western side of the town and located on a beautiful stretch of coastline is the **John Muir Country Park**. American patrons, will feel at home here for this park was named in honour of the man who himself emigrated to the States and founded America's first national park. Dunbar is his home town, and today the Sierra Club of America regularly visit the town in memory of the man who provided them with perhaps one of the most important elements of their national heritage.

Lovers of self-catering will discover a real haven at **Bowerhouse**, an impressive 19th century mansion standing in 25 acres of beautiful gardens and grounds just outside Dunbar. Taking the Bowerhouse turning off the A1 Dunbar bypass, if you continue along this road and take the right fork, the mansion entrance can be found on your left. After passing the Lodge, wend your way along the lovely treelined driveway and Bowerhouse awaits you. Accommodation is provided in two cottages and the East Wing of the mansion house, equipped with every modern facility for complete comfort. Guests are welcome to walk through the grounds, which offer a wealth of bird and animal life and a truly outstanding walled garden that is a riot of colour in spring and summer.

Bowerhouse, Dunbar. 0368-62293 Map Ref: G3

Again we must leave the sea and take the A1 back inland across the southern Lothians towards Haddington. Before we alight there however there are a few places worth seeking out on the way.

Set within 160 hectares of lush farmland just off the A1 near East Linton, **Knowes Farm Shop** is one place not to be missed and can be reached via the A1 at the junction with the A198. Owners Peter and

Hilary Cochran were winners of the 1990 and 1992 Scottish Farm Shop award and in 1991 Hilary was Farmwoman of the Year. The farm shop is housed within an old Lothian bothy and offers a comprehensive range of fresh, homegrown fruit and vegetables and eggs from the Cochran's own chickens for which they were the 1992 winners of the UK Egg Quality Award. Hilary makes her own range of delicious-looking preserves and pickles as well as soup, paté, cakes, biscuits and numerous other 'goodies' to tempt you and everything is well laid out, making shopping here a real pleasure.

Knowes Farm Shop, Near East Linton. 0620-860010 Map Ref: G3

At **East Linton**, just off the A1 is **Preston Mill and Phantassie Doocot**. The watermill is probably the last of its kind still in working order in Scotland. The Doocot or Dovecote without doubt one of the strangest looking buildings in Scotland, and once home to over 500 doves.

The Drovers Inn, 5 Bridge Street, East Linton. 0620-860298
Map Ref: G3

179

In the heart of the picturesque village of East Linton you will find a super refreshment stop at **The Drovers Inn**. Built in 1708, this charming inn has instant appeal, with its lovely hanging baskets adorning the stone walls and once enticed in, you won't want to leave. As you cross the threshold you feel as though you have taken a step back in time, with exposed wooden floors, various comfy armchairs of different shapes and sizes dotted about and super decoration throughout. Upstairs you will find a very intimate restaurant ideal for that special meal out, with a superb menu complemented by beautiful crockery and cutlery, and candelabras on each table lending an air of class. Downstairs the cosy bar serves fine Real Ales and the adjoining Bistro proves a popular venue for a less formal evening meal.

The village also hold a real 'hidden' gem, the **Ken Lochhead Gallery**, a wonderful establishment which has a veritable wealth of artistic delights. The creative talents of both Ken and Sheila Lochhead are beautifully displayed alongside a wealth of other locally produced crafts which will have you lingering for hours. Ken has been an artist for over twenty years and his watercolours have gained wide recognition. Sheila's skill lies in the beautiful knitwear and cushions she produces, an art which began merely as a hobby. To add to the attraction, across the road from the gallery lies a lovely cosy coffee shop owned by Sheena McDougall, where you can enjoy a refreshing drink and delicious homemade cakes and snacks.

Ken Lochhead Gallery, 9 The Square, East Linton. 0620-860442
Map Ref: G3

Another excellent hostelry is **The Red Lion Hotel**. Originally known as the Golden Lion, this former inn was built to provide refreshment and accommodation for the navvies working on the Great Eastern Railway which runs across the road from here.

Preston Mill, East Linton

Structurally, it has changed little over the years, but current owners Nancy and Tony O'Neill have breathed new life into the place since their arrival almost two years ago and it is now a very popular place.The cosy bar offers a wide selection of fine ales and tasty homecooked meals and accommodation is provided in seven comfortable, well furnished guest rooms, making The Red Lion Hotel an ideal place to pause on your journey.

The Red Lion Hotel, 3, Bridgend, East Linton. 0620-860202
Map Ref: G3

For lovers of aeroplanes and everything airborne, a visit to the **Museum of Flight** at East Fortune Airfield is a must.

Museum of Flight, East Fortune Airfield, Near Berwick.
0620-88308 Map Ref: G3

It is only a short drive from East Linton to this former WWII fighter station, now scheduled as an historic monument. It is a fascinating museum where you can see no less than thirty aircraft, including a Supermarine Spitfire, a Sea Hawk and a 1930 de Havilland Puss Moth. A large part of the museum is devoted to a collection of aero engines which include pre-1914 models to those of the present day and there is also a display of rockets, which includes the museum's pride and joy 'Blue Streak'. With a wonderful 'aviation shop' for your mementos and a café for welcome refreshment, your day out is easily filled.

For those of you following the story of Mary Queen of Scots, there is another piece of the jigsaw back across the A1 at **Hailes Castle**. The ruins date from the 13th and 15th centuries. Mary was brought here by the Earl of Bothwell, her third husband, on her flight from Borthwick Castle in 1567.

Haddington is one of those rare towns that has come into the twentieth century with its elegance and character intact. You're sure to be delighted to find that it was indeed a magnificent town, with many lovingly restored houses and shops, a mixture of both Georgian and Victorian buildings.

Situated on the main street next to the old Corn Exchange, the **Plough Tavern** is a popular stopping-off point for visitors and locals alike. Renowned for its excellent range of tasty homecooked food which comes in substantial portions and at very reasonable prices, this is as much a restaurant as an inn and Allan and Alison Inglis are friendly hosts whose hard efforts have won them due recognition and a regular clientele. The Tavern is beautifully furnished and decorated throughout in lovely traditional style, providing a warm welcoming atmosphere in which to savour fine ale and pleasant conversation.

Plough Tavern, 11/13 Court Street, Haddington. 0620-823326
Map Ref: F3

Unfortunately, the town lay directly in the path of invading

English armies and was repeatedly destroyed before reaching more prosperous days in the 18th century. Since then, its biggest threat came from the river Tyne that runs around it, flooding it in 1775 when it rose to a height of seventeen feet above its normal level. As recently as 1948 the Tyne rose above all recorded levels, forming a torrent some eight hundred yards across.

The George Hotel, set in the heart of the town, is a magnificent base from which to explore the Borders, Edinburgh and beyond. Originally built in 1674, its outward appearance has changed little over the centuries and careful refurbishment has provided every modern facility without detracting from its character and charm. One of the first Post Houses situated on what was once the Great North Road, it was here that teams of horses would be changed before continuing their journey. All the guest rooms are equipped to the highest standards, with beautiful decor and en-suite bathroom for maximum comfort. Defoe's Cocktail Bar is named after the famous author of Treasure Island who was a regular patron and in the Poacher's Restaurant you can sample the excellent à la carte menu which is highly praised by all who eat here, for its variety and quality and after staying here you are sure to feel that friendly proprietor Alan Cope has succeeded in his pursuit of excellence.

The George Hotel, High Street, Haddington. 0620-823372
Fax: 0620-822485 Map Ref: F3

Campers, caravanners will discover a real 'gem' at **The Monks' Muir**, an outstanding caravan and camping park situated just off the A1 near the town. Over the past couple of years, dedicated owners Douglas and Deirdre MacFarlane have created a very special place to stay, with first class facilities deservedly awarded a 4 tick grading by the Scottish Tourist Board. Set within seven acres of wooded grounds

The Pulpit, St. Mary's Kirk, Haddington

The Monks' Muir is ideally situated as a touring base, being close to Edinburgh, the Borders and the beautiful Scottish coastline. A warm welcome greets your arrival and a friendly relaxed atmosphere pervades throughout. In addition to the usual facilities one expects from a park of this calibre, there is an excellent restaurant and a shop which sells all the basic essentials plus a range of gifts and holiday mementos. All in all this special place has something for everyone and is well loved not just by its owners, but by the many visitors who use it time and again.

The Monk's Muir, Haddington. 0620-860340 Map Ref: F3

Should you choose to make Haddington a base for exploring the area there are many local places of interest. Nearby **Athelstaneford** off the B1343 is the church where Scotland adopted the cross of St. Andrew as its national flag, one flies permanently on the site, floodlit at night. A little further north, near Drem, is **The Chesters Fort**, one of Scotland best Iron Age forts.

To the south of Haddington on the B6369 is **Lennoxlove House**. Originally named Lethington, it was owned for centuries by the Maitland family, one of whom was secretary to Mary Queen of Scots. In 1672 the Duchess of Lennox, La Belle Stewart who was model for Britannia on the coinage, bequethed it to Lord Blantyre, stipulating it be renamed in memory of her love for her husband. Owned by the Duke of Hamilton it is open on Easter weekend and on Wednesdays, Saturdays and Sundays from May to September.

Three miles south of Haddington lies the delightful hamlet of **Bolton** and it is here that you will discover a lovely holiday base at **Under Bolton Farmhouse**. Set within pleasant gardens and surrounded by beautiful views, this Georgian farmhouse is the charming home of Mrs. Steven who provides excellent accommodation in three attractive guest rooms, two with en-suite facilities. A warm welcome is followed by tea and biscuits on arrival, making you immediately feel at home. Mrs. Steven also offers alternative accommodation in three superbly equipped self-catering cottages sleeping between four and eight people, which carry a Four Crown Commended rating by the Scottish Tourist Board. Whether you stay in the farmhouse or cottages, Mrs. Steven will happily provide an evening meal by prior arrangement.

Under Bolton, Nr Haddington. 0620-81318 Map Ref: F4

The roads south of here take you into the beautiful Lammermuir Hills, which rise to to over 1700ft at Meikle Says. There are plenty of opportunities to explore on foot and the opportunity to test your car on the climb from Gifford over to Danskine, on the B6355.

For first class farmhouse accommodation, make your way to **Eaglescairnie Mains,** a splendid Georgian farmhouse near Gifford.

Eaglescairnie Mains, Gifford, By Haddington.Tel/fax: 0620-810491
Map Ref: F4

To find this somewhat 'hidden' place, take the B6368 Humbie road out of Haddington towards . A few miles along this road after Bolton, turn off left at the sign for Eaglescairnie and Gifford and you will see signs for the farm on your left. Barbara and Michael Williams are friendly hosts who have been welcoming guests here for over four years. Accommodation is provided in rooms of varying sizes ranging from singles to twins and doubles, several with en-suite facilities.Breakfast is a substantial affair, enjoyed in the comfort of the conservatory with beautiful views over the garden and the surrounding countryside.

Sat in the heart of the picturesque and unspoilt **Gifford** the **Goblin Ha' Hotel** has an unusual name, but here you will find everything you need by way of fine ale, good food and very comfortable accommodation in an atmosphere of warm hospitality. Owned and run by Max and Susan Muir and their son Douglas, Goblin Ha' has been in the family for over 30 years. Traditionally furnished throughout, there are seven well-equipped, en-suite guest rooms and the hotel restaurant proves very popular, with an extensive menu of tasty homecooked food, much of the produce supplied by the hotel garden. Outside, you can relax on the patio, make use of the boule court, or simply stroll around the beautiful garden and admire the wonderful views.

Goblin Ha' Hotel, Gifford. 0620-8144 Map Ref: F4

Set in two acres of beautiful wooded grounds at the foot of the Lammermuir Hills, **Newlands House** is a self-catering enthusiast's dream. Perfect for that 'get-away-from-it-all' break, the house enjoys a secluded and peaceful location three miles south east of the picturesque village of Gifford. The Four Crown Highly Commended rating by the Scottish Tourist Board gives you an indication of the standard of facilities you can expect. Accommodation is provided in a fully equipped ground floor flat sleeping two which occupies a single storey wing of the main house, but has its own private entrance, parking space and small garden. Regretfully children under 16 and pets cannot be accommodated.

Did You Know...

The Hidden Places Series

Covers most of Britain?

For our full list see back of book

A few miles south of Garvald and little further from Gifford, just off the B6355 you will discover a lovely place to stay at **Carfrae Farm**, a grand farmhouse which forms part of an 800 acre working mixed farm. Dating back to 1844, this impressive ivy-clad house is surrounded by the most delightful gardens creating a real picture postcard effect.

Carfrae Farm, Nr Garvald, Haddington. 0620-83242 Map Ref: F4

This is the charming home of the Gibsons, Mr. Gibson having been born here, and the interior is just as attractive as the outside. Beautifully decorated and furnished throughout, the atmosphere is cosy and homely and very comfortable accommodation is provided in two spacious, en-suite guest rooms. With the Borders, Edinburgh and

189

Northumberland all within easy reach, Carfrae makes a peaceful and relaxing touring base.

The beautiful countryside of East Lothian is ideal for exploring on horseback and at **Bughtknowe Farm** in **Humbie** you will discover a super riding and trekking centre. If you take the B6368 out of Haddington towards Humbie, you will see the sign for Bughtknowe on your left just prior to the village. James and Patricia Nisbet are friendly hosts who employ a resident qualified riding instructress, catering for both experienced and novice riders, although if you are not a keen horse rider, you can come and participate in day to day farming life. The house is comfortably furnished in keeping with its original character and you can't fail to notice the beautiful stained glass window near the staircase. There are two lovely guest rooms each with private bathroom and guests are well looked after, with a farmhouse breakfast each morning and a packed lunch and evening meal by prior arrangement. Whether you explore by foot or on horseback, this is definitely a country lover's retreat.

Bughtknowe Farm, Humbie. 0875-33601 Map Ref: F4

From Humbie our route meanders through Fala and Tynehead to the A7 and **Borthwick Castle** and Church near North Middleton. The highest tower house in Scotland and in many respects one of the best preserved and most impressive of our medieval buildings. Bothwell and Mary Queen of Scots came here a month after their marriage before being forced to flee. In 1650 Cromwell sent the tenth Lord Borthwick, a Royalist, a letter threatening to 'bend his cannon' unless he capitulate. Cromwell did indeed need his cannons but Borthwick surrendered before any substantial damage was done. Today the castle, so full of Royal tragedy and treachery, is a hotel and surely one of the most exciting and romantic places to stay in the Lothians.

The local church, associated with the Borthwick family and clan, is mainly Victorian; though it does retain an aisle and vault from the 15th century, an apse from the 12th century and two 15th century effigies, amongst the best preserved in Scotland.

Continuing north on the A7 brings you to the Scottish Mining Museum at **Newtongrange**. A whole town was built around the **Lady Victoria Colliery**. Everything was built and run by the mine company; the mines own powerhouse supplied the the towns electricity and they provided homes, baths, a cinema and institute (pub) for their employees. The mine manager's word was law and a man fired would never work in the Scottish coalfields again. One manager inspected his employees' gardens every Sunday and any found wanting would be seen to, at the miners expense. Another forced the miner's sons underground by threatening their fathers with the sack.

The pithead is much as it was the day it closed, around ten years ago, covered in coaldust, and a fitting tribute to the men who toiled deep underground to win coal. There is a magnificent pit winding engine in working order, though the shaft has been filled, and tours are conducted by former miners. The visitors centre, in the old mine offices, describes life in a Victorian pit village. Keep an eye out for Pick and Shovel, the museum's canaries. This type of bird was once the miner's best friend, being used to detect the presence of dangerous gases, and some are still used today.

Dalkeith, the next town along our northerly path, once stood on a Roman road as it stands today on one of the main routes to Edinburgh, situated on the River Esk. There are interesting houses here to look at, most notably the Palace which, although not open to visitors, has had celebrated guests such as James IV, George IV and Queen Victoria.

A few miles from Dalkieth on the A6094 lie the towns of Bonnyrigg and **Lasswade**. Sir Walter Scott lived at Lasswade Cottage for the first six years of his married life, and during this time Scott began to establish himself as a poet and was in turn visited by William and Dorothy Wordsworth.

Yet another noted literary figure, Thomas de Quincey, came to live at a cottage a mile away at Polton Station, from 1840 until his death in 1859. Lasswade is said to be the location of Gandercleugh in Scott's 'Tales of my Landlord'. While Dorothy Wordsworth stayed here she recorded in her diary her impressions of this part of the Esk Valley, and in particular the Glen of Roslin that is a mile downstream from Polton. She noted that she had "never passed through a more pleasant dell", and remarked upon the ruins of **Rosslyn Castle** and the Chapel

. Roslin Glen is now a public park and well worth a visit. After all, what better recommendation could you have than that of a Wordsworth?

The castle is believed to have been founded by Sir William St Clair, having reputedly won the lands in a wager he made, betting his head against the lands, that two of his hounds would bring down a deer by the time it reached a certain spot. Fortunately for Sir William the deer was killed and he was awarded the estate. The Lady Chapel was the beginning of a much larger project that Sir William had intended as a monument of himself. Unfortunately he died when the project was only partially completed. The remains are somewhat dilapidated, though what is left gives indications that, had it been finished, the church would have been one of the most remarkable medieval buildings in Europe.

Anyone visiting Rosslyn Chapel around three hundred years ago may well have lingered at the cottage adjacent to this old Midlothian church. Built around 1660, it was then The Old Roslin Inn. Famous patrons included King Edward VII when he was Prince of Wales, Sir Walter Scott, Robert Burns and William and Dorothy Wordsworth. The inn is though to have closed its doors for the last time in 1866. Also in the glen is **Hawthornden Castle**, which dates from the fifteenth century. It was the birth place of William Drummond the poet, 1585-1649, and remained in the Drummond family until the 1970s. It is now a retreat for poets and writers.

The small Midlothian town of **Penicuik** has its fair share of visitors, many of them attracted to the **Edinburgh Crystal Visitor Centre** on the edge of the town. Penicuik is an excellent centre for the Pentland Hills, which are a long stretch of uplands that run south from the edge of Edinburgh. If you would like a rest from the enjoyable but tiring rigours of the cities and towns then why not abandon yourself to this nearby haven? You will find the grazing lands and the numerous reservoirs a picturesque and refreshing tonic. As many of the hills are over 1500ft in height, you will of course be rewarded with many lovely views.

Wending our way northwards around the hills, using the A702, A720 and A71 brings us to **East Calder**, as well as giving ample opportunity to admire those barren heights. **Almondell and Calderwood Country Park** resides here and offers the visitor extensive riverside and woodland walks as well as displays on nature, local history and a large freshwater aquaria in the visitors centre.

After a refreshing break we plunge back in to the urban landscape once more, passing the new towns of Livingston and Bathgate to **Armadale**. The Dale, as it is better known to most of its inhabitants, is situated in an area once famous for its wild pig hunting. Until 1790 there was nothing much here, however, Lord Armadale purchased a house here as a weekend retreat from his law practice in Edinburgh, and when the Glasgow to Edinburgh highway was completed Armadale became perfectly situated and turned into one of the new towns of the Industrial Revolution. Armadale contains a wealth of stories and characters from the past, and its development over the last century is fascinating. Being halfway between the two cities, a regular stage coach route was established, and passengers would break for a rest and perhaps have a meal while the horses were changed in the middle of this twelve hour journey. There was also a toll house here, and it was once described as a "small one-roomed hut with a window lookout in each wall". Presumably this was to keep an eye open for those who might try to slip by without paying.

For those interested in pre-history the area has the fascinating Cairnpapple Hill, off the B792 near Torphichen. Originally a neolithic sanctuary it was rebuilt in the early Bronze Age, around 1800BC, as a monumental open-air temple with stone circle. Later around 1500BC the site was despoiled and built over with a cairn, which in itself was enlarged several centuries later.

Cairnpapple's significance to early man may be explained by its position on the summit of the Bathgate Hills. On a clear day the view extends right across Scotland, from the Isle of May in the Firth to Goat Fell on distant Arran. The site has now been excavated and laid out but still retains the mystery of its ancient worshippers and their rites.

Set high up in the same hills, two miles out of Linlithgow, Beecraigs Country Park is the largest of its kind in West Lothian and offers a whole range of activities and outdoor pursuits to appeal to the whole family. The beautiful surrounding countryside is home to a variety of bird and wildlife and provides a wealth of lovely walks. The nearby Deer Farm with its pedestrian walkway and viewing platform gives visitors the opportunity to observe the majestic red deer while they graze undisturbed and at the Trout Farm, the rearing ponds detail the life cycle of the trout. Beecraigs also has a lot to offer the sports enthusiast with a wide variety of activities and courses available, ranging from canoeing and climbing to archery and mountain biking. Although open to passing visitors, a day is not really long enough to fully enjoy all that Beecraigs has to offer and for those wishing to stay, there is a fully equipped caravan and camping site which carries the prestigious five tick award for the high standard of facilities it provides. It is hard to imagine a more picturesque or tranquil setting for a caravan and camping site than Beecraigs and a modern toilet block, barbecue sites and disabled facilities ensure maximum comfort during your stay. Also within the grounds of Beecraigs, the newly established restaurant is rapidly gaining a well-deserved reputation for its superb cuisine and service, where the discerning guests can choose from both an à la carte and table d'hôte menu. Immaculate and beautifully furnished throughout, it provides the perfect setting for a relaxing lunch or intimate dinner and makes Beecraigs the ideal holiday base, providing all you need for a memorable family holiday.

Beecraigs Country Park, Linlithgow. 0506-844516 Map Ref: B3

We are now close to **Linlithgow** and its famous palace. On Linlithgow lochside this solid and imposing building has its origins back in the 1200's. Ruined in 1313 and rebuilt in 1350 by King David II it went on to become a favourite residence of the Scottish kings. Burnt out in 1424 it was again rebuilt much as we see it today. When Mary Queen of Scots was born here in 1542, her father, James V, lay dying in Falkland Palace across the Forth. Mary's son, James VI, had much done to the palace, having the north wing, where his mother was born, rescued from dereliction. Later Cromwell garrisoned it, Bonnie Prince Charlie captured and abandoned it and finally men defeated by the Prince sought sanctuary there and accidently burnt it down. And so it remains today, there have been various projects mooted to reroof it but in the meantime it stands massive and gaunt, brooding over the past. Next door to the palace is St. Michael's, one of Scotlands finest examples of a medieval church.

Linlithgow stands on the Union Canal, built 1822, which joined Edinburgh to the Forth-Clyde Canal near Falkirk. Some of the 31 miles of the canal can be enjoyed aboard the Victoria, a replica Victorian Steam Packet that takes half hour trips along it. The boat can be found at the Manse Road basin along with the Canal Museum. Sited in the former Canal stables the museum features records, photographs, audio-visual displays and relics of the history of the Union Canal.

EDINBURGH AND THE LOTHIANS

Exploring the great houses always brings pleasure, discovering how the aristocracy and gentry lived and a taste of a centuries old way of life that World War I swept away. The southern shores of the Firth of Forth, close to the capital, are scattered with a rich variety of these fascinating windows into history. Three in particular offer rewarding exploration.

The House of Binns is situated just off the A904 south of Blackness and in common with its neighbouring grand houses offers extensive views over the Firth. Built between 1612 and 1633, by the Dalyells, the house admirably reflects the transition of the Scottish manor house architecture from fortification to mansion. The interior has fine plaster ceilings and an outstanding family collection of paintings, furniture and porcelain. Occupied for over 350 years the house is now in the capable hands of the National Trust for Scotland and open everyday except Friday from 1st May to 30th September between 2pm and 5pm.

Just a few miles along the A904 near Abercorn is **Hopetoun House**. Family home of the Hopes it was built in the grand manner, starting in 1699 to a Sir William Bruce design it was considerably enlarged in between 1721 and 1754 by William Adam and his son, John. With paintings by Canaletto, Gainsborough, Rubens and Titian on display inside, a rooftop viewing platform with panoramic views and magnificent gardens and deer parks in the grounds it is certainly one of the great houses of Scotland. Looked after by a preservation trust the house and grounds are open daily between Easter and September from 10am to 5pm.

The third of this cluster of wonderous country piles is along the coast past South Queensferry at Dalmeny. **Dalmeny House** has been the home of the Primrose family and the Earls of Rosebery for over 300 years. The splendid Tudor Gothic house seen today was largely built in 1815 by William Wilkins. Inside the Gothic abounds with hammerbeamed hall, vaulted corridors and classical main rooms. The interior also features a collection of 18th century portraits, tapestries, many pieces of 18th century French furniture, porcelain from the Rothschild Mentmore collection and the Napoleon collection. The grounds feature a 4 mile walk along the shoreline to Cramond. Still in the Primrose family the house is open to the public 2pm to 5.30pm Sunday to Thursday between May and September. Whatever your interest, architecture, the arts or just plain ancient atmosphere these three house from very different ages are highly recommended.

The village of **Cramond**, with its huddle of cottages and narrow winding steps has changed little since its Roman fishing village origins and it is here, enjoying a pleasant quayside location, that you will discover **Cramond Gallery Bistro**. Alan and Evelyn Bogue are friendly, experienced hosts who have created a culinary haven for non-smokers, with a regularly changing menu of delicious homecooked food, incorporating fresh produce such as local fish and steak according to availability. Set within an old timbered building with lovely views across the Forth, Cramond Gallery Bistro provides the perfect setting for a romantic meal out and although the premises aren't licensed, you are welcome to bring your own wine with you.

Cramond Gallery Bistro, 4/5 Riverside, Cramond, Edinburgh. 031 312-6555 Map Ref: C3

As you may now appreciate The Lothians though a compact area are certainly one of the country's most populous and are packed with history and hidden places. And we haven't quite finished. Our route now returns the short distance to **South Queensferry**.

St. Mary's House, Kirkliston Road, South Queensferry. 031 331-2550 Map Ref: C3

On the edge of this historic town you will discover a lovely place to stay at **St. Mary's House** on Kirkliston Road. Originally a vicarage, St. Mary's House was built some 120 years ago and can be found by travelling along the High Street and up the hill. Welcoming hosts Norah and Robert Smith offer very comfortable accommodation in four attractively furnished guest rooms, each with colour TV and hot drinks facilities. A warm welcome is extended to all guests and on your arrival you are greeted with a hot drink and biscuits in the comfort of the guest lounge. With many attractions within easy reach and Scotland's beautiful, historic capital city a relatively short drive away, St. Mary's House makes an ideal touring base.

The **Queensferry Arms Hotel** has an enviable location right on the shore front. It's a delightful holiday base, being just seven miles from the historic city of Edinburgh and within easy reach of various places of interest such as Dalmeny House and The House of the Binns. Beautifully furnished throughout, most of the guest rooms are en-suite and each provides colour TV, hot drinks facilities and direct dial telephone for maximum privacy and comfort. Dining is a rare treat, with the River View restaurant offering a spectacular panoramic view of the brightly lit Forth Rail Bridge, a splendid backdrop for the superb à la carte menu which features chargrilled Scottish beef and local produce as a speciality.

Queensferry Arms Hotel, 17 High Street, South Queensferry. 031 331-1298 Map Ref: C3

The town is dominated by the two **Forth bridges**. The rail bridge comes right over the town and is best viewed from the shore front - which incidently has an original hexagonal Victorian post box . Built over 100 years ago it is still a breathtakingly audacious structure. A mile and more long this double cantilever bridge is 361ft high and takes three years to paint from end to end, having 135 acres of exposed steel. Magnificent though it is, the modern road suspension bridge somewhat lives in the shadow of its neighbour. This bridge, opened in 1964 by the Queen, ended 800 years of ferrying people and goods across the Firth.

And it is this bridge that takes us from the Lothians into the Kingdom of Fife, but remember to have your loose change handy as it is a toll bridge!

Forth Bridge

CHAPTER SIX

Kingdom of Fife

Falkland Palace

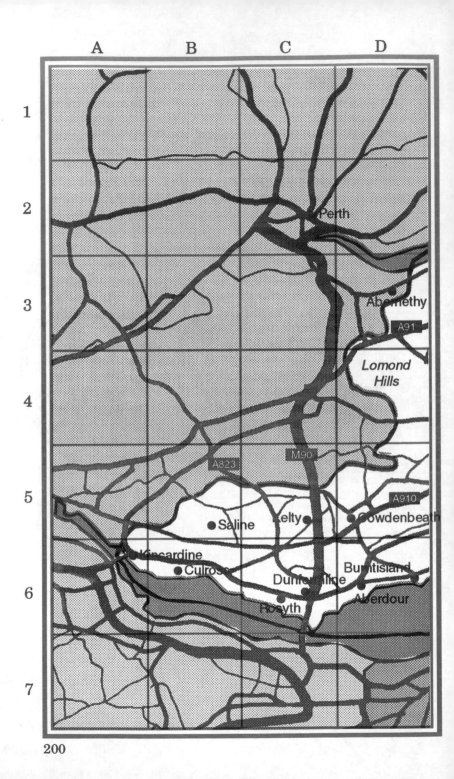

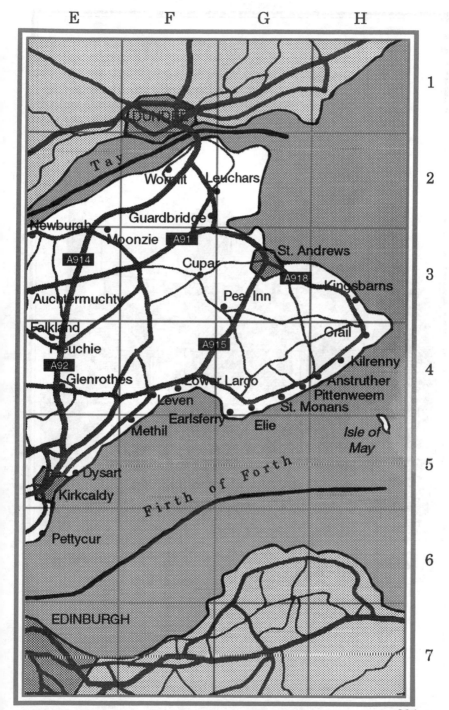

Earlshall Castle, Near Leuchars

CHAPTER SIX

The Kingdom of Fife .

From the high bridge over the Forth the first views of Fife are of the once great naval dockyards of **Rosyth**. Here in the glory days, when Britannia did rule the waves, the battleships of the fleet were built and maintained. It was from Rosyth that Admiral Beattie's ill-fated squadron of Battlecruisers sailed; joining Jellicoe's Home Fleet to meet the German Grand Fleet at Jutland in 1916. Three ships were lost; Invincible, Indefatigable and Queen Mary, together with their 3000 crew. Only the self-less actions of a turret gunner, who flooded a burning magazine, saved Beattie's own flagship, Lion, from a similar fate. The days losses led to Beattie's oft quoted understatement 'There appears to be something wrong with our bloody ships today'. Times have changed since the days when the Navy could muster over forty Dreadnoughts and Rosyth is now a shadow of its former self.

Gaining land once more we arrive in **Dunfermline** in no time at all. This ancient town was the seat of many Scottish Kings and Queens and in fact was once itself the capital of Scotland. The palace now lies in ruins beside Dunfermline Abbey , which contains many royal graves including most notably that of Robert the Bruce who died in 1327. During restoration work on the abbey in 1818, workmen who were excavating came across a vault containing a stone coffin, in which was a skeleton wrapped in thin lead. Some of the teeth were still in the head and there were shreds of gold cloth still clinging to the bones. Any doubt that this was the body of Robert the Bruce was removed when it was noticed that the breastbone was sawn away so that his heart could be removed by Sir James Douglas. You might recall how Sir James was pledged to take the heart of the king for burial in the Holy Land. Before the new tomb was ready the king lay in state and many hundreds of people came to pay their respects.

Situated in the heart of Dunfermline in Bruce Street, overlooking the City Chambers towards the Abbey, **The New Victoria Restaurant** is a licensed establishment, ideally located for a lunchbreak and traditional High Teas served daily while you explore this lovely historic city. It is said to be the oldest eating establishment in Dunfermline and can be found on the second floor, with a turn of the century turretted frontage. It became The New Victoria Restaurant some seventy years ago and for the past twenty one years has been run by the current owner Alistair McEwan and since then has established a reputation as a real family restaurant. Immaculately decorated throughout, it offers a cosy, welcoming setting in which to savour fine homecooked food, with an extensive menu which caters to every taste. Open from 9.00am - 9.00pm seven days a week, snacks are available all day, but for weekend evenings, it is advisable to book.

The New Victoria Restaurant, 2 Bruce Street, Dunfermline.
0383-724175 Map Ref: C6

Dunfermline boasts a list of interesting buildings and some lovely parks. One of the town's most famous sons was Andrew Carnegie who went to America and became a self-made millionaire in the iron and steel industry. The cottage where he was born in 1835 is now a museum, and the town contains many fine buildings housing galleries and museums donated by Carnegie.

From Dunfermline, travel a few miles to the east on the A92 to the small town of **Aberdour**, which is famous for its silver sands and its attractive position between dramatic cliffs. It was here that an amorous young Frenchman propositioned the young Queen of Scots, and was beheaded for his unwelcome attentions. The village itself is steeped in history. The quaint harbour is still here and there is also a 12th century church, 14th century castle and an interesting circular doocot, or dovecote.

It would be hard to find a more hospitable or welcoming place to stay than **The Kingswood Hotel** which lies on the coastal road near **Burntisland** in Fife. This delightful hotel was originally built as a private residence in 1850, but today it is a Four Crown Commended hotel where comfort, service and a warm, relaxed atmosphere blend comfortably to provide guests with the ideal holiday retreat. Rankin and Kathryn Bell are the friendly resident owners whose hard efforts have created a very special place indeed. The beautifully panelled cocktail bar provides the perfect setting for an aperitif before you make your way to the cosy restaurant to savour the mouthwatering delights of an extensive menu and after dinner, what could be nicer than relaxing in front of a roaring log fire in the lounge bar.

The Kingswood Hotel, Kinghorn Road, Nr Burntisland.
0592-872329 Map Ref: D6

Staying on the coast road our journey wends its way past Kinghorn. A small family resort that merges with the village of **Pettycur**. Curiously the name Pettycur appears on many old roadside milestones throughout the Kingdom, for once it was the northern end of a long gone ferry route across the Firth to Leith. Still heading west the road and railway share a narrow path below the towering cliffs. It was from these cliffs that the last Celtic King of Scotland, Alexander III, accidently plunged to his death in the spring of 1286

Situated on the coast road between Burntisland and Kinghorn, **Pettycur Bay Holiday Park** enjoys a magnificent location with unrivalled seascape views over the bay. Here peace and tranquillity are offered in an idyllic setting. Boasting the prestigious Thistle Award and carrying a Four Tick rating by the Scottish Tourist Board, you are assured of the highest quality accommodation. The luxury and executive caravans are equipped to a superior standard. In the restaurant and lounge bar which overlook two miles of golden sands, you can enjoy a good variety of freshly prepared and varied cuisine served by professional and friendly staff who are courteous and considerate. The excellent facilities on this park are a credit to the Wallace family, who by hard work and determined effort over the past nine years have developed it into a real gem of a place.

Pettycur Bay Holiday Park, Kinghorn.   0592-890321/890913
Map Ref: E6

We travel onto **Kirkcaldy**, a thriving town that developed through the linen trade into the manufacture of linoleum. The latter was apparently discovered when a local family had the idea of making more durable cloth that would be suitable for the covering of floors. It was originally made from cork imported from Spain, and whale oil. This combination at one time gave the town a rather unique smell.

There is a wealth of interesting buildings throughout the town, including Raith, probably built by MacDuff and Balwearie, which has strong connections with the renowned wizard, Michael Scott, whose practices and proficiency in alchemy and astrology earned him a fearful reputation. He even has a mention in the eighth Circle of Dante's 'Inferno'.

Adam Smith, the economist, was born here, and it was here that he retired to write his famous book 'The Wealth of Nations' which appeared in 1776. Interestingly the last two duels to be fought in Scotland, in 1822 and 1826, took place in Kirkcaldy.

Kirkcaldy is also known as "the long town", and if you take the time to walk down its four mile long main street you will find out why it was so named. There are libraries, an award winning museum and galleries throughout, which make interesting viewing. **Ravenscraig castle** stands on a promontary between Kirkcaldy and Dysart. Though of no great historical significance it does have perhaps two claims to fame; it is probably the first castle in Britain designed and built to deliver and withstand artillery attack and undoubtably the first to be overlooked by a high-rise blocks of flats.

Dysart village lies just to the north of Kirkcaldy, and is worth a visit to stop and take in the delightful harbour with its rows of pantiled fishing houses now restored by the National Trust.

The name Dysart itself actually means desert or hermitage, and it was in the 6th century that St. Serf settled at Culross and established a retreat at Dysart. St. Serf is credited with the conversion of Fife to christianity and he reputedly kept a pet robin. His life abounds with rumour and legend; one source claims that he was the son of a Caanite king and an Arab princess, while another says that he was pope for seven years. Dysart once did a brisk trade with the Continent in salt, though by the end of the 18th century, nailmaking had become its principal industry, with over twelve million nails produced each year.

The villages of **East** and **West Wemyss** take their name from the old word for sea-caves, as does Pittenweem along the coast. The story of the caves is told by the environmental education centre in East village. During the summer months the centre hold occasional open days that include walks and displays on the history, wildlife and industry of the area. The ruins of Macduff's Castle stand nearby, once probably occupied by the historical original of the Thane of Fife in Shakespeare's Macbeth.

Keeping to the coast passing through the towns of Buckhaven and Methil our journey pauses in **Leven**. Here a Mr Bissett adorned his cottage garden with seashells, eventually covering it from top to bottom. Sadley the late Mr Bissett's efforts are no more but his shell covered bus remains triumphant, every square inch bar the windows adorned with crustaceans.

Once the estate house for a large estate, which is now unfortunately long since gone, **The Hawkshill Hotel** is situated close to Leven town centre and makes a super holiday base from which to explore the area.

The Hawkshill Hotel, Hawkslaw Street, Leven. 0333-426056
Map Ref: F4

Since Marie and Mark Rossiter took the hotel over, complete refurbishment has created a first class establishment, well-deserving of the Three Crown Commended status awarded by the Scottish Tourist Board. Outside there is ample parking and a lovely gardens, including a beer garden to the front. The four bedrooms are all cosy and tastefully furnished, one with en-suite bathroom and the comfortable bar area provides a relaxing setting for a pre-dinner drink before savouring the delights of the restaurant menu.

Continuing along this beautiful coastline we enter East Nuik, the corner of Fife that juts out into the North Sea. Along the shore some of the prettiest fishing villages you'll find anywhere in Britain, strung along the coast like a chain. For centuries these village traded with the continent, and many of the buildings reflect this featuring 'crow-step' gables that are common in Belgium. The main industry of herring fishing has declined in recent years but many of these small harbours still retain a fleet.

At Lundin Links, the most southerly of the East Neuk villages, you will discover an excellent holiday base at **The Lundin Links Hotel**. Awarded a Three Crown Commended rating, this Tudor style hotel opened nearly 100 years ago and has eighteen en-suite guest rooms all equipped for maximum comfort, plus a self-catering cottage in its own grounds. Situated only 11 miles from St. Andrews, and with another 35 18-hole courses with a 25 mile radius, the hotel specialises in Golf Packages and sporting breaks. This sporting theme is reflected in the restaurant's 'Golfer's Menu' which is open to non-residents all year round.

The Lundin Links Hotel, Lundin Links. 0333-320207 Fax: 0333-320930 Map Ref: F4

Every village offers the visitor something different. **Lower Largo,** with its fine beaches, was the birthplace of Alexander Selkirk whose experiences marooned on the island of Juan Fernandez, off the coast of Chile, inspired Daniel Defoe's 'Robinson Crusoe'. A statue of Selkirk, in the dress of a castaway, looks out over the sea from the village. There are many delightful walks in the area, and for the energetic the climb to the summit of Largo Law is particularly rewarding the whole of East Nuik unfolding before you as you climb.

The villages of **Elie** and **Earlsferry** nestle between Chapel Ness and Sauchar Point. Together they are one of Fife's favourite resorts, offering a mile and more of safe sandy beach and a large harbour popular with yachtsmen and windsurfers. There is history here as well. Earlsferry took its name from the time when Macduff, in flight from the murderous King Macbeth, took a ferry from here. In slightly more recent times Elie gained its Lady's Tower, built as a bathing box for noted 17th century beauty, Lady Janet Anstruther. Legend has it that she would send a servant through the streets, ringing a bell and warning villagers to avert their eyes whilst she bathed. How times have changed!

For a refreshing drink or a tasty homecooked meal, visitors to Elie would be well advised to call in at **The Ship Inn**. Situated in the heart of the town overlooking the beach, as well as being a popular watering hole, this is one of the most well patronised restaurants in the area. Originally built as a cottage in 1794, it has been an inn since 1838 and is beautifully decorated throughout, with lovely pew style seating and wooden tables, enhancing its character and charm. The 'ship' theme is emphasised with new and old ships photographs adorning the walls and the cosy restaurant provides an intimate setting in which to enjoy the excellent menu whilst admiring the wonderful views over the Firth of Forth.

The Ship Inn, The Toft, Elie. 0333-330246 Map Ref: G4

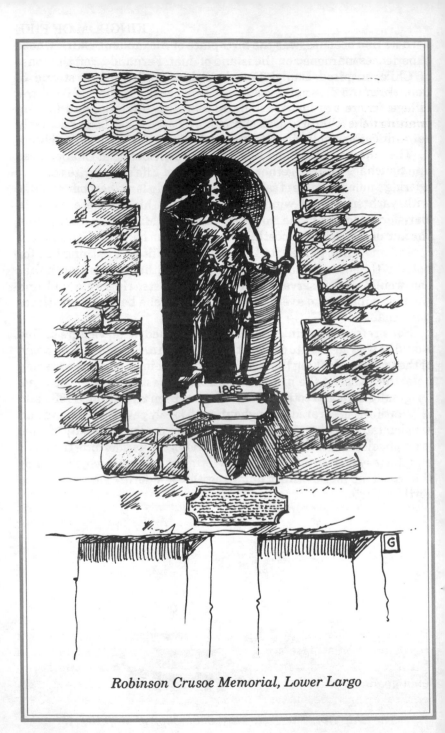

Robinson Crusoe Memorial, Lower Largo

For all self-confessed gastronomes who find themselves close to Elie, a visit to **Bouquet Garni** is an absolute must. Situated on the High Street, this superb restaurant is double fronted on the outside and split into two halves within. On entering there is a cosy area where you can sit with an aperitif whilst ordering your meal and waiting for it to be prepared. You then find yourself taken through to a beautifully decorated dining area, comfortably furnished to provide a relaxing and intimate setting in which to savour the mouthwatering menu which is both extensive and varied, catering to the most discerning palate. With a welcoming smile which lingers throughout your visit, this gastronomic paradise is one place you are sure to return to and one which will leave you with memories you can truly savour.

Bouquet Garni, 51 High Street, Elie. 0333-330374 Map Ref: G4

It's hard to image, gazing over the tranquil sea-lapped harbour at **St. Monans** that it was once one of the busiest harbours in Scotland with scarecely a quiet hour. Not that the sea has been forgotten here, for the 18th century boatyard still builds and repairs wooden fishing vessels. Above the village on a headland are the remains of Newark Castle (yet another) that once belonged to General Leslie, 1st Earl of Leven, a key Covenanter.

Just along the coast is **Pittenween**, with its harbour still busy with 'the fishing'. Many of the little houses in the village have been restored by tha National Trust for Scotland and away from the harbour the quiet streets and lanes invite exploration. Its name is, as mentioned, derived from an ancient word for sea-caves and surely enough amongst the houses is St. Fillan's Cave. Once a retreat of the early christian missionary it has for the most part been respected as a shrine for many centuries, though fishermen did once store nets in it. Re-dedicated in the 1930's, services are still held in this unusual holy place.

The nearby town of **Anstruther**, pronounced 'Anster', is, with its close neighbour **Cellardyke** the largest in East Nuik. With its strong connections with the sea it is fitting that it is home to the **Scottish Fisheries Museum**. Established in 1969 in buildings dating back as far as the 16th century the museum the visitor vivid insight into the hard and dangerous work of the fisherman. Using tableaux, models and striking paintings the story is told. It covers every aspect of the fishing industry, including whaling and industrial salmon farming, as well as the lifes of those who worked ashore, in its heyday there were four ashore for every one at sea. In the harbour you can explore 'Reaper' and 'Zulu'a pair of lovingly restored fishing vessels. The museum also has the pogniant Memorial to Scottish Fishermen Lost at Sea.

Situated behind the Scottish Fisheries Museum in Anstruther, the **Cellar Restuarant** is a 'hidden place' well worth seeking out. The county of Fife is blessed with an abundant variety of splendid places to eat, from country inns of character to elegant dining rooms with fine cuisine. The atmosphere of both is cleverly combined with great success at the **Cellar**, a former 16th century cooperage.

Cellar Restaurant, Anstruther. 0333-310378 Map Ref: H4

It is approached through a walled garden courtyard, to an interior of stone walls, beamed ceiling and two open fires. Chef proprietor Peter Jukes - a sassanach from Wolverhampton, has been here for ten years and is one of Britain's Master Chefs. Fresh seafood predominates here and his treatment is both simple and masterly, earning his restaurant 3 AA Rosettes. To complement the food his fabulous wine list is bettered by few in Scotland. The size of the Cellar and its popularity make booking essential, but a meal here is one you will remember for a long, long time. A must for all food and wine enthusiasts.

Anstruther's other maritime museum spent forty years helping protect seafarers. **North Carr Lightship** was stationed at the notorious Carr Rocks off the Fife coast and is now a tribute to the men who served on lightships all around our coastline. From 1933 to 1975 her 500,000 candle-power lamp swept the Firth of Forth and her foghorn boomed out a melancholy note. They were a rare breed the men who manned her through the worst the North Sea storms, keeping her vital generators running, standing four hour watches on her open deck and living with the non-stop clamour of her engines and the crashing of the waves.

Exploring the streets is a rewarding experience, one of Anstruther's curiosities is **Buckie House**. 'Buckie' is the is local dialect for shell and the eccentric who owned the house covered it inside and out with shells. He even requested that he be buried in a shell-encrusted coffin.

Visitors to the town will find a super touring base when they stay at **The Spindrift**, an impressive Victorian-built house which is the charming home of Eric and Moyra McFarlane.

The Spindrift, Pittenweem Road, Anstruther. 0333-310573
Map Ref: H4

This licensed guest house was originally built in 1872 for a Captain Smith and today offers excellent accommodation in eight beautifully furnished en-suite guest rooms for which it carries a Three Crowns Highly Commended rating by the Scottish Tourist Board. Arguably the best room in the house is The Captain's Room on the top floor which is furnished and equipped as a replica of a ship master's cabin, with a small east facing window looking out across the sea. Eric

North Carr Lightboat, Anstruther

and Moyra are super hosts who go out of their way to ensure a memorable stay for their many guests, creating the relaxed feeling of staying with old friends.

Cellardyke produced many fine whaler and tea-clipper captains and one of their former houses has an archway forme from the jawbone of an Arctic whale.

As you follow the old meandering streets through Cellardyke towards the harbour, you will discover a superb restaurant, very aptly named **The Haven**. Run by friendly hosts David and Dianne Barnett, this is a very popular establishment, renowned throughout Fife for the excellent and varied menu which caters for every taste, specialising in local fish dishes. Originally built during the 18th century as a bakery, David and Dianne bought it as such in 1947 and it continued as a bakery until 1978, when the bakery business moved across the road and The Haven was created. Overlooking the famous Cellardyke harbour, this is a restaurant with an unrivalled location, the beautifully laid out gardens, complete with tables and chairs, providing the perfect 'al fresco' setting for a delicious lunch or dinner.

The Haven, 1 Shore Street, Cellardyke. 0333-310574 Map Ref: H4

It is from Anstruther harbour that, tides and weather permitting, those of you with sea-legs can take the five mile voyage to the **Isle of May** out in the Firth. Centuries ago the home of Benedictine priors dedicated to St. Adrian, murdered on the island in 870AD, it is now a haven for razorbills, shags and guillemots. The island is also the site of Scotland's first lighthouse, built in 1636 and now preserved as an ancient monument. There is still a light on the island which dates from 1816 but is no longer manned. During World War II the waters around the island were used as practice ranges by torpedo bomber crews. 21

aircrew gravestones in Crail churchyard, on the mainland, bear witness to the courage and dedication of the fliers.

For a relaxing, peaceful break away from it all **Rennyhill House** at **Kilrenny** is ideal. Jim and Anne Wotherspoon are welcoming hosts who have completely refurbished this lovely old laird's country house. To find Rennyhill, take the road out of Anstruther towards Crail and as soon as you see the sign for Kilrenny, turn left and after about 1/4 of a mile, Rennyhill House is on your right. Outside there are beautiful walled gardens and inside, the house is a delight, attractively furnished throughout and offering first class accommodation in three spacious guest rooms which carries a Commended Facilities Listed rating. The adjoining cottage provides excellent self-catering accommodation which carries a Four Crown Highly Commended rating, with bedrooms and bathroom on the ground floor and upstairs a studio lounge which offers wonderful views towards the Firth of Forth.

Rennyhill House, Kilrenny, Nr Anstruther. 0333-312234
Map Ref: H4

Crail itself is the last and most easterly of the East Nuik ports. It has one of the most photographed harbours in Scotland but picture postcard as it may be it is also home to Fife's crab and lobster fleet, a working port. The red tiled houses tumble down to the harbour and it is indeed a delightful sight. During the summer on Sundays the town's small museum run guided walks and they really give you a flavour of these little fishing ports lives over the centuries. Amongst the many fascinating buildings are the early 16th century Tolbooth, which now doubles as library and Town Hall, with it fishy weather vane and the striking Dutch Tower which has a bell cast in Holland and dated 1520. Somewhat 'hidden' in the picturesque village of Crail, **Selcraig**

House is one of those very special places you come across from time to time. Built over 200 years ago, this magnificent house has been sympathetically upgraded over the years to offer every modern comfort without losing any of its original character and charm. Awarded a One Crown Commended rating by the Scottish Tourist Board, this is the welcoming home of Margaret Carstairs, a friendly lady who goes out of her way to make her many guests feel at home. Her excellent cooking includes a choice of breakfast as well as an optional homecooked evening meal. With an attractive conservatory to relax in looking out over well kept gardens, staying at Selcraig House is a real treat.

Selcraig House, 47 Nethergate, Crail. 0333-50697 Map Ref: H4

Crail churchyard not only holds the graves of those brave airmen but also a large boulder that, so the story goes, the Devil hurled from the Isle of May. Why he threw it no one knows but he missed anyway. A good thing too, as the church is one of the oldest and most interesting buildings in the village.

Situated on the High Street in the village, **Caiplie Guest House** makes an ideal holiday and touring base for visitors to this lovely part of Scotland. Built during the 1880s, this splendid house looks deceptively small from the outside and yet within, provides very comfortable accommodation in seven attractively furnished guest rooms. Jayne Hudson is a welcoming hostess who goes out of her way to make her guests feel at home. A full Scottish breakfast sets you up well for a day's exploring and on your return you can look forward to an excellent three course dinner. It comes as no surprise then to learn that Caiplie Guest House is Taste of Scotland and Ashley Courtenay Recommended and carries a Scottish Tourist Board Two Crown Commended grading.

Caiplie Guest House, 53 High Street, Crail. 0333-50564 Map Ref: H4

Tucked away down Rose Wynd, you will discover **Crail Pottery**, a 'hidden' gem. This is a success story that began in 1965 when Stephen and Carol Grieve, then newly-weds, moved north from the Lake District, bought a caravan which was to be their home for the next two years and with the rest of their money, just £250, bought a near derelict cottage. Today, that same cottage is a thriving pottery industry with a delightful courtyard providing the perfect display area for beautiful handcrafted pots and domestic stoneware. The business is a family venture with Stephen and Carol working successfully alongside daughter Sarah, son Ben and daughter-in-law Jane. For a unique holiday memento or special gift for someone, this is definitely the place to come.

Crail Pottery, Rose Wynd, Crail. 0333-50413 Map Ref: H4

The A917, that we have followed along the coast, now turns north, passing Fife Ness and **Cambo Country Park**. With its nature rambles, seashore walks and adventure play area it's a great place for all the family to relax. Cambo is also an important rare breeds centre helping to preserve many of the less common breeds of farm animal once familiar sights all over Scotland.

Situated on the main A917 coast road near **Kingsbarns** you will find **Cambo House**, an impressive listed building which is the hub of one of Fife's great estates. Those staying will find a variety of accommodation with or without four poster beds. There is very comfortable en-suite bed and breakfast accommodation situated off the grand sweeping staircase within the main family part of the house, and fully equipped self-catering accommodation provided in several apartments within the house, plus two traditional farm cottages situated less than a mile from Cambo House itself. The owner, an internationally renowned photographer, uses this wonderful house and grounds as the a most spectacular photographic portrait studio. Set in magnificent grounds this fine house has an enchanting, romantic walled garden that is open to the public all year round. This charming 2-acre garden, centred on an oriental summerhouse and bridge over a waterfall by a weeping willow, is full of delights and surprises from the carpet of snowdrops and snowflakes in January, through to the fall of the multicoloured leaves in the autumn and the array of berries and coloured barks in the winter.

Cambo House, Kingsbarns, Nr St. Andrews,.0333-50313 Fax: 0333-50987 Map Ref: H3

Stood on the A917 at Kingsbarns, the **Cambo Arms Hotel** makes an ideal stopping-off point in any journey. Purpose-built in 1780 as a coaching inn, it formed part of the great Cambo Estate and was leased up until 1989, when the present owners, Alistair and Anne Fraser bought it. A traditional Scottish feel is enhanced by attractive tartan furnishings and clan prints and in these comfortable surroundings you can savour excellent homecooked country fare and fine ale. For those wishing to stay, there are two very comfortable and attractively furnished guest rooms and on fine days there is nothing nicer than relaxing at one of the outdoor tables with a drink and a bite to eat.

Cambo Arms Hotel, Kingsbarns. 0334-88226 Map Ref: H3

For the best in self-catering in the area **Morton of Pitmilly** really cannot be bettered. Awarded a Five Crown Highly Commended rating by the Scottish Tourist Board, this collection of houses enjoys a delightful setting within a working farm, with magnificent views in every direction. It would be hard to imagine a more idyllic location for a family holiday and first class facilities ensure maximum comfort and relaxation.

Morton of Pitmilly, Kingsbarns. 0334-88466 Fax: 0334 88 437
Map Ref: H3

The original farm courtyard has been tastefully converted into a delightful central patio area complete with flagstone paths, a well, waterpump, pond, fountain and cobbled patio area. Each of the ten houses is beautifully appointed and equipped to a standard that many housewives would envy. In addition, there is a comprehensive leisure complex for guests to use which includes a heated indoor swimming pool, sauna, fitness room, games room, sunbed, video library, children's play area, bicycle hire service and much more besides. Open all year round, Morton of Pitmilly really is a holiday haven of the highest calibre.

With its lovely coastal location, two miles from St Andrews on the A917 Crail Road, **Kinkell Farm** makes a delightful base from which to explore the beautiful surrounding countryside. A working arable farm, Kinkell is set within 250 acres of land which stretches down to the sea. Sandy and Frippy Fyfe are welcoming hosts who provide first class accommodation in three very comfortable guest rooms, each with en-suite or private facilities. The atmosphere is so welcoming and relaxed that you immediately feel like part of the family and the excellent homecooking makes the optional evening meal a tempting alternative to venturing further afield. For self-catering enthusiasts, Sandy and Frippy also provide accommodation in a fully equipped, attractively furnished cottage which sleeps up to eight.

Kinkell Farm, Kinkell, St Andrews. 0334-72003 Fax: 0334 75248
Map Ref: G3

It is now only a short drive to the ancient burgh of **St. Andrews**. The calm of the town today gives no hint of the violent and bloody struggles that took place here during the Reformation. One particular churchman, Cardinal David Beaton, was particularly relentless in the punishment of considered heretics, watching more than one victim burning at the stake. He in turn was murdered by the Reformers, who were joined by John Knox and occupied the castle, until the French attacked in 1547 forcing a surrender. Knox was taken away and subjected to the life of a galley slave for eighteen months. He swore to return to St Andrews for vengeance upon the places of worship, and indeed came back to Scotland eventually in 1559 to incite his followers to destroy the cathedral.

Despite Knox's attentions the cathedral remains still give a vivid impression of the scale and splendour of what was once Scotland's biggest church. From St. Rule's Tower, in the grounds, there are superb views of the town and surrounding countryside.

Today there is a far more peaceful air in the town, and the place attracts holiday makers and visitors to its stretches of safe, sandy beaches with delightful dunes and wonderfully clear waters. St. Andrews is also home to Scotland's oldest university, founded by Papal decree in 1411. It has many fine old buildings right in the centre of the town; which are only accessible to the public during July and August when twice daily guided tours operate, the Tourist Information office on South Street will have the details.

During term time Sunday afternoons are a colourful affairs as the students stroll up and down the stone piers of the harbour in their red robes, a tradition that goes back centuries. The pier, incidently, contains stone from both the cathedral and the castle.

No Scottish town with so rich a history could be complete without a castle. St. Andrews is no exception and the castle has as long and bloody history as any. There is a bottle dungeon hollowed out of solid rock - from which death was the only release, as well as a mine and counter-mine hacked out beneath it during one of several seiges. Cardinal Beaton was murdered here in 1546 and the first round of the Reformation was fought out in the seige that followed.

And, of course, there is golf, with St Andrews, home to possibly the most famous golf course in the world at the Royal and Ancient Golf Course founded in 1754. The history of the game is much older and has its origins in the 14th century. Its popularity in the 1400's led to its banning in 1457, the Scottish parliament feeling it took people away from archery practice. The ban was repeated by James IV as he found the game 'unprofitabill' for his subjects. The Stuart kings were ardent players and so to, it was rumoured, was Mary Queen of Scots. St. Andrews naturally is home to the **British Golf Museum**, which uses the latest in audio-visual displays and touch activation to tell the 500 year story of Golf, fascinating even if you've never tee'd off.

The delightful small village of **Guardbridge** lies approximately three and a half miles from St. Andrews on the A919 and it is here, on

River Terrace that you will find an excellent touring base at **The Larches,** home of Valerie and Barry Mayner. Originally built in 1919 as a Memorial Hall to the villagers killed in the war, it remained as a Community Hall until the 1970's and was then sold and used for various things including a playschool and a bank, until the Mayners bought it six years ago, by which time it was very run down. Today, totally refurbished it provides first class accommodation in an atmosphere of friendly hospitality, with three attractively furnished guest rooms, each with that extra personal touch, and two private bathrooms. Awarded a One Crown Commended grading, the emphasis at The Larches is clearly on guest comfort, an area in which Valerie and Barry most definitely succed.

The Larches, River Terrace, Guardbridge Tel / fax: 0334-838008
Map Ref: F2

Two mile further on is the town of **Leuchars,** where the jets of the RAF fly overhead on their way to and from the training grounds of the far north. The airbase annually hosts the Battle of Britain Airshow in September, an opportunity to marvel at the planes of old and the latest flying technology. History of an older but no less dramatic kind can be found at **Earlshall Castle,** a mile or so east of the town.

Earlshall, despite its five foot thick walls, battlements and musket loops, has a feeling of warmth and welcome about it. It is relatively new as Scottish castles go, being built in 1546 by Sir William Bruce. His ancestors, the Baron and Baroness Earlshall, retain the castle as their private family home to this day.

Inside the castle has a renown long gallery, it coved painted ceiling depicts the arms of the principle families of Scotland, together with many fabulous and fanciful mythical beasts. The walls are lined with over a hundred Scottish broadswords, reminders of a more bloody age.

Here too you can see the romantic 'Lynkit' hearts symbol, which incorporated the initials of Sir William Bruce, great grandson of the builder, and his wife Dame Agnes Lindsey. The motif is still used, over 350 years later, on the estates signs.

In 1561 Mary Queen of Scot visited and her bedchamber with its period furnishings is on view. There are many other articles and artifacts from the Jacobite period displayed throughout the castle. Sir Andrew - The Bloody Bruce - is said to haunt the castle, his ghost's footfall heard on the staircase from time to time. The pastimes of hunting shooting and fishing are celebrated in the Rod and Gun room, with its antique firearms, old sporting guns and fishing tackle from past generations. The museum room contains many military trophies, including a set of bagpipes played at Waterloo in 1815.

The castle grounds were relaid over a hundred years ago by renown Scottish architect Sir Robert Lorimer. They feature a magnificent Yew topiary, herbacious borders and a series of small gardens within gardens. There is also a fine herb garden and a 'secret garden'. All this exploring may leave you a little thirsty and sustenance is available in the castle tearoom. In the lovely wood panelled room traditional Scottish fare, baked in the castle kitchens, is served, together with a reviving cuppa.

North east of Leuchars is the **Tentsmuir Point National Nature Reserve**. It is a large reserve of some 47 acres that runs from Tentsmuir forest down to the forshore at Abertay Sands, and is a haven for a wide variety of birds and animals. The B945 takes us past the nature reserve, through Tayport, where once ferries plied across the Tay to Broughty Ferry and on to Newport on Tay. Keeping with shoreline along the B946, we pass through the small village of **Wormit** at which point the railway from Edinburgh to Dundee crosses the Firth on the infamous Tay Bridge.

The Sandford Country House Hotel at Wormit provides a wonderful holiday and touring base for this lovely part of Scotland. Built at the turn of the century by the famous architect Baillie-Scott, it is very impressive both inside and out. The gardens are simply beautiful, with a delightful courtyard complete with wishing well and the unusual feature of the floodlit Haggis Hatchery. Inside, the decor and furnishings are commensurate with the hotel's Four Crown Highly Commended rating and the sixteen en-suite guest rooms are all equipped for maximum comfort. You can relax with a drink in the ornately carved wood bar before making your way to the restaurant where Head Chef Steven Johnstone will tempt you with a mouthwatering menu which has earned him a fine reputation throughout the area.

The Sandford Country House Hotel, Newton Hill, Wormit.
0382-541802 Fax: 0382-542136 Map Ref: F2

Along the coast from here, along an unclassified road, is **Balmerino Abbey**. Founded by Queen Ermingade, second wife of William Lyon, in 1229 this Cistercian abbey met its fate, along with many others, during Henry VIII's Reformation.

Sticking to unclassified roads our journey meanders south from Balmerino, across the A914 and on to **Moonzie**. The name is a probable derivation of the Gaelic for corn plain, and indeed this area known as the Howe of Fife is a fertile land of rolling hills covered with the checkerboard fields of arable farming. The old kirk of Moonzie, standing on a hilltop used to be known as the 'Visable Kirk' by sailors who caught sight of it on the skyline as they sailed the Tay. Ruined Lordscairnie Castle was the stronghold of a 15th century Earl of Crawford; a fearsomely hirsute character, called Earl Beardie behind his back. His involvement in a failed attempt to overthrow James II saw him forced to dress in beggars rags and grovel for forgiveness before the King's court.

For self-catering enthusiasts, **Mountquhanie Holiday Homes** have a variety of properties within St. Andrews and the beautiful surrounding countryside, all equipped to the highest standards and graded between Four Crown Commended and Highly Commended to the coveted Five Crown Deluxe rating by the Scottish Tourist Board. Mountquhanie itself is a splendid 19th century country house lying five miles north of Cupar, home of the Folicity and Andrew Wedderburn and their family who have been in the self-catering business for over twenty years. There are three self-contained apartments within the house offering guests a taste of luxurious elegance and within the grounds there is a tennis court which guests are welcome to use, also nature trails and one and a half miles of river fishing. You can even enjoy tailormade golf packages should you wish. Whichever of the Mountquhanie Holiday Homes you choose, a wealth of beautiful countryside and places of historic interest are within easy reach and various sporting and leisure pursuits readily available, ensuring a truly memorable holiday.

Mountquhanie Holiday Homes, Cupar. 0826-24252 Map Ref: F3

Short drive down the A913 and you're in **Cupar**. Here, in Duffus Park, You'll discover the **Sir Douglas Bader Garden for the Disabled**. This famous World War II fighter pilot worked tirelessly for the cause of the disabled until his death a few years ago and this garden is a tribute to his works. Designed to be worked on and enjoyed by the disabled, it features raised beds, water gardens, aviary and rock garden.

Eden House Hotel, Pitscottie Road, Cupar. 0334-52510
Map Ref: F3

On the outskirts of Cupar on Pitscottie Road stands **Eden House Hotel**, a splendid Victorian building awarded a Three Crown Commended rating by the Scottish Tourist Board. A haven for golfing enthusiasts, Eden House lies just eight miles from St. Andrews and a host of historic attractions. Carefully refurbished by present owners, Paul and Louise Meredew, the hotel is beautifully furnished in keeping with its age and character and accommodation is provided in nine delightful, en-suite guest rooms. In the friendly atmosphere of the bar you can enjoy a 'wee dram' with the locals before savouring the mouthwatering cuisine in the very popular restaurant. With both table d'hôte and à la carte menus to choose from, every taste is catered for and a fine accompanying wine list completes your meal.

There are several interesting place to explore within striking distance of Cupar. On the A916 two miles south of the town is the unusually named **Hill of Tarvit**. An Edwardian country mansion designed by Sir Robert Lorimar, who you may recall rebuilt Earlshall Castle, for Mr Fredrick Bonar Sharp. Mr Bonar Sharp was a noted art collector and the furnishings, paintings, tapestries, Chinese porcelain and bronzes reflect his admirable tastes. The house also has well laid out gardens as you may expect from Sir Robert. Almost next door to the house is **Scotstarvit Tower**, a finely preserved five story L-plan castle which lost one of its heraldic fireplaces to the Hill of Tarvit.

Housed within an old coaching inn which dates back to 1750 and is now a listed building, **The Peat Inn** can be found by the crossroads in the village of the same name and is one of those very rare 'hidden' gems where you can experience the finest in gourmet cuisine and luxurious accommodation.

The Peat Inn, Peat Inn, By Cupar. 0334-84206 Map Ref: G3

227

David and Patricia Wilson are experienced, welcoming hosts whose appreciation of fine things is apparent in the beautiful decor and furnishings both within the restaurant and adjacent Residence, which houses eight superior, en-suite apartments. The highlight of a visit here is of course, the superb food for which David has earned an international reputation and won numerous awards, including being made Chef Laureate in 1986. His hobby is wine which means that in addition to a fine dinner menu, you can choose from a select wine list.

Near to Cupar on the A91 you may come across the **Scottish Deer Centre**, which is a unique opportunity to see, and even feed and touch these noble beasts. The centre makes an ideal day out for all the family, with many attractions and picnic areas. There are super facilities for the young ones, with adventure playgrounds both indoors and outside.

Somewhat 'hidden' away but well signposted off the A914 at **Letham, Fernie Castle Hotel** is an impressive establishment which carries a Three Crown Commended rating by the Scottish Tourist Board. This wonderful hotel is ideal for a romantic break away and even has its own ghost! With records dating as far back as 1353 when it was owned by Duncan the 13th, Earl of Fife, this is a place full of character and history and sympathetic refurbishment has retained many original features whilst providing the highest standards of comfort and service. The sixteen guest rooms are all en-suite and equipped for complete comfort. The Keep Bar provides a cosy and unique setting for a quiet drink and in the relaxed, candlelit atmosphere of the restaurant you can savour the finest in Scottish cuisine.

Fernie Castle Hotel, Letham, Nr Cupar. 0337-810381
fax: 0337-810422 Map Ref: F3

Lindores is just a short drive from Letham and its 12th century abbey stands untended on the edge of the village. Two miles away is

Newburgh which has many fine old buildings. Keep an eye out for the marriage lintel at 60 High Street, where the names of the newlyweds has been carved alongside a sailing ship, showing the husband was a master mariner. The harbour looks across the Tay to wide expanses of reed bed on the north shore. These are still harvested every winter for roofing thatch.

Set within 400 acres of land and with panoramic views on all sides, **Easter Clunie Farm** is a charming 19th century farmhouse situated two miles east of **Abernethy** on the A913. This is the welcoming home of Kathleen and David Baird, who offer everything that is good about farmhouse bed and breakfast. In addition to the beautiful location, a friendly welcome is complemented by excellent homecooked food and fine accommodation in three tastefully furnished guest rooms, one with en-suite bathroom. Adjacent to the farmhouse is a splendid Victorian walled garden and for the walking enthusiast, the surrounding countryside provides a wealth of scenic walks.

Easter Clunie Farm, Newburgh. 0337-840218 Map Ref: E3

To the south is the town with that most delightful name, **Auchtermuchty**. Well; delightful until you discover it is Gaelic for 'Upland for Swine'!

In the heart of the Royal Burgh you will find a welcoming hostelry, **The Forest Hills Hotel**. This traditional inn dates back to the 1750's and careful refurbishment has retained all its original character and charm. The copper topped tables and beamed ceilings in the Cocktail bar enhance the deliberate olde worlde theme, whilst the lounge provides a comfortable setting in which to relax. The candlelit Restaurant serves a varied selection of tasty, homecooked food accompanied by an interesting wine list and later in the evening you can retire to one of the ten attractively furnished guest rooms, each equipped with every modern facility, eight with en-suite bathroom for maximum comfort. For a small fee, residents can make use of the leisure facilities at The Lomond Hills Hotel in Freuchie village. STB Three Crown Commended.

The Forest Hills Hotel, The Square, Auchtermuchty. 0337-28318
Map Ref: E3

To the south west lie the Lomond Hills. The hills contain a number of weird rock formations, formed by the erosion of soft underlying rock leaving sandstone boulders doing a balancing act. Easiest to get to is the **Bannet Stane** or Bonnet Stone, so named for its shape. On the west side of the hills is Carlin Maggie - Maggie the Witch - who so irritated the devil that he turned her into stone for all eternity. She stands here, a 40ft column of shattered basalt, admiring the view.

Beneath the hills is **Falkland** and its splendid palace. The buildings, in Renaissance style, date from 1501-41 and were the favourite seat of James V who died here in 1542, and of his daughter Mary Queen of Scots. There is a rather grisly story that Robert the Second died here after being imprisoned and forced by starvation to eat his own flesh. A woman in an adjoining cell, who is said to have fed him for a while from her own breasts, was put to death for her trouble. When James VI was here he was forced to listen to the preachings of John Knox the reformist. Legend has it that the King kept interrupting the preacher until he was reminded in no uncertain terms that the King was merely "God's silly Vassal". Apart from being a fine palace with some exemplary architecture of the period, the gardens contain the original royal tennis court, the oldest in Britain, built in 1539.

Enjoying a magnificent countryside setting a mile south of Falkland and just twenty minutes drive from the M90, **Templelands Farm** makes a peaceful and relaxing holiday base. Awarded a One Crown

Commended grading by the Scottish Tourist Board, this is the place to come if you want warm, friendly hospitality in a caring, homely atmosphere. Mr. and Mrs. McGregor have been providing first class bed and breakfast service for many years and offer their many guests very comfortable accommodation in two spacious, attractively furnished bedrooms. The tasty farmhouse breakfast sets you up for the day and if you wish, a packed lunch and homecooked evening meal can be provided by prior notice.

Templelands Farm, Falkland. 0337-857383 Map Ref: E4

Situated in the heart of the picturesque village of **Freuchie** and just a few miles from Falkland Palace, **The Lomond Hills Hotel** is a delightful establishment awarded a Four Crowns Commended grading by the Scottish Tourist Board.

The Lomond Hills Hotel, Freuchie. 0337-57329/57498/58180
Map Ref: E4

Falkland Palace

Dating back in some parts to 1720, this former coaching inn is still full of character and charm, yet has many unexpected, but welcome surprises. Among these are the beautiful heated indoor swimming pool and comprehensive fitness centre complete with solarium and sauna. If first class cuisine is what you are after, indulge yourself in the candlelit Restaurant where your needs will certainly be well catered for. With twenty five superbly equipped, en-suite guest rooms providing first class accommodation, it seems you have everything you need for a perfect holiday.

As already mentioned Fife is rich in arable land and its coastal waters teem with life but the prize its hinterland holds is deep underground - coal. Though coal is still being won below our feet you'd be hard pushed to find much evidence of the areas industrial past. New industries are replacing the old though and the town of **Glenrothes** has a fast developing electronics industry.

Horse riding enthusiasts will love **Glenrothes Riding Centre** which is set within 40 acres of fine grazing land just out of Glenrothes as you head for Balgeddie. Mr and Mrs Gilbert have a wealth of knowledge and experience with horses which shows in the excellent facilities and the well-kept animals. The rides cover Corporation Bridleways around the town and every age and ability is catered for, with mounts ranging from 12 hand ponies to 16.3 hand horses. Hacks last for one or two hours and the indoor arena provides a welcome alternative when the weather changes for the worse. Whilst here, make sure you look out for the original round house with its outstanding interior roof which is still intact. This is where in olden times, the horse would walk round and round, turning the machinery to grind the flour. Whether riding is in your blood or just something you fancy trying, you won't leave Glenrothes Riding Centre disappointed.

Glenrothes Riding Centre, Balgeddie Farm, Glenrothes.
0592-742428 Map Ref: E4

Also near Glenrothes for a good place to stay you might seek out **Redlands Country Lodge**, at Ladybank near Glenrothes, a lovely Norwegian style pine lodge which is situated in tranquil surroundings just half a mile from the centre of Ladybank village. Friendly hosts Ken and Maureen Robinson have four delightful guest rooms which carry a Three Crown Commended rating by the Scottish Tourist Board. Each has its own en-suite shower room, colour TV and hot drinks facilities and returning to your room in the afternoon you will find a welcome plate of home baked 'goodies'. Maureen's excellent cooking continues into the evening with a fine daily changing dinner menu incorporating homegrown produce wherever possible and accompanied by a glass of wine. Breakfast is another delight, with freshly baked rolls accompanying a substantial meal that sets you up perfectly for the day.

Redlands Country Lodge, By Ladybank. 0337-31091 Map Ref: E4

We now take a drive to do some 'real' driving. By taking the B921 to Auchterderran, following the A910 to Cowdenbeath, then the A909/B914 we arrive at our destination. But not before a passing the doorstep of **The Butterchurn Restaurant**. Set in 25 acres, part of a working farm dating back to 1773, it is housed within old cowsheds and dairy buildings and is a very special place, one not to be missed. The blackboard style menu is outstanding, with every meal freshly prepared and homecooked to the highest standards. Beautifully arranged on the display stand you will see meatloaf, home cooked ham, fresh salmon, herring rolls, nut rissoles and vegetarian pie. To complete your meal, the adjacent display houses an equally mouthwatering selection of sweets, all homemade and very tempting. With panoramic views on all sides and a wonderful relaxed atmosphere, this really is a gastronomic haven.

The Butterchurn, Cocklaw Farm, Kelty. 0383-830169/831614 Map Ref: C5

It has been a twisty route to here but not as tortuous as the hairpins and bends of **Knock Hill Racing Circuit,** Scotland's national motorsport centre. Between Easter and October scarcely a weekend goes by without the roar of engines and the screech of tyres. Every sort of car, motorcycle and even trucks can be seen being pushed to the limit and beyond! And if you'd like to find your own limit then the race and rally school will be happy to oblige. For details of the racing programme call 0383-723337, budding Nigel Mansells should call 0383-622090.

Minutes along the B914 on the outskirts of the village of **Saline,** you will find an excellent place to stay at **The Saline Hotel** which is Scottish Tourist Board Listed.

The Saline Hotel, West Road, Saline 0383-852798 Map Ref: C6

Irene Gordon, the friendly proprietor has a wealth of experience in the hotel trade and has created a welcoming traditional hostelry here, where locals and visitors mix easily in a warm, relaxed atmosphere. In the cosy bar you can enjoy a wide range of well kept ale and Irene offers excellent homecooked food throughout the day, with High Teas provided at weekends. Very comfortable accommodation is provided in three chalet style guest rooms, all en-suite and well furnished, which are located in converted outbuildings adjacent to the hotel.

About 5 miles south of Knock Hill, on the bank of the Forth, is Culross, and a very different world. Pronounced 'Cooross' this fascinating village has been very carefully looked after by the National Trust for Scotland. It's a remarkable example of a 16th and 17th century small town, having changed little in 300 years. The small 'palace' was built between 1597 and 1611 by Sir William Bruce, who developed the seagoing trade in salt and coal from Culross. Featuring crow stepped gables and pantiled roofs outside and painted ceilings inside it is indeed an outstanding building. Others well worth finding include The Study, Town House, The ark and the nunnery. On the outskirts of the village there is also the remains of the 13th century cistercian abbey, the choir of which is the present Parish Church.

It is just a short journey upstream to Kincardine Bridge, where we leave Fife. If the name is familiar to the traveller it is because the name seems to appear on signposts all over Scotland, there is only one other place that appears more frequently and that by way of coincidence is also in the Central Region, which lies across the river and in the next chapter.

Central Region

Stirling Castle

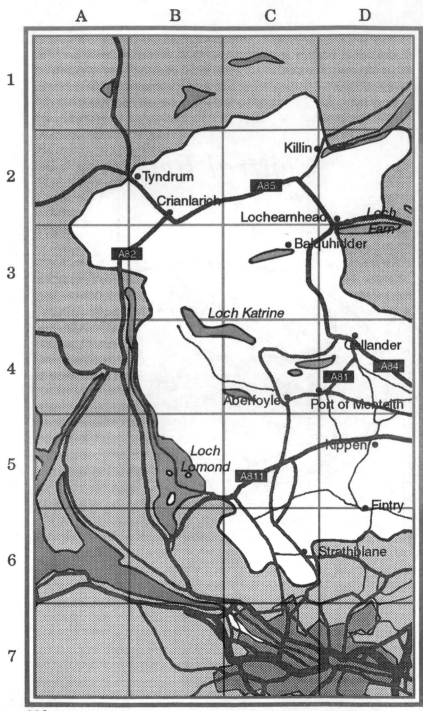

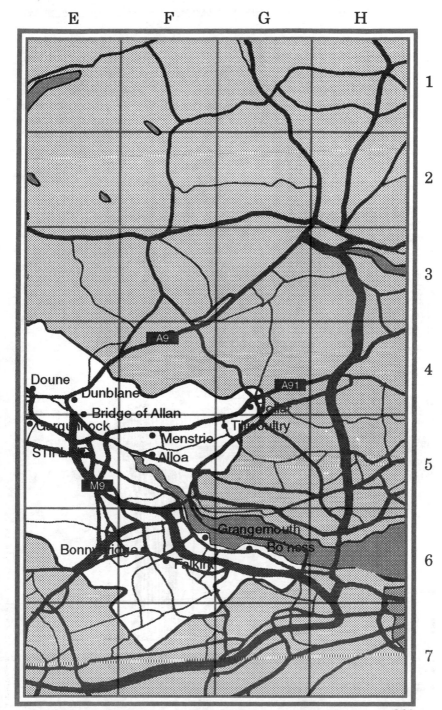

Robert the Bruce, Stirling Castle

CHAPTER SEVEN

Central Region.

Uninspiringly named it may be but the Central Region is certainly no disappointment. There are plenty of treasures to discover and an accessible taste of what the north of Caledonia has in store.

We start on the south bank of the mighty Forth River at **Dunmore Park**, a couple of miles upstream of the Kincardine Bridge on the B9124. Here is a hidden gem of rare quality, one of Britain's finest follies, the Pineapple. Quite why, in 1761, John Murray, 4th Earl of Dunmore felt compelled to have a 53ft stone fruit built is anyone's guess, but if you have a taste for the unusual you'll be glad he did. This strange building was supposedly built as a garden retreat and must have astounded the locals who would never have seen a pineapple.

Two hundred years later the pineapple is no longer a rare and exotic luxury but the building hasn't lost its ability to amaze the onlooker. It is not open to the public, but it can be rented! If you like the idea of a week in Britain's most bizarre holiday cottage call The Landmark Trust (0628-825925), who let all manner of unusual buildings all over Britain.

Near **Grangemouth**, a little south of the bridge, the world's petroleum industry had its humble beginnings. In 1851 Dr James 'paraffin' Young established Young's Paraffin and Mineral Oil Company. At its height the Scottish shale-oil industry employed 40,000 at 120 different sites. You can discover many of these for yourself by following the Paraffin Young Heritage Trail, which starts in the town. The last shale-mine closed in 1962, shale oil refining having been rendered uncompetitive by the crude oil gushing from wells in Arabia. Young's company still exists as part of BP, who have a huge refinery here that dominates the shore front. Incidentally Young anonymously financed David Livingstone's many expeditions to Africa.

When **Grangemouth Sports Stadium** opened on 9th July 1966 it was the first all-weather track in the United Kingdom and it continues as the heart of Scottish athletics, hosting a large number of championships and major fixtures every year, in addition to the local authority's own programme of competition.

The tree hedge on the embankment around the arena has matured and provides a continental atmosphere and with a fine grandstand the facility is second to none for athletes, footballers, cyclists, officials and spectators alike to enjoy their sport. Floodlit 5-a-side pitches, a wall mirrored gymnasium and a thriving cafeteria further enhance the venue which enjoys easy access with the M9 motorway at junction 5. Open Monday-Friday 8.00am - 9.30pm and weekends 8.00am - 4.00pm.

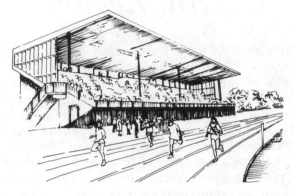

Grangemouth Sports Stadium, Kersiebank Avenue, Grangemouth.
0324-483752 Map Ref: F6

Polmonthill Ski Centre, just off the M9 motorway at junction 4, has a 110 metre artificial ski slope and a 15 metre starter slope, both of which are floodlit. The main run, on the historic setting of the Antonine Wall, is lubricated with a sprinkler system and is serviced by a button style ski lift. The facility is staffed by qualified instructors and caters for all ages and standards of groups and individuals. Advance bookings and ski hire are available at the Ski Lodge, a listed building recently refurbished, where you can also relax aprés ski in the Antonine Coffee Bar.

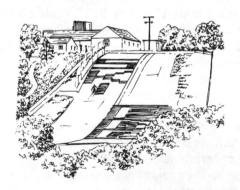

Polmonthill Ski Centre, Polmont Farm, Falkirk. 0324-711660
Map Ref: F6

The Pineapple, Dunmore

The next town downstream is Borrowstounness, better known now as the less tongue twisting **Bo'ness**. The town flourished for many years on the industrial success of the area, a story recalled in a fine museum at the nearby Kinneil House and estate. Another legacy of the industrial revolution admirably preserved is the **Bo'ness & Kinneil Railway**. The volunteers of the Scottish Railway Preservation Society run steam and diesel trains at weekends between April and October, and daily from Mid-July to late August. Their Victorian station was painstakingly moved from Wormit in Fife and reassembled in Bo'ness. As well as all the paraphernalia of a working railway there are the additional attractions of a working man's home of the 1920's, in Hamilton's Cottage, opposite the station and at the other end of the line Birkhill Fireclay Mine, set in the side of Avon Gorge.

A little to the south at Belsyde, set in over 100 acres of land above the Union Canal is **Belsyde House.** The house enjoys a secluded setting and boasts wonderful views northwards to the Ochil Hills, though the M8, M9, and M90 are all within 10 minutes drive, and it is only 30 minutes to Edinburgh Airport, making this a readily accessible holiday base. This charming 18th century farmhouse is the home of welcoming hostess Nan Hay, who enjoys sharing it with her many guests. Awarded a Two Crown Commended grading, Belsyde House has four very comfortable and well-equipped guest rooms, one with en-suite facilities, plus a private guest lounge. Breakfast is always a substantial affair ensuring all guests are well set up to make the most of a day's exploring or local fishing and golf.

Belsyde House, Belsyde, Linlithgow. 0506-842098 Map Ref: G6

The nearby town of **Falkirk** boasts Britain's shortest street. Tolbooth Street still manages to accommodate a tearoom, pub and shoe shop in its 20 paces - end-to-end. The A803 takes us west from here to **Bonnybridge** and **Rough Castle**. Though the approach looks unpromising Rough is the best preserved of the Roman forts along the Antonine Wall. The earthworks of the barracks, headquarters, granary and bath-house are clearly visible, and through the centre the military road that the connected the forts along the wall. Started only ten years after the more famous Hadrian's Wall, it was built and originally manned by Legions recruited in Italy.

Our route passes through nearby Denny and takes the B818 travelling westwards, leading up above the Kilsyth Hills, and into the Campsie Fells. The road runs up to Carron Bridge, and along through the Carron Valley, with its reservoir and forest, the road weaving its way between the high fells, some of which reach nearly 2000ft. **Fintry** is hemmed in on both sides, by the Campsie Fells to the south and the Gargunnock Hills to the north. The peaks of Earl's Seat and Stronend dominating the village.

If you would like to spend some time exploring the Campsie Fells then there is a delightful place to stay on the south side of Earl's Seat at **Strathblane**. Surrounded by fifteen acres of beautiful parkland yet conveniently situated on the A81 Glasgow to Aberfoyle road,

The Country Club Hotel, Milngavie Road, Strathblane.
0360-770491 Map Ref: C6

The Country Club Hotel makes an ideal holiday retreat, offering both peaceful seclusion and ready accessibility. Originally built 110 years ago as a family home, it has been a hotel for the past fifty years and sympathetic refurbishment has created a holiday base full of character and charm which offers first class comforts in an atmosphere of friendly hospitality. This proves a popular venue for wedding receptions and private parties or functions, but at the same time offers the passing traveller or holidaymaker a very comfortable place to stay, with ten beautifully furnished en-suite guest rooms and a restaurant with a deserved reputation for its fine Scottish cuisine.

At Fintry the road divides, the B818 continues on towards the east bank of Loch Lomond and the B822 turns northwards. We follow the latter up towards **Kippen**. The parish title 'The Kingdom of Kippen, might seem very grand for such a small village, but was bestowed upon the village by James V.

History relates that whilst residing at Stirling Castle, the King sent out his men to catch venison from the nearby hills. On returning with the venison, the men happened to cross the land of John Buchanan who ambushed them and relieved them of their bounty. When the King's men tried to reason that the venison belonged to the King, Buchanan replied that James might be the King of Scotland but he was the King of Kippen. James V was amused and rode out to meet his neighbouring majesty. John Buchanan was cordial to the King, and became so great a favourite that he was often invited as 'King of Kippen' to meet his brother sovereign at Stirling.

The Black Bull in Kippen is not a pub, as you might think, but rather a nice building that has been restored through the National Trust for Scotland. The building dates back to 1729 and was once the principal hostelry in the village, standing on the back road from Stirling to Dumbarton. It retains its original style of twelve pane glazing and has scrolled skewputs on the gables.

There are still a small number of industries in Kippen which have been going for 200 years or more. The blacksmiths for example, where the Rennie family have been shoeing horses for all that time. Andrew Rennie, the last of that long line, worked until his death in 1985, at the age of 97, at the Smiddy which is still in operation and is now owned by the National Trust for Scotland.

From Kippen we take the road to Stirling, on route stopping at **Gargunnock**. The Gardens here are delight and are well worth a visit to appreciate the blaze of colours, textures and sheer magic of narcissi, azaleas, rhododendrons and many other flowering shrubs and trees. The combination and sheer beauty of these in any season is a great pleasure, and there is also a small wood here with a charming walk. The gardens are in the grounds of an impressive house that was built between the 16th and 18th centuries, and unfortunately not open to the public without prior written arrangement. Indeed the gardens themselves are something of a rare treat as they are only open on Wednesday afternoons from one o'clock until five between April and October.

Stirling is surely one of the most atmospheric of Scottish towns, and today retains much of the feeling and charm of days gone by. The

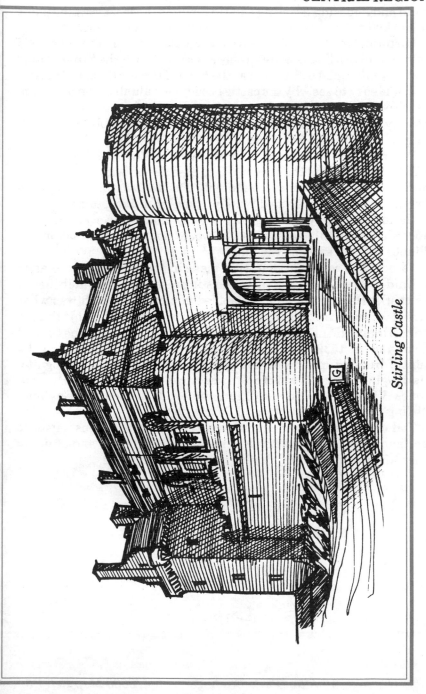

Stirling Castle

grand and imposing **Stirling Castle** remains the most striking point on its skyline, challenged only by the Wallace Monument.

Historically, the castle played a crucial role in the country's history, and Stirling is more closely associated with the Stuart kings than any other place. Situated at the head of the Forth on a strategic rock, it is easy to see why the castle became so valuable. Indeed it was the site of many a Pictish stronghold long before the castle was actually built. It is even said to have been the Round Table upon which King Arthur trained his forces.

When James I returned from captivity in England, he held his court at Stirling, and thus began a long association with the castle for the Stuart dynasty. James II reputedly tried to curb the power of the Douglas' when he persuaded William, the eighth Earl, to come to the castle for dinner by offering him safe conduct. However, he then proceeded to kill his guest when he would not agree to break off an alliance that threatened the king.

James IV, a colourful character, made improvements to the castle and laid out the Kings Knot', a garden still preserved in outline beneath the castle. He also apparently dabbled in alchemy, which was what passed for science at the time. James V also spent much of his time at the castle and did much to improve it, including rebuilding the Chapel Royal and, in 1539, building the palace. Incidentally he was in the habit of dressing up in disguise and walking around the town incognito. His daughter Mary Queen of Scots was crowned here in 1543. Her son, James VI, was also crowned here but when he left for England, Stirling's importance as a Royal Seat declined.

Today you can hire the Royal apartments for functions. Historic Scotland (031 244-3144) can arrange everything, here, and at many other historic houses and castles throughout Scotland.

The Heritage, 16 Allan Park, Stirling. 0786-473660 Map Ref: E5

248

Situated in Allan Park, at the foot of Stirling's Castle Rock, you will discover **The Heritage**, an elegant Georgian hotel and restaurant which carries a Three Crown Commended rating by the Scottish Tourist Board. Here, surrounded by exquisite antique furnishings and beautiful paintings, you can savour the finest international cuisine prepared by the resident chef and owner, Frenchman Georges Marquetty. Highly recommended by a number of leading guides, The Heritage is renowned for its superb restaurant, which offers an extensive international menu to please the most discerning palate, accompanied by an excellent wine list. To complete an evening out, you can choose to stay in one of the four lovely en-suite guest rooms, each attractively furnished in keeping with the hotel's age and character.

Much of the cities original character has been preserved, together with a large collection of buildings from the nineteenth century, when the town rapidly expanded. The walk down from the castle passes many places of interest including Mar's Wark, the Tolbooth and Mercat Cross before bringing you to Stirling's street markets, which have been held since medieval times. There is so much of interest in the old town, and helpfully the place abounds with plaques and notices to help you on your meanderings.

For visitors to Stirling looking for somewhere special to stay, **Park Lodge Hotel** provides a truly luxurious base from which to explore this historic city, with lovely views of Stirling Castle and the Campsie Fells Hills.

Park Lodge Hotel, 32 Park Terrace, Stirling. 0786-74862
Map Ref: E5

This impressive part Victorian and part Georgian hotel carries a Three Crown Commended rating although after staying here you may well rate it higher, with beautiful antiques, original paintings and sumptuous furnishings enhancing an air of timeless elegance. Guests here will feel like royalty in surroundings that have an almost palatial aura and yet the atmosphere is relaxed and friendly, with first class service being the order of the day. All ten en-suite guest rooms are equipped to the highest standards, some with four poster beds and the restaurant is renowned for its superb cuisine which is accompanied by a fine wine list and comes Michelin recommended.

Stirling's antiquity and position has ensured that the town has occupied a central role in many great historical events that have shaped Scotland's history. As Scotland's historic capital, the town has more than its fair share of ghostly inhabitants. many, like the tragic 'green lady' are known throughout Scotland, others are familiar only to local residents. This rich legacy provides the raw material which inspires the **Stirling Ghost Walk**. Guests are taken on an atmospheric exploration of the Old Town of Stirling. Throughout, guests are entertained with a leavened mix of comedy, drama and the occasional fright! Unique amongst this type of walk, the Stirling Ghost Walk centres on a full dramatic show using six actors, with guests touring the ancient nooks and crannies that give the Old Town such character. Can guests be really sure that a phantom glimpsed is simply an actor or something altogether more sinister? The Walks run five nights a week throughout the summer season and pre-booking is advised.

Tickets can be booked by telephone or in person and Local Tourist Information Centres can also supply tickets.

Stirling Heritage Company Ltd, 17-19 Irvine Place, Stirling.
0786-450945 Map Ref: E5

Situated in a very pleasant residential area in the heart of the city, **8 Victoria Place** is a well-appointed Victorian guest house owned and run by Paul and Suzanne Howarth. Open all year, this charming house is ideally situated as a base from which to explore Stirling and its surroundings, with the famous castle just a short walk away. Attractively furnished in keeping with its age and character, the house provides very comfortable accommodation in three spacious guest rooms and is set within lovely gardens, all of which adds up to a peaceful and relaxing holiday base. The Howarths have a dog and four cats, by the way, which many visitors enjoy, but obviously some might not.

8 Victoria Place, Stirling. 0786-479360 Map Ref: E5

South of the town lies the site of the Scots greatest victory over the English. **Bannockburn** saw the freeing of the nation, when Robert the Bruce led his forces in defeating a huge army of Edward I. You can follow the stirring events of June 1314 through a series of exhibitions and admire the huge statue of Bruce astride his warhorse.

Swanswater Fishery and Smokehouse, Sauchieburn, Stirling.
0786-814805 Map Ref: E5

251

Nearby fishing enthusiasts will discover a real haven at **Swanswater,** an excellent fishery, somewhat hidden but well worth seeking out. Situated on the site of the famous Battle of Bannockburn, Swanswater can be found by taking Junction 9 off the M9, marked Stirling Services, then heading for the Bannockburn Heritage Centre and turning left just before it, towards Chartershall. Turning right at the end of this road, you will see Swanswater signposted. Once here, visitors have the choice of fishing from the bank or going out in one of three boats, but either way you are assured of a satisfying day's fishing, with a wide variety of both small and large fish to tempt anglers of all abilities. With a superb smokehouse producing the finest Scottish smoked fish, you need not leave without a tasty memento of your visit.

On the northern side of the town is one 'hidden' gem well worth seeking out, **The Birds & Bees,** which can be found on Easter Cornton Road. Whatever your requirements, this first class restaurant/bar caters for everybody. In Le Bistro which is open at lunchtime and each evening from 5.00pm till late, you can savour a wide range of tasty meals, from 'tattie skins' to steaks, while in the main bar you can enjoy an excellent pint of real ale with your bar lunch or supper. The Bumble Bee Club is specifically designed with families in mind and the 'bumble bee' menu includes a wide selection for children. With a permanent barbecue situated in the courtyard beer garden and regular Petanque Evenings (French bowls to the uninitiated!), this is definitely one place not to be missed.

The Birds & Bees, Easter Cornton Road, Stirling. 0786-473663
Map Ref: E5

The Wallace Monument also stands on this side of town and is highly recommended, not least for its unrivalled views of the town and castle. This rather strangely shaped tower commemorates the Scots victory over the English at nearby Stirling Bridge in 1297. Sir William Wallace led the force that defeated Edward I's army of over 10,000. Though Wallace was ultimately defeated at Falkirk, and met a gruesome end - being hung drawn and quartered, he provided the catalyst that inspired King Robert the Bruce to lead the nation to freedom in 1314 at Bannockburn. The tower itself is 220ft high and was built in the 1850's, when a tide of nationalism swept the country. Today there is Hall of Heroes, displays that tell the story of Wallace's victory and history of the surrounding countryside, while the viewing platform, at the top of 246 steps, gives you views that stretch from the Forth Bridges to Ben Lomond.

The monument overlooks the village of Kildean and it is here, close to the auction rooms that you will find a super restaurant, appropriately called **The Riverway**. Enjoying a picturesque location on the riverbank, you can savour wide range of food from the lunchtime table d'hôte and à la carte menus or call in later for a traditional Scottish High Tea to a backdrop of wonderful countryside views from the large picture windows. Children are most welcome and Archie's Menu caters specifically for them and Archie the Parakeet is a feathered friend that they can talk to! During the summer months you can enjoy a barbecue and for a taste of rural Scottish life, join the local farmers in The Wheatsheaf self service restaurant and bar every Wednesday and Thursday lunchtime.

The Riverway Restaurant, Kildean, Stirling. 0786-475734
Map Ref: E5

The monument also lies on the road to **Alloa**, which happens to be our next destination. This strange name comes from the Celtic and means 'swift ford'. Its origin no doubt refers to the magnificent sweep of the Firth of Forth which stretches out beneath the town.

Before the river silted up it had formed part of Scotland's naval dockyard in the 16th century. Here in 1511, James IV launched the great flagship of the Royal Scottish Navy, the 'Great Michael'. which had reputedly taken up all of the woods of Fife to build. With 300 guns she was far ahead of other ships of the time, and was to be the pride of the King and Navy.

She spent her first two years docked for want of a better purpose, and when finally taken out, entrusted to the Earl of Arran, who had never actually been to sea. It is to this day a mystery as to what happened to this extravagant and costly ship. Rumour has that a wrecked hull, found years later at the port of Brest in France, was indeed all that was left of the Great Michael.

Our travels take the north road out from Alloa to **Tillicoultry** where you may like to pause for refreshment.

Sterling Warehouse on Moss Road in Tillicoultry has always been renowned for its furniture showrooms, but now there is a further attraction in the form of a super restaurant, **The Butterfly Inn**. This excellent self-service licensed establishment is designed with families in mind and provides a perfect alternative when you don't feel like cooking for yourself. Here you can savour fine homecooking throughout the day (10.00am - 8.00pm Monday to Saturday and 11.00am - 7.00pm Sunday) at surprisingly reasonable prices. In attractive surroundings with delightful butterfly motifs adorning the ceiling, the whole family can enjoy the treat of a meal out and ramp access for wheelchair users plus highchairs for younger children means that everyone's needs are catered for.

The Butterfly Inn, Moss Road, Tillicoultry. 0259-751596
Map Ref: G5

A little further up the A93 is **Dollar**, scene in 877 AD of the defeat of the 'Scots' in battle by the Danes. The Dollar Academy is a fine building here well worth a look, being a good example of Classical Georgian style built by Sir William Playfair in 1819. Sir William also designed the Academy and National Gallery in Edinburgh.

In Glen above Dollar sits **Castle Campbell** , commanding long views over the plains of the Firth. Built at the end of the 15th century, it was burned by Cromwell, although the ruin is still quite impressive. The castle was once known as Castle Gloume, set as it is between the glens of Care and Sorrow and by the waters of Grief. It's a mystery why the area should feature so much verbal depression.

Another castle with an interesting past can be found in **Menstrie**, which lies westwards on the A91. Early in the 17th century the owner of Menstrie, Sir William Alexander suggested to James VI that creating and selling baronetcies in Nova Scotia could raise funds to develop this 'New Scotland' in Canada. Though poorly subscribed the Baronetcies were created and in the castle's Nova Scotia Room 109 baronet's shields are on display. The castle has been converted into flats and a library but is open on Wednesday, Saturday and Sunday afternoons from May to September.

Westwards, on the A9, is the delightful town of **Bridge of Allan** and enjoying a central location there, the **Old Manor Hotel** which makes an excellent holiday base, with Stirling only three miles away and both Glasgow and Edinburgh readily accessible via the excellent motorway network nearby.

Old Manor Hotel, 129 Henderson Street, Bridge of Allan.
0786-832169 Map Ref: E4

Originally built some 250 years ago as a private dwelling, sympathetic restoration has ensured that whilst offering every modern comfort, the Old Manor has lost none of its original character and charm. Set within beautiful grounds with ample parking space, this is friendly, family-run establishment which proves a popular venue for wedding receptions. Very comfortable accommodation is provided in seven spacious and well-equipped guest rooms, five with en-suite facilities. The hotel restaurant is open to non-residents and offers a superb menu, with a varied selection to suit every palate.

Visitors would also be well advised to call in at **The Crooked Arm**, a welcoming traditional inn situated on Allanvale Road, a quiet backwater on the western side of the town. Unimposing from the outside, this is a cosy old inn run by Stuart Galloway and his friendly staff and its warm, relaxed atmosphere makes it a popular venue with visitors and locals alike. The lunchtime bar menu offers a wide range of tasty homecooked meals and there is a daily changing selection of blackboard specials which make an ideal accompaniment to the fine range of ales served here.

The Crooked Arm, Allanvale Road, Bridge of Allan. 0786-833 830
Map Ref: E4

Crossing the A9 we headed towards **Doune**, keen to have a look at one of the best medieval castles to survive more or less intact. Doune Castle was built during the late 14th and early 15th centuries by the Regent Albany, who was later executed in 1424, implicated in the murder of James I's brother David. It became part of the crown and Royalty visited from time to time; including Mary Queen of Scots. During the '45 rising it became a Jacobite garrison and in fiction Scott's hero in 'Waverley' come to the castle as well.

Interestingly, the village bridge across the river was built by one Robert Spital, tailor to James IV, in order to spite a ferryman who had refused him passage.

There is a splendid motor museum here about two miles north of Doune, off the A84, which houses a marvellous collection of vintage and post vintage cars. Collected and owned by the Earl of Moray, most of them are in running order. Other interesting local attractions to be found locally include the Blair Drummond Safari Park, which is a delight for youngsters - of all ages! The park can be found two miles to the south of Doune.

We now forsake the A84, for the time being, in a quest for Aberfoyle and Loch Katrine. Our route takes us past the Lake of Menteith and its priory. Accessible by boat from **Port of Menteith**, Inchmahome Priory sits on an island in the middle of the lake. Founded by Augustinian monks in 1238, the house proved an ideal refuge for the infant Mary Queen of Scots over three hundred years later.

It would be hard to imagine a more spectacular or tranquil location for a relaxing holiday than that of **The Lake Hotel**, which as its name suggests, lies on the shores of the Lake of Menteith in the Trossachs. Beautifully refurbished throughout, this splendid establishment is well deserving of its Four Crown Highly Commended status and provides discerning guests with that extra touch of luxury and comfort that makes staying here such a pleasure. The spacious conservatory restaurant with its panoramic views across the Lake makes dining a treat and at the end of the day, you can retire to one of thirteen tastefully furnished and well equipped en-suite guest rooms.

The Lake Hotel, Port of Menteith. 0877-385258 Map Ref: D4

Driving on through the Menteith Hills takes us on to Loch Ard Forest and **Aberfoyle**. For those keen to get out into the great wide open this is the place, the **Queen Elizabeth Forest Park** has over sixty miles of waymarked walks and cycle trails. The Visitors Centre is packed full of displays and information on the forest and its flora and fauna, as well as shop, cafeteria and toilet facilities.

It is also from here that those who prefer to take in the scenery from the comfort of their car can get details of the **Achray Forest Drive**. Using Forestry Commission roads the drive takes you into the heart of the forest, amongst the conifers, oaks and birch to observe the combination of logging, conservation and recreation. There are plenty of places to stop and picnic, and an all important play area and toilets at the halfway point.

As you explore the spectacular scenery of The Trossachs, you will discover an excellent touring base at the **Inverard Hotel**, which enjoys a beautiful setting overlooking the River Forth in Aberfoyle. Originally an old hunting lodge built in 1860 by the Duke of Montrose, this welcoming hotel provides excellent accommodation in seventeen well-equipped guest rooms, twelve of which are en-suite. The emphasis here is very much on friendly efficient service and various sporting activities such as fishing, golf and mountain biking can be arranged to suit guests' requirements. At the end of a day's exploring, the cosy restaurant provides the perfect setting in which to savour a varied menu of freshly prepared local produce, accompanied by a fine wine list and excellent range of ales and malt whiskies.

The Inverard Hotel, Lochard Road, Aberfoyle. 0877-2229
Map Ref: C4

At the northern edge of Loch Ard Forest is **Loch Katrine**, set right in the heart of the Trossachs. The loch is ten miles long and its name derives from gaelic 'Cateran' or Highland robber. Stronachlachar, which stands near head of the Loch, is accessible by road from Aberfoyle and gives unrivalled views of the loch and Ben Lomond. The loch lies in Clan MacGregor country and the Clan graveyard is still to

SS Sir Walter Scott, Loch Katrine

be found at the head of the loch, as is Glengyle House, birthplace of Rob Roy MacGregor who's adventures were immortalized by Sir Walter Scott. Indeed it was Scott's colourful description of this area that prompted the first tourist to venture into highland Scotland. So fittingly the Steamer on the loch is named after him.

The ship itself has an interesting history. She has been taking sightseers up and down the loch since 1900 and is the only remaining screw steamer in service in Scotland. Built on the Clyde, she was bought overland from Loch Lomond to Stronachlachar in kit form and ever since has provided leisurely pleasure cruises, to this day still using her original engines.

Following the road as it twists and turns through the hills and forest our journey arrives at **Callander**. Tucked midway between east and west coasts at the gateway to the beautiful Trossachs, it is an ideal base from which to explore the Scottish Highlands. The town is known world wide as 'Tannochbrae', made famous in the 1960's by the popular television series 'Dr. Finlay's Casebook.' Many readers will no doubt remember Arden House, the home of Drs Finlay and Cameron. Today it's a guest house that welcomes visitors from all over the world.

Situated on Station Road, **The Dreadnought Hotel** is an impressive establishment built during the 18th century by one of the chiefs of the Clan McNab and it gets its name from the clan's motto, meaning 'fear nothing'.

The Dreadnought Hotel, Station Road, Callander. 0877-30184
Map Ref: D4

Now owned by the North British Trust, this rather grand hotel carries a Three Crown Commended rating by the Scottish Tourist Board and provides very comfortable accommodation in spacious and well-equipped en-suite guest rooms. There are two private guest lounges which in addition to offering guests somewhere to relax in peace, can also be hired for private functions, as can the elegant McNab Restaurant. Here you can choose from an extensive and varied menu which caters for every palate, with the finest local produce prepared to the highest standards.

The **Bracklinn Falls** is a delightful bar and restaurant situated on the Main Street. Its relatively plain exterior belies the beautiful surroundings inside where beamed ceilings, soft lighting and attractive furnishings provide a lovely setting in which to savour the finest traditional Scottish cuisine. Amelia Melvin is a welcoming hostess who has developed The Bracklinn Falls into a first class restaurant where visitors can call in throughout the day for anything from a relaxing drink and a light snack, to a full three course dinner. Closed only on New Years Day, this really is a place for all seasons and is ideally situated for visitors exploring Callander and the picturesque surrounding countryside.

The Bracklinn Falls, 63 Main Street, Callander Tel: 0877-30622
Map Ref: D4

Callander is also home to the **Rob Roy and Trossachs Visitors Centre**. Here the visitor is taken back three centuries to rediscover the daring adventures of Scotland's most colourful folk hero and all about his wild and beautiful homeland.

There is a simply delightful holiday base on Tulipan Crescent at **Tulipan Lodge**, a large Victorian house built over 110 years ago. Originally built as the home for a local doctor, it was formerly known as Tulipan House and later changed its name, shortly after which the rest of the houses in the crescent sprang up. Present owners Bob and Sheena Lane insist on the personal touch and Bob prepares all the meals, buying fresh local produce each morning. Both he and Sheena pride themselves on the friendly, informal atmosphere which makes all their guests immediately feel at home. The excellent accommodation comprises five en-suite guest rooms, each with full facilities for maximum comfort and downstairs there is a large residents lounge and dining room. Awarded a Three Crown Commended rating, Tulipan Lodge is set back from the road and provides ample parking in private grounds.

Tulipan Lodge, Tulipan Crescent, Callander. 0877-330572
Map Ref: D4

Travelling out of town on the Stirling Road, you will come across the ideal stopping-off point at **Myrtle Inn**, a charming 18th century former couter's house.

Myrtle Inn, Stirling Road, Callander. 0877-30919 Map Ref: D4

Sympathetic refurbishment over the years has retained many original features including exposed stonework and a large old fireplace, re-discovered and now put to good use on those chilly autumn evenings. Jim and Eileen Davidson are warm, welcoming hosts who have built up a well-deserved reputation for their excellent restaurant and the inn is almost better known now for its food than its ale, although visitors can always enjoy a fine pint here. The restaurant menu is both extensive and varied, catering to the most discerning palate and making Myrtle Inn a popular place to eat with visitors and locals alike.

We continue north once more back on the A84, which leads up into the Strathyre Forest and along the beautiful shores of Loch Lubnaig. Strathyre itself has much to offer the visitor and has great charm and character. The surrounding countryside is enchanting, and was reputedly the inspiration behind Sir Walter Scott's 'The Lady of the Lake'.

A little distance from the head of the loch is a small road that leads to **Balquhidder**. Here, buried with his family, is Rob Roy MacGregor. In the kirk they lie, and their numerous visitors have included no less a personage as Queen Victoria. This Robin Hood of the North, born in 1660, was apparently a decently educated man who possessed a strong physique and a masterful ability with the sword. He set out to become a cattle dealer, but he lived in times of constant feuding and rivalry between clans. Faced with the poaching and pilfering rife around him, Rob Roy was forced to put together a band of men to protect his interests from other greedy landowners and landlords.

He was at one time an officer in the Pretender's army at the Battle of Sheriffmuir in 1715. Eventually the government set a price of one thousand pounds on his head, though he managed to escape capture and the scaffold. He spent ten years on the run and on at least one occasion, was caught and escaped from his captors, until he was eventually pardoned in 1727, and became a convert to Catholicism. He died peacefully in his bed in 1734.

Visitors to Balquhidder will find there are two very good reasons for seeking out **Stronvar House** which stands on the banks of Loch Voil. As well as being a superior country house hotel, it is also the home of **Bygones Museum & Balquhidder Visitor Centre**, a fascinating place where you can take a nostalgic journey back in time to yesteryear, with a varied collection of memorabilia beautifully laid out within this splendid Laird's mansion.

Guests staying at Stronvar House will find very comfortable accommodation provided in luxuriously furnished en-suite guest rooms, some with four poster beds and all offering spectacular countryside views. With the use of the private guests bar plus optional evening meals available, this really is a very special holiday base.

Stronvar House, Balquhidder. 0877-384688 Map Ref: C3

To the east of the main A84 at the head of Glen Ample lies Edinample Castle. Once a MacGregor stronghold, its present owner is in the process of restoring it to its 16th century appearance.

The A84 joins the A85 at **Lochearnhead** and heads for Crainlarich, passing through Glen Ogle. This is a wild glen, its heathery hillsides cut by lines of rocky cliffs. A five and a half mile trail along the glen starts in Lochearnhead and follows riverside and woodland paths and part of the old 18th century military road before turning back along the trackbed of the Callander to Oban railway, passing the huge rock fall that provided the excuse for closing the line in the Sixties.

Enjoying an enviable location on the banks of Loch Earn, it would be hard to equal the **Clachan Cottage Hotel's** idyllic surroundings.

Clachan Cottage Hotel, Lochside, Lochearnhead. 0567-830247
Map Ref: D2

Awarded a Three Crown Approved rating by the Scottish Tourist Board and Two Stars by the RAC, this charming hotel dates back some 300 years, when it was then a row of cottages. Sympathetic conversion and refurbishment has created a 21-bedroom hotel of character where locals and visitors mix easily in a warm, relaxed atmosphere. The restaurant has been awarded 'The Taste of Scotland' and offers the finest Scottish cuisine in a daily changing table d'hôte menu and after dinner you can relax in the friendly ambience of the lounge bar with one of the excellent range of malt whiskies.

As mentioned at the end of Chapter Five there is only one place that seems to feature on more signposts than Kincardine Bridge, way back on the Forth, and that is the tiny community of **Crianlarich**. The railway once followed our self same route and Doune, Strathyre and Balquhidder all had stations, now no more. Though the Caledonian Railway route is gone, Crianlarich still has a station, and is the junction on the West Highland line where the routes to Fort William and Oban separate.

Peaceful and remote, Crianlarich is on the famous West Highland Way walking route from Glasgow to Fort William, and as such makes an ideal base for those wishing to explore the beautiful West Highlands of Scotland. There is an abundance of wildlife, and deer roam the surrounding hills; eagles and other rare birds have also been spotted.

To the south is Glen Falloch and the **Falls of Falloch**. A picnic site marks the start of a short footpath to the hidden and impressive falls where the River Falloch, striking of jagged ledges, plunges into a dark shadowy pool. Originally a cattle drovers route, the road through the glen was improved as part of the pacification of the Highlands following the '45 Jacobite rising. As late as 1845 there was a battle here of sorts when workers from rival railway companies set about one another, though it would be another 49 years before the North British Railway would open the route.

A few miles to the north of Crianlarich is the small village of **Tyndrum**. The surrounding area was aptly described, in 1876, by Queen Victoria as being set in a "wild, rugged, picturesque glen surrounded by high rugged mountains". The name Tyndrum itself comes from the phrase, 'tigh an droma', which translates as 'the house on the ridge'. Small though it may be the village boasts two stations, Upper and Lower. The two lines from Crainlarich having to share the same valley as the road, only diverging beyond the village. Tyndrum is as far as we come west in this chapter but we shall be back near here later.

If we had not followed the A85 all the way from Lochearnhead we could have turned right after five miles towards Loch Tay on the A827.

At **Killin** however, you'll discover a quiet village which the enchanting Falls of Dochart rush through the centre of. On the Island of Inchbuie on the river is the burial ground of the Clan MacNabb. Nearby, are the ruins of Finlarig Castle , which was a Campbell seat associated with the notorious Black Duncan, whose beheading pit can still be seen here.

Enjoying an idyllic setting beside the Falls on the edge the village, **The Clachaig** is a small family-run hotel, ideal for a peaceful, relaxing break away from it all. Sympathetically refurbished over the years, this charming 200 year old listed building has lost none of its original character and guests will find a warm welcome awaits them from friendly hosts John and Maureen Mullinson. There are nine attractively furnished en-suite guest rooms and the candlelit restaurant provides the perfect setting in which to savour freshly prepared traditional Scottish fare for which the hotel is Egon Ronay and Les Routiers Recommended. After dinner, the cosy bar is the perfect place to enjoy a 'wee dram' and trade fishing or golfing stories with your fellow guests. With beautiful countryside offering a wealth of walks plus abundant fishing, golf and even shooting available, your holiday break is complete.

The Clachaig Hotel, Falls of Dochart, Killin.   0567-2270
Map Ref: D2

Standing in its own beautiful grounds on the banks of the River Lochay in the village, the **Dall Lodge Hotel** makes an ideal holiday base. Sporting activities are readily catered for here, with walking, fishing, golf, pony trekking and a wide range of water sports all easily arranged. However, should you just wish to relax, Dall Lodge is ideal for that too. The twelve beautifully furnished guest rooms are designed with comfort in mind and one is converted for use by disabled guests.

The dining room offers the finest Scottish cuisine traditionally prepared to the highest standards and after dinner, what could be nicer than to relax with a drink in the peaceful conservatory. You will also find an excellent place to call in for snacks and pick up a holiday memento at the nearby Shutters Restaurant which is owned by Lesley Kettle, Dall Lodge Hotel's friendly manageress.

Dall Lodge Hotel, Main Street, Killin. 0567-820217 Map Ref: D2

The towering form of **Ben Lawers**, some three thousand nine hundred and eighty four feet above sea level, provides an impressive sight from here. Ben Lawers has long held a reputation as a botanical paradise and, if you have the energy to climb to its summit, there are magnificent views stretching from the east coast to the west. The National Trust has issued a guide book, but be warned as there is a sign warning against the removal of any plants.

Strictly speaking the mountain lies in Tayside and so the next chapter but it seemed appropriate to finish the Central Region on a high note.

Pipe Major

CHAPTER EIGHT

Tayside.

RRS Discovery

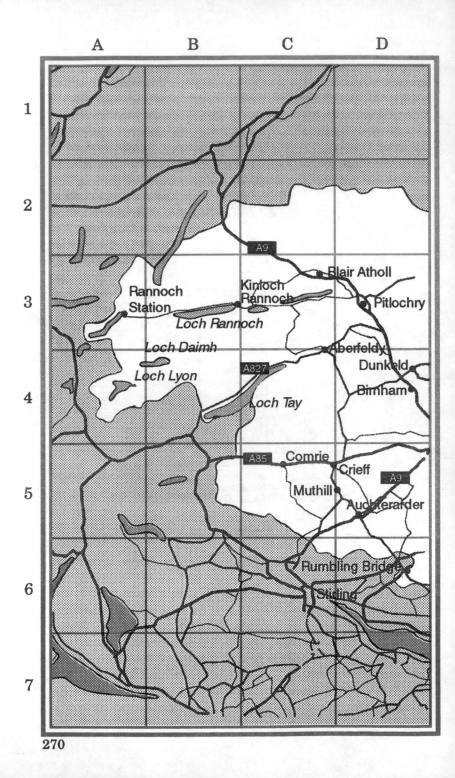

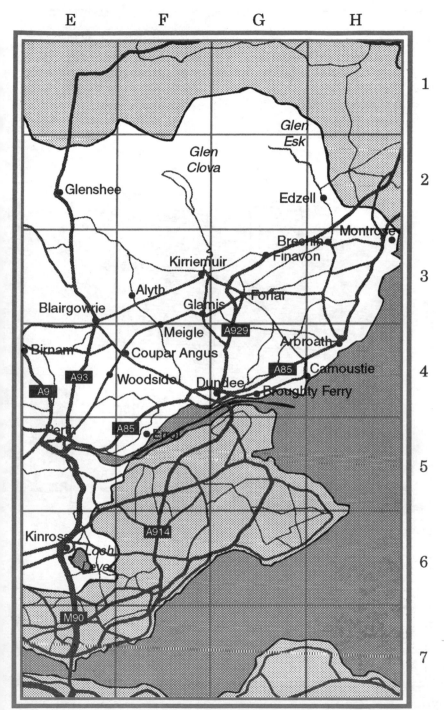

Claypotts Castle, Broughty Ferry

CHAPTER EIGHT

Tayside.

We have already paid a visit to **Dollar** in the previous chapter, and it is near here that we start our journey around Tayside.

Just east of Dollar is **Rumbling Bridge**, where the River Devon falls through a ravine spanned by three bridges. A footpath from the north side gives good access to the spectacular gorges and falls, one of which is known as the Devil's Mill. Another, Cauldron Linn, is a mile downstream, with Vicar's Bridge, a beauty spot, a mile beyond this. The village's unusual name comes from the sound the river makes beneath the bridges.

The A977 takes us across to **Kinross** on the west side of Loch Leven. Just before you enter the town, adjacent to the motorway roundabout and services. is a fascinating selection of attractions clustered together. **Kin-kraft** was started by six local enthusiasts in 1990 and now has evolved into a major showcase for a huge range of crafts created all over Scotland. There are regular demonstrations of the various crafts and of course the opportunity to buy most of the wares on display.

Findlay Clark Tropical Butterfly House is one of the largest butterfly farms in the country. As British summers sadly seem to bring fewer and fewer butterflies this is a perfect antidote. Numerous tropical varieties of every size, colour and hue glide gracefully around the palms and pools. Next door to the butterflies are natures equivalent of the jet fighter - birds of prey. At the **Scottish Centre for Falconry** these elusive and magnificent creatures can be watched at really close quarters. At regular intervals displays of falconry take place, and members of the public are encouraged to join in. The Hawk Walk gives unrestricted views of the birds that the whole of Scotland once teemed with. The Centre is involved in special breeding projects and, thanks to closed circuit TV, visitors can see chicks being fed by their parents. Budding falconers might also like to ask about the expert tuition available. There is also a garden centre, golf shop and cafe on the site, so there is something for everyone.

In the Kinross town centre there is an interesting tolbooth that dates back to the 16th century and that was restored in 1771 by Robert Adam. Kinross House has a fine Renaissance exterior and was built for Daniel Defoe between 1685 and 1690. The gardens of the house are most interesting and are open from May to September.

There is also a museum in the town that gave us an interesting insight into the history of the town and the loch, with its famous castle. **Loch Leven** was where Mary Queen of Scots was kept prisoner during 1567, until her daring escape eleven months later in 1568. With help from the gaoler's son she locked her guards in the castle and made away in a boat, throwing the castle keys into the loch. The accidental discovery of a bunch of keys in the lock 300 years later would seem to confirm the story. A boat from Kinross takes visitors to the island and castle. Mary was held in the small round tower which is separate from the main keep.

The Loch Leven National Nature Reserve is the most important area for freshwater breeding and migratory wildfowl in Britain. In the winter months the loch is a favourite breeding ground for wild geese, ducks and other wild fowl.

Travel down to the south of the loch and you will have the chance to observe and even partake in one of the most exhilarating of all activities, gliding. At Portmoak Airfield in Scotlandwell visitors are welcome to view the gliding, and if inclined, to be taken for a trial instructional flight.

North of Kinross situated on the B996 two miles south of Glenfarg, you will discover a delightful holiday base at **Cuthill Towers**, the welcoming home of Susan and Arthur Lawrie.

Cuthill Towers, Milnathort, Kinross 0577-830221 Map Ref: E6

This somewhat eccentric looking property forms part of a 350 acre working farm. The impressive entrance porch with its thick stone pillars is guarded by a stone lion lying above it and at one end of the house there is a tall ornately detailed tower. Despite its unique

274

appearance, there is nothing unusual within, where a warm, homely atmosphere pervades throughout. There are three comfortable guest rooms and the dining room with its display of cups for prize-winning Ayrshire cattle provides the setting for a full farmhouse breakfast each morning.

Our route west from Kinross passes the massive white 'golf ball' of a radio communications station on the wartime Balado airfield before following the A91 along the foothills of the Ochils. Then it turns north on to the A823, which cuts across these rounded and often forested hills. Along the narrow Glens of Devon and Eagle the road follows the line of an old cattle drovers route, down which herds from the Highlands were walked to the great livestock markets of Falkirk.

However you choose to arrive in **Auchterarder** the journey is scenic. The town has a wealth of delightful antique shops, and the Great Scots Visitors Centre. As well as featuring weaving displays and the last steam-driven factory engine in Scotland the centre has 'Great Scots'. This is the history of Scotland told using a huge map and computerized lighting effects. There is also the worlds only Barrs Irn Bru bar, which for the uninitiated is a soft drink, as well as a millshop. A little to the south of the town is Gleneagles Hotel; built by the London Midland and Scottish Railway after the Great War, which would explain why it has its own station whose platform has a telephone connected directly to the hotel. Gleneagles is of course world famous for its King's and Queen's golf courses, owned by the hotel and scene of some of the top events in the golfing calendar.

It rarely pays to be in a rush when you're exploring and with this in mind our travels wend their way northwards to **Muthill**. Though only small the village contains some lovely examples of buildings from the mid-1700's; non survive from earlier times as the Earl of Mar burnt the all houses to the ground after the failure of the 1715 Jacobite rising. Only the old Parish Church survived, though it too is now a ruin, worshipping having finished in about 1818. Parts of it date as far back as the early 12th century and the graveyard features some rather startling headstones that feature skulls and crossed bones, hour glass and the words 'Tempus Fugit'. Near the village is Drummond Castle and its Italian style gardens. These are the largest formal gardens in Scotland and were first laid out in 1630 by the John Drummond, 2nd Earl of Perth. In around 1830 the ornamental area was Italianised and embellished with many fine figures and statues from Italy. The centre piece must be John Mylne's obelisk-type sundial, a feature retained from the original layout. These spectacular gardens are open from 2pm to 6pm between 1st May and 30th September and should undoubtedly be on the garden enthusiasts itinerary.

Rather that head straight into nearby Crieff from Muthill we take to the unclassified roads west to find **Comrie** and **Loch Earn**. Comrie is a pretty little village with the odd nick name of The Shaky Toun, due to the number of tremors the village has felt, sitting as it does atop the Highland Boundary Fault. Records go back some 400 years and to this day movement is recorded at the Earthquake House. This was built in 1869 and had its first seismometer installed in 1874; recently restored its instruments are now sensitive enough to detect earthquakes world-wide. Though the building isn't open to the public it can be viewed through the door and windows and there's plenty of information on panels on the outside walls.

The village is also home to the **Museum of Scottish Tartans** in Drummond Street, which houses the largest collection of material relating to tartans and Highland dress in existence. The Tartan Room has over 450 different examples and there is a history of Highland dress exhibition. Incidentally following the failure of Bonnie Prince Charlie's Jacobite rebellion of 1745 the kilt was banned and the bagpipes outlawed as an offensive weapon.

Comrie's other great attraction is the **Auchingarrich Wildlife Centre**. Set in 100 acres of beautiful Perthshire hill country it has a whole host of running, flying, swimming, burrowing, grunting and squawking animals and birds. In addition there is a unique wild bird hatchery, rural museum and antique farm machinery display and a spectacular 600ft viewpoint. Then there's Rosie the pig - all 47 stone of her! All in all a full day out for everyone.

Fishermen amongst you will find a visit to **Drummond Fish Farm** a real treat. In addition to being able to see and feed the thousands of trout on the farm you can indulge your passion amongst the specially created complex of ponds. There is a pond set aside for children and all you'll need can be hired on site. No need to go back empty handed either the farm shop has fresh and frozen trout; as well as other quality Highland salmon, venison and pheasant.

Westwards from Comrie is Loch Earn, it was here at Ardvorlich on the southside, that Rob Roy's family, the MacGregors, reputedly beheaded a forester of the king's against whom they had a grievance, and presented his head on a plate, with a crust of bread between his teeth, to his sister.

Eastwards is **Crieff**, a charming place, popular with visitors who's town signs proclaim it to be 'The Holiday Town'. The Visitors Centre is certainly welcoming and gives you the opportunity to tour two fascinating factories, Thistles Pottery and Perthshire Paperweights, to discover the secrets of hand throwing pottery and blowing glass. There is also a factory shop, well stocked garden centre and restaurant, which offers Taste of Scotland specialities. Right across the road from the Centre is Stuart Crystal's Strathern Glassworks. Here you can see the skills involved in the decoration of full lead crystal wear. There is a museum display with glassmaking video, coffee shop and the opportunity to have your purchase personally engraved.

Probably one of Scotland's best known hotels, the **Crieff Hydro Hotel** is a magnificent example of Victorian architecture at its best and offers the discerning guest the perfect combination of old-fashioned Scottish hospitality and service, with up-to-the-minute facilities ensuring a complete and relaxing holiday. Awarded a Four Crown Commended grading by the Scottish Tourist Board and a member of Consort, a consortium of select hotels, guests at Crieff Hydro know the quality of facilities they can expect. Accommodation comes in various forms ranging from standard rooms to honeymoon suites and for those who prefer greater independence, wooden chalets tucked away on the wooded hillside to the rear of the hotel. Whichever you choose, the furnishings and facilities are exactly as you would expect of a hotel of this calibre.

Crieff Hydro Hotel, Crieff. 0764-655555 Map Ref: C5

The high point of a holiday here, however, is probably the outstanding leisure complex and full range of outdoor and indoor activities available, leaving guests spoilt for choice as to what to do next. The Lagoon Pool Leisure Complex caters for visitors of all ages and abilities, with a separate children's pool for younger family members, plus a children's chute and for the more accomplished swimmer a 20-metre heated pool. In addition, there is a spa bath, sauna, fitness centre and steam room, complete with refreshment area to relax in after your 'workout'. The hotel's sports hall is equally well-equipped offering almost every indoor sport you can think of and outdoors, the new golfing centre is proving another major attraction. With horse riding, tennis, an all weather bowling green, croquet, football and even a children's adventure playground, not to mention a range of indoor entertainment including a 96-seater cinema, the Crieff Hydro really does cater for every guest's holiday needs.

Scotland's oldest distillery is here in Crieff, **Glenturret** was established 1775 and to this day its selection of single malt whisky are award winners. There are guided tours, a visitors centre with displays and exhibitions telling the story of Glenturret and whisky, and two excellent restaurants, plus of course a whisky tasting bar. Those of you with a taste for something sweeter might like to find your way to West High Street and Gordon and Durward's, where you can watch traditional confectionery being made and pick up the odd quarter of something.

Visitors to this historic town will discover a super holiday base at **Murraypark Hotel**, a Four Crowns Commended establishment where the warmth of the welcome is only surpassed by the superb accommodation and fine cuisine. Noel and Ann Scott are friendly hosts who developed Murraypark into a first class hotel which proves popular with visitors and locals alike. Renowned for its imaginative and varied menu, the elegant candlelit dining room provides the perfect setting in which to savour the finest local produce, including fresh fish and game when in season, and after dinner, what can be nicer than relaxing with a 'wee dram' in front of a roaring log fire before retiring to one of the 21 beautifully furnished en-suite guest rooms.

Murraypark Hotel, Connaught Terrace, Crieff. 0764-653731
Fax: 0764-655311 Map Ref: C5

The A822 north from the town runs through Sma' Glen, where in a few miles you get a taste of all the scenic attributes the Highlands can offer. The narrow glen has towering hills awash with purple heather, with the River Almond gushing along the valley floor. This was once a strategic route from the Lowlands to the Highlands, know as far back as Roman times. General Wade chose Sma' Glen as one of the routes for his military roads, designed to allow quick access for the King's army if the Highlanders should rise again. Ironically Bonnie Prince Charlie's 1745 campaign made fullest use of it during his advance and retreat.

The next town, **Aberfeldy**, will always be associated with a new era in the Highlands that began with the formation of the Black Watch. It was on this spot on the Tay in 1739, that the first of these regiments was incorporated into the British army, in an attempt to bring into line and control the warring factions and clans of the Highlands. The name Black Watch came about as the tartans worn by the men were darker in contrast with the red coats of the regular army. A memorial to the regiment was erected in Queen Victoria's Jubilee Year of 1887. The large cairn topped by a kilted soldier stands alongside General Wade's bridge over the Tay, which lies just north of the town on the B846. Built in 1733 this bridge is considered his finest, being designed by William Adam, who's work is found all over Scotland.

This area has strong connections with General Wade, who stayed in Weem Inn whilst he was directing the building of the bridge. Wade was sent to Scotland originally to assess what measures were necessary to subdue the rebellious Highlanders, and his reports culminated in his appointment as Commander-in-Chief in Scotland. Whilst in office, he directed the construction of military roads, bringing the north and west of Scotland within easy reach of those south of the border. Wade eventually died in 1748, and has the fourth verse of the National Anthem dedicated to his honour.

Weem Inn, or Hotel as it is now, still stands on the B846. The history of the hotel is fascinating. Part of the building dates back to the 16th century, a time when it offered the guest a rather less comfortable nights stay, which, depending on your ability to pay, might have ranged from a heap of heather or straw to a straw mattress, with a blanket and pillow being extra. It was also the watering place of the Clan Menzies, with their ancestral home next door, who came here to drink the home-made whisky and ales. **Castle Menzies** itself is a fine example of a Z- plan castle, called so because they featured two diagonally opposite towers to cover the buildings four walls.

This was the Menzies third home, the first at Comrie and earliest one on this site having been destroyed. The family line died out in 1918 and was eventually rescued from advanced decay by the Clan Menzies Society, who are slowly restoring it to former glories.

To the east of the town along the A827 is the hamlet of Grandtully and at Pitcairn Farm, St. Mary's Church. This 16th century church has a stunning painted wooden ceiling that depicts heraldic and symbolic subjects. The church is kept locked and the key is kept at the farm but available at any reasonable time.

From Aberfeldy it is a short drive to **Loch Tay** and Ben Lawers, which we visited in the last chapter. At **Fortingall** on an unclassified road to the north of the loch is the Fortingall Yew. This great tree stands in the churchyard and is claimed to be 3000 years old, and so the oldest in Europe. The village is also claimed to be the birth place of Pontius Pilate - born here during the Roman occupation. He was sent to Rome as a boy slave and rose to become Governor of Judea in AD 26. There are even suggestions that on his downfall he returned here to die. Today the village itself is very pretty having been rebuilt in 1900 with many thatched houses.

Our journey however now takes us north to **Kinloch Rannoch**, at the head of Loch Rannoch. The roads either side of the loch take you eventually to Rannoch Station on the West Highland Line but no further - it is a dead end that looks out over wastes of **Rannoch Moor**. This is a remote land with signs of human habitation few and far between, the station was originally built to service a few shooting lodges set here high in the Grampian mountains, though it does now have a hotel. For all its isolation there is much beauty here and it is well worth taking the round trip up and down the loch for the scenery is stunning.

From Kinloch Rannoch we take the road through Glen Errochty to join the A9 at Calvine. It is worth pausing here to take in the **Falls of Bruar**. There are three sets of which the upper is most impressive and altogether they drop over two hundred feet. When Robert Burns saw the falls he remarked they were missing something. So he asked the Duke of Atholl, a great arboriculturalist, to clothe the banks in trees to complete the picture. The Duke obliged Burns and now the waters cascade through pinewoods, with paths and bridges giving great views. Back on the main road is Clan Donnachaidh Museum. The Clan comprised of the Reid, Robertson, MacConnachie, Duncan and MacInroy families and their story is told here.

It is less than five miles south now to **Blair Atholl** and its celebrated castle. Blair is a white turretted baronial mansion and the seat of the Duke of Atholl, chief of Clan Murray. The oldest section, the Cumming's Tower dates from around 1269 but most of what we see was restored in 1869. It has had amongst its famous visitors Mary Queen of Scots and Queen Victoria. The castle was renowned for its generosity in the

Blair Castle, Blair Atholl

entertainment of its visitors, and there is an account of Mary's visit in 1564 when two thousand clansmen were employed to drive the game from the surrounding area. The final bag included 360 deer and five wolves. This gave Blair a reputation as one of the finest hunting chateaux in Europe. It also has the distinction of being the last stronghold in Britain to be besieged, in 1746, when forces loyal to Bonnie Prince Charlie attempted to capture it. The Duke is the only British subject allowed to maintain a private army, the Atholl Highlanders. The castle today has many fascinating collections of furniture, portraits, china, arms, armour, as well as some exceptional Rococo style plaster ceilings. It also has extensive facilities, parklands, pony trekking and an excellent caravan park - and a piper plays outside the castle on most days!

Almost next door to the castle is **Atholl Country Collection**, a unique little folk museum that is a real slice of Highland rural life. As well as a smiddy, crofter's stable and byre, there are displays of flax growing and spinning, once the main economy of the district. No one gets left out with road, rail and postal services, the school, the kirk, vet and gamekeeper all featured.

Blair Atholl village, which provided the setting for TV's 'Strathblair', has its own little piece of history in the The Mill. Built in 1613 this water mill still produces traditional oatmeal and flour which can be bought in the shop, or sampled straight away in the tearoom.

Less than four miles south is **The Pass of Killiecrankie** and Soldiers Leap, the famous wooded gorge where in 1689 Government troops were routed by Jacobite forces led by 'Bonnie' Viscount Dundee, who met his end in the action. Though the force was later stopped it was difficult to contain the Highlanders and the trouble that this caused ultimately led to the massacre at Glencoe four years later. Soldiers Leap was so named after Donald MacBean made his death defying leap across the gorge to evade his Highland pursuers.

Pitlochry is minutes travel from Killiecrankie and has been described as the "jewel in Perthshire's crown", and it certainly is set amidst some magnificent scenery with plenty of first class accommodation and a wide range of activities. There are two distilleries here that, if you are fond of a tot, you may like to find out more about, one reputedly the smallest distillery in the world. Edradour has been making whisky since 1825, but it wasn't until 1986 that the proprietors decided that the old place was worthy of greater recognition and set up the visitor centre. Come along to see the production process and take away a sample of their wares. The other distillery is the Blair Atholl Distillery, owned and managed by Arthur Bell & Sons plc. This is production at the other end of the scale and there is a tour to help you understand the distillery process. There is also a shop here with a wide range of single malts and blended whiskies for sale. Afterwards there's the opportunity to relax over a cup of coffee.

Set in three and a half acres of grounds on Dunfallandy Road just outside Pitlochry, **Dunfallandy House** is an impressive Georgian mansion which offers a secluded setting for a relaxing break away from it all. Originally built in 1790 for General Archibald Fergusson, careful and sympathetic refurbishment has created a superb country house hotel, well-deserving of its Three Crown Highly Commended rating. Retaining many of its original features, it is full of character yet provides every modern facility for maximum comfort. Dining is a treat, with a superb dinner menu offering a mouthwatering selection to tempt the most discerning palate, accompanied by an extensive wine list. Afterwards, what could be nicer than retiring to one of the beautifully furnished, individually designed en-suite bedrooms for a refreshing night's sleep.

Dunfallandy House, Logierait Road, Pitlochry. 0796-472648
Map Ref: D3

One of Pitlochry's major attractions is the Salmon Ladder, at the hydro-electric power station on Loch Faskally, five minutes from the town centre. Here there is an observation chamber for visitors to watch the salmon by-passing the dam by a series of connecting pools. This is quite a feat, and the fish can be seen gathering their strength for a final push up into Loch Faskally. Best seen in May and June during the spring run and again in September, although fish can be seen most of the summer.

Set in beautiful grounds overlooking Loch Faskally, the **Green Park Hotel** has been owned by the Brown family for over thirty years. The Hotel is located at the north end of the town, within easy walking distance of the centre. The world renowned Festival Theatre and the fascinating Salmon leap are both just a stroll around the loch. There are numerous golf courses in the area; together with lots of other activities, from Quad-biking to walking. Beautiful scenery abounds whatever pursuit you choose. The Hotel provides putting, table tennis, and sailing or windsurfing for the more adventurous.

During fine weather teas, coffees, lunches and pre-dinner drinks are served on the front lawn, allowing you to relax and enjoy the sunshine in wonderful surroundings. The Hotel is open to non-residents for all meals and Graham and Anne Brown , together with their staff, look forward to welcoming you.

Green Park Hotel, Clunie Bridge,Road, Pitlochry. 0796-473248
Map Ref: D3

The **Pitlochry Festival Theatre** is set on the banks of the River Tummell and offers entertainment throughout the summer which is of a very high standard. Their resident repertory company proclaims visitors 'may stay six days and see seven plays'. It makes sense to have a look at the programme and book ahead if possible.

For that relaxing break away from it all, where comfort and a cosy, welcoming atmosphere are all important, look no further than **Rosemount Hotel**, which is situated above the town of Pitlochry in Higher Oakfield. Originally built as a private residence, this attractive stone-built country house is owned and run by Keith and Anne Urry whose hard efforts have created a super hotel where the warmth of the welcome is equalled only by the excellent facilities. The 21 guest rooms are all en-suite and equipped to a standard commensurate with the hotel's Three Crown Commended status. Freshly prepared local produce forms the basis for the bar and restaurant menus and you can always make use of the gymnasium and sauna to work off a few calories.

Rosemount Hotel, 12 Higher Oakfield, Pitlochry. 0796-472302
Fax: 0796-474216 Map Ref: D3

Dunkeld is some 12 miles to the south of Pitlochry and no one would suspect from the appearance of this charming little town that it possessed such a turbulent history. In fact, Dunkeld became the religious centre of Scotland in the 9th century, and before that was the ancient capital of Caledonia (the name itself means 'fort of the Caledonians').

This small town was the home of kings and the site of at least one bloody battle in the 17th century when, after the Battle of Killicrankie, a raw regiment of Cameronians were ordered to hold the town against the Jacobites. As the rebellious army advanced, they did great damage to the town, causing the Cameronians to retreat to the cathedral and Dunkeld House. Here, running out of ammunition, they were forced to rip the lead from the mansion's roof in desperation. Somehow they succeeded in driving the Jacobites off and even pursued them, singing hymns as they went. Many years prior to this the Vikings attacked the town. They managed to do this by bringing with them a number of small horses aboard their ships, which enabled them to invade further inland than was previously possible. On at least one occasion, they were successful, and managed to capture and devastate Dunkeld.

Today Dunkeld is a little more tolerant of her visitors and this very attractive town has lots to offer the visitor. In a building that once was the City Hall is a unique business, **The Highland Horn and Deerskin Centre**. They make and sell a range of things in deerskin and horn that cannot be obtained anywhere else in the world. The Little

Cottages project in the town centre, completed by the National Trust, has restored the cottages of Cathedral Street providing us with a glimpse of a highland town as it would have been two hundred years ago. Close to the picturesque River Tay, is the cathedral, set in lovely grounds. Refounded in the 12th century on an ancient ecclesiastical site, much of the ruins dating from the 15th century. Only the choir is intact and is still used as parish church. Further along the Tay, is one of Thomas Telford's finest bridges, built in 1809. A riverside path leads from here downstream to the famous Birnam Oak, which is the sole remainder of Macbeth's Birnam Beeches.

To the west of the town lies a pleasant one and a half mile wooded walk along the river Braan to The Hermitage, a folly built in 1758 and restored in 1986. Nearby is **Birnam**, Dunkeld's close neighbour and the inspiration for Beatrix Potter's popular tales. She came here for holidays as a child and one picture-letter she sent to a friend later developed into 'The Tale of Peter Rabbit'. Her timeless characters are celebrated in the Beatrix Potter Garden, where sculptures of Peter Rabbit and his friends can be enjoyed by fans young and old.

Perth, the 'fair city', has a proud historical tradition - it was once Capital of Scotland - that has left it with a legacy of fascinating places to visit. The area was first settled over 8000 years ago, and succeeding waves of Roman Centurions, Pictish peoples and Celtic missionaries established themselves here. They all enjoyed the favourable climate, fertile farmlands and an ideal defensive and trading location at the edge of the Highlands. Though few relics of the distant past survived the centuries, Perth's natural advantages remained, and helped the town to become a thriving commercial, religious and cultural centre by the middle ages.

Perth's rise to pre-eminence was also largely due to Kenneth MacAlpine, who in 838 AD became the first King of a united Scotland. He bought to nearby Scone the legendary Stone of Destiny, and many coronations took place atop this mystical symbol. A great abbey grew up on the site, and, even after Edward 1 of England stole the sacred Stone in 1296, Scone (pronounced Scoon) remained at the centre of royal life.

Helped by royal and religious patronage Perth prospered. Its position on the navigable River Tay enabled the the town to become an important trading port, and it has retained its busy harbour to this day. Salmon, wool and other agricultural products are exported, with claret from Bordeaux a major import. Perth also established itself as a cattle trading centre, perfectly situated on the drovers route from the north and its Bull Sales are still internationally renowned. By the 16th century another of the towns products had begun to take city's name around the world - Whisky. Today Bell's, Dewar's and Famous Grouse continue to distil their fiery elixirs here. Reminders of medieval times are plentiful. In the city centre stands the striking **St. John's Kirk**, founded in 1126 and now largely restored. Perth was known for a time as St. John's Toun, and it was from the kirk that John Knox preached the inflammatory sermon which sparked the Reformation's wholesale destruction of monastries and churches, amongst them Scone. The church was restored in 1923 as a memorial to the fallen of the Great War.

One of the best ways to explore any town centre is on foot and the **Old Perth Trail** - leaflet available from Tourist Information Centre on the High Street - is a great guide. Everywhere plaques and memorials commemorate historic events, famous visitors and notable residents; with street names such as Ropemaker Close, Horners Lane and Glover Street giving clues to the towns medieval trades. The narrow Cow Vennel was a route taken by livestock being herded to the common grazing meadows which bordered the town centre. Those parklands survive today as the North and South Inch, and are overlooked by elegant Georgian Terraces.

The North Inch was the scene of the infamous Battle of the Clans in 1396. Scores of men from the Chatten and Kay Clans were slaughtered when King Robert III attempted unsuccessfully to put an end to the feuding between Highlanders. The Battle forms the backdrop to Sir Walter Scott's novel 'The Fair Maid of Perth', which in turn inspired Bizet's opera of the same name. Nearby, one of Perth's oldest buildings, now a craft shop is known as the **Fair Maids House**.

Incidentally the Old Council Chambers on the High Street feature a wonderful Fair Maid stained glass window, together with other Scott characters, Victoria and Albert and Robert the Bruce. The building occupies a site that has for centuries been the hub of civic and judicial life in the city, though the present building dates from 1896. It is still used by the Leisure and Recreation Department, but visitors are welcome to this most fascinating of hidden places. Also adjacent to the North Inch is Balhousie Castle, home to the **Black Watch Museum**, which tells the story of Perthshire's famous Royal Highland Regiment.

The Fergusson Gallery in Marshall Square, near the South Inch, is a must for art lovers. Housed in Perth's first ever water works - now a grade A listed building - it is the largest single collection of the works by Scotland's foremost colourist John Duncan Fergusson.

At the northern edge of the town, the Caithness Glass Factory and Visitors Centre, famous for its paperweights, shows the skills of glassmakers at work. Tours of Dewar's Whisky Bottling Plant are always popular, while those wishing to discover more about the area's rich agricultural heritage can visit the the auction market or see the magnificent Clydesdales at the Fairways Heavy Horse Centre.

There is plenty to discover within easy striking distance of the city. To the west alongside the A85 stands the impressive **Huntingtower Castle**, formerly known as Ruthven Castle. This splendid place is a 15th century mansion that was the scene of the raid of Ruthven in 1583, when James VI found himself captive at the hands of his nobles who demanded the removal of certain royal favourites. The King tried to escape (he was 16 at the time) but found his way barred and was kept virtual prisoner for ten months, being forced to sign proclamations declaring himself a free agent. The nobles managed to hold on to some power for a few months, though the Earl of Gowrie (Lord Ruthven), who had originally invited the King to his hunting seat, was eventually beheaded in 1585. James waited a full eighteen years to take revenge on the remainder of the family, and the Earl's grandson and his brother were killed in mysterious circumstances, their dead bodies tried for treason and their estates forfeited to the Crown. The name of Ruthven was abolished by an Act of Parliament, and the castle's name changed to Huntingtower. The castle has some fine painted ceilings, murals and plasterwork, as well as unusual decorative beams in the Hall.

If you enjoy walking there is plenty to see within minutes of the city centre at **Kinnoull Hill Woodland Park**, and the adjoining Binn and Deuchny Hills. The well marked wooded walks on Kinnoull lead you to the summit and fantastic views that stretch across the city, the Tay estuary and over the rolling Fife countryside to the Lomond Hills. Looking north the views extend over the Highlands from Ben More in the west to Lochnagar amongst the Cairngorms in the north east.

Out to the east is **Elcho Castle**, the handsome fortified mansion of the Wemyss family, looking out from the north bank of the Tay. Built with comfort as well as defence in mind the castle has a profusion of round and square towers and still retains the original iron grills protecting the windows. A little further east, in the village of **Errol**, The Errol Railway Heritage Centre celebrates the golden age of the train. The station recreates a typical 1920's style Scottish country station with plenty of railway artifacts and a slide show. Only open on Sundays between May and September it is worth finding for nostalgia and railway buffs alike. Close to Errol village is **Megginch Castle Gardens**. The grounds around the 15th century castle have 1000 year old yews and feature a walled kitchen garden, 16th century rose garden and 19th century sunken garden, as well as a gothic courtyard with a pagoda-roofed dovecote. There is also a topiary with a golden yew crown. Opening times through the year vary so it is advisable to call 0821- 222 to avoid disappointment.

For country lovers who enjoy a real 'house party' atmosphere, **Waterybutts Lodge** in nearby Grange is a real haven. Originally built during the 15th century as a friary attached to the Abbey at Coupar Angus, this rather grand house stands in beautifully laid out grounds with a splendid herb garden. The seven guest rooms are all en-suite and furnished to a standard commensurate with the Lodge's Three Crown Highly Commended rating. Rachel and Barry Allenby-Wilcox are friendly, welcoming hosts and dining is a treat, with guests joining together around a magnificent 16' Charles I refectory table to savour superb cuisine in true dinner party style. With the choice of chauffeur driven limousines or pony and trap transport, not to mention a wealth of country activities available, this is definitely a holiday base for the discerning guest.

Waterybutts Lodge, Grange, by Errol. 0821-642 894 Map Ref: F5

Northwards on the A93 is **Scone Palace**, the crowning place of all the Scottish kings from 843 until 1296. The coronations were performed upon the Stone of Scone, which originally came from the western isle of Iona. It was stolen in 1296 and taken to Westminster Abbey where it still is, or should be. In 1951 a group of patriot Scots removed the stone and took it to Arbroath Abbey. In due course it was returned but many believe that a copy was made by a local stonemason and the stone that sits beneath the Coronation Chair in Westminster is fake. The palace we can explore today was built in 1803 and incorporates the 16th century and earlier palaces. It contains a magnificent collection of porcelain, furniture, ivories, 18th century clocks and 16th century needlework, home to the family of the Earl of Mansfield it is open to the public everyday between Easter and October.

Scone is on the road to **Blairgowrie**, our next destination. On the approach to the town stands the unique Meikleour Beech Hedge. Planted in 1746, the hedge is now over 650 yards long and nearly 100ft tall and has earned a place in the Guinness Book of Records. Blairgowrie, Gaelic for 'field of goats', sits, with its sister community of Rattray, astride the fast flowing River Ericht, which is famed for its salmon. 'Blair' as it is known locally is situated in the heart of fruit growing and farming countryside. The altitude and soil seem to combine to give just the right growing conditions for what are described as the raspberries to match any other. These raspberries are largely picked for the jam factories of Dundee.

In the centre of the town is **Keathbank Mill**. Visitors here can gaze in wonder at the huge 1862 mill steam engine, admire Scotland's largest waterwheel, enjoy watching the trains on what is thought to be Britain's largest model railway and discover all about the ancient art of heraldry.

There is a first class recreational centre in Blairgowrie with many facilities including a swimming pool, games hall, gymnasium and sunroom. There are also excellent walks in the vicinity, spring time brings the valley into true beauty, and the wildlife reserve at Loch of the Lowes welcomes many migratory visitors, including ospreys. Summer is packed with events, including Highland games and sheepdog trials. Then of course there is the legendary fruit picking that is available in the autumn months. The autumnal colours are quite unforgettable on the heather-clad hills, and in the winter Blairgowrie comes alive as sports enthusiasts come up for skiing at **Glenshee**.

There are no less than 26 lifts stretching up either side of the A93 giving downhill skiers a choice of 38 pistes. Cross country enthusiasts are also catered for in the area at Glenisla to the east, where there are 40 miles of forest trails to explore. Apart from skiing, visitors may go pony trekking, touring, walking, fishing or play golf, tennis and squash.

To the south is the abbey town of **Coupar Angus**. Its network of streets and closes is one of the best preserved medieval patterns in Scotland, though the buildings have changed over the centuries. The abbey was established here in 1164 and prospered well leading to the creation of the town. By the 16th century its incomes matched those of Holyrood and exceeded those of the border abbeys of Melrose and Kelso. From such heady heights the abbeys fall was swift, its estates were disbanded following the Reformation and the abbey fell into disuse, becoming a valuable source of quality stone for the locals. All that remains is a gateway arch.

Situated on the edge of Coupar Angus on Station Road, you will discover The **Red House Hotel**, which despite its name is in fact not a place to stay. Originally built as a hotel, the name has remained, but today this impressive red brick building offers a variety of facilities, including a complete leisure complex with squash courts, gymnasium, sauna and snooker room, as well as two very comfortable bars and a functions room which is perfect for wedding banquets and parties. However, the main reason for coming here is the outstanding cuisine, with menus which incorporate the finest local produce imaginatively prepared and beautifully presented to tempt the most discerning palate, all accompanied by a fine wine list.

The Red House Hotel, Station Road, Coupar Angus. 0828-28500
Map Ref: F4

Another building of note in the town is the Tolbooth Tower. This square Clock Tower or steeple was built by public subscription in 1762. Part of the building was once used as the town prison. Nearby on Calton Street stand Cumberland Barracks. The town lies at the southern end of two military roads into the Highlands and many a soldier must have spent his last night of relative comfort in the barracks, which were named after The Duke of Cumberland, who finally defeated Bonnie Prince Charlie at Culloden. The barracks were restored by the burgh council in 1974 and converted into flats.

You will find a welcoming hostelry at **Enverdale Hotel,** which stands set back on Pleasance Road. Originally built in the 1870's as a private residence, it was once the home of a Dundee Jute Baron, but today is a small hotel owned and personally run by a friendly couple, Martin and Rosemary Price. This is the ideal place to call in for a quiet drink or a delicious meal and the Harvester Restaurant is well renowned for its menu selection, hence its entry in the Taste of

Scotland. Attractively furnished throughout, period and modern furniture blend easily and the five guest rooms, two of which are en-suite, provide very comfortable accommodation for those wishing to stay.

Enverdale Hotel, Pleasance Road, Coupar Angus. 0828-27606
Map Ref: F4

To the south-west of the town on the A94 is the small village of **Woodside** and **The Woodside Inn**, originally an old drovers inn. It makes a welcome stopping-off point in your journey. Steve and Alice Mee are friendly proprietors who pride themselves on the quality of homecooked food and Real Ales they serve.

The Woodside Inn, Main Street, Woodside, Nr Coupar Angus.
0828-7254 Map Ref: E4

Visitors and locals mix easily in the cosy, relaxed atmosphere of the oak beamed bars and the comfortable restaurant provides the perfect setting for a quiet meal out. The food is always freshly prepared using local produce wherever possible, including wild salmon and venison, with the Woodside Mixed Grill proving a regular favourite.

It is only a few miles east of the town, along the same A94, to the little village of **Meigle**, which has a fascinating museum dedicated entirely to ancient carved stones. This magnificent collection is the largest of its kind, with some 25 examples Celtic Christian sculptured monuments found in or near the old churchyard.

To the north is the attractive small town of **Alyth**, with its burn flowing through it alongside the main street. Here there is a charming folk museum which has interesting displays of life in the local community and in the surrounding countryside.

Close to Meigle is **Glamis** and its famous Castle , mentioned by Shakespeare in 'Macbeth', 'Lord of Glamis' was the second of the titles which the witches foretold for Macbeth. There have been many famous visitors to this castle, including James V, and his daughter Mary Queen of Scots. Sir Walter Scott was another guest here, and it was the childhood home of Queen Elizabeth, the Queen Mother, whose father was the fourteenth Earl of Strathmore. Princess Margaret was born here in 1930. The castle with its turrets and parapets has a romantic fairy tale appeal, but above all remains a family home, much lived in and loved by the Strathmore family, who have been residents since 1372. There are extensive grounds and gardens to explore as well as the castle and a restaurant to recover in in comfort. It is open everyday from Easter through to Mid-October.

In the village square of Glamis, a few minutes walk from Glamis Castle, you will discover a rare gem called The **Strathmore Arms**.

The Strathmore Arms, Glamis. 0307-840248 Map Ref: F3

Although at first glance it looks like an ordinary, traditional pub, The Strathmore has a secret, for it is in fact a locally renowned restaurant serving the best international cuisine in the area. Thanks to the skill of Mr. Zaari, the friendly and highly skilled proprietor, visitors here can enjoy a superb range of dishes to tempt the most discerning palate, accompanied by an equally select wine list. Before dining, you can relax in the cocktail lounge with an aperitif, where open stone walls are adorned with a collection of copper pans and there is a crackling log fire to toast your toes by. The functions room proves popular for parties and wedding receptions and the coffee lounge and bar provide the perfect setting for a post-dinner liqueur.

Kirriemuir lies to the north of Glamis on the A926 and is frequently described as the 'gateway to the Glens of Angus'. Most of the town retains its original 18th and 19th century character, when it was an important centre for handloom weaving. The square is dominated by an even older tolbooth dating from around 1604, a reminder of the towns connection with the Douglas, Earls of Angus. It is also the birthplace of J.M. Barrie, creator of Peter Pan, born at Nine Brechin Road. He gifted the cricket pavilion on Kirriemuir Hill to the townsfolk, and it houses one of only three surviving camera obscura in Scotland, which gives panoramic views of Strathmore and the Glens.

The fliers of the RAF are paid tribute to in a private museum in the former council offices on Bellies Brae. Richard Moss has amassed a huge selection of wartime photographs, uniforms, medals, models, newspapers and memorabilia. Open to the public everyday in summer there is no admission but donations for local charity are welcome.

The renowned **Angus Glens** are each very different; Isla, Prosen and Clova offer great beauty and are all worth exploring. The entry to Glen Prosen is dominated by the Airlie Monument Tower, which commemorates the 11th Earl of Airlie, who was killed during the Boer War. Keep an eye out too for the Captain Scott and Dr Wilson Memorial on the roadside. Prosen was Scott's favourite glen and he and Wilson planned their ill-fated South pole expedition near here.

Situated on the main road in Dykehead, bordered by two of the most beautiful glens in Scotland, the **Royal Jubilee Arms Hotel** provides a charming touring base from which to explore the surrounding area. This is a place that caters for everyone, visitor and local alike. The Ceilidhs and High Teas always prove popular and there are facilities for parties of up to 120 people. The 28 guest rooms are all en-suite and well-equipped to ensure a comfortable night's sleep and the restaurant provides a wide selection of excellent homecooked food to appeal to every palate. With a choice of three bars to relax in, a snooker room for the games enthusiast and a wealth of activities on the doorstep the Royal Jubilee Arms has all you need.

Royal Jubilee Arms Hotel, Dykehead, By Kirriemuir.
0575-4381/382 Map Ref: F3

Before going south, back towards the Tay, there is the ancient town of **Forfar** to explore. Administrative capital of Angus today, the town has held higher station, being the site for King Malcolm Canmore's Parliament of 1057, and King William the Lion 's Scottish Parliament, convened at the castle in the early part of the 13th century. The castle itself was destroyed by followers of Robert the Bruce, who brought it down on the heads of its English garrison - it was never rebuilt and a modern tower marks the site. Just outside the town, on the B9113, are the ruins of Restenneth Priory.

To the north east on the A94 is the scattered hamlet of **Finavon**, which has two interesting features that are worthy of our attention. A side road to the south east starts deceptively on the straight and level, then hairpins steeply up the Hill of Finavon. On the summit is the very peculiar vitrified fort. Clearly created by great heat, there has been much speculation how this 8th century fort and others like it became so. What is known is that the drystone walls of this type of fort were often strengthened by internal timbers, and if they caught light the lack of oxygen in the wall would cause them to burn at a very high temperature fusing the stone together. Finavon is also home to Scotland's largest Dovecote or Doocot, it now contains an exhibition on the Doocots of Angus and can clearly be seen by passing traffic on the A94.

We now head for **Dundee**, Scotland's fourth city, set against the majestic backdrop of the Sidlaw Hills and fronted by the Tay. There is much to see and do in the city, which has a rich heritage befitting its dramatic setting.

R.R.S. Discovery, Discovery Point, Dundee

King William the Lion made it a royal burgh in 1191 and it grew to become a major trading port. The growing wealth attracted raiders and it became subject to frequent attacks. In 1547 the forces of Henry VIII held the town for a short period, before laying waste to a greater part of it. In the 17th century the Duke of Montrose stormed the town and only the timely intervention of a relief force saved further destruction. But it was General Monk who did most damage to Dundee, when in 1657 he devastated important buildings, put many towns' people to the sword and looted its treasures. It would be many years before the town recovered.

The city as we see it today was founded on one product - jute. At the turn of the century over half the population worked in the jute mills and the city was nicked named 'Juteopolis'. The world's largest jute works, Camperdown Works, still stands, dominated by a massive chimney known as Cox's Stack, the buildings redeveloped into a new housing, shopping and leisure complex. The former Verdant Works have been taken over by Dundee Industrial Heritage to be developed as a living museum of jute and its importance the world over.

Shipbuilding also became an important industry and the shipwrights built sleek clippers to carry the jute from India and sturdy whalers to cope with the demands of high seas, fierce winds and the ice. Their expertise led to a commission to build one of the most famous ships in the world - **R.R.S. Discovery**, Captain Scott's antarctic expedition vessel, launched in 1901. She now lies alongside at Discovery Point and you can discover for yourselves just how tough life aboard was for the explorers and their crew. In the comfort of a special auditorium the ships story is told and you can try the accommodation for yourself aboard the ship.

Another piece of floating history moored at Dundee is **HM Frigate Unicorn**. She is the oldest British built ship still afloat and can be found in Victoria Dock. Built in Chatham, Kent, in 1824 this classic sailing frigate was fast and usefully armed, one of the most successful designs of her age. She still performed a useful role during the last war as home to the naval planners covering the North Sea. Today Unicorn tells the story of the Royal Navy under sail.

Two bridges leap the Tay at Dundee and one is infamous the world over. Work on the original **Tay Railway Bridge** was started in 1871 and finished in 1878. Built to a design of Thomas Bouch it was, at 10,711ft, the longest in the world. Queen Victoria crossed it soon after it opened, Bouch was knighted and his bridge was held up as an example British engineering supremacy.

Tragedy struck on the last Sunday of 1879 during a fearful storm, when the entire centre section of the bridge fell into the Tay, taking a train and its 75 passengers with it. Sir Thomas' career swiftly followed it and all work on his bridge across the Forth was stopped. It would be 1887 before trains would once more cross the Tay. The stumps of Bouch's bridge still stand out of the river alongside its replacement. What isn't generally known is that much of the new bridges iron work was taken from the old one; and that the doomed train's engine, Number 224, was pulled out of the Tay and worked east coast expresses for many years. No driver would cross the bridge with her though, until, on December 28th 1908, the 29th anniversary of the disaster, when she worked the same Dundee mail train. She wasn't scrapped until 1919.

One of Dundee's most famous sons was the self-styled poet, William McGonagall, whose unique approach to theatre and verse was to make him renowned, if not for the skill of his work then for its infectious delivery. The disaster inspired 'Beautiful Railway Bridge of the Silvery Tay' one of his more memorable pieces and today the city is quite proud at having the world's worst poet. The city has many other famous sons and daughters: Frankenstein's creator Mary Shelley was brought up here, the inventor of marmalade John Keiller was a Dundee grocer and Dennis the Menace, Oor Wullie and Desperate Dan were all born here in the studios of D.C. Thomson, publishers of the Dandy and Beano amongst many others.

You'll encounter characters far more alive and of a very different nature at **Camperdown Wildlife Centre**. Set right in the heart of the city the centre has one of the finest collections of Scottish and European wildlife in the country. In addition to members of rare species that survive in Scotland they have examples of those that haven't; the Brown Bear, Wolf, Arctic Fox and lynx. There is also an important collection of farm breeds that have all but disappeared. The centre is at the forefront of wildlife conservation, with captive breeding programmes aimed at bringing the Capercaillie, Pine Marten and Red Squirrel back to Scotland in significant numbers.

Once a fishing village, **Broughty Ferry** is now a very individual suburb of Dundee. At the height of the Jute trade it was the favoured residence of city businessmen, and the huge mansions they had built were said to form 'the richest square mile in Europe'. Another example of Victorian opulence can be admired on the Monifieth road where a substantial arch stands in celebration of Queen Victoria's Jubilee. Broughty Ferry also boasts two castles. Claypotts Castle stands rather incongruously next to a roundabout on the A92 in the middle of Dundee's urban sprawl, and was once the home of John Graham of Claverhouse, 'Bonnie Dundee', hero of Killiecrankie. If the word cute could ever be applied to a castle then this surely must be a candidate.

Queen Victoria Jubilee Arch, Broughty Ferry

Built of pink sandstone, with its modest proportions and rounded corners it looks like its on the set of a film. Broughty Castle is of a much more solid countenance. It stands four square on the river and was built to protect the village and guard the Firth. In later life it became a War Office gun battery and is now a local history museum.

Along the Firth from Broughty is the famous resort of **Carnoustie**, internationally famed as host to the British Open Golf Championship and many other big golfing tournaments. There are four links here, and the championship course is widely recognized as being a major challenge. Chasing the little white ball isn't all Carnoustie has to offer though. There's a magnificent beach with sailing, windsurfing and fishing facilities and a little inland **Barry Mill**. In continuous use from the 18th century to the early 80's this water mill rolled oats from local farms and their labourers, who received meal and oats as part of their wages, and so played an important role in the community. Now restored to working order by the National Trust for Scotland it provides a window into a way of life now long gone. North of Carnoustie there are two Country Parks, Crombie and Monikie. Both were developed around lochs created to supply water to Dundee in the late 1800's and which had became redundant. They are now havens for wildlife and visitors alike, whatever the season. There's a host of birds and animals to see on and around the lochs and woodlands, including woodpeckers and roe deer, and a Ranger service to help you spot them. There are well marked walks in both parks and Crombie has an orienteering course, whilst at Monikie there is the opportunity to get out on to the water.

Back on the coast our travels take us to **Arbroath**, home of the famous 'smokies', haddock straight from the sea cured over oak fires. Angus' largest town, its busy harbour area still captures the feel of the east coast's fishing heritage. You'll find outlets for the smokies around here, fresh from the backyard curing houses of the fishermen. On the seafront is the tall white Signalling Tower, that once guided mariners and acted as the depot for the lighthouse at Bell Rock in the North Sea. It is now the town museum with a special emphasis on fishing and the sea.

Visitors to Arbroath will discover the ideal holiday base at **Scurdy Guest House**, the charming home of Jim and Irene Leckie. Situated in a pleasant conservation area a stone's throw from the harbour, guest staying at this two hundred year old house will find a warm welcome and very comfortable accommodation with seven well-equipped guest rooms, some of which have en-suite facilities. The name 'Scurdy' means favourite place and with its lovely display of flowers outside it may well become a favourite place of yours. An additional attraction is the licensed restaurant which offers a varied menu ranging from toasted sandwiches and baked potatoes to full steak dinners.

Scurdy Guest House, 33 Marketgate, Arbroath. 0241-72417
Map Ref: H4

Arbroath Abbey holds a special place in Scottish history. Here in 1320, before Robert the Bruce, gathered Scottish nobles signed a Declaration of Independence. The red sandstone abbey was founded by King William the Lion in 1178, whose tomb lies here, and its distinctive ruins can easily be found in the town centre.

A few miles north, just off the A92 is **Lunan Bay**. Four miles of clean golden sands formed in a sheltered crescent, with a spectacular cliff backdrop, that provides an ideal escape on a sunny day. Overlooking the bay are the rather grim ruins of Red Castle. At the northern end of the bay is Boddin and the Elephant Rock, which does really look like one strolling into the surf. Though you can't help but wonder what it was called before anyone had seen an elephant.

The port of **Montrose** became notorious in the 18th century as a centre for smugglers, the numerous coves and inlets on the coast ideal for hiding from the Customs men. The port has long had a fishing fleet and still has strong connections with the sea acting as a service port for the North Sea oilfields. Montrose is also proud to be station number one for the R.N.I.B., their first lifeboat, 'Mincing Lane', being launched in 1869. An unmissable feature of the town is the 2000 acre tidal basin behind it. It provides an ideal habitat for seabirds and waders all year round. Ornithologists literally flock to this spot and rare birds are quite often spotted, blown off their migratory course by the fierce winds of the North Sea.

On the inland edge of the basin is the splendid **House of Dun**. This fine Palladian house was designed by William Burns and has been extensively and sensitively restored. The house contains royal mementoes of the William IV period, wonderful plasterwork in the saloon by Joseph Enzer and affords outstanding views out over the estate and basin as well. In the courtyard there is a loom weaving display, a gardeners bothy and gamekeeper's room to look over too.

The nearby town of **Brechin** is perhaps best known for the small cathedral which today serves as a parish church. It has its origins in the founding of the Diocese of Brechin by David I in the mid 12th century. Over the years 'improvements' and neglect have altered its appearance but the latest restoration has, as far as possible, returned it to its medieval glory. The tall thin round tower next to the Cathedral pre-dates it and was originally free standing. There are only two such towers in Scotland and it is a striking example of Celtic Culdee architecture. Built between AD990 and 1012 as a refuge for the clergy in times of invasion by the Northmen, it is all that remains of a college that once stood here. The door is some six feet above ground level making it somewhat difficult to gain entry. The cathedral itself is actually eighty-six feet high, if you don't count the roof cap which was added a later date. The carvings inside also point to a Celtic influence, one showing a crucifixion with the legs of Christ uncrossed, in the Irish tradition. In the churchyard is a Plague Stone, built into the south gate pillar, a reminder of one of the saddest episodes of the town's history when in 1647 some two thirds of Brechin's citizens died in just four months.

There are many historic sites and buildings in the area, and Brechin Museum gives a penetrating insight into local history. The Mechanics Institute, centre of learning in the 1800's, has recently been restored and now makes for an impressive sight. Other mechanical marvels can be enjoyed at Brechin Station. **The Brechin Railway Society** have restored the station buildings and the magnificent glass canopy and now run both steam and diesel trains to the Bridge of Dun. The line used to run from Perth, through Forfar and on to Montrose and once carried the London and North Western Railways crack expresses to Aberdeen. The last passenger trains ran in 1952 and the line finally closed to freight in 1981. Like many other preserved railways the staff are all volunteers and it runs on summer Sundays only, for timetable details call 0674-81318.

Our final destination in Tayside is the pretty village of **Edzell**, right on the border with Grampian Region, winner of several best kept village awards. Entry to the village is through the Dalhousie Arch, erected in 1887 by the tenants and friends, to the memory of the 13th Earl of Dalhousie and his Countess, who died within hours of each other. Just outside the village is Edzell Castle, which once occupied an important strategic position at the foot of Glen Esk. During various upheavals and occupations the castle survived but following the second Jacobite uprising a military detachment set about dismantling the castle to prevent further misuse. The ruination continued when the then owners became bankrupt and roof, floors and windows were removed to raise funds. Around the same time some stone work was also used in local projects, a then common occurrence. Edzell's jewel though is its pleasance, a walled garden built by Sir David Lindsay in 1604. The heraldic and symbolic sculptures set in the walls are unique in Scotland, and the flower filled recesses add to the beauty of these outstanding formal gardens.

High in the hills above Edzell is **Glenesk Folk Museum**. The building was once a shooting lodge known as 'The Retreat' and now tell the story of everyday life in Glenesk from 1800 to present times. Further up the Glen is Invermark Castle, a stronghold that once guarded several hilly passes from its prominent position on the eastern edge of Loch Lee. Looking out from the castle today it is hard to believe that the area was busy with the mining of iron and silver 300 years ago, so complete is the peace and tranquillity.

There couldn't be a better place to finish this chapter than the foothills of the Grampian Mountains. It has been a long journey from Rumbling Bridge, back south of Perth, and one full of contrasts and certainly packed with history. Before us is the Grampian Region which promises more to intrigue and delight the traveller.

Highland Cattle

The Grampians.

Strathisla Distillery, Keith

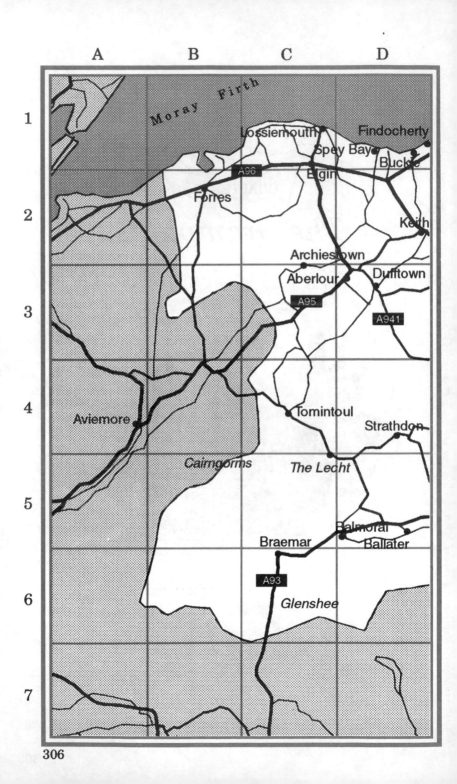

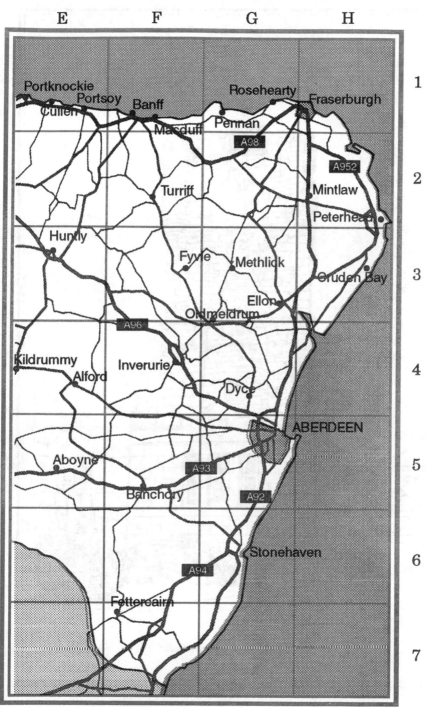

Dufftown Clocktower

CHAPTER NINE

The Grampians.

Our exploration of the region begins only a few miles north of where we left off in the last chapter, on the B966 in the small village of **Fettercairn**. A rather impressive gothic stone archway greets the visitor approaching from the south, erected to commemorate a visit to the town by Queen Victoria and Prince Albert in 1861. The village is home to the second oldest licensed distillery in Scotland, Fettercairn. Half a mile north of the village is the magnificent **Fasque House**, one of the best preserved Victorian stately homes anywhere. No museum but a living house Fasque has been the family home of the Gladstones since 1829, the sixth generation living here today. Its most famous occupant was William Gladstone, four times Prime Minister to Queen Victoria. Inside the house, specially 'downstairs' very little has changed since William's day. The kitchens and sculleries contain a wealth of domestic implements from a by-gone era. 'Above' stairs there are the staterooms, drawing room, library and cantilever staircase to admire. At the front of the house red deer roam in the park. Fasque is open in the afternoons between May and September, except on Fridays, and is certainly worth the visit.

If you have chosen to head straight into Deeside the B974 will take you over the pass and on to Banchory. The road climbs past the tiny tearoom at Clatterin' Brig and up to the **Cairn O'Mount summit,** 1493ft above sea level. Up here you'll catch your first glimpse of the tall poles that line the roads of the high mountains, when the snow is several feet deep they act as a guide for the ploughs. At the bottom of the pass is the **Bridge of Dye**. This graceful single high-arch bridge was built in 1680 and is one of the earliest in the north-east. In the wall of the house nearby is what looks rather like a pill box, disguised as part of the wall no doubt at the insistence of the house owner. There are a number of pill boxes in the Grampians, part of a grid defence system against German invasion.

Our route shall visit Banchory shortly, but from Fasque we head east to the coast just south of Stonehaven. Our first stop is the village of **Kinneff**, on the coastline and just off the A92. Part of the Old Church here formed the original buildings in which the crown jewels of Scotland were hidden during the Civil War. They were hidden under flag stones for nine years after being smuggled past Cromwell's besieging army at **Dunnottar Castle**. The castle itself is an impressive ruin standing on rocky cliff 160ft above the sea just south of Stonehaven. Known as the 'Scottish Camelot' this stronghold of the Earls Marischal was besieged in 1650 by the Roundheads. The castle had been chosen as the safest place to keep the crown jewels during the upheavals, these were smuggled out to Kinneff before the castle capitulated due to a lack of food. The Earl Marischal threw his lot in with the 1715 Rising and a year later Argyll rendered the castle harmless. In recent years its spectacular position and appearance landed it a part in Mel Gibson's film 'Hamlet'.

Stonehaven is a former fishing port spread around Stonehaven Bay. At the north end of the bay is Cowie village, the old fishertown quarter of the harbour. The Tolbooth here, situated on the quay, is a former 16th century storehouse of the Earl's Marischal. It was later used as a prison, and between 1748-49 Episcopal ministers lodged inside it, baptising children through the windows. Today it is the town museum, with displays on local history, archeology and in particular fishing. To the north of the town is **Muchalls Castle**, just off the A92. Overlooking the sea, this tiny castle was built in 1619 by the Burnetts of Leys. Inside there are plasterwork ceilings, fine fireplaces and a hidden staircase. Only open a few days a year it is never the less a lovely place.

From Muchalls we turn inland taking the B979 across to the A93, passing **Storybook Glen** on the way. The Glen is an ideal place to take younger children, with more than a hundred nursery rhyme characters spread amidst 20 acres of beautiful gardens and parklands. At Mains of Drum, on the A93, is **Drum Castle**, a rather impressive 13th century tower house that has been added to over the centuries. The Royal Hunting forests of Drum were conferred on William de Irwin by Robert the Bruce in 1323. The family line remained unbroken until 1975 and the death of Mr Forbes-Irvine, when the castle passed into the hands of the National Trust.

We head west along the A93 now heading into Royal Deeside and our next castle, **Crathes**. Pronounced 'Crathess' the castle dates back to the 16th century and is also well known for its 18th century gardens. The painted ceilings with their accompanying rhymes and proverbs are delightful. Outside the huge yew hedges, planted in 1702, have been clipped into elaborate topiary, and the famous walled Blue garden shouldn't be missed.

We follow the A93 along the Dee, through the small town of **Banchory** and on to Aboyne. A little north of **Aboyne** on the road to Tarland is **Tomnaverie Stone Circle**. One of many pre-historic sites scattered along the valley of the Dee. The remains of this recumbent stone circle date from around 1800-1600BC and has yet to be excavated. To the north-east of **Tarland** is another example of ancient Scotland, **Culsh Earth House**. This is a well preserved example of a souterrain or underground store house. The still air and even temperature made them ideal for preserving produce for a village that would have been somewhere nearby.

Midway between Aboyne and Ballater is the **Muir of Dinnet National Nature Reserve**. This area of outstanding natural beauty includes the lovely Burn O'Vat and Kinord and Daven Lochs. An ideal place to stretch your legs, there is an information centre, nature trails and, of course the views of the mountains. Within the reserve is the rather magnificent Kinord Cross-slab. The intricately carved cross covers all one side of the slab and was probably sculpted in the 9th century AD. A little further north on the A97 at Logie Coldstone is another example of a Cross-slab, the Migvie Stone. Rougher, taller and rather more crudely carved than the Kinord slab, it also features a horse and rider on the back.

Back on the banks of the Dee is **Ballater**. Pananich Lodge, the original spa, was founded in 1785 and was so successful that the facilities were expanded and the Spa town was soon established.

Enjoying an enviable location near the bridge in the town, quite literally on the banks of the River Dee, the **Monaltrie Hotel** is ideally situated as a touring base for the beautiful surrounds of Royal Deeside and the emphasis here is on first class service and facilities, provided in a warm, relaxed atmosphere.

Monaltrie Hotel, Bridge Square, Ballater   03397-55417 Ref: D5

Awarded a Four Crown Commended rating by the Scottish Tourist Board, the Monaltrie boasts two restaurants. In the elegant surroundings of the à la carte restaurant you can savour the finest Scottish cuisine prepared using fresh local produce, or if you prefer you can tantalise your taste buds with authentic spices and flavours of the Orient in the Thai Orchid restaurant . After dinner, what could be nicer than to relax with a nightcap in front of a roaring log fire before retiring to one of the twenty five en-suite guest rooms, each attractively furnished and equipped for maximum comfort.

The railway station of this pretty town was originally the station from which Queen Victoria would alight when travelling to Balmoral. If you have a sweet tooth you can indulge your habit at **Dee Valley Confectioners** in the Station Square. There is a visitors viewing area where you can see your favourites being made and naturally the opportunity to stock up for the journey. Many of the town's shops display the Royal Warrant. On the western edge of the town is the Church Hotel, an unusual conversion of a redundant kirk.

Centrally located in Bridge Square, you will discover a delightful licensed restaurant called **The Hayloft**. Originally the stone-built stables and hayloft belonging to the adjacent hotel, careful conversion a couple of years ago has created a lovely place with a bistro-style atmosphere, where you can call in for mid-morning coffee and pastries or enjoy a mouthwatering homecooked meal. Brodie Hepburn is the friendly proprietor and he prides himself on using only the finest local produce for all his dishes, ranging from delicious home-made soups and smoked goose breast to marinated herrings, venison and salmon. Open seven days a week from 11.00am for lunch and dinner, this is one place not to be missed while you explore this lovely part of Scotland.

The Hayloft, Bridge Square, Ballater. 03397-55999 Map Ref: D5

Another lovely place to stay in the town is **Dee Valley Guest House**, the charming home of Sandy and Evelyn Gray. Providing very

312

comfortable accommodation in four spacious and well equipped bedrooms, one en-suite, Evelyn is the longest serving landlady in Ballater and has been welcoming guests of all nationalities here for almost thirty years. Originally a private nursing home run by Dr Sir George Middleton the Queen's physician, the Duke of Kent apparently had his tonsils out here! Today, however, guests here are no longer patients, but visitors seeking a comfortable touring base and as the house provides ample tourist information, you can easily plan your trips out from here.

Dee Valley Guest House, 26 Viewfield Road, Ballater. 0339-755408
Map Ref: D5

Just outside the town you will discover a wonderful holiday base at **The Willows** in Cambus o' May, home of a very welcoming couple, Roger and Fiona Barnes.

The Willows, Cambus o' May, Ballater. 03397-55892 Map Ref:: D5

This beautiful Edwardian country house offers both bed and

313

breakfast accommodation and self-catering, with two lovely en-suite bedrooms within the main house and three exceptionally well-equipped self-catering units, one of which is suitable for the disabled. With Two to Four Crowns Highly Commended ratings for the self-catering units, you know the standard of facilities you can expect, but even if you're not looking for a place to stay, The Willows is well worth visiting if only to sample some of the excellent homecooking which Fiona and her staff provide in the delightful coffee shop. Their High Tea is a treat not to be missed.

The most famous place on the Dee is **Balmoral Castle**, summer home of the Royal Family for over a century. The earliest reference to it, as Bouchmorale, was in 1484. Queen Victoria visited the earlier castle in 1848, and fell in love with the location. Prince Albert bought the estate in 1852, and had the castle rebuilt by William Smith of Aberdeen. Public access is limited to the grounds and Ballroom, with it paintings and works of art, during May, June and July. Balmoral stands under 3791ft Lochnagar mountain, which stands to the south. Some years ago Prince Charles wrote a childrens tale 'The Old man of Lochnagar', no doubt inspired by the scenery and the myth and legends of the Highlands. The story went on to be published and an animated film with the Prince as narrator.

Not far from the castle at **Crathie** is the Royal Lochnagar Distillery. The Distillery was granted a Royal Warrant of Appointment by Queen Victoria in 1848 and has a visitors centre.

Crathie has a small church, built in 1895, which is attended by the Royal Family when it is in residence at Balmoral. Nearby Balmoral Bridge carries the B976 over the Dee near the castle. Commissioned by Prince Albert as part of the improvements to the Estate, and designed by Isambard Kingdom Brunel, its construction took the public road away from the castle, creating better privacy and was a more solid replacement for the original suspension bridge. Another bridge of great note is the military one upstream at Invercauld, built in 1752 by Major Edward Caulfield.

Our next town, **Braemar**, is famous for the 'Gathering' held every September, and attended by the Royal family. This is the largest Highland Games in Scotland, dating form 1832. Here you can see the tossing of the famous Braemar Caber, nearly 20ft long and weighing 132lb. Highland Games uphold a tradition that goes back into the mists of the past. The earliest were held more than a thousand years ago under the sponsorship of clan chiefs and kings, proving very useful for recruiting staff; race winners made good messengers and the strongest men bodyguards. Down the centuries villagers gathered once a year, perhaps their only holiday, to take part in competitions

Tossing the Braemar Caber

based on the tools of their trades, throwing hammers, tossing tree trunks, carrying boulders and running races, all activities now incorporated in the modern games. It also became opportunity to salute the clan chief with a march past to pipe bands and flying the clan colours. At Braemar the Queen takes the salute, a tradition begun by King Malcolm in the 11th century.

The castle at Braemar was built in the early 17th century. It was the work of the Seventh Earl of Mar, who held it for the Government during the Early Jacobite rising of Bonnie Dundee in 1689, falling into Jacobite hands when the Earl died. Twenty five years later the next Earl of Mar raised the Jacobite standard on the Braes of Mar starting the 1715 Rising. In 1748 following the failure of the '45 Rising the Government rented the then semi- derelict castle from the Farquharsons of Invercauld, who had bought it off the disgraced Mar , and who own it to this day. The road south of Braemar climbs the highest main road pass in the country at Cairnwell.

We return to Balmoral and turn north on to the B976 which joins the A939 at Gairnsheil, where there is a particularly fine example of a stone high single arch bridge still in use. Just north of here there is a well preserved section of military road running over the hills to Corgarff. Stood here in the remote hills of Upper Strathdon is **Corgarff Castle**. This lonely tower house has seen plenty of history despite its location. It was built in 1537, only to be destroyed in 1571, when a party of Gordons from Auchindoun Castle fired the castle, taking with it the Lairds wife, Margaret Forbes, and 26 others; part of an endemic rivalry between the Catholic Gordons and the Protestant Forbes. The castle suffered a second burning in 1689 when Jacobites put a torch to it, aiming to prevent its use by forces of the King. In 1715 the Earl of Mar encamped here before raising the Jacobite standard at Braemar. After Culloden the castle was garrisoned by Government troops having been modified in a similar style to Braemar. The final episode in the castle active life came in 1827-31 when a captain, Subaltern and 56 men were stationed here to help the excisemen stamp out whisky smuggling. After then it drifted into disuse, though it has now been restored.

The road over **The Lecht** is narrow, steep, twisting and often blocked by snow in the winter. At the top of the pass you will see the mechanical monsters of the ski tow, skiers flocking to these hills because of that very snow. Two miles north of the summit is the Well of Lecht. Above the small natural spring a white stone plaque dated 1754 records that five companies of the 33rd Regiment built the road from here to the Spey. This marks one section of the military road that starts in Blairgowrie, passes the garrisons of Braemar and Corgarff, over the bridges of Invercauld and Gairnsheil and on to Ruthven Barracks on the banks of the Spey at Kingussie. The isolation of the road is broken by the small town of **Tomintoul**. Tomintoul Museum features displays on local history, wild life and the changing environment. There are also reconstructions of farmhouse farm kitchen, and blacksmiths shop. A day out with a difference can be arranged at Tomintoul Tourist Information Centre. Here you can book to take a safari around a working Highland estate. These Ranger guided tours of the Glenlivet Estate by Land Rover, cover its history, landscape, wildlife and work.

As far as far as this chapter is concerned we have reached a dead end and must return over the Lecht to Corgarff, to take the A944 to **Strathdon**. For keen gardeners there are two gems to discover near the village. Candacraig Gardens is a Victorian walled garden with 1820 Gothic style summerhouse, formal and modern rose gardens and period fountains. **Old Semeil Herb Garden**, three miles to the south east is a specialist herb plant nursery, with a display herb garden, plant nursery, and garden centre selling garden pottery, books, seeds, gifts and unusual plants.

Our travels now take us north along the A97 and on to a pair of interesting castles. Grampian is castle country, as you may have noticed, and contains some of the finest examples of the 1200 that are spread across Scotland. **Glenbuchat Castle**, five miles south of Kildrummy, is a non-nonsense Z-plan castle, Glenbuchat stands foursquare above the ravine through which flows the Water of Buchat. It was built in 1590 by the Gordons. Brigadier-General Gordon of Buchat supported both the '15 and '45 Jacobite Risings. He avoided retribution by fleeing to France. Though he kept his head, his land and castle were forfeited to the Earl of Fife.

Kildrummy Castle ruins, a mile or so south of the village, are the best preserved example of a 13th century castle of enclosure. Seat of the Earls of Mar, it was dismantled after the '45 Rising. There is a beautiful shrub and alpine garden in the adjacent ancient quarry below the castle. In Kildrummy village there is an unusual rectangular bow fronted Kirk which replaced the pre-reformation kirk in 1805. The old kirk still stands on a grassy mound in the kirkyard, though it has lost its font, reused in the new one.

It is only a short drive from here to **Alford**, home of the **Grampian Transport Museum**. This houses an extensive collection of historic road vehicles in a purpose built exhibition hall. Climb aboard exhibits include a huge MAC snowplough, vintage steam roller and an armoured car. There is a recreation of a sixties transport cafe, a driving simulator and video bus featuring motorsport and road transport history. During the summer the museum is host to many events, with car and motorcycles of all ages being put through their paces on the race circuit. In the village is **Alford Railway Museum**. The station depicts the advent of the railway in Alford, the period booking office containing a photo exhibition.

South of Alford on A980 at Muir of Fowlis is **Craigievar Castle**. A perfect example of a fairy-tale castle, built in 1626 and unchanged inside and out since then. Built of soft pink stone, the L- plan tower house is plain and simple up to the fourth floor, where it breaks out in a riot of conical turrets, serrated gables, chimneys and balustrades. A masterpiece of Scottish baronial architecture it was built for William Forbes; known as 'Danzig Willie' because he made his fortune exporting fish and woollen goods to the Baltic. Home of the Forbes family until the 1960's it is now in the care of the National Trust for Scotland.

Heading back along the A944, off to the north is **Castle Fraser**. Begun in 1575, it belongs to the same period of native architecture that produced Crathes and Craigievar Castles, and is the largest and grandest of the castles of Mar. There is a splendid Great Hall and what remains of an eavesdropping device known as the 'Lairds lug'. Not far from the castle is Cluny Old Kirkyard. Its most striking feature is the neo-classical mausoleum of 1808, dedicated to Miss Elyza Fraser from the castle. It cost £353 and is the finest classical tomb in the north-east. In front of the mausoleum are four mortsafes, iron cages topped with heavy granite slabs, these were placed over coffins to prevents the bodies being snatched.

From Castle Fraser we journey east to **Aberdeen**, Scotland's third city, and most prosperous in recent decades, also known as the 'Granite City' due to the profusion of wonderful grey granite buildings at its heart. As you would expect in a major city there are plenty of things to see and do. The city offers theatre, cinema, a vast array of sports facilities, some very fine shopping and eating out to suit every palate. There is large selection of accommodation available but at certain times of the year it can be in short supply, due to the oil industry.

We plan to concentrate on some of the fine buildings, of which there are very many. The present townscape that prompted the nick-name is a result of the Aberdeen New Streets Act of 1801, which inaugurated a hectic half century of civil engineering and construction. Huge town planning changes were implemented, the most dramatic being the creation of **Union Street** in 1801, which involved the removal of the sand and gravel St. Katherines hill and the erection of a series of great arches and bridges. This undertaking very nearly bankrupted the city, a boom in trade rescuing it from financial ruin.

Here in the centre of the city the visitor is surrounded by granite - dull or sparkling according to the light - which came from the city quarries in huge quantities. Many of the city's most beautiful buildings are to be found here, and it is well worth setting aside a little time just to wander around, and wonder at, the architecture. We cannot hope to tell you about all of them but one or two are rather special. At the western end of Union Street is **St. James'**, built of pink granite the church has an odd appearance as the spire originally planned was never built. Behind the church in Justice Mill Lane is something altogether different - **Satrosphere, The Discovery Place**. Great for kids of all ages, it is a hands on science & technology centre, exploring sound, light, energy and the environment with nearly a hundred DIY experiments.

The west end of Union Street became a highly desirable residential area during the city's expansion, as the wealthy moved out of their town houses on the waterfront. **Bon Accord Square** and Crescent are a triumph of the near austere. Their simple facades covering Georgian elegance and spaciousness. Close-by is the **Old Post Office**. What could have been merely plain and utilitarian has the all the style and appearance of a Baronial Scottish mansion.

Across Union Street at the end of Union Terrace is Rosemount Viaduct and **His Majesty's Theatre**, opened in 1906. The exquisite Edwardian interior has been restored and it is Aberdeen's main theatre, seating 1500, and hosting ballet, opera, musicals, concerts and plays. Next door are the Church of St. Mark's and the City library - the three being affectionately known as Education, Salvation and Damnation'. In the next block is the City Art Gallery, which house a fine collection works from the last three centuries.

Along Schoolhill and to the right on Broad street is **Provost Skene's House**. Erected in the 16th century, this house bears the name of its most notable owner, Sir George Skene, Provost of Aberdeen 1676-1685. The Provost being chief administrative official of a Scottish Burgh. One of few remaining town houses in the city it has remarkable painted ceilings and interesting relics. Across Broad Street is **Marischall College**. This imposing 1906 granite structure has a soaring Tudor Gothic frontage and a quadrangle, entered by a fine archway, around which are older buildings of 1836-44, and the graceful Mitchell Tower.

A minutes walk is St. Andrews Cathedral on King Street. Cathedral Church of the Scottish Episcopal Diocese of Aberdeen and Orkney. One of few sandstone buildings this part of Aberdeen, it contains the Seabury Memorial, which commorates the consecration of Samuel Seabury of Connecticut, the first Bishop of the USA, in Aberdeen in 1784. There is also an exhibition showing some of the distinct features of Christian heritage of the North-East.

Aberdeen is still one of Britain's major fishing ports, and the story of this ancient port is told at the **Maritime Museum** in the **Provost Ross's House** on Shiprow. One of Aberdeen's oldest buildings built in 1593, it was saved by conservationists in the 1950's with the help of the Queen Mother. The museum uses models, paintings and audio-visual displays to tell the story of local shipbuilding, the fishing industry and North Sea oil and gas developments.

Along the harbour front is **Footdee**, bound in on one side by the bustling harbour quays and protected from the elements by the sea-wall at the south end of Aberdeen Esplanade. 'Fittie' is a peninsula village with a quite separate atmosphere from the rest of the city. Its sturdy stone cottages, ranged around squares, were built early in the 19th century for fishermen and harbour pilots, the pilotage authority is still based at the Round House. Nearby Pocra Quay is a supply base for North Sea oil platforms and shipyards here launched many of the phenomenally fast tea- clippers, whose times were virtually unrivalled in the races to bring back the first crop of the season in Victorian times. Some Small scale shipbuilding and repairs still goes on. Aberdeen is also the port to catch a ferry to Shetland from, the voyage taking 14 hours.

To the north of the city is **Aulton**, or Old Town. The Aulton has always maintained a separate identity to the 'new' burgh and port on the River Dee. Stood on the south bank of the River Don it has many older buildings and a typical medieval street layout. The High Street is dominated by **King's College Chapel**. The university was founded in 1494, and this was its first building. The chapel interior has some of Scotland's finest medieval woodwork and the exterior is crowned by an imposing crown spire. In sharp contrast is Grant's Place, a row of simple single-storey cottages built in 1732. Also on the High Street is the Town House, a splendidly proportioned municipal building with a small clock tower erected in 1788. A more unusual house is to be found down on the river. **Wallace Tower** is fine example of a simple tower-house, like a castle in miniature, built in 1616. Originally it stood near the harbour but redevelopment led to it being move here stone by stone in 1964.

Along the river to the east is **Brig O'Balgowie**. Also known as the 'Auld Brig o'Don' this massive 62ft wide arch spans a deep pool of the river. It was completed built around 1320 and rebuilt in 1607. In 1605 Sir Alexander Hay endowed the bridge with a small property, which had so increased in value that it built the New Bridge of Don, a little down stream, in 1830 at a cost of £26000, as well as bearing the cost of the Victoria bridge and contributed to many other public works. Another bridge of interest crosses the Dee on the south-western outskirts of the city. **The Bridge of Dee** was built in 1520's by Bishop Gavin Dunbar, during the reign of James V. Its seven arches span 400ft and the medieval solidity of the structure is enlivened by heraldic carvings.

We now venture away from the city taking the A96 then the A947 to **Dyce**. To the west of the village at Old Dyce Kirk are a pair of fine examples of Pictish symbol stones, one covered in ancient symbols including a large beast with a fine plume and muscles. The other is an intricate Cross-slab. It is not completely clear what function these stones performed but at least some were involved in burial rituals, the stone commemorating an ancestor of rank, as well as providing descendants with a form of title. That many now stand in ancient churchyards may be the result of Christianization of existing Pictish burial sites.

From Dyce our journey rejoins the A96 and take us towards **Inverurie**, a pleasant market town surrounded by rich farmland, with excellent walks over the lovely hill of Bennachie to the west. Two miles to the south on the banks of the River Don are the ruins of Kinkell Church. An early 16th century parish church with some fine ornate details including rich sacrament house of unusual design dated 1524. Within the churchyard is the graveslab of Gilbert de Greenlaw, killed in the battle of Harlaw in 1411, which bears an unusually detailed carving of an armoured knight This slab was reused by the Forbes in 1592. To the west is **Easter Aquhorthies** recumbent stone circle, sign posted from the town. An impressive stone circle, the recumbent, its flankers and the circle are all of different stone, some from many miles away. Recumbent stones were Neolithic sites of communal and seasonal ritual, some later becoming cremation burial sites. The huge recumbent stones weighed anything up to 20 tons and would have needed many men to move then even a short distance.

Across the main road at Deviot is Loanhead Stone Circle, perhaps the best known example of a wide spread group of recumbent stone circles in east Scotland. From the stone circle we cut across country, on to the A920, and into **Oldmeldrum**, which retains much of it old character. To the east are several interesting places to find. The smallest stands in **Udny Green churchyard**, to the south of A920. In the corner is a rather plain circular building that could easily be mistaken for a rather substantial toolstore. A second look at the strength of the walls, lack of windows and stout oak door, reveals an ingenious solution to problem of bodysnatchers. Coffins were placed in the Mort house, postponing the burial until the body was unsuitable for sale. Four separate key holders were need to unlock the door and sliding inner iron gate. Ironically it was built in 1832, when a law was passed that solved the problem of bodysnatching by ensuring a legal supply of bodies.

To the north of Udny Green are the **Great Gardens of Pitmidden**. These wonderful formal gardens have been brilliantly restored to their original 1675 layout. There are huge geometric flowerbeds, marked out with box and yew hedges, as well as pavilions fountains and sundials. Three of the four parterres or flowerbeds follow designs used at Holyrood house in Edinburgh, while the fourth is the family crest of Sir Alexander Seton who started the gardens. There is also a Museum of Farming Life, which has an impressive selection of agricultural equipment from the last century.

It is only a very short drive along the B999 to **Tolquhon Castle**. Once a seat of the Forbes family, it was originally known as Preston Tower and a simple rectangular keep. William Forbes, the 7th Laird, was responsible for its expansion into a more spacious accommodation. We can be sure when the work was done because one of the outer walls contains the inscription 'Al this worke excep the Auld Tour was begun by William Forbes 15 April 1584 and endit be him October 1589'. Sold to the Farquharsits it passed onto the 2nd Earl of Aberdeen, and was abandoned as a residence by 1800. William Forbes and his wife are laid to rest nearby in Tarves Churchyard, his fine altar-tomb showing an interesting mix of gothic and renaissance styles.

A little further along the B999 is **Haddo House**. Designed by William Adam for William, 2nd Earl of Aberdeen, in 1731, Haddo replaced the Old House of Kellie, home of the Gordons of Methlick for centuries. When the fourth Earl, George came into his inheritance in 1805 he found a treeless waste surrounded the neglected house, the third or 'wicked' earl having lived away with his mistresses. He set to work with a will, his 80 foresters planting trees across the estate, he made other major improvements and laid out the gardens. He was less successful in political life, having become Prime Minister in 1852 he became unhappily embroiled in the debacle of Crimea. Much of the interior is 'Adam Revival' style carried out about 1880 for John, 7th Earl and 1st Marquess of Aberdeen and his Countess, Ishbel. A large area of the 4th earl's forest is now a country park that adjoins the house grounds.

Formerly the manse attached to the village church, **Gight House Hotel** enjoys a tranquil location beside the River Ythan in **Methlick** and is an ideal touring base from which to explore local places of interest such as nearby Haddo House and Fyvie Castle. Families are most welcome here and the acre of surrounding gardens include a beer garden with a play area for children. Les and Carole Ross are welcoming hosts who pride themselves on offering a wide selection of fine ale and an extensive menu of homecooked food which includes vegetarian dishes, fresh fish and shellfish and local game when in season. For those wishing to stay, very comfortable accommodation is provided in three lovely guest rooms, two of which are en-suite.

Gight House Hotel, Sunnybrae, Methlick. 0651-806389 Ref: G3

Our next destination not only has an unusual name but is also a real hidden place. **Remains to be Seen** is off the B9005 at Quilquox, east of Methlick. It is a fascinating exhibition of period clothes and accessories, lace and jewellery, and has a porcelain room. The surrounding gardens were specially planted by an ornithologists to attract wild birds. North-west of Methlick at Kirkton, near Millbrex is the **Fluffsfield Donkey Sanctuary**. They have over 76 rescued donkeys in their care, and visitors are welcome every day of the year.

We now follow the B9005 to **Fyvie** and its castle. The oldest part of **Fyvie Castle** dates from the 13th century, with subsequent generations adding to the grand structure over the years. Today its five towers enshrine five centuries of Scottish history and its is now a fine example of Scottish baronial architecture. Its most famous features are its 'Wheel' staircase and the important collection of fine portraits, including work by Raeburn and Gainsborough. Most of interior was created by 1st Lord Leith of Fyvie and reflects the opulence of the Edwardian ora. Three miles north of the village is the much smaller but no less interesting castle Towie Barclay. An ancient stronghold of the Barclays dating from 1136, it has recently been reconstructed, together with its walled garden, by the present owners and has won major European restoration awards. Incidentally a descendant of the Barclay family, Prince Barclay de Toille, became a Russian Field Marshal and was immortalised in Tolstoy's 'War and Peace'.

Following the A947 north brings us to **Turriff**. In 1913 Turriff became known throughout Great Britain when a local farmer, Robert Paterson, refused to join Lloyd George's new National Health Insurance Scheme. One of his cows was impounded and Sheriff's Officers tried to auction it to cover the payments, a riot ensued and they were chased out of town. Similar attempts in Aberdeen met with little more success and eventually his neighbours bought the cow and after parading through the streets presented it back to Paterson. The 'Turra Coo' as it was known made front page news and there was a healthy souvenir industry of 'coo' postcards, mugs, plates and the like. Today the two-day Turriff Show is one of Europe's major agricultural events attracting 50000 visitors.

Two miles east of the town is **Delgatie Castle**. A stout tower house, home of the Hays of Delgatie, dating back to the 11th century, it features a magnificent turnpike stair of 97 steps.

Mary Queen of Scots stayed here for three days in 1562, a portrait hanging in the room she used. The beautiful colour ceilings were installed in 1590 and amongst the interesting contents are many pictures and arms.

Several miles east of Turriff is the village of **Mintlaw** and **Aden Country Park**. Something like 220 acres of an estate that once covered 10000 have been turned into this very attractive country park. Footpaths explore broadleaf and conifer woodland, pass a wildfowl lake which used to hold a head of water for the mill and crosses a footbridge over the winding South Ugie Water. This mixture of habitats attracts many kinds of birds and small mammals; and visitors early or late in the day my catch sight of the roe deer feeding on the open ground. Aden's beautifully restored semi-circular range of farm buildings houses a series of displays illustrating the lives of the estate workers. The 18th century mansion house is now a gaunt ruin, but it is easy to imagine how opulent it must once have been. There is also an interesting ice-house, this underground store would be packed with tons of snow and ice that would see the estate through to the next winter. Part of the park is now a 20 acre working farm where north-east farming in the 1950's is brought to life.

To the north is **Mormond Hill**, a prominent Buchan landmark with an RAF signal station on its summit. A large white horse and white stag were cut into is flanks in the 18th century by Captain

Fraser of Strichen. The horse can easily be seen from the Strichen to New Pitsligo road. The stag is clearly visible on the opposite side of the hill above New Leeds on the A92.

Directly east from Mintlaw is **Peterhead**, Europe's busiest fishing port. Dozens of boats a day land their catches, and there is a very busy fishmarket early every weekday morning. The history of the towns long connection with the sea is told at the **Arbuthnot Museum and Art Gallery** in St. Peter Street. There are displays on the development of the fishing and whaling industries, with special Arctic exhibits, a section on local history, and photograph and coin exhibitions. On Golf Road at the mouth of the River Ugie is the oldest salmon fish house in Scotland. **Ugie Salmon Fish House**, was Built in 1585 for George Keith, 5th Earl Marischal of Scotland, and still supplies tasty fresh and smoked salmon today.

On the coast south of Peterhead is **Cruden Bay**, a rocky cliff spectacular, with the Bullers of Buchan as its masterpiece. This is a vast sea chasm 200ft deep, where the sea rushes in through a natural archway open to the sky. Stood on the cliffs above the bay are the extensive ruins of **Slains Castle**. Built in 1597 and remodelled in the gothic style in the 19th century, only to fall into disuse. Once home of the Dukes of Erroll, Johnson and Boswell stayed here on their Highland journey, as did Bram Stoker, who got inspiration for his gothic horror masterpiece 'Dracula' here. Cruden Bay is famous in golfing circles for its course, so popular late last century that the Great North of Scotland Railway Company built a 140 room hotel. Both it and the railway are now distant memories.

The road north up the coast passes the wild empty **Rattery Head**, where 70ft sand dunes overlook the vast endless beach. The landscape is almost lunar, the eeriness being added to in foggy weather by the mournful fog horn at Rattery Head lighthouse. The head is very popular with birdwatchers as the **RSPB Loch of Strathbeg Reserve** lies to the north, as does our destination, **Fraserburgh**. Unlikely as it may seem today the fishing port of Fraserburgh, once had a university. Built in 1595, with a grant from the Scottish Parliament, it soon withered away when the principal was flung in jail by James VI for defying his ecclesiastical policy. The only remnant is the Moses Stone, a carved stone, that now stands at South Church. At **Kinnaird Head**, north of the harbour, is an interesting lighthouse. When an Act of 1786 demanded a light at the most northerly part of Aberdeenshire the tower house built in the 16th century by Sir Alexander Fraser, 8th Laird of Philorth, was in an ideal spot and provided a ready made platform for the light. It was first lit on 1st December 1787, becoming the first lighthouse in Scotland. Originally the light was fixed and used whale-oil lamps, but even so on a clear night its beam could be seen up to 14 mile away. Though much modified it is still in use today. On the rocks below the lighthouse is the Wine Tower, a mysterious building that is thought to have been a private chapel. Built in the 1400's the tower features in many local legends and is reputed to be haunted. South of the harbour the sandy town beach stretches for three miles and has won international awards for cleanliness.

Unable to go any further north of east we turn west along the coast to **Pitsligo Castle** near **Rosehearty**. This ruined castle dates from 1424 and passed through various families on to the 4th and last Lord Pitsligo, an ardent Jacobite, who is remembered for his generosity to the poor and successful attempts to evade capture following the '45 rising. It was purchased by an American descendant of the Lord, Malcolm Forbes the multi-millionaire publisher, who had the buildings structure secured prior to his death in 1990.

It is only a short drive from Rosehearty to the hidden and delightful fishing village of **Pennan**. This Beautiful old smugglers haunt stands at the foot of mighty cliffs, hidden by the overhang until you are right on top of it. Pennan was the location for the film 'Local Hero' which told the topical tale of how a small Scottish Community hoodwinked a giant American oil company. Interestingly the villages public phone box is a listed historic monument. The cliffs nearby are full of caves and secret bays that made life very hard for the excisemen chasing the smugglers.

Along the coast is **Macduff**, a bustling fishing port on the eastern bank of the River Deveron. The harbour is overlooked by the imposing War Memorial, a 70ft high octagonal tower erected in 1923, with the names of the fallen carved on slabs. Doune Church is unusual having a clock tower with four faces, one of which is blank. This faces across the river to Banff and marks the indignation felt by the folk of Macduff to those of Banff when they advanced their clocks to bring forward the execution of local outlaw James MacPherson's execution to ensure he could not be pardoned. The empty clockface is meant to ensure that Banffers never again know the time.

Across the Deveron is the royal and ancient burgh of **Banff**. The town contains a great number of 17th and 18th century buildings, the town houses of Laird and prosperous tradesmen, The Banff Preservation Society have helpfully placed information plaques on many of them and there is a trail leaflet available from the Tourist Information office to guide you around. In the centre of the historic quarter of the town is the Plainstones, or market place. Here you will find a well preserved Mercat Cross from the 16th century, the very ornate Biggar fountain and a cannon captured at Sevastopol during the Crimean war; these are all overlooked by the strangely conical-shaped tolbooth steeple. It is only a short walk from here to Sandyhill Road and something rather different. **The Sculpture Garden** features a number wondrous and unique garden sculptures, carved from huge pieces of tree trunk, that really fire the imagination.

Nearby **Duff House** is very different again but still does its best to overpower the senses. Although incomplete, William Adam's splendid and richly detailed mansion is amongst the finest works of Georgian baroque architecture in Britain. Started 1730, of all William Adams creations this is the most assertive, most brash, specially when compared with the relative restraint of Haddo, which he was building at the same time. The explanation lies in Adam's ability to interpret a clients demands. In William Braco he had one that was determined to impress, if not daunt his visitors.

Braco was one of the richest men in Aberdeenshire, thanks to his fathers banking interests. He became Lord Braco in 1735 and Earl of Fife in 1759. Adam responded to his clients wishes to the letter, proposing a swaggering and vainglorious proclamation of wealth, work beginning in 1730. What we see today is only half the intended pile. A dispute between architect and customer in 1736 left the house without its pair of intended pavilions and the sweeping colonnades that would have joined then to the main house. The dispute remained unresolved at the time of Adams death in 1748, and such was Braco's bitterness he could never bring himself to live in it, drawing the blinds of his carriage whenever he passed it. Eventually occupied by the second Earl and his descendants, it has since been a hotel, nursing home and army billet before being rescued by Historic Scotland, who intended to house works of art from the national collection here.

To the west of Banff is the beautifully preserved town of **Portsoy**, built around a picturesque small harbour. Many of the houses of the town were skilfully restored in the 1960's, among them the Old Star Inn of 1727 and the oldest, Soy House, built 1690's and much of the town is now designated an outstanding conservation area. Portsoy Marble, taken from a vein that runs across the braes to the west of the town, has been greatly appreciated for its beauty, some finding its way into The Palace of Versailles. These days Portsoy Marble Workshop, housed in a renovated building overlooking harbour, continues the tradition of crafting the local marble.

Almost directly inland from Portsoy is a well kept secret, **Fordyce**. This secluded village nestling under Drum Hill, though small, has its own castle, which sits right in the centre of the village. Built in 1592 by Sir Thomas Menzies of Drum, this four story L plan tower house in pink sandstone is a diminutive model of a 16th century Scottish

Fordyce Castle

baronial architecture. Today Fordyce is a fine conservation village, its narrow streets flanked by lovingly restored cottages it really is one of the undiscovered gems of the region. Back on the A98 near the turning for Sandend is Glasshaugh Windmill, known locally as the Cup and Saucer because of its unusual shape.

Sandend, as its name suggests, stands at the end of a broad sandy bay that is one of the most popular beaches in the area. The row of old fishermen's cottages on the shorefront are all lovingly looked after, and are unusually painted; the edges of the rough hewn stones painted black and the mortar lines painted white to give a regular block pattern appearance. Along the cliffs to the west of Sandend is **Findlater Castle**. This spectacular ruin is built into the rock-face, its empty windows look out over a sheer drop of 50ft. The heavily fortified castle was built by the Oglivies in 1455. Unsuccessfully besieged by Mary Queen of Scots in 1563, it was abandoned in the 16th century and today its crumbling remains cling on to a windlashed rock, overlooked by the taller cliffs. On those cliff on the path down to the castle is a recently restored white Doocot, or Dovecote.

From Findlater it is only a couple of miles into **Cullen**, which has a fascinating and unusual history. When the old village got a little too close to the Laird of Seafield's planned house extensions his solution was to pull down the existing village, and build a new one some distance from the big house. Work started in 1821 and everything was to be provided; Town Hall, Library and Hotel, all centred around a town square. The original village's Mercat Cross was transported to the square and mounted on an ornate octagonal base.

The Seafield Arms Hotel, Cullen. 0542-840791 Map Ref: E1

Standing in the heart of Cullen beside the old Town Hall, **The Seafield Arms Hotel** is an impressive former coaching inn, built by the Earl of Seafield in 1822. Here you will find very comfortable accommodation in 25 attractively furnished bedrooms, each equipped to a high standard and all with private facilities. The comfortable lounge and elegant dining room both feature carpets specially woven from the Grant tartan, enhancing the warm, relaxed atmosphere in which you can savour the finest ale and Scotch whisky and sample a rich variety of traditional Scottish fare, imaginatively prepared from the finest local produce. With a wealth of sporting activities and outdoor pursuits readily available and some wonderful coastal walks on your doorstep, The Seafield Arms Hotel makes an ideal holiday base.

The most striking thing about Cullen is the series of towering railway bridges that snake between the town and Seatown, the existing fishing village on the shoreline. They were built in 1886 by the Great North of Scotland Railway Company, the result of being refused permission to cross part of Cullen House grounds by Countess of Seafield. The biggest is nearly 100ft high and has eight arches, while the eastern one is a prominent feature of the centre of the new town. The line eventually closed in 1967 and much of it is now a footpath. Out in Cullen Bay are the Three Kings, a triumvirate of isolated sea-stacks.

Walking along the cliff to the next village gives fine views of the **Bow Fiddle Rock**, which looks not unlike its namesake. That next village, **Portknockie**, unlike its near neighbours, is not on the shoreline, there being no room between the foot of the cliffs and the sea, but along the clifftops over looking the harbour, which is the only one in the area accessible regardless of the tide. Our walk along the cliffs continues to **Findochty**, with its brightly painted cottages clustered around its pretty tidal harbour. The custom of decorating the houses arose from the need to use oil paints to keep the weather out, the vivid colours becoming now an established tradition, with each household vying with its neighbours to keep the paint fresh and neat. The third of this cluster of old fishing harbours is **Buckie**, once the largest town in the old county of Banff and still one of the largest in Moray District. Still a fishing harbour, with a market around 8.30 to 10.00 am, when catches have been landed. Buckie's two boatyards still build and repair traditional wooden boats. **Buckie Maritime Museum**, in Cluny Place, has displays of fishing methods, cooperage, lifeboats, navigation and local history, and the Peter Anson Gallery houses watercolours showing the development of fishing in Scotland. Nearby is the **Seamen's Memorial**, a small chapel, with beautiful stained glass windows, dedicated to local fishermen who have lost their lives at sea since 1946. Opened by the Queen in 1982 access can

Strathisla Distillery, Keith

be gained by collecting the key from 6 New Street. Keep an eye out for the town's war memorial, which is held to be one of the finest in North-East Scotland.

St. Ninians Chapel at nearby Tynet, just north of A98 between Portgordon and Fochabers is the oldest post-Reformation Catholic Church still in use in Scotland. This unassuming place of worship was originally a sheep-cote and was given by the Laird to the local Catholic Community in 1755, for use as a clandestine church during the anti-Catholic period. Back on the coast at **Spey Bay** are two very different but equally fascinating finds. **Tugnet Ice House** stands near the B9104 south of the village. Its permanent exhibition tells the story of the River Spey, its salmon fishing and wildlife. This historic ice house is possibly the largest in Scotland and dates from 1830. It was the centre of a complex salmon fishing station. During the netting season salmon would be packed in ice prior to their journey south, initially by sea and later by rail. At its high in the late 1800's 150 people were employed here and it would have been an important part of the local economy. A little to the south off the same B road is **Speymouth Railway Viaduct**. Built in 1886 and stretching over the Spey, this awe inspiring iron structure is almost 330 yards long. Now part of the Speyside Way, walkers on the bridge can the admire this cathedral of girders, as well as cross the river with ease.

We head back the short distance south to **Fochabers** with is unusual Folk Museum. An old church has been converted to house a large collection of horse drawn carts on the top floor and on the ground floor a varied collection of items that tell the history of Fochabers over the past 200 years. Nearby is the famous **Baxter's Foods Factory** and visitors centre. George Baxter set up his grocery store in the village 125 years ago and now the family's tinned soups are famous the world over.

From Fochabers we follow the A96 South-east to **Keith**. Though much of the town owes its existence to the fashion for developing planned towns, Keith's history goes back to at least 700AD. It was here in 1700 that the outlaw James MacPherson was captured, and sent to be hanged back at Banff. Forty six years later the last successful action of the Jacobite army took place here, when a section of the Government forces were take by surprised and routed. The great development of Keith that we see today took place starting in 1750, when the Earl of Findlater laid out New Keith. The town is on the famous Speyside Malt Whisky Trail, which take those fond of a tot on a 70 mile journey around the beautiful countryside, visiting eight distilleries and a cooperage. Speyside is covered in distilleries, many open to the public. There are 56 in and around Moray District, out of the 116 in Scotland. The four in Keith include **Strathisla**, which is on the trail, and famous for its Chivas Regal blended scotch which is exported all over the world.

Keeping heading south-east brings us to the once strategically important town of **Huntly**, which commands the route from Aberdeen and Strathdon into Moray. As a result it has had an eventful history, the defensive site between the rivers Deveron and Bogie having been fortified since the days of the Norman earls, though the two standing stones in the town square suggest much earlier occupation. From 1776 the town was expanded by the Duke of Gordon and the regular street pattern formed which is still a major feature today.

Enjoying a central location on Gordon Street in Huntly, just a stones throw from the castle and golf course, **Greenmount** is a welcoming Three Crown Commended guest house run by George and Evelyn Manson. This impressive Georgian building dates back some 150 years and since 1973 has been providing passing travellers with very comfortable accommodation and warm, Scottish hospitality. The dining room, with its attractive display of fishing flies provides a cosy setting for a substantial breakfast each morning as well as a wholesome evening meal, by prior arrangement. Four of the eight guest rooms are en-suite and each is attractively furnished, with the useful addition of a comprehensive information pack to help you plan your stay in this beautiful part of Scotland.

Greenmount, Gordon Street, Huntly. 0466-792482 Map Ref: E3

Almost in the heart of the town is **Huntly Castle**. An imposing ruin of rich golden stone, which replaced medieval Strathbogie Castle, it was until 1544 was the seat of the Gordons, the Marquesses of Huntly, and the most powerful family in the north until the Mid-16th century. The castle, now surrounded by a wooded park, was destroyed and rebuilt several times. The family's support for Charles I led to its final destruction during the Civil War in the mid-1600's.

Situated above the ruins of Huntly Castle, set in its own well kept grounds, overlooking the Deveron Valley, with wonderful views of the Clashmach Hills, the **Castle Hotel** is a magnificent 18th century house originally built as a home for the Dukes of Gordon, when it was known as Sandston. Later, in 1769, refurbished and extended using stones from the ruins of Huntly Castle, it was renamed Huntly Lodge, and it eventually became the Castle Hotel in 1946. As you would expect from the imposing exterior the rooms inside are extremely spacious and furnished in keeping with the hotel's age and character. All the rooms are en-suite, and the hotel dining room offers a superb menu of traditional Scottish fare, including venison, haggis and Arbroath smokies. Good fishing for salmon and sea trout on the Deveron as well as shooting and stalking. With a golf course situated adjacent to the hotel, and numerous others a short drive away golf enthusiasts are well catered for. Forest and other walks also abound in the area and the whisky and castle trails are literally on our doorstep.

The Castle Hotel, Huntly. 0466-792696 Fax: 0466-792641
Map Ref: E3

Travelling on the Huntly Ring Road, close to the roundabout you would be well advised to call in at the **King George V Garden Centre**.

Apart from having obvious appeal to the gardening enthusiast, this is much more than just a garden centre and has something to offer the whole family. As you browse, looking round the vast selection of shrubs and trees, over 100 varieties of pot plants, planters, pots and hanging baskets and other garden accessories, the children can run off energy in the adventure playground, complete with dodgem cars.

The floral department offers a complete florist service and has the largest selection of real and silk flowers in the area, while the gift shop will provide you with a wealth of ideas for that perfect present or memento. There is also a well-stocked book shop and a super restaurant which offers traditional Scottish fare, ranging from teas and snacks to freshly cooked main meals and the Centre's excellent modern facilities include toilets for the disabled and a unit for nursing mothers, ensuring everyone's needs are catered for.

King George V Garden Centre, Huntly. 0466-793908
Fax: 0466-793098 Map Ref: E3

Several miles south of the town on the B9002 is a country seat from a different era, **Leith Hall**. The mansion house of Leith is at the centre of a 286-acre estate which was the home of the head of the Leith and Leith-Hay family from 1650. The house contains personal possessions of successive Lairds, most of whom followed a tradition of military service, a story told in the 'For Crown and Country: the military Lairds of Leith' exhibition. The grounds contain an 18th century curved stables, not unlike the one back at Aden Country Park, as well as informal gardens and woodland walks.

To the north of Huntly off the A97 is the fascinating **Cloverleaf Fibre Stud**. This working farm breeds llama, alpacas, guanacos, reindeer, and goats bearing cashmere, cashgora and mohair,; as well as rare breeds of sheep In the farm shop everything from spinning fibre to finished garments are available.

The road from Huntly to Dufftown wanders along the valley of the Deveron before climbing over the spectacular Dough of Invermarkie and dropping into **Dufftown**. In 1817 James Duff, 4th Earl of Fife, founded Dufftown, or Balvenie as it was initially named, to create employment after the Napoleonic wars. Like other new villages of the period Dufftown has spacious streets laid out in a regular plan. The four main streets converge on **The Clocktower**, which was completed in 1839. It was originally the town jail, then burgh chambers and now houses the Tourist Information Centre and a small museum. The clock comes from Banff and is the very one that was put forward an hour to ensure that James MacPherson was hanged, and is known locally as 'the clock that hanged MacPherson'. Dufftown is at the centre of the whisky distilling industry, being surrounded by seven malt distilleries, the most famous probably being **Glenfiddich**, which is on the whisky trail and open to the public.

Not far from the distillery is **Balvenie Castle**, this picturesque 13th century moated stronghold was originally owned by the Comyns. During a turbulent history it was visited by Edward I in 1304, by Mary Queens of Scots in 1562, during her campaign against the Gordons. It gave refuge to Montrose in 1644 and was stormed by Royalists 1649, occupied by victorious Jacobites after the Battle of Killiecrankie in 1689 and finally held by Government troops in 1746. Also within walking distance of the town square is **Mortlach Church**, founded in around 566AD by St. Moluag. Undoubtedly one of the oldest places of Christian worship in Scotland, it has been a in use ever since. Parts of the present building date from 11/12th century, though it has been substantially reconstructed in 1876 and again in 1931. Legend has it that in 1016 it was lengthened by 3 spears length on the command of King Malcolm II, in thanksgiving for his victory over the Danes. Inside the church has some very fine stained glass and in the graveyard is a weathered Pictish cross, one side depicting two fish monsters, a relief cross and a grotesque beast, the other a serpent, bull's head and a horseman. In the vestibule of the church is an even earlier Pictish symbol stone, the 'Elephant Stone'. Later monuments around the graveyard include a fine heraldic gravestone dated 1417 and a recumbent effigy of Alexander Leslie of Kininvie in full armour dated 1549, as well as lots of distillers tombs. There is also a watch-house, used to guard against bodysnatchers.

To the south-east in Glen Fiddich is **Auchindoun Castle**. A massive ruin that stands on an isolated hillside, and can be seen from miles around. The keep, encircled by Pictish earthworks, was built by Robert Cochran, a favourite of King James III. It went on to become a stronghold of the Ogilvies, and later the Gordons. It met its end in 1592, burned in a feud with the MacIntoshes. The only access to these rather dangerous ruins is a walk up a rough track from the A941. North-west of Dufftown is **Aberlour**, and its fascinating Village Store, on the main street. This old village general store has all the original fittings, records and stock dating back to the 1920's, and is a window

Elgin Cathedral

into the past. North of the village on the A941 is **Craigellachie Bridge**. One of Thomas Telford's most graceful designs, the 152ft single span iron bridge carried the main road until 1973 and is probably the oldest iron bridge to survive in Scotland.

West of the bridge, along the B9102 is **Archiestown**. Named after its founder, Sir Archibald Grant of Monymusk, Archiestown preserves the feel of a small planned settlement of the 18th century. Close to the village is **Ladycroft Agricultural Museum**, a museum dedicated to the time when all the farm implements were worked by horses.

The administrative and commercial capital of Moray District, **Elgin**, is only a short drive north from here. The medieval street plan of Elgin is well preserved. The main street widens to the old cobbled market place, now known as the Plainstones, and is dominated by **St. Giles Church** of 1825, it position on an island site means both ends are equally prominent, one all Greek and columned, the other an eclectic round tower. A few buildings still retain the arched facades which were typical of early 18th century Elgin. One of the best examples is **Braco's Banking House** on the High Street. Built in 1694, the building takes its name from William Duff of Dipple and Braco, an ancestor of the Earl of Fife, who built Duff House in Banff.

Elgin's most famous old building is undoubtably the **Cathedral** on North College Street. When it was complete it was perhaps the most beautiful of Scottish cathedrals, known as the Lantern of the North. It was founded in 1224, damaged by a fire in 1270, but in 1390 it was burned by the 'Wolf of Badenoch', Earl of Buchan, together with the towns of Elgin and Forres. Rebuilt it did not finally fall into ruin until after the Reformation. The lead was stripped from the roof in 1667, and on Easter Sunday 1711 the great central tower fell in. The ruins were used as a 'common quarry' until 1807, when steps were taken to preserve what we see today.

Elgin is well known for the fine fabrics from **Johnstons of Elgin Mill**. Here you can watch the process that, using only the purest Cashmere from Mongolia and China and the finest Lambs wool from Australia, sees fibres dyed, spun, woven and finished at Newmill. Established nearly 200 years they are now the only British mill to convert natural raw cashmere into finished garments. In addition to the mill tours there is a shop where these high quality garments can be bought.

Not every abbey in Scotland is a ruin, by taking the B9010 south-west and turning right on to an unclassified road you will discover **Pluscarden Abbey**, originally founded in 1230. In 1390 the church was burned, probably by the 'Wolf of Badenoch', who burned Elgin. It became a dependant priory of the Benedictine Abbey at Dunfermline in 1454 until the suppression of monastic life in Scotland in 1560. Thereafter it fell into ruin, until 1948, when a group of Benedictine monks from Prinknish Abbey, Gloucester, returned to restore it. The surrounding countryside is certainly a suitably serene location for that most rare of modern ecclesiastical sights a working abbey, a status it regained in 1974. Visitors will find the Monastic services are open to the public.

Out from Elgin on the road to Lossiemouth is **Moray Motor Museum**, a unique collection of over 40 cars and motor-cycles, housed in an old mill building, that should keep any transport buff engrossed for a few hours. By keeping with the A941 we pass RAF Lossiemouth, home to powerful Jaguar ground attack jets and the Sea King Search and Rescue helicopters. Up on the Moray Firth at **Lossiemouth** you may be fortunate enough to catch a glimpse of one of only two resident populations of bottle-nosed dolphins in Britain. On a calm sunny day walkers on the coast between here and Cullen can be almost sure of seeing a group of 20 or so leaping and playing, sometimes quite close to the shore.

To the south-east of Lossiemouth is **Duffus Castle**. The massive ruins of a fine motte and bailey castle are surrounded by a moat, still complete and water-filled. The 14th-century tower that crowns the Norman motte, has caused subsidence of the motte fracturing it in an impressive fashion. Our route now takes us still westwards to our final Grampians destination, Forres. We pass the regions other RAF station along the way. RAF Kinloss is base for the long range Nimrod reconnaissance aircraft that patrol far out over the Northern Atlantic and often help guide the air- sea rescue helicopters from Lossiemouth to ships in distress.

The name of **Forres** has been made famous by Shakespeare, who set the opening scenes of 'Macbeth' here. As you enter the town from the east you will be met by **Sueno's Stone**. This, the tallest and most complex piece of early medieval sculpture in Scotland, most probably commemorates an heroic battle campaign, possibly against the Norse settlers of Orkney. The elaborate carvings tell the story of a great victory, the stone being a sort of war report. Discovered buried in 1726 it is now housed in a glass structure to protect it from the ravages of the weather. West of the town is **Brodie Castle and Gardens**, just off the A96. There have been Brodies at Brodie for 800 years, 25 Lairds in all, this structure being the work of the 12th Laird, Alexander. The castle being largely rebuilt after the earlier structure was burned in 1645.

Based on a 16th century Z plan house, with additions in 17th and 19th centuries, it remains, outside, stout simple and uncluttered.

Inside the story is a little different. The house contains fine French furniture, English, Continental and Chinese porcelain, and a major collection of paintings. The plasterwork of the Dining Room is exceptionally intricate, in each corner dusky brown maidens and vines spill from a blue background, appearing to represent the elements: Earth, Air, Fire and Water. Back outside a woodland walk has been laid out in the gardens by edge of 3 acre pond, which was intended to be the centre piece of a much grander scheme, until the money ran out. It is only a mile or so from Brodie to the border with our next chapter, so it is here we leave the Grampians.

Coastline at Pennan

CHAPTER TEN

The Highlands and Islands.

Tioram Castle, Moidart

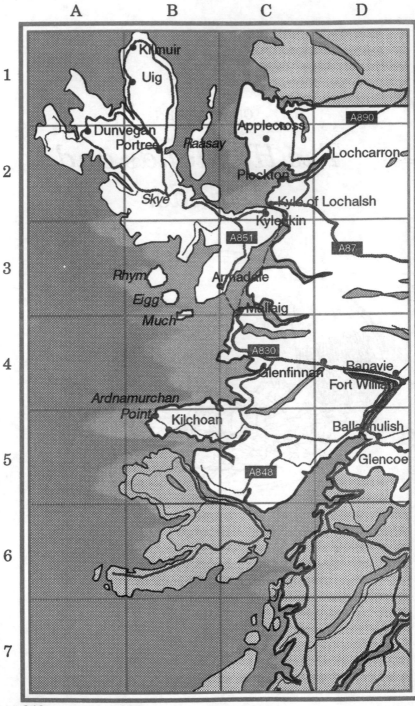

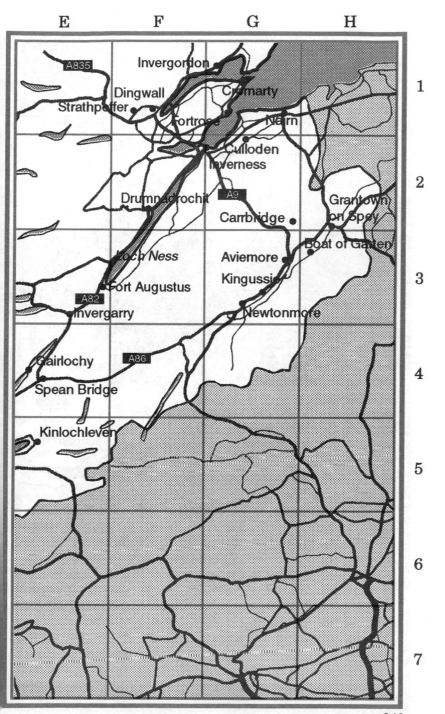

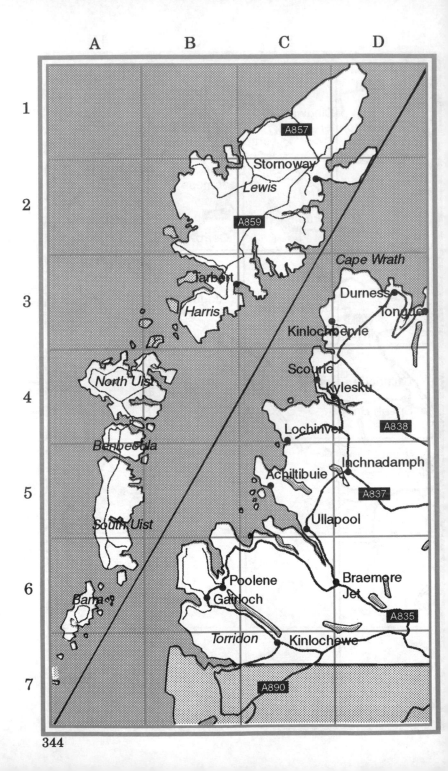

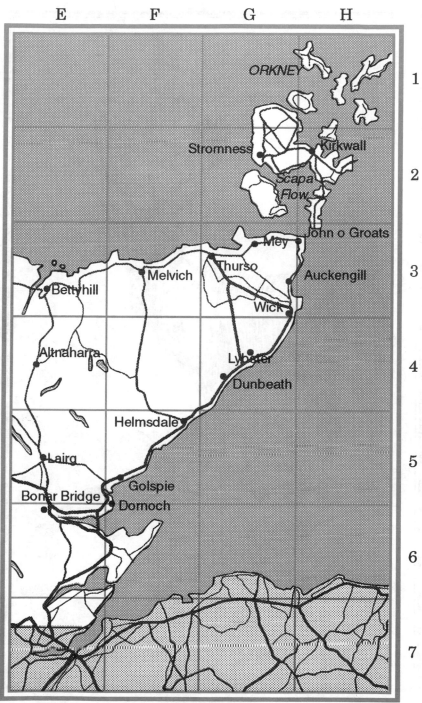

Monarch of the Glen

CHAPTER TEN

The Highlands and Islands.

Ceud Mile Failte - a Gaelic hundred thousand welcomes to the Highlands and Islands, the biggest region on our journey and the one of the last remote wilderness of Western Europe.

We start this epic in **Nairn**, an attractive county town and holiday resort. In Laing Hall on King Street is Nairn Fishertown Museum. It houses a collection of photographs and articles connected with the Moray Firth and herring fishing industry during the days of steam drifters. The remains of an industry of a very different nature stands just up the coast at Whiteness Head. The giant skeleton of the oil platform construction yard stands idle as testament to the boom years of the North Sea oil exploration. Just along the coast is **Fort George**. Built out into the Firth on a promontory the fort was built in 1748 as a result of the '45 Rebellion. It is an imposing sight, all massive ramparts and solid walls. Inside there is Regimental Museum of the Queen's Own Highlanders, who are still barracked here, as well as displays on the Seaforth Highlanders, Queen's Own Cameron Highlanders and the Lovat Scouts. The surrounding area is used for manoeuvres, so don't be at all surprised if a clump of bushes stands up and walks off!

Inland is a fortress of a different era, **Cawdor Castle**, which stands in the village of the same name. The old central tower dates back to 1372 and is surrounded by 16th century additions. Shakespeare's Macbeth was Thane of Cawdor and the castle is one of several traditional settings for the murder of Duncan at the hands of the real Macbeth, Shakespeare's 'Scottish Play', being loosely based on real events.

From Cawdor our route heads south joining the A939 near Rayburn. A little to the south of here at Ardclach stands a lone bell-tower. The parish church here was set so low down on the river bank that the peel of its bell would never have carried; so the tower was built in 1655, calling the locals to worship or warning of attack. Near the junction with the A940 an unclassified road heads west to Lochindorb. On a small island stands the ruined **Lochindorb castle**, once seat of the Comyns. In 1371 it became the stronghold of the Earl of Buchan, the vicious 'Wolf of Badenoch', who terrorised the area. James II ordered its destruction in 1458 to prevent any further misuse.

The main road now crosses the wide-open Dava Moor before entering **Grantown on Spey**, one of Queen Victoria's favourite villages. Originally laid out in the 18th century around a central square this traditional Highland resort grew in stature when Victorian doctors recommended it for its healthy air. A little way out of the village on the A95 at Dulnain Bridge is the Speyside Heather Garden Centre. Here the Heather Heritage Centre houses an exhibition on the historical uses for heather. It was made into weaving ropes, doormats, baskets and used in thatching. as well as in medicine, drinks and dyeing wool. Outside the landscaped show garden has approximately 300 varieties on show. There is also the opportunity to buy heather for your own garden, or gifts from the heather craft shop.

Boat of Garten was originally named after the ferry here across the Spey. Today it is the northern terminus of the **Strathspey Steam Railway**. Discover the magic of steam on the old Perth to Inverness line between here and Aviemore Speyside. The line was originally closed in 1965, but in 1978 trains started running once more. The trains are run by a mainly volunteer team of enthusiasts who have plans the route through to Grantown on Spey. In the restored station buildings at Boat of Garten there is a small display of railway relics and rolling stock. From outside the station you can take a vintage coach trip up to the RSPB's **Loch Garten Reserve**. Ospreys nest here every year and visitors can watch the from the well-equipped visitor centre.

At the southern end of the Strathspey railway is **Aviemore**, the main year-round holiday resort in the Spey Valley, dominated from the west by the birchwood cliffs of the Craigellachie. In the other direction the huge bulk of the Cairngorms fills the south- eastern skyline. Much of the village was built during the 1960's to provide facilities for the growing number skiers.

On the way out of the village to the mountains you pass the steam railway station and its engine shed full of burnished locomotives. The shed itself is original but the station buildings came from Dalnaspidal, and the turntable from Kyle of Lochalsh. Further up the road at Coylumbridge a right turn takes us up to Loch Morlich and the **Cairngorm Reindeer Centre**, where visitors may accompany the guide to see the Scotland's only reindeer herd free-ranging in their natural surroundings. Bending south the route becomes the 'ski road', climbing steadily above the forest to the high level car parks which in Winter and early spring service the Cairngorm Ski-lifts. The whole year round a chair-lift operates to the Ptarmigan Restaurant, which at 3600ft is the highest building in Britain.

Back down the valley floor we head south on the old A9 for seven miles to find the **Highland Wildlife Park**. Owned and run by the Royal Zoological Society of Scotland it has breeding groups of Scottish mammals past and present in a beautiful natural setting. The drive through the reserve has red deer, bison and Highland cattle roaming free, whilst the walk around area has capercaillie, eagles, wolves and wildcats. In the visitors centre there is an exhibition on 'Man and Fauna in the Highlands'. A different history unfolds down in **Kingussie**, at the Highland Folk Museum. Based at an 18th century shooting lodge much of the museum is open air and features a 'black house' from Lewis and a wide variety of farming equipment. Indoors the farming museum has fine displays of all manner of articles, as well as a exhibition on Highland tinkers.

South of the village on the B970 are the substantial ruins of **Ruthven Barracks**. Stood on a site originally occupied by a fortress of the 'Wolf of Badenoch', the barracks were first built in 1716 to keep the Highlanders in check following the 1715 Rising and were added to by General Wade in 1734. After the debacle of Culloden some Jacobite forces rallied here hoping Bonnie Prince Charlie might once again take the field. When they realized the cause was hopeless they destroyed the barracks. A little further along the A9 at Balavil Brae in **Newtonmore** is the unique Waltzing Water Show. This unusual and stunning combination of water, lights and music is great all weather entertainment for all the family.

Newtonmore is as far south as this part of our journey gets so we now leap back up the A9 to **Carrbridge**, a few miles north of Aviemore. The stone bridge that gave the village its name in 1717 still survives, an elegant single high-arched span. The imaginative **Landmark Visitors Centre** here includes a sophisticated audio-visual history of the Highlands. Outdoors there is a boardwalk maze and even - securely raised on timber stilts - a tree-top- level trail and a 65ft tall observation tower.

From Carrbridge the road climbs over the lonely summits of Slochd and Tomatin, both over a 1000ft above sea level, running neck and neck with the railway line. The views over Inverness and the Moray Firth as you descend off the summit are a wonderful, but we don't head straight into the Highlands capital taking a right turn at Daviot in search of one of Scotland's saddest places - **Culloden**. This bleak moor was the site for the last land battle on mainland Britain, and saw the final demise of the Jacobites attempts to regain the throne of Britain and the end of the Highland tribal system.

In April 1746 1500 clansmen lost their lives fighting at Bonnie Prince Charlie's last stand. The actions of the victors has gone down as one of the most shameful events in the long proud history of the British army. After the battle orders were given to kill every Highland survivor, starting with the wounded. The English army carried out its orders with ruthless efficiency. Men were shot, bayoneted and burnt alive, then the army went on the rampage through the Highland camp slaughtering the women and children. The killings spread across the Highlands as Clan chiefs loyal to the crown exterminated hereditary enemies. The King extracted his revenge on the Jacobites in thorough fashion; lands were forfeited, the kilt was banned and the bagpipes deemed an offensive weapon. The story of the battle and the Prince's flight are told in an exciting audio-visual show at the visitors centre. Outside you can wander the battlefield, and see the many graves of the clans. This melancholy moor seems a desperately inglorious place for such high dreams to have died.

It is just a short drive into **Inverness**, the transport, trading, shopping and administrative centre of the vast Highland Region. The River Ness flows briskly through the centre on its way to the Moray Firth and many of the towns most interesting features are clustered round its bank. The 19th century castle, a fine red-sandstone building still serves as courthouse and council offices, it stands on the same site as the castle where Macbeth murdered Duncan in the play. The Town House is ornamented Victorian Gothic, where Lloyd George called the first cabinet meeting outside London. Across the road is the impressive Corinthian columned Royal Bank of Scotland. On Huntly Street is Balnain House, Home of Highland Music. Balnain Trust is dedicated to preserving every aspect of Highland music. The exhibitions present a huge selection covering everything from heroic warrior songs to Gaelic rock n'roll. There are a dozen listening stations and you can try the instruments for yourself - or perhaps not. The house itself has quite a history. Built for a merchant in 1726, it was used as a government field hospital following Culloden. In the 1880's it was a base for Royal Ordnance making the first survey map of the Highlands.

Just two minute's walk from the centre of Inverness, **Culduthel Lodge,** on Culduthel Road, is a superb guest house owned and run by David and Marion Bonsor. Awarded the prestigious Three Crowns Deluxe rating by the Scottish Tourist Board, the attractively laid out gardens and rather grand exterior of this impressive house are equalled by the elegant interior, with twelve spacious and beautifully colour co-ordinated, en-suite guest rooms all equipped to the highest standards. A warm Scottish welcome greets your arrival and in addition to a substantial breakfast each morning, the daily changing dinner menu offers a mouthwatering variety of fine Scottish fare, imaginatively prepared with something to tempt every palate.

Culduthel Lodge, 14 Culduthel Road, Inverness. 0463-240084
Map Ref: F2

Getting away from the hustle of a busy city centre is easy in Inverness. Just a few minutes walk from the centre and you cross the footbridges that link up the wooded Ness Islands and watch the anglers casting for salmon in the fast running water. Another beautiful place is more unexpected. A local boast is that Inverness has the best-placed burial ground in the world. Tomnahurich cemetery occupies a wooded hilltop above the Caledonian Canal, and a favourite walk is to the viewpoint at it summit.

Ryeford, 21 Ardconnel Terrace, Inverness. 0463-242871   Ref: F2

Also enjoying an elevated location in Ardconnel Terrace, above the town is **Ryeford** is the charming home of Catriona and Simon Forsyth who offer a warm welcome to their many guests.

Built approximately 140 years ago, Ryeford is typical of a Victorian terraced house and is tastefully furnished throughout, providing very comfortable accommodation in six attractive and well equipped guest rooms, two with en-suite facilities. There are wonderful views of Inverness from some of the bedroom windows and in the pleasant surroundings of the elegant dining room you can savour Catriona's full Scottish breakfast, a substantial meal which sets you up perfectly for a day's exploring.

An exhibition in Falcon Square 'correlates the fossil evidence of the Plesiosauridae with advanced studies of the morphology of the biomass', or more simply presents the research into the Loch Ness monster. Appetite whetted we head off in search of the Loch and its tenant.

Luckily for us there are roads both sides of **Loch Ness**, and so the opportunity for an excellent round trip. If you'd prefer to see the loch from the water there are plenty of cruises to choose from. The loch itself is 24 mile long, as much as a mile wide, and up to 900ft deep. The greatest expanse of fresh water in Europe, its waters are clouded by peat hiding anything that may lurk in its depths. One hidden monster the loch has given up recently is a WWII Wellington bomber, the last of its type, that had crashed landed on the surface in 1941. It is now being restored at Brooklands in Surrey, where it was built.

For some miles the A82 hugs the lochside, until it turns away to curve through the villages of **Drumnadrochit** and Lewiston. The Loch Ness Monster Centre here displays photographs, drawings, sonar scans, and some rather speculative claims about one of the world's greatest mystery phenomenons. Expeditions from all over the world have searched high and low for the vital piece of evidence that something lurks in the Loch and their endeavours are also recorded here.

The road rejoins the lochside above **Urquhart Castle**. These dramatic ruins were once one of the largest castles in Scotland. Its strategic position led to it changing hands several times, until, finally it was blown up in 1692 to prevent its being occupied by Jacobites. Not far beyond is a memorial to John Cobb, the land speed record holder who was killed on the water near here in 1952, attempting to set a new water speed record in his jet-engined craft Crusader.

The A82 is a very pleasant road on this part of the lochside, with the Forestry Commission spruce plantations on the hillsides and the ancient birch, rowan and alder fringing the loch. At the head of the loch is **Fort Augustus**. A flight of lochs here lifts the Caledonian Canal up from the level of the loch as it travels south. Close at hand is the **Great Glen Exhibition**, which illustrates the story of the canal, as well as local history. St. Benedicts Abbey, open to visitors, stands in beautiful surroundings on the edge of the village. Some of the Abbeys buildings were part of the old fort here, still standing when the site was given to the Benedictines in 1876.

As you travel through Fort Augustus, you will discover a super stopping-off point when you call in at the **Lock Inn**, a delightful old stone-built pub full of atmosphere and charm. The olde worlde atmosphere of the cosy bar is enhanced by old photographs of Fort Augustus lock and ships on the walls and you can choose from a wide selection of ales and malt whiskies. The high point of a visit here however, is the excellent restaurant upstairs which provides an extensive menu of the finest Scottish produce imaginatively prepared and beautifully presented. With such culinary delights as Haggis with Whisky Sauce, Nessies Dragon Pie, and Lochness Mud Pie with cream to choose from, there is something here to whet the most jaded appetite.

Lock Inn, Fort Augustus. 0320-6302 Map Ref: E3

Beside the Abbey entrance our route bears left and along the southern bank of the loch. This road follows the route of General Wades original military road through the Great Glen. The first village you will encounter is Foyers. Here in 1891 opened Britain's first aluminium smelter. The main attraction of the location were the **Falls of Foyers** and the hydro- electric power they could supply. Though the smelter closed in 1967 the falls have never really recovered. The road runs on, high above the loch, only dipping to its level at Inverfarigaig. Here you have the option of keeping with the lochside or heading east through the foothills of the Monadhliath Mountains and on to join the A9 south of Inverness. Which ever road is chosen our journey now turns directly north for the long drive to the roof of Britain, calling at some interesting places along the route.

Where there was once the ferry across Beauly Firth now stands the magnificent Kessock Bridge carrying the A9 north on to the **Black Isle** - which is neither black nor an island. North Kessock gave its name to the small sweet herrings caught in the Moray Firth during summer and sold in the local shops, a delicacy worth seeking. Eastwards is **Fortrose** and its magnificent ruined Cathedral, which rivals the majesty of Elgin. Around it are the tombs and mausoleums of Clan aristocracies. On the northern tip of the isle is **Cromarty**, a real gem and an almost perfect example of an 18th century Scottish seaport. The failure of the fishing in Moray Firth, and the coming of the railway saw the port go into decline. The decay and neglect that threatened it for so long has now been reversed and restoration of the rope works, brewery, fisher-cottages, civic buildings and merchants houses is well under way. Of particular fascination is the award winning Courthouse, which uses computer controlled animated figures to bring the court back to life. Another piece of history is the car ferry that still crosses the Firth to Nigg during the summer, the last ferry in the area. We briefly forsake the new A9 to follow its old course to **Dingwall**, a traditional bustling market town that serves much of Easter Ross. The towns history stretches back over a thousand years, its name Norse for Place of the Council. From being a southern outpost of the great Norse Earldom of Orkney, it became a strategic fortress of the Celtic Kings, a stronghold against the Vikings to the north and the wild and rebellious Highlanders all around. Visitor can't miss the tall monument tower, which stands in Mitchell Hill cemetery, overlooking the town. It was erected in memory of General Sir Hector MacDonald, an outstanding soldier who served with the Gordon Highlanders, and known as 'Fighting Mac'.

Above the town on the Heights of Brae is the **Neil Gunn Memorial**, which overlooks the Cromarty Firth and the Black Isle, the inspirations for his Highland novels. From here is only a few miles into the Victorian Spa town of **Strathpeffer**. Full of genteel villas and grand houses, it is a marked contrast to the wild hills and moors nearby. You can still take the waters at the restored pump room in the village square. Sulphurous and pungent with a lingering aftertaste, the waters were held to be a fine restorative - something to judge for yourself. Outside the village is the Eagle Stone, a Pictish stone that has an eagle and horseshoe shape etched on it. Across the road from the stone is the long closed Strathpeffer Station. Though the trains are gone the building is still very much alive, full of craft shops and the **Museum**

Sir Hector MacDonald's Monument, Dingwall

of Childhood, a fascinating look at bringing up children in the Highlands.

The road from Dingwall follows the shore of Cromarty Firth, rejoining the A9 at the northern end of the second of the great new bridges across the Firths of Easter Ross. If you look up to the left here you many spot an unusual monument high on the hillside above. This is the **Fyrish Monument,** a replica of the gateway of Negapatam. This Indian city was captured in 1781 by Sir Hector Munro, and he had the monument built in 1782 providing work during a time of great unemployment in the area. A two mile long steep rocky path leads up to it, but the climb is worth it for views across the Firth.

We leave the trunk road behind again and take the B road into the Firthside town of **Invergordon.** Planned as a model village to encourage local trades, today the town is the centre for the repair and refitting of North Sea oil rigs. There are often as many as a dozen scattered around the Firth, and you can get really close to these man-made creatures of the deep by driving along the front. To the east is **Tarbet Ness.** There are several pictish stones on the Ness, and indeed all over Ross-shire, each intricately carved. Perhaps the most impressive here are at Shandwick and Nigg. At Hill of Fearn is **Fearn Abbey,** built in the 13th century. It was converted into a Parish church, but in 1742 the roof collapsed killing 42 of the congregation. The nave and choir of the abbey were restored, and are still used as the parish church, whilst the north and south chapels remain roof-less.

While the movement of goods has benefited greatly from the huge bridge building programme over the three Firths in the area it means a journey searching for hidden places can miss out on so much, so we will stick with the old route along the Dornoch Firth to Ardgay and its twin village of **Bonar Bridge** a mile apart at the head of the Dornoch Firth. It was once a major east coast bridging point and still is an important junction though the A9 now uses the impressive bridge opened by the Queen Mother in 1991. It is only a short detour inland to **Lairg,** that sits at the southern end of Loch Shin and at the centre of Sutherland's road network. The Lairg lamb sales are the biggest one-day sales in Europe, a reflection on the importance of sheep farming in the north to this day. Not far from the village are the picturesque Falls of Shin. The water crashes through a rock gorge that is famous for its leaping salmon. Also nearby is **Carbisdale Castle,** Scotland's most impressive Youth Hostel. Stood overlooking the Kyle of Sutherland it was commissioned by the Dowager Duchess of Sutherland and completed in 1914, two years after her death, and gifted to the Scottish Youth Hostel Association in 1945.

Sat at the mouth of the Dornoch Firth, **Dornoch,** an attractive seaside town, is dominated by the 13th century tower of the Cathedral. As well as miles of excellent and deserted beaches, there is the famous Royal Dornoch golf course, ranked in the world top 12. As well as the Cathedral to admire there is the 16th century Bishop's Palace, now a hotel and the Old Jail, now a craft centre. Dornoch was also the site of the last witch burning in Scotland in 1722, the poor woman being tarred feathered and then roasted alive. Just north of the town is Skelbo Castle, on the shore of Loch Fleet, originally built in 1259 it's now a rather dangerous ruin best seen from the roadside. **Loch Fleet** itself is a massive salt water basin at the mouth of the River Fleet, home to seals, ducks and waders and a Scottish Wildlife Trust Reserve.

A little further up the coast is **Golspie**, a picturesque town that is the administrative centre of Sutherland. Beinn a'Bhragaidh overlooks the town and is crowned by a monument to the first Duke of Sutherland, reached by a steep climb from the town. The Big Burn Walk at the north end of the village is well recommended as is a visit to the Orcadian Stone Company's workshops and geological exhibition.

On the outskirts of the town is **Dunrobin Castle**, ancient seat of the Earls and Dukes of Sutherland. Parts of the castle date back to the 1200's, although most was built in the 19th century in the style of a French chateau. The Sutherland family have a rather colourful history, full of treachery and intrigue, presiding over many of the Highland clearances of last century amongst many other earlier miss-deeds. There are fine gardens to explore and a museum that houses a collection of archaeological remains and hunting trophies from the world over. The castle has one of the most exclusive railway halts in Scotland. Rustic Dunrobin Castle Station was built as a private stop and last regularly used in the Sixties. Though it no longer appears in the timetable during the summer British Rail organises excursion trains from Inverness.

Helmsdale stands on one of the great Salmon rivers of the north, and the village owes its origin to the herring boom of the last century. Boats still land fish here but the boom days are sadly gone. Surrounded by steep hillsides and crofts it also has a rocky shoreline where fossils and gemstones have been discovered. Helmsdale is also home to **Timespan**, which uses the latest in audio-visual technology to tell the dramatic story of the Highlands. A short drive up the Strath of Kildonan takes you to Baille an Or and Suisgill, scenes of the Sutherland gold rush of 1869. You can still pan for gold today but don't bank on becoming rich overnight.

North of Helmsdale, the A9 climbs to the Ord of Caithness, 1300ft above the close-by sea. From this high point there are wonderful views north to the Caithness coastline, south over East Sutherland and, on a clear day across the Firth to the Moray coast and the Grampian Highlands beyond. A little north at Ousdale a footpath leads from a lay-by to ruined croft houses of Badbea, perched above the cliffs. This lonely settlement was founded by tenants evicted from the inland straths during the infamous 'clearances'. Tradition has it that the livestock and children of the village had to be tethered to prevent them being blown over the cliffs.

At **Dunbeath** the Dunbeath Heritage Centre features interesting displays on the natural and social history of the area and a fine audio-visual presentation. The village is the birth place of the author Neil Gunn, the surrounding area and its people providing this renowned highland story teller with the inspiration for many of his tales. A mile north of the village is **Lhaidhay Croft Museum**, an original longhouse dating from around 1842 which contains many examples of implements and furniture used by 19th century crofters. The small harbour at Latheronwheel is specially picturesque and there are many pleasant walks around it. Nearby Latheron is the home of the **Clan Gunn Centre**, which as well as having displays on the clan has many displays relevant to the history of the area.

The village of **Lybster** boasts a fine harbour and an interesting Celtic Cross, now protected from the elements with a cover, standing on the south side of the churchyard. Just north of the village a minor road leads to the Neolithic **Grey Cairns of Camster**, chambered burial cairns dating back to the 2nd and 3rd millennia BC. North of Lybster near Halberry Head is further evidence of ancient civilization in the area. At the **Hill O'Many Stones**, early Bronze Age stone rows in an array of 22 rows with an average eight stones each. At Ulbster is the **Cairn of Get**, which measures over 80ft in length and nearly 50ft wide. Opposite the sign for the cairn are Whaligoe Steps, which descend the spectacular cliffs to a small harbour where boats used to land their catches. In the middle of the last century over 150 fishermen lived on the cliff tops and the women folk would climb the 300 steps from the harbour with the full herring-baskets and them walk the six miles to the fishmarket at Wick. The harbour is long abandoned but the steps have been repaired, though they can be precarious in wet and windy weather.

Wick was once the busiest herring port in Europe, and today there is plenty to see in this friendly town. The award winning Wick Heritage Centre includes a cooperage , blacksmiths shop, kippering kilns and an outstanding collection of photographs. Wick has its fair share of castles too. Oldwick Castle, to the south of the town, is one of the earliest stone castles in Scotland, and there are the three castles of

Sinclair's Bay. Girnigoe and its once siamese brother Sinclair stand adjacent, clinging on to the cliff edge above the southern end of the bay. One time strongholds of the Earls of Caithness, Girnigoe is the older, dating from the end of the 15th century and Sinclair, built in 1606/7, was developed from it. Attacked by a force from Keiss in 1679 both were abandoned and within 20 years were ruins. At the northern end of the bay stands Keiss Castle. As with its southerly brothers it is built on a rock promontory in typical Caithness style defending against attack from land or sea. Another fortress of the Sinclairs, they abandoned it in 1755 for Keiss House, and is now a sorry if impressive ruin.

Just beyond Brough Head at the top of the bay is **Auckengill** and the John Nicolson Museum. The displays tell the archaeological history of Caithness, concentrating on the unique Iron Age brochs of the county, and on John Nicolson, a Victorian antiquarian. Of special interest is a 4000 year old beaker which would have contained food or drink to sustain the dead person on his or her journey to the afterlife.

From here it is only a short run on to **Duncansby Head**. The lighthouse on the head commands a fine view of Orkney, the Pentland Skerries and the headlands of the east coast. A little to the south are the three Duncansby Stacks, huge stone 'needles' in the sea. The high sandstone cliffs are severed by great deep gashes running inland, one of which is bridged by a natural arch. Seabirds wheel between the rock faces and the seals sunbathing far below. Though much of Caithness is relatively flat the cliffs here ably demonstrate that we are still hundreds of feet above sea level.

Quite literally round the corner from Duncansby the A9 finishes at **John o'Groats**, the furthest point from Land's End on the British mainland. Though neither are extreme compass points it is the longest uninterrupted run on the mainland - a full 876 miles separates them. There are many attractions to look around , including John o'Groats Pottery, Caithness Candles, the First and Last Shop and the Last House Museum. You can also have your photograph taken beside the famous signpost, with your hometown and mileage specially placed on it. A small ferry crosses from the little harbour to Orkney offering interesting day trips. We now turn westwards, not that there is much choice.

The **Castle of Mey** in the village of the same name is Queen Elizabeth the Queen Mother's holiday home. The Royal Gallery in the Castle Arms Hotel is a unique collection of photographs of the Queen Mother and the Royal family in Caithness. The locals would have you believe that she has been known to pop in for a drink when holidaying at the Castle.

North-west of Mey is **Dunnet Head,** the most northerly point on the Mainland of Britain, but unlike its pretender to the east not as well remembered. From here it is nearer to the Arctic Circle than London. Above the lighthouse, amongst the remains of the wartime radar station, is a viewfinder table. This identifies the far distant mountains of Ben Loyal and Ben Hope, visible on a clear day, the Old Man of Hoy off Orkney, and the other landmarks around. It is also an excellent place to watch the ships in the busy shipping lanes of the Pentland Firth.

It is a short drive from here into **Thurso,** whose origins date back to Viking times. Entry to the town is greeted by the rather bizarre Thurso Castle lodge. It is a wild piece of gothic, a folly if ever there was one, all over sized battlements and towers, with a top heavy gateway that looks set to topple in the slightest breeze. The town itself has an excellent **Heritage Museum,** amongst the exhibits are a reconstruction of a crofter's kitchen, a runic cross discovered at Old St. Peters Kirk and a collection of the plant and fossil specimens gathered by the 19th century naturalist, Robert Dick.

Old St. Peter's Kirk itself is situated down near the harbour, in the restored old town. Some of its ruins date as far back as the 12th century. The Meadow Well stands nearby, it was once the main water supply for the town and is now covered by an unusual round building. Next door to Thurso is the port of Scrabster, where the ferries from Orkney dock and where we head to catch one.

The Orkney and Shetland Archipelagos were governed by The Norse for some 400 years. It wasn't until 1468 that the islands were ceded to Scotland as part of a marriage settlement. The Norse influence has remained strong and still today the local accent is as much Scandinavian as anything else. Many of the place names are pure Norse, and as late as last century the ancient Norse language of Norn was still in use on Shetland. They are a very independent folk, the Orcadians and Shetlanders. Both see the Scots as being as foreign as the English, though that doesn't mean you won't receive a warm welcome.

Orkney offers much to see and do. Places not to be missed include the Italian Chapel on the tiny island of Lamb Holm, built by Italian prisoners of war from scrap metal, and beautifully painted inside. The Kitchener Memorial, overlooking the sea at Marwick Head, where the warship carrying him was sunk in 1916. Then there's Britain's most northerly real-ale brewery, Orkney, at Quoyloo, with its additive free Raven Ale and Dark Island. The islands are an ornithologists and naturalists dream as well.

Sailing into the port of **Stromness** is a memorable experience.

THE HIGHLAND AND ISLANDS

Soon after leaving Scabster, and crossing the Pentland Firth, you pass the **Old Man of Hoy**. An inspiring 450ft stack, not climbed until 1966, that stands off the high cliffs of Hoy, guarding the approaches to the little port of Stromness, which has been a safe harbour since Viking days and through the centuries has played host to whaling, herring and battle fleets.

The islands abound with evidence of long ago cultures that scratched out a living here. There are Megalithic, Neolithic, Stone Age and Iron Age sites everywhere. To the east of the port is **Maeshowe**, a vast neolithic tomb. Built with huge stones some weighing up to 3 tons, it is 25ft high and 115ft in diameter. Originally filled with treasure, in 1150 it was looted by a group of Norsemen, who left runic graffiti recording their act of vandalism. To the west is **Skarabrae** a complete Stone Age village uncovered by great storm in 1850 after some 4000 years under the sand.

Kirkwall is the capital of Orkney - never 'the Orkneys' - and, together with Stromness, is on the rather confusingly named Mainland, the largest of Orkneys 66 islands. The ferry to Shetland docks here. The town is most famous for its great **Cathedral of St. Magnus**, founded in 1127. At the time of the Reformation the protestations of the people of Kirkwall saved it from destruction. A mere hundred yards away is **Earl Patrick's Palace** which has been described as one of the finest pieces of Renaissance architecture left in Scotland. Built in 1607, by the tyrannical Earl Patrick Stewart, it is a fine looking ruin and must have looked magnificent in all its glory.

To the south of Mainland island is **Scapa Flow**, a huge natural harbour, used in both world wars as a major naval base. Under the cliffs of Gaitnip, in eastern Scapa, lies the battleship Royal Oak, sunk within five weeks of the outbreak of WWII in an audacious submarine attack. She is the grave of 800 men, her position marked by a buoy and the traces of fuel oil on the sea surface, still seeping from her bunkers. Royal Oak is not the only battleship in Scapa Flow. After the Great War the German High Seas Fleet was interned here. Their skeleton crews carried out one last defiant and dramatic act and scuttled the entire fleet. Many were raised for scrap, but battleships, cruisers and destroyers still lie where they finally came to rest in 1919.

Our next port of call out here in the Northern Atlantic is **Fair Isle**, Britain's most isolated community. The island is famous for its intricately pattern knitwear and as a staging post for thousands of migrating birds. As you can imagine access to the island can be tricky. There is a twice weekly mailboat and scheduled flights, both from Shetland, but the weather can easily leave the island isolated for weeks.

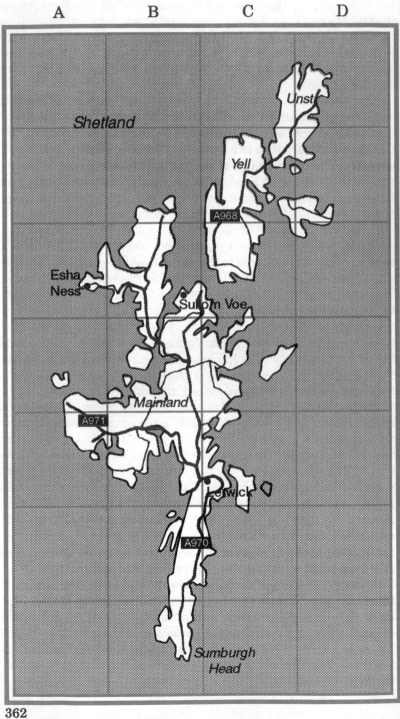

THE HIGHLAND AND ISLANDS

The sea is a part of everyday life in **Shetland**, Britain's northernmost islands, some 100 in all. Such was the reputation of Shetlander's sea faring skills that nearly 3000 were serving with Nelson's fleet during his great victories. The islands are so far north that during Summer there is scarcely any night, just the dimming of the sky around midnight, know locally as simmer dim. The skies above the main town of **Lerwick** light up on the last Tuesday of January as well, when the islanders celebrate **Up-Helly-Aa**. The men of the town dress as Vikings and parade through the streets with a replica Norse Galley, which is put to the torch in a flaming declaration of Viking ancestry. The very luckiest of visitors to Shetland many be treated to the most spectacular light show on earth - Aurora Borealis - the Northern lights. This amazing natural phenomenon comes from the polar horizon and once seen is never forgotten.

As well as the total peace and tranquillity there are plenty of things to discover on the islands. **Jarlshof** at Sumburgh Head is a remarkable site, where seven distinct layers of civilization can be identified amongst its ancient dwellings. One of the most remarkable archaeological sites in Europe, its oldest, Iron age, dwellings are very similar to Skarabrae on Orkney.

Mousa Broch stands on the small island of the same name. It is the best preserved of the Brochs or forts unique to the northern tip of Scotland and the northern and western islands. It stands over 40ft high, its inner and outer walls containing a rough staircase the can be climbed to the parapet. There are nearly 200 of these brochs on Orkney and Shetland, yet we know very little about their builders, and they stand as monuments to a people whose careful defences failed against an unknown enemy.

Near to the town of Lerwick is **Scalloway Castle**, built by the Earl Patrick Stewart in 1600. It fell into disuse just 15 years later when the notorious Earl was executed. He had paid for its construction, and that of Earl's Palace on Orkney, by the simple means of extracting free materials and labour from his tenants on pain of forfeiture of their own lands and properties.

Wildlife abounds all over the islands, tiny ponies roam free and there are seals, otters and fabulous colonies of seabirds to be studied. The scenery is at once bleak, windswept and fantastic, specially the coast at Esha Ness, with its spectacular sea stacks. A long journey here will never be forgotten and many come back time and again, caught under the spell of both these groups of islands.

Our must now return to the mainland, and once more to Scrabster, to journey across the roof of Britain, heading west. Our first encounter looks like it's straight off the set of a science-fiction film. The Atomic

Energy Authority's **Dounreay** site houses Britain's oldest nuclear reactor, built in 1955. It is to be closed, part of the move away from nuclear power but in the meantime you can discover all about atomic energy in a free exhibition and in the afternoons everyone over the age of 12 can join a guide tour around the reactor.

Along the coast road is **Melvich**, lying at the mouth of the River Halladale, which drains much of Sutherland's interior. A beautiful beach lies on the river estuary, surrounded by massive cliffs. Nearby is the **Split Stone**. Legend has it the Devil split it in a fit of temper, having chased an old woman round and round it. The A897 follows the course of the river inland, crossing the vast, bleak and uninhabited hinterland before emerging on the south-east coast at Helmsdale.

Further along the spectacular coast road is one of North Sutherland's biggest villages, **Bettyhill**. It is a crofting community situated beside the striking Farr Beach. As with many coastal settlements it owes its existence to the notorious 'Highland Clearances' of the last century. The history of those troubled times is well told in **Strathnaver Museum** in the village. To the south of Bettyhill is a witness of the clearances, Achanlochy village, now just bare outlines in the turf.

The story of the clearances is very sad, greed overcoming the traditions of the Highlands., The clans had lived happily in settlements like Achanlochy for centuries. Their chief was the clan 'father' responsible for administering justice, receiving no rent, but able to rely upon the young men to serve him in times of trouble. Culloden changed everything. Lands were handed over to loyal chiefs, who lost most of their powers and simply became landlords. The rents that their new tenants could raise were not enough though, to maintain their new lifestyles.

An easier means of raising the money to live in comfort did appear; the Cheviot sheep, which was hardy enough to withstand the winters and gave better quantities of quality meat and wool. The draw back was that they needed the land the clansmen lived on. With their new found position in society to maintain many chiefs turned their backs on the clans, ignoring their ancient obligations to look after them in times of hardship, and simply evicting them to make way for the sheep. The people left passively, bewildered and unable to understand why their protectors would cause them such misery, sent to poor coastal lands or forcibly emigrated to America.

The single largest land owner in the area was Lord Stafford, later first Duke of Sutherland. He was English and his wife had inherited the chieftainship of the people of Sutherland. In his name the factors (Scottish Land Agents) organized clearances with increasing ruthlessness and brutality. Many thousands were displaced between

1800 and 1841. Even as late as 1853 Mrs MacDonell, widow of the 16th chief of Glengarry, oversaw the burning of her peoples cottages, a ship standing by to take them to America. Those who resisted were left without shelter to die in the hills. It wasn't until the 1880's that laws were introduced to put a stop to the clearances. There are many other beautiful crofting townships like Bettyhill along the coast, easily reached by taking short detours from the main road, and well worth discovering for their magnificent beaches and cliffs. It is only a few miles further to **Tongue**, which stands above the Kyle of Tongue in the centre of Sutherland's north coast. The village has a fine church with a lairds loft or private gallery, and close by are the ruins of Caistail Bharraich (Anglicised to Castle Varrich), a MacKay stronghold that may date back to Viking times. The village also boasts what is possibly the world's most northerly palm tree, a reflection on the mild weather the coast enjoys. The Kyle itself is crossed by a long causeway that offers panoramic views of Ben Loyal and Ben Hope. There is again the opportunity to strike inland from here, down to **Altnaharra** and its hotel, renowned in the Highlands for its hospitality to the weary traveller. The tiny settlement sits in the heart of Sutherland, in the true wilderness of the Flow Country. This type of wetland country is rare in world terms and anyone passing through the area cannot help but be impressed with the scale of it all.

Back on the coast it is a long drive around **Loch Eribol**. A very deep sea-loch, once a rendezvous point for wartime convoys, it is now scattered with fish farm cages. Our journey along the roof of Britain finally turns south at **Durness**. Rather than a compact village Durness is a number of scattered settlements. To the west is Balnakeil and the remains of its 17th century church, which has a monument to Rob Donn, a famous Celtic bard. **Balnakeil Craft Village** is housed in buildings that were once a cold war early warning station, and visitors are welcome to watch the wide variety of crafts being made. On nearby Balnakeil Beach the grave of a Viking warrior was recently discovered. To the north is Faraid Head, noted for its cliffs and seabirds.

To the east is **Smoo Cave**, three vast caverns at the end of a deep cleft in the limestone cliffs with waterfall. The entrance to the first resembles a Gothic arch and the second can be viewed from a platform. A boat is needed to enter the third chamber and see the 80ft waterfall. For information about trips enquire at Durness Tourist Office.

It is possible to go further north and west, but not with your own vehicle. **Cape Wrath** is only accessible by the small, summer only, passenger ferry across the Kyle of Durness. A mini-bus takes you along one of the loneliest roads in Europe, the 11 miles to this the north-western tip of the British mainland. Even on a clear bright day it's easy to imagine that the Cape is more than capable of living up to its foreboding name. The lighthouse here was built in 1827 and on a clear day you can see Orkney to the east and Lewis to the west. To the south of the Cape Clo More cliffs reach up 920ft, teeming with seabirds they are the highest mainland cliffs in Britain. Much of the wild moorland inland is used as an army firing range.

The main road runs down the shore of the Kyle of Durness, a stretch of water a deeper blue and cleaner than many a tropical sea, but most definitely not as warm. At Rhiconich it is well worth diverting west along the B801 to **Kinlochbervie**. Lying at the mouth of Loch Inchard, Kinlochbervie is the most north- westerly of the mainlands great white-fish landing ports. It's worth the detour to see the fish being landed and the boats tied up at the jetty alone, but what is more amazing is the sight of the huge articulated lorries that collect the fish. The road to the village from the south is a typical Highland single track road, narrow, twisting and full of brows. It must take skill and great patience to guide these leviathans of the highway safely. To the west of the village are the crofting townships of Oldshoremore, Oldshorebeg and Sheigra, which have beautiful sandy beaches and wonderful opportunities for pleasant walks. It is another five miles on foot to the spectacular Sandwood Bay and its sea stack, possibly Britain's remotest beach, but worth the effort.

They are cutting a new path for the road south to **Laxford Bridge**, no doubt to ease the passage of the fish lorries. One of few junctions in this area, the traveller has a choice of returning south-east, past Loch Shin, towards Lairg and Dornoch. This long long road passes through one of the least inhabited areas of a sparsely populated region. Driving along you get a real sense of isolation passing one or two lodges and the occasional croft. The first few miles are dominated by the white mountains of Arkle and Foinaven. Arkle is build like a rampart, a brutal pile of a mountain. Directly across the glen is Ben Stack, a total contrast, with its tall spire of a peak, looking just as a mountain should look . At Achfary, beneath the Ben, is Britain's only black and white telephone box. Achfary Estate have been given special permission by British Telecom to paint the local kiosk in keeping with the estate's colour scheme. In the 37 miles to Lairgs the route starts in the mountains, opening out on to moorland along Loch Shin and finally running through lush green pasture approaching the town.

The other option at Laxford Bridge is to continue south which our journey does. The next settlement you'll come across is **Scourie**. It is a picturesque crofting community with a safe bathing beach in the bay. Fishermen amongst you may like to pause here as Scourie is at the heart of a famous Brown Trout fishing area. The village also has a notable war memorial, it's a sad fact that even the smallest remotest communities in these Highlands and Islands have need of a memorial to the war dead. Scourie's is a fine example, its seventeen names guarded over by a kilted soldier.

To the north of Scourie Bay is **Handa Island**. Until as recently as the first half of the 19th century the 12 families that inhabited the island upheld the eldest widow as their leader, the Queen of Handa. They survived on the numerous seabirds, providing meat, eggs and feathers, which they bartered for wool. On the northern coast is The Great Stack, an isolated pillar in a u- shaped inlet. The bird-catchers reached its flat grassy top by rope - going hand over hand 300ft above the waves! The only inhabitants today are the Scottish Wildlife Trust warden and the thousands of puffins, fulmars, shags, gulls, kittiwakes, skuas and auks. Day trips to this 'twitchers' paradise can be arranged with local fishermen in Scourie and nearby Tarbet. RSPB members can stay a little longer as the island has a well- equipped bothy accommodation available to them.

In a landscape of old rock the idea of a concrete bridge blending in seems highly improbable, and yet the bridge that takes the A894 across the lochs at **Kylesku** achieves just that. A graceful design, it has won many awards since being opened by the Queen in the mid-eighties, replacing one of the few mainland to mainland ferries left in Britain. There is a lay-by next to the northern end of the bridge, it offers an ideal spot to pause and take in the view of the bridge and beyond. In one corner of the lay-by there is a Memorial Cairn, erected in 1993, to commemorate the men of the XIIth Submarine Flottila who gave their lives in action. The top secret midget submarine flotilla trained in the local waters, and perhaps their best remembered feat was to seriously damage the German Battleship Tirpitz in a Norwegian fjord.

From Kylesku village pleasure boats take visitors up the lochs to see the seal colonies and **Eas Coul Aulin**, Britain's highest waterfall with a drop of 658ft. It's possible to reach them on foot but be prepared for a walk that will take half a day. Back in the village there's a little inn well worth finding, it's not often you can watch seals play while enjoying a drink.

Just south of the bridge is a side road westward perfect for the dawdler, rolling around the coastline down to the fishing port of Lochinver. Should you be in more a hurry the main road south will get you there quicker, but not by much. This route is dominated by Quinaig to the west, flanked on three sides by roads that each give such different aspects of it, that you could be forgiven for thinking that it was three different peaks. To the south of the mountain lies **Loch**

Assynt. The rather sorry remains of Ardvreck Castle stand on a spit in the loch.

It is at Loch Assynt that the 'fast' road to Lochinver turns west. **Lochinver** has been a major herring port since the 17th century. It is now the largest village in West Sutherland and investment in recent years has seen the construction of a new quay and the port is, together with Kinlochbervie and Ullapool, a major white and shell fish centre. The twisting narrow road to the south demands the drivers complete attention, so undoubtedly the best way to enjoy the glorious scenery is to get out into it on foot.

At the eastern end of Assynt is **Inchnadamph** and its Hotel, which still sells petrol as once did many of the roadside resting places of the Highlands years ago. To the south is Ledmore Junction. Just a few crofts and a telephone box, it again offers the traveller a chance to return to Easter Ross, or as we do press on south and into Inverpolly. At the first hamlet on the road, Elphin, there is the **Scottish Farm Animal Visitors Centre**. Children will love this croft where they can meet many of the traditional breeds of Scottish farm animals, including the seaweed- eating Soay sheep, hairy Highland cattle and thirty other breeds. Almost next door is Knockan and its spectacular cliff. **The Cliff Visitors Centre**, offers two very different trails along and up the cliff, one looking at flora the other at the local geology. Both are fascinating and at the end of the climb you'll be rewarded with great views of the Inverpolly reserve spread out before you.

The land between Loch Inver and Loch Broom is remote and almost uninhabited area of bog, moorland, woodland, cliffs and towering summits. A desolate but beautiful wilderness. At its heart is the **Inverpolly Nature Reserve**, home to many rare plants and animals. The coastline is a shambolic riot of lochs and tiny islands the work of the last ice age, some 10000 years ago. The area is as much water as land, over three hundred lochs and lochans scattered amongst the magnificent mountains. Described by renown Scottish writer Jim Crumley, as 'a glimpse into Valhalla'.

Inverpolly has few settlements and the largest is **Achiltibuie**, reached by the winding road that passes right beneath Stac Pollaidh and through the empty Coigach mountains. Here you will discover on of the most unusual hidden places of Scotland, **The Hydroponicum**. Robert Irvine built this prophetic 'garden of the future'; a garden without soil. With its three distinct climates - Hampshire, Bordeaux and the Canaries - and the spectacle of Strawberries hanging overhead, ripening bananas, passion fruit lemons, figs, vines, flowers and vegetables growing in the far north-west it is an astounding place. The gift shop stocks special growing kits, so you can have a go yourself.

Stac Pollaidh, Inverpolly

Food of a different and more traditional kind is on offer at The Smokehouse. Discover the secrets of smoking and curing of salmon, fish, meat and game at this purpose built smokery, with its viewing gallery and well stocked shop, that has a mail-order service.

Across Badentarbat Bay are the **Summer Isles**. The biggest, Tanera Mor, has been busy for a 1000 years and more. The Anchorage, a sheltered bay, has been used since Viking times; they called the island Hawrarymoir - the island of the Haven. Cruises from Ullapool tour the islands, seeking the seabird colonies and seals, and boats across from Achiltibuie. It is even possible for the fully equipped camper to stay on the island.

In all the 140 miles of coast between Thurso and Fort William there is only one other town, **Ullapool**. Today the main port for the Northern Hebrides, it is the focal point for the sparse and wide spread communities of Wester Ross, and was purpose-built as a fishing centre in 1788 by the British Fishery Society to a plan by Thomas Telford. Now a major tourist centre it still retains a real frontier town feel, specially during the autumn fishing season, when Loch Broom is full of fish factory ships from Eastern Europe and the streets ring with strange tongues from faraway places. The town has a fine hostelry, the **Ferry Boat Inn**, which stands on waterfront. As well as offering meals and B&B, for the real ale enthusiast it offers hand-pulled ales, very much a rare commodity in the Highlands. Directly across the loch is the Altnaharrie Hotel, which is only accessible by private launch from Ullapool, and has an international reputation for its cuisine.

The ferry from Ullapool takes three and a half hours to reach Stornaway, on the Hebridean island of Lewis. The **Outer Hebrides** stretch for 130 miles, a string of islands that in most places rise no more than a few hundred feet, battered by the full force of the Atlantic. Sail west, and the first land you reach is the coast of Labrador. It sounds desolate but you will discover mile after mile of empty beaches with dazzling white sand, unbelievably clear water and breathtaking sunsets. There is also a fascinating range of flora and fauna here, with most islands having at least one nature reserve. The islands have been inhabited for over 6000 years and today some 31,000 people live on the twelve populated islands. The people are Gaels and guardians of a rich culture, perhaps most accessible to visitors in its music. You shouldn't pass up the chance to attend a ceilidh (pronounce Kaylee). There are rich Scandanavian influences here as well. The Vikings ruled the islands from the 9th century until 1280 and many place names are of Norse origin, specially in the north.

It's important to remember that Sundays are treated with a degree of reverence on these islands that has long since vanished in England

and are one of the features that makes life here different. Some ferries don't run on the Sabbath, most Hotel bars and pubs are closed and some B&B establishments would prefer if you book a Sunday night stay on Saturday.

Lewis and **Harris** are actually one island, a pair of siamese twins. Although solidly joined they are very different lands. Lewis is largely moorland, flat and boggy and scattered with a thousand tiny lochs that offer some of the finest and most expensive fishing in Europe. Harris is mountainous, one of the peaks rising to 2622ft. It's western coast has spectacular beaches, the work of the crashing Atlantic waves, whilst the east shelters several small fishing villages.

Stornoway is the capital, and the biggest town in the Outer Hebrides. With the exception of this town of 6000 people Gaelic is the first language of all these islands. It's many years, however, since the death of the last islander to speak no English at all. North of Stornoway is the Black house at Arnol, a vivid re-creation of the old island way of life. There's also a very good local museum at Shawbost. Another sight not to be missed are the famous **Standing Stones of Callanish.** This great stone circle, with its avenues radiating from it, is one of the best preserved sites in Europe. Legend has it that the stones are giants turned to stone for refusing to be baptized by St. Kieran. Just a few miles away is **Dun Carloway,** an Iron Age Broch similar to those on Orkney and Shetland.

On Harris is St. Clement's Church at Rodel or Roghadel (many of these islands places being bi-lingually named). One of the finest churches in the west of Scotland, it contains the magnificent sculptured tomb of Alasdair Crotach Macleod, a tomb he built nineteen years before his death in 1547. The ferry from port of **Tarbert** plys the Little Minch, connect the island with Uig on Skye and Lochmaddy on North Uist. Throughout the islands you'll find men and women hard at work weaving the Harris tweed. The Harris Tweed Association, formed in 1909, prevents imitations. it's a real cottage industry, most houses having a loom on which to work in odd moments. Moves to allow the use of power looms were smartly stopped by the weavers in 1975.

Below Harris are the islands of **North Uist, Benbecula, South Uist,** which are connected by a causeway. Beyond South Uist lie the smaller islands of Eriskay, Barra and Vatersay. There are also innumerable smaller islands, some of which are inhabited. It was from Rossinish on Benbecula that Bonnie Prince Charlie made his famous escape aided by Flora MacDonald. She had, at first, been unwilling to help him, but was eventually persuaded by his famous charm. A cairn stands at the site of her birthplace on South Uist.

Eriskay has made the headlines twice in its long history. First as the spot where Bonnie Prince Charlie landed on his arrival from France in 1745. More recently S.S. Politician was wrecked here with a cargo of 20,000 cases of whisky in 1941. This was the raw material for Sir Compton Mackenzie's hilarious novel 'Whisky Galore', and the wonderful Ealing comedy of the same name. Those bottles are now collector's items, and can be worth several thousand pounds. As an aside Sir Compton owned the Shiant Islands off the coast of Lewis.

Barra is the southernmost of the larger Hebridean islands. It has the only airfield in Britain that is under water twice a day - the scheduled flights landing on the beach at Castlebay. Kisimul Castle stands on a small island in the bay. This was the home of the MacNeils, once notorious for their piracy and vanity. It's said that a servant was employed to stand on the battlements everyday and announce 'MacNeil has dined; Kings, Princes and the rest of earth may now dine'! After decades of neglect an American descendant of the MacNeils has now restored the castle to its former glory.

The islands of **St. Kilda** can safely lay claim to being Britain's most hidden place. The three islands, Hirta, Soay and Boreway lie 50 miles west of Harris, open to the full force of the Atlantic. The main island Hirta has a majesty and power all its own, surrounded on the most part by towering cliffs a thousand feet high. The highest at Conachair, at 1397ft, are the highest in Britain. Incredibly the island was inhabited for centuries by a community of around 200, who clung to life on this barren rock. They finally left in 1930 when their numbers had dropped to an unsustainable 72. The island is now home to a National Trust for Scotland warden and the military, who arrived in the 1950's, building a radar station to monitor the missile test firings from Benbecula. Trust organized summer working parties are the only way for the public to land on Hirta. Britain does have a more remote spot than Hirta, but Rockall 230 miles out in the Atlantic is a pinhead of rock surrounded by the endless ocean.

The choice and frequency of the Hebrides ferry services mean that it is quite possible to island hop starting and finishing your journey at several ports on the mainland. Our journey however returns to Ullapool, to pick up our trail southwards.

Only a few minute drive out of the town, on the A835, is the **Leckmelm Shrubbery and Arboretum.** This ten acre arboretum and two and a half acre walled garden was originally laid out in the 1870's. It lay unattended for 45 years until 1985 and is now gradually being restored. A few miles further along the road is **Corrieshalloch Gorge**, one of the most accessible spectacular sights in this area of the Highlands. A mile long, many rare plants cling to the side of out of harms and the sheep's way. The Falls of Measach tumble 150 feet into the gorge The best view point is the Victorian suspension Bridge which dangles over the falls. Not for the vertigo sufferer, the bridge has a sign recommending that no more than two people go on it at a time!

Just beyond the gorge is Braemore Junction and a choice of roads. The A835 continues through Dirrie More, past Loch Glascarnoch, with its big dam and lonely inn and on back to Easter Ross. Our travels take the A832, keeping with the coast. After following the shore of Little Loch Broom the road turns briefly inland before dropping down to the golden sandy beaches of **Gruinard Bay**. During the last war the island in the bay was used for biological warfare experiments and landing on it was prohibited on it until the Mid-Eighties, when it was cleaned up at great expense. The next bay along is **Loch Ewe**. In the 1940's supply convoys to Russia gathered here and the sides of the loch are scattered with the remains concrete bunkers, pill boxes and anti-aircraft platforms, the castles of the 20th century. There is still a NATO refuelling jetty in the loch. On the surrounding hillside are **Inverewe Gardens**. Plants from many countries flourish in this garden created by Osgood MacKenzie over 120 years ago. They feature eucalyptus from Australia, giant forget-me-nots from South America and Himalayan lilies, giving an almost continuous display of colour. You can take guided walks with the gardening staff and there is a caravan and camping park, restaurant, petrol and plant sales.

Gairloch is very popular with those who love the great outdoors; attractions include golfing, angling, windsurfing, canoeing and boating. Gairloch Heritage Museum has won awards for its displays on the past life of a typical West Highland area from prehistoric time right up to the present day. From Gairloch the road travels down Loch Maree, its banks swathed in ancient Caledonian pinewoods of the sort that once covered much of Scotland. Queen Victoria visited the area in 1870 and at Slattadale the falls were renamed in honour of her visit. The eastern end of the loch is dominated by the mighty Slioch, all 3215ft of it.

Kinlochewe, at the inland end of Loch, was, during the clan wars, one of the most dangerous places in Europe. It lies on the north- east edge of the **Beinn Eighe National Nature Reserve**, the home of the red deer, golden eagle, pine marten and the very rare and shy Scottish wild cat. **The Torridons** are a magnificent part of that Reserve. Held to be the oldest rocks on earth, the bedrock of these mountains are at least 2000 million years old. We tend to see mountains as permanent features but they are no such thing, the Torridons are the mere stumps of much greater peaks, beaten by wind, rain and ice into the peaks of Ruadh Stac Mor, Liathach and Beinn Alligin and their lesser brothers and sisters. These three mountains, all well over 3000ft, overwhelm the landscape with their presence, running a very close second to the Cuillins of Skye as the most individual range of rock in the Highlands.

At Torridon village is a visitor centre with an audio-visual display the describes the wildlife of the reserve, whilst nearby is a static display on he life of the red deer. At the nearby village of Sheildaig there is the opportunity to take a detour around the **Applecross peninsula**. A tortuous round trip takes you on one of the last great motoring adventures of Britain. In good weather, often in short supply, the gradients, hairpins and the 2000ft summit of Bealach na Ba will still leave vivid memories. In winter the road can become a game of Russian roulette. Those who live in Applecross were grateful for the opening of the new road to Sheildaig in 1970, a long diversion but at least an escape route.

After the excitement of Applecross the country calms a little, at least by Highland standards, as our chosen path leads down to **Lochcarron**. Once known as Jeantown it is a lovely little village laid out in typical 18th century style. Along an unclassified road to the west stands Strome Castle. After you have driven around the loch head to Stromeferry it is well worth taking the short detour to the lovely little harbour of **Plockton**. There can't be many villages that have a main street lined with palm trees but this is one of them. From here it is only a short drive to **Kyle of Lochalsh**, until the arrival of the railway from Inverness in 1897 just a bare and rocky headland. It is for now the main ferry port for Skye, as well as the shopping centre for a wide area of Wester Ross. We board the ferry here, there's no booking, just join the queue for the five minute crossing.

There is little subtlety about the scenery of **Skye**, it is dramatic and beautiful whatever the season. Above all it is a paradise for the serious walker and climber. The peaks of the **Black Cuillin** are unlike any other in the land, a landscape from another planet, with towering summits. In winter they offer a special challenge held to be more difficult than any in the Alps and even admiring them from the safety of a road side lay-by it is easy to see why they demand and gain respect from everyone who ventures up their flanks.

Most visitors land at small town **Kyleakin** after a five minute journey across Loch Alsh, taking the ferry gives a real sense of travel that the coming of the new bridge will sadly take away. Near the pier are the forlorn remains of Dunakin Castle, once a stronghold of the MacKinnons of Strath it is now called Castle Moil - 'the roofless castle'.

Along the A850 from Kyleakin is **Luib Folk Museum**. The theme here is the crofting life of Skye early this century. Skye still has

THE HIGHLAND AND ISLANDS

hundreds of crofts - smallholdings which usually have some arable land, a share of the hill grazings and the use of communally held peat banks where fuel can be cut for free, except for the labour involved. Just along the coast is Sconser and the car-ferry to the small island of **Raasay**. Between 1913 and 1919 an ironstone mine was in operation, worked for a time by German prisoners during World War I. The abandoned workings were never tidied up but slowly nature is hiding them again. **Sligachan Hotel** is perhaps the most famous hotel on Skye, standing at the junction of the A850 and A863 it has long been a favourite base for climbers, standing as it does on the doorstep of the Cuillins.

Portree is the capital of Skye and the touring centre of Skye built around a harbour and bay sheltered by the bulk of Raasay. There are many hotels and guest houses to choose from, offering that special Highland hospitality and plenty of shoreline, clifftop and hill walks starting from here to work off all that hospitality. The oldest building is Meall House, which once served as the jail and it is now the local visitors information centre. The tourist information officer working from the condemned cell.

North of Portree even reluctant walkers you can get a taste of the islands flamboyant rock architecture by taking the 45 minute walk up to the hollow beneath the Trotternish Ridge. here stands the **Old Man of Storr**, a 160ft rock pinnacle that looks as if one shove would have it over. The area has the makings of a giants adventure playground, with its colossal boulders, high pinnacles and dramatic overhanging cliffs.

Around the head of the peninsula at **Kilmuir** there is a cluster of thatched dwellings that make up the **Skye Cottage Museum**. Nearby is the graveyard that contains Flora MacDonald's Celtic Cross Memorial Grave. She was the Jacobite heroine who, in the words of the song which recalls a most daring escapade, brought Bonnie Prince Charlie disguised as her maid 'over the sea to Skye'. Today getting to the Outer islands is a lot easier with frequent sailings from the jetty at **Uig** to Harris and North Uist.

Following the road around eventually brings you to **Dunvegan** and its famous castle, which has been the home of the Macleods for at least 700 years. It's full of fascinating and bizarre relics, ranging from the 'Fairy Flag' to letters from Dr Johnson. There are also many items from Jacobite times including a lock of Bonnie Prince Charlie's hair. Legend says the 'Fairy Flag' brings luck in battle and photographs of it were carried by members of the family serving with the RAF during World War II.

Just as members of the Macleod clan head for Dunvegan, members

Flora MacDonald's Memorial Grave, Kilmuir

of the Clan Donald head for Armadale, in the South-east of the island. Here the award winning **Clan Donald Centre** is set in forty acres of restored 19th century exotic gardens. The story of the Macdonalds and the Lord of the Isles is told in a restored section of the castle. From **Armadale** it is possible during the summer to take the ferry to Mallaig. Our journey however returns to the Kyle of Lochalsh, for there is still much to see on our route south.

Along the A87 at the confluence Loch Alsh, Loch Long and Loch Duich stands the castle that is the image of Scotland, **Eilean Donan**, and chosen for the cover of this book. Its picture postcard appeal should perhaps be tempered by the bloody truth of it history, but regardless of it past it remains the most photographed, most painted - irresistible to all who pass this way for the first time. Originally the chief stronghold of the MacKenzies of Kintail, who became Earls of Seaforth, it was later looked after by their bodyguards the MacCraes. In 1331 Randolph, Earl of Moray, decorated the walls with the corpses of 15 men executed in a 'territorial' dispute. Twice besieged, in 1304 and 1579 it met its end during the abortive Jacobite rising of 1719. Garrisoned by Spanish troops under William MacKenzie, fifth Earl of Seaforth, it succumbed to gun fire from three English warships. It remained a ruin until Colonel MacCrae-Gilstrap had it restored as the MacCrae family seat in the 1930's.

At the head of Loch Duich the road plunges up **Glen Sheil**. The five sisters of Kintail and The Saddle cram its air space on both sides. Described as 'the loveliest glen in the west Highlands' it certainly has a bigger landscape than even Glencoe and though blood was shed here aplenty it shares non of that glens perpetual melancholy nor its infamy. Below the mountains at Sheilbridge there is a narrow road into Glenelg, built by General Wade. The road takes us into the land that inspired Gavin Maxwell's book **'Ring of Bright Water'** the wonderful story of his life with the otters. He had a house on the coast; which burned down in 1968 claiming the life of his otter Edal, within a year he was dead, his ashes scattered over the site of his home near Sandaig.

The A87 joins the A82 at **Invergarry**, just a few miles from Fort Augustus, which we have already visited.

In Invergarry village, you will discover a tranquil holiday haven at the **Invergarry Hotel**, a Three Crowns Commended establishment owned and run by Robert MacCallum and his friendly team of staff. Catering to everyone's needs, this charming Victorian hotel offers superb accommodation in ten beautifully furnished and well equipped en-suite guest rooms. The comfortable bar proves a popular meeting place where guests and locals mix easily, exchanging tales of the day's activities over a drink. There is a selection of over forty malt whiskies to choose from, complemented by a wide range of bar meals available both at lunchtime and in the evening. For more formal dining, the hotel's à la carte restaurant offers an extensive menu incorporating the finest Scottish produce freshly prepared to the highest standards to tempt the most discerning palate. Between Easter and October, guests and passers-by can also make use of the hotel's self-service restaurant which serves a wide variety of snacks and meals throughout the day, making this an ideal stopping-off point as you explore the wonderful surrounding countryside.

Invergarry Hotel, Invergarry. 0809-3206 Map Ref: E3

We turn south-east along the Great Glen and the banks of Loch Lochy, before making the climb up to the **Commando Memorial** above **Spean Bridge**. This inspiring sculpture was erected in 1952 to commemorate the Commandos who trained in these mountains and gave their lives in the struggle for freedom. There can be few more worthy spots to contemplate the brave deeds of others, with the wonderful mountains spread out before you.

Just a few hundred yards from the memorial you will find a delightful place to stay at **Old Pines**, a Three Crowns Highly Commended Scandinavian style pine and stone lodge set in 30 acres of breathtaking scenery with views of Ben Nevis from the front door. Charming hosts Niall and Sukie Scott have been welcoming guests here for the past three years and provide very comfortable accommodation in eight lovely en-suite guest rooms, four of which are suitable for the disabled. Beautiful pine furniture and attractive furnishings throughout enhance the Scandinavian feel of the house and all the rooms have that extra personal touch. The spacious conservatory dining room provides the perfect setting in which to savour Sukie's wonderful cooking, with imaginative use of fresh local produce creating a menu to tempt the most discerning palate.

Old Pines, Gairlochy Road, Spean Bridge. 0397-712324
fax: 0397-712433 Map Ref: E4

From the memorial it is a short drive into Spean Bridge Village. Situated off the A86 on the eastern outskirts of Spean Bridge, **Barbagianni Guest House** stands in delightfully laid out grounds which overlook the Ben Nevis mountain range.

Barbagianni Guest House, Trindrish, Spean Bridge. 0397-712437
Map Ref: E4

Sadie and Robert Baldon are warm, welcoming hosts who enjoy sharing their charming home with their many guests. Awarded a Three Crowns Highly Commended rating, Barbagianni Guest House provides very comfortable accommodation in seven attractively furnished, en-suite guest rooms and a varied menu of tasty homecooked fare in the dining room. As you explore both the house and its surrounding grounds, you will find owls are a special feature here, with a collection of over 250 of all shapes and sizes!

There are two routes from Spean Bridge into Fort William. The A82 is fast and direct, but for those of you content to meaner and explore the B8004 from the memorial, passing the Old Pines, and travelling into **Gairlochy** may be a better alternative. This small hamlet that sits on the Caledonian Canal, there are two locks and a swing bridge here and it is a great place to relax and watch the boats as they negotiate the lochs down to the sea at Corpach. Just beyond the bridge you may follow the canal down to the sea or swing right and follow the road up to Loch Arkaig. Up here at Achnacarry is the **Clan Cameron Museum**, housed in a typical 17th century Highland croft house. During his flight from the government forces following Culloden Bonnie Prince Charlie found refuge here, a story told here with the help of many Jacobite artifacts. As well as Clan Cameron memorabilia there are displays covering the histories of the Cameron Regiment, Queen's Own Cameron Highlanders and the Commandos. Open in the afternoons between April and October it is a hidden place well worth discovering, not least for the drive to it. Back at Gairlochy, if you follow the road along the canal down to **Banavie** you will come across the delightfully named Neptune's Staircase, a series of eight locks that raise the canal 64ft. The canal itself was designed by Thomas Telford and completed in 1822.

From here it is only a short drive into **Fort William**, and our first set of traffic lights and roundabout since Thurso! The town is the capital of the Western Highlands and business centre for the whole region. The **West Highland Museum** holds many displays of great historical interest. Be sure not to miss the 'secret portrait' of Bonnie Prince Charlie, a meaningless smudge of colour until viewed in a cylindrical mirror. It dates from a time when any one caught possessing his image would receive the death sentence.

On the edge of Fort William on the Inverness Road, you will find **The Distillery House**, a charming establishment situated within the grounds of the former Glenlochy Distillery on the banks of the River Nevis. The house was originally three semi-detached dwellings used to house distillery staff which have since been converted into a welcoming hotel which carries a Two Crown Highly Commended rating. All seven en-suite guest rooms are beautifully furnished and colour co-ordinated whilst downstairs there is an elegant reading lounge to relax in, complete with leather chesterfield sofas and the unusual feature of an antique wooden crib. With a wealth of sports and leisure facilities available in the area, The Distillery House makes an ideal touring base.

The Distillery House, Nevis Bridge, North Road, Fort William
0397-700103 Map Ref: D4

The town stands at the foot of **Ben Nevis**, the highest mountain in Britain at 4406ft. Thousands who have never climbed a mountain before, or since, have struggled up to the summit, their personal Everest. Though it is perfectly possible to walk up it in a day you need to be wary of the rapidly changing weather, you may never be out of sight of the town but it is a mountain and needs to be treated with the same respect as the peaks of the far north. The easiest route is up the bridle path from Achintee in Glen Nevis, though it has challenges for every level of mountaineering competence. It goes without saying that on the few and far between clear days the views are wonderful.

Achintee Farm, Glen Nevis, Fort William. 0397-702240
Map Ref: D4

Visitors to the beautiful area of Glen Nevis will find a super touring base at **Achintee Farm,** the home of Dianne and Maurice Young which lies adjacent to the walkers route up Ben Nevis. In addition to providing first class accommodation in five beautifully furnished guest rooms, two of which are en-suite, within the house, the Youngs also have two well equipped self-catering flats, a delightful 350 year old cottage and two bunkhouses located in the extensive grounds, which makes this a popular base for climbers and walkers. Dianne's culinary skill makes dining a treat and the farm's location, surrounded by breathtaking countryside, makes this such a peaceful place to stay, you are sure to feel you have finally succeeded in 'getting away from it all'.

Just off the A82 Ballachulish road, overlooking Loch Linnhe and just ten minutes walk from Fort William is **The Grange.**

The Grange, Grange Road, Fort William. 0397-705516
Map Ref: D4

Originally built in 1884, this splendid white house has been sympathetically refurbished by the current owners John and Joan Campbell who for the past three years, have taken great delight in sharing their charming home with their many guests. The Grange's Two Crowns Deluxe rating gives you an idea of the high standard of facilities you can expect and lovely fabrics and antique furniture enhance an air of comfort and elegance. Superior accommodation is provided in three lovely guest rooms, two with spectacular loch views and the attractive dining room provides a relaxed setting in which to savour a full Scottish breakfast.

Driving along the banks of Loch Linnhe it is not far on to Onich and Ballachulish, but to do that would be to miss out on the peninsulas of Ardnamurchan, Moidart and Morvern to the west. So from Corpach where the Caledonian Canal meets the sea we venture westwards, along Loch Eil and on to **Glenfinnan**. There is much to see and admire in this quiet and remote place. Glenfinnan Viaduct carrys the West Highland railway extension from Fort William to Mallaig. The line was built by Sir Robert MacAlpine between 1897 and 1901, and was the first to use concrete in its construction. The 21 arches stand as tribute to 'Concrete Bob' who pioneered its use in construction. **Glenfinnan Station Museum** uses the redundant station buildings to tell the story of the line. The introduction of radio signalling in 1988 swept away three quarters of a centuries working practices and the museum aims to preserve atmosphere of the railway from those times.

South of the station at the head of Loch Sheil stands the impressive **Glenfinnan Monument**. It was at this point that Bonnie Prince Charlie raised his standard in August 1745 and began rallying the clans to support his rebellion. A visitors centre tells the story of the Princes endeavour, which reached as far south as Derby and ended at Culloden.

Less than 12 miles along the A830 at Loch nan Uamh there is a memorial cairn that marks the spot from which Bonnie Prince Charlie sailed for France in September 1746, having wandered the Highlands as a fugitive with a price of £30,000 on his head. He died in 1788, a forlorn drunk. The road from the Loch runs up to **Mallaig**, terminal of the West Highland Line. Once one of the remotest communities in the West Highlands, only accessible by a 40 miles of rough track, it became a major ferry and fishing port. From here you can catch boats to the inner Hebridean islands of Rum. Eigg, Canna and Muck, as well as summer services to Skye and Kyle of Lochalsh.

The road to Mallaig is a dead end, unless you use a ferry, so our journey returns to Lochailort and joins the southbound A861, travelling down through the wonderful scenery of Moidart, in search of one of Scotland's best hidden castles, Tioram on the southern shore of Loch Moidart. Reached by a north bound unclassified road, **Tioram Castle** stands in an islet in the loch. Once the seat of the MacDonalds of Clan Ranald; it was burned on the orders of the then chief when he joined the 1715 Jacobite rising, fearing it might fall into the hands of his enemies the Campbells. Accessible at low tide it offers fine views along the loch.

Continuing south we travel on to **Ardnamurchan**. Almost an island, the tip of this peninsula is the most westerly point on the British mainland, a good 20 miles east of Land's End. The landscape is wild, wind swept and beautifully rugged. It is best not to try to hurry along the road to the point. The single track road has no concept of the straight line, meandering along in a time sapping way. Near the point

Glenfinnan Viaduct, West Highland Line

is the village of **Kilchoan**, where you can cross to Mull on the ferry. Naturally the point is a cul-de-sac, so we must retrace our steps to the A861 heading up Loch Sunan to the village of **Strontian**. If the name seems a little familiar it may be because the village lent it name to the radio active isotope Strontium, discovered here in 1790.

Just beyond the village there is the opportunity to keep heading south on to the Morvern peninsula. We head for **Corran**, and one of the few surviving mainland to mainland ferries in Scotland. This deposits us on the A82 just north of Onich and saves a very long drive around.

Enjoying a peaceful setting on the shores of Loch Linnhe at **Onich**, **Cuilcheanna House** is a welcoming family-run establishment, awarded 3 Q's by the AA and winner of the Guest Accommodation Good Room Award.

Cuilcheanna House, Onich, By Fort William. 0855-3226
Map Ref: D5

Surrounded by wonderful scenery, the small hill to the rear rewards climbers with the most spectacular views. There are eight attractively furnished en-suite guest rooms plus a residents' lounge, dining room and a very comfortable lounge bar in which to relax. A full Scottish breakfast provides the perfect start to the day and each evening you can enjoy traditional Scottish fare, freshly prepared on the premises using the finest local produce. Within the grounds of the house alternative accommodation is provided in a small caravan site with nine fully equipped modern caravans and three cottages. Self catering guests are welcome to make use of the bar and dining facilities.

Right on the banks of Loch Linnhe, **Nether Lochaber Hotel** in Onich makes a delightful base from which to explore this lovely area of Scotland. This charming Victorian Highland inn has been in the same family for over 70 years and is currently run by Sarah Mackintosh, a friendly hostess who offers a warm welcome to her many guests. The cosy bar offers visitors the opportunity to chat with the locals as they enjoy a pint of Scottish ale or a scotch and in the comfortable surroundings of the dining room you can enjoy fine homecooked meals. The four guest rooms are all attractively furnished and well equipped, most with en-suite facilities and the magnificent views across Loch Linnhe are simply breathtaking.

Nether Lochaber Hotel, Onich, By Fort William. 0855-3235
Map Ref: D5

Although the direct route to Glencoe now uses the impressive Ballachulish Bridge to cross Loch Leven, the old road takes a circuitous route around the loch. At its head is the small industrial town of **Kinlochleven**. For over eighty years aluminium has been smelted in this seemingly unlikely place. It was cheap electricity that brought industry here, using the water pouring off the hills to generate the huge amounts needed for the process. The loch also provided access to the sea, essential once for the raw materials in and the finished product out to destinations all over the world. The story of the smelter and the community that grew around it is told at **Kinlochleven Visitors Centre** on Linnhe Road in the town.

Those choosing to cross Ballachulish Bridge may spot the James Stewart Monument overlooking its southern end. James of the Glen had his story immortalized in Robert Louis Stevenson's book 'Kidnapped'. On the southbank the road here splits, the A82 heading east toward **Ballachulish** village and Glencoe, the A828 following the coast of Loch Linnhe south to Oban.

Set on the banks of Loch Leven and boasting magnificent views, the **Ballachulish Hotel** offers the discerning guest superior holiday comforts. As you enter the grand hall with its beautiful array of flowers, the warm, welcoming atmosphere is immediately apparent and you can't help but relax. The thirty en-suite guest rooms are individually styled and furnished to the high standards commensurate with the hotel's Four Crowns Commended grading. In the comfort of the guest lounge with its open log fire you can forget your cares and enjoy a refreshing aperitif before making your way to the elegant surroundings of the dining room, where an extensive menu will tempt your palate with imaginative dishes using the finest fresh local produce, including fish and game, when in season.

The Ballachulish Hotel, Ballachulish. 0855-2606 Map Ref: D5

From here we head west into the village Ballachulish. Keep an eye open for the rather forlorn Caledonian Railway distant signal stood at the roadside, the sole remnant of the branch line that ran from Oban to Ballachulish. For many years the Slate quarries here provided slate for roofs all over the country. The story of the quarries is charted at the Ballachulish Tourist Information Centre. The quarries themselves have been thoughtfully landscaped and now offer pleasant walks in stunning scenery.

Just outside Ballachulish and overlooking the tranquil waters of Loch Leven, you will find a very restful holiday base at **Lynleven**, the charming home of John Alick and Priscilla Macleod. Surrounded by lovely, well-tended gardens, Lynleven is a licensed establishment which carries a Three Crowns Commended rating and is AA and RAC Acclaimed. The eight guest rooms are attractively furnished and equipped for maximum comfort, each with en-suite shower/wc. The spacious dining room offers lovely southfacing views and provides the perfect setting for both a full Scottish breakfast and a tasty homecooked dinner each evening, prepared from fresh local produce. With friendly hosts to welcome you and spectacular surroundings inviting exploration, your relaxing holiday break is complete.

Lynleven, Ballachulish 0855-2392 Map Ref: D5

Glencoe is know the world over for the infamous massacre that took place here in 1692. The story has been told and retold until it has become a legendary tale of treachery. The reality is rather different. King William III and his government realized that to contain the Highland clans by force would be impractical, and so was tempted into using a single act of severity to frighten the clan chiefs. All the clans were ordered to sign an oath of allegiance to the King, MacDonald of Glencoe had been late in giving his, due partly to truculence and partly because of bad weather.

Government troops billeted with the clan, and led by Captain Robert Campbell of Glenlyon, were ordered to make an example of them. It was a botch of a job, at dawn on the 13th of February 38 were slaughtered but 300 escaped. Though there is no excuse for such a bloody act this small clan had an ill-name for thieving and were hated by those on whom it preyed. There have been far worse atrocities committed between the clans yet Glencoe still offends, perhaps because of the abuse of Highland hospitality, and is the one that is remembered. Even today the sign on the **Clachaig Inn**'s door proclaims 'Nae Campbells'. The Signal Rock, near the inn, marks the spot where it all began.

The mountains finish abruptly as the glen opens out on to **Rannoch Moor**. This trackless expanse of peat bog is a daunting sight to even the hardiest of souls. Flat as a loch on a still day, it will take the determined walker three days to cross on foot. Those who have will tell you that after the elation of reaching a summit is long forgotten the memories of crossing Rannoch still burn bright. A charming and yet repellent place, the feeling of desolation the moor imparts penetrates even the cocoon of a car

The West Highland Line runs around its eastern flank, floating on a causeway structure invented by the Romans. In this sea of nothing there are two stations, Rannoch which we have already visited and Corrour, the unlikeliest station in Britain. Inaccessible by road, everything and everyone must come and go by rail (or on foot), the station serves a Youth Hostel and two hunting lodges.

We say farewell to the Highlands here, crossing the Black Mount plateau, having come a very long way from Nairn. Undoubtedly a world apart, the Highlands and Islands give the traveller a taste of a very different way of life.

Tioram Castle, Moidart

CHAPTER ELEVEN

Argyll and Dumbartonshire.

Castle Stalker

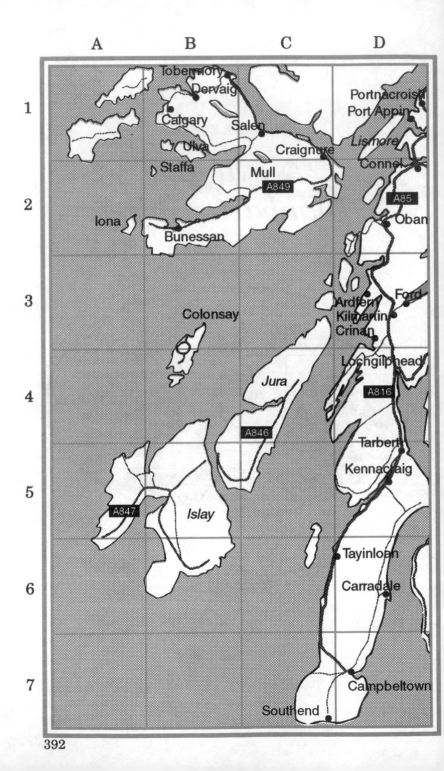

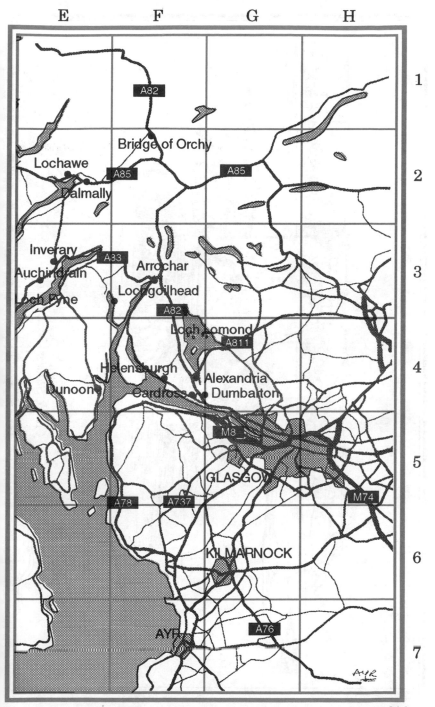

E   F   G   H

A82

1

Bridge of Orchy

Lochawe   A85   A85   2

Dalmally

Inverary   A83   Arrochar   3

Auchindrain   Lochgoilhead

Loch Fyne   A82

Loch Lomond

A811

Helensburgh   4

Dunoon   Cardross   Alexandria   Dumbarton

M8

5

GLASGOW

A78   A737   M74

KILMARNOCK   6

AYR   A76   7

393

Castle Stalker, Loch Linnhe

Argyll and Dumbartonshire.

Once a county all its own, Argyll is now part of the vast Strathclyde Region. We pick up our journey where we left the Highlands, on the A82 high on the Black Mount plateau.

The road comes down off the Black Mount in spectacular style, dropping steeply to Loch Tulla and into the hamlet of **Bridge of Orchy**. There still is a bridge here, though the main road no longer crosses it, as well as a hotel, railway station and a few houses. The former coaching house still sells petrol, once a common occurrence in the Highlands in the days before self-service garages. The original road north from here passed to the east of the Loch until rebuilt in the 1930's, and a stump still runs up to the lonely and historic Inn at Inveroran and a pair of shooting lodges before petering out - the Tarmac having been reclaimed by nature.

A little to the south of the village the B8074 veers south-west off the main road through Glen Orchy and it is this route between the mountains and trees that we take, heading for **Dalmally** and **Loch Awe**. In the village a side road to the south leads up to Monument Hill where, from the memorial rotunda to Gaelic poet Duncan Ban MacIntyre, there is a superb panorama over Ben Cruachan, the two northern arms of Loch Awe and the wooded islets scattered around them. Beyond the village is Kilchurn Castle. Once surrounded by the waters of the loch, this dramatic ruin was built by Sir Colin Campbell of Glenorchy in 1440 and abandoned during the Jacobite rebellions. From the pier beside the railway station at Lochawe village summer cruises round the islands are run by the Edwardian peat fired steam launch Lady Rowena. The Pullman Carriage Tearoom on the pier serves wonderful views to go with its cuppas and sticky buns.

The road now splits, with the A819 heading south toward Inverary. We stay with the A85 and head into the Pass of Brander. At Inverawe at the Smokery and Fishery there is a detailed exhibition on curing and smoking fish in the old tradition, as well as the opportunity to catch some of your own in the trout lochs. Above the pass stands mighty Ben Cruachan, all 3695 feet of it. Hidden inside the mountain is a massive storage power station, water is pumped 1,200ft up the mountain into a vast cavern when electricity demand is low, and at the push of a button released back into Loch Awe creating 400,000 kilowatts for everyone's morning coffee. The only visible evidence of all this is a dam high on the hillside.

At the end of the pass is **Taynuilt** village on the shore of Loch Etive and **Bonawe Iron Furnace**, the preserved remains of a charcoal furnace, or 'bloomery' for iron smelting. Established in 1753, it worked until 1876, forced to close when all the forests had gone.

Self-catering enthusiasts will discover a super place to stay at **Bonawe House,** which lies in secluded grounds just under a mile from Taynuilt village. Within the main house there are four beautifully appointed apartments sleeping between two and six, each equipped and furnished to a very high standard for maximum comfort. Ronnie and Margaret Dalgleish are friendly hosts whose hard efforts have created a very special holiday base for the independent traveller. Within the lovely grounds of Bonawe House there are six self-catering cottages again sleeping between two and six, each with its own individual style and equipped to the same high standards as the apartments. Surrounded by breathtaking countryside offering a choice of various leisure activities, including cruise trips from Oban which is only 12 miles away, your relaxing holiday is complete.

Bonawe House, Taynuilt. 0786-462519 Map Ref: E2

Along the Lochside at **Achnacloich** are some delightful woodland gardens. From the lawns round the castellated mansion the view west is to Mull and east to Ben Cruachan. The gardens are sheltered by oak woods and tall larch and stay free of frost bursting into life early in spring with daffodils, primulas, magnolias and shrubs. It is only a short drive now to **Connel** and its unusual bridge. When the railway still ran north to Ballachulish road and rail traffic shared the bridge, though it was controlled by the railway signalman and trains took priority. In 1966 the line closed but the bridge still remains, today used solely by the motor car.

By crossing the bridge we can explore the coastline north towards Ballachulish, visited in the last chapter. The waters around the west coast teem with life and there's no better place to find out about it all than the **Sea Life Centre**. From loveable seals to the sinister conger eels the centre presents unique display of the native marine life in a stunning setting. The shoreline restaurant has won 'Taste of Scotland' awards and the views could win them as well. As we travel north the road winds its way around the edge of Loch Creran and brings us to **Portnacroish** and one of a handful of views that could only be Scotland - **Castle Stalker**. This tall simple tower keep stands on an islet in **Loch Linnhe** with the mountains of Kingairloch as a backdrop and has been the worthy subject of countless photographs. Home to the Stuarts of Appin it was fortified after the '45 Rising and became a garrison before being abandoned to the elements. In 1965 work began to restore it and it is possible, via a boat trip, to visit it. An appointment is needed and you should call 0883-622768 in Surrey for details.

Close by is **Port Appin** and **Linnhe House** in the village is a large, well appointed Victorian House set in its own grounds and boasting fabulous views over Loch Linnhe and the mountains beyond.

Linnhe House, Port Appin. 0631-73245 Map Ref: D1

Doreen and Roger Evans are the lucky owners of this charming house and they offer their many guests superb accommodation in four beautifully furnished en-suite guest rooms. In addition to a substantial breakfast, evening meals and packed lunches can be provided by prior arrangement, as can various outdoor activities such as pony trekking, fishing and bicycle hire. The accommodation is not suitable for children under five. Pets are not allowed indoors.

From Port Appin you can catch the passenger ferry to **Lismore** out in Loch Linnhe. Only eight miles long and a mile wide, the island was once an important religious centre. The Pictish St. Moluag brought Christianity to Lismore in the sixth century, and the parish church, on the site of the 13th century cathedral of the diocese of Argyll, retains his name. So does the nearby hollowed boulder known for hundreds of years a St. Moluag's Chair. An Iron Age broch stands at Tirefour and the 13th century ruin of Castle Coeffin is perched on a headland facing the mainland of Kingairloch. North of the restored cottages of Port Ramsay, a long-disused lime-kiln moulders, a monument to better trading days. From Achnacroish there is a vehicle ferry service to Oban.

Back on the mainland our journey retraces it steps back across Connel Bridge and turns south toward Oban. **Dunstaffnage Castle** stands off the A85 at Dunbeg. It is a well-preserved example of a 13th century castle with a massive curtain wall and round towers. Originally built by the MacDougal, Lords of Lorne, it was passed to the Earls of Argyll and held on their behalf by the hereditary captains of Dunstaffnage from the late 16th century, falling into disrepair after 1810 when the captains moved out. Angus, twentieth Captain of Dunstaffnage had some of the buildings restored in the 1930's. Though successfully seiged by Robert the Bruce in 1308, Dunstaffnage was always on the side of the government during the Civil War and Jacobite risings

The handsome and lively Victorian port of **Oban** bustles with trade and tourists heading to and from the islands. From the harbour the ferries of Caledonian MacBryne criss-cross the waters around the inner and outer Hebrides. The town is overlooked by one of Britain's finest and most unforgettable follies. John McCaig was a local banker and adhered to the Victorian philosophy that wealth obliged the holder to better the education of the less fortunate. **McCaig's Tower** is an impressive, if ill-remembered, imitation of the Colosseum of Rome, which he'd seen on a visit to Italy. Built between 1897 and 1900, it provided unemployed masons in the area with work and was also intended to house a museum, art gallery and monument to the McCaig family. None of this came about and the hollow shell stands as a folly to his aspirations.

If you are looking to satisfy an appetite then **Heatherfield House,** situated on Albert Road in Oban, is quite clearly a first class restaurant with rooms. Alasdair and Jane Robertson are friendly proprietors who have established a reputation for outstanding cuisine and fine wines and they now feature in many of the leading good food guides. The all-pervading atmosphere is one of comfortable relaxation and your only dilemma is what to choose from the mouthwatering and extensive menu, which incorporates only the finest local produce, with much emphasis on seafood. Having enjoyed a superb dinner, your evening out ends perfectly when you retire to one of seven very comfortable and attractively furnished guest rooms, two of which are en-suite and all equipped to a high standard.

Heatherfield House, Albert Road, Oban. 0631-62681 Map Ref: D2

There is plenty to see around the town. It has its own distillery, founded in 1794, that produces the famous **Oban West Highland Malt** in Stafford Street.. You can take a free trip around the distillery but they would appreciate a call beforehand on 0631-64262. The mysteries of working with glass are revealed at **Oban Glass** on the Lochavullin Estate. Part of the Caithness Glass Group they take the raw materials and transform them into beautiful paperweights. Visitor are invited to see the process from start to finish and they can buy examples of what they've seen made in the factory shop. Collectors of porcelain figures will delight in discovering **Highbank Porcelain Pottery** on Gallanach Road. Here you can take self-conducted tours a see for yourself how their hand-painted china model animals are made.

Situated on the outskirts of the town with excellent views across the bay, **The Manor House** is a superb Four Crowns Highly Commended establishment ideally situated for ferry travellers. Dating back to 1780, The Manor House was built in late Georgian style and was originally the principle residence of the Duke of Argyll's Oban estate. Today, sympathetic refurbishment and decoration has retained its former grandeur and character, whilst providing guests with every modern comfort. Beautifully furnished throughout, all the guest rooms are en-suite and many boast wonderful views over the bay towards the adjacent islands. The elegant dining room provides the perfect setting in which to savour an extensive menu which incorporates a blend of both traditional Scottish and fine French cuisine to appeal to every palate, accompanied by an excellent wine list and after dinner malt whiskies.

The Manor House, Gallanach Road, Oban. 0631-62087 Fax: 0631-63053 Map Ref: D2

Animal lovers of all ages will enjoy a trip to **Oban Rare Breeds Farm Park** where you can meet a variety of rare breed animals seldom seen on modern farms.

Oban Rare Breeds Farm Park, Oban. 063177-608/604 Map Ref: D2

Set within thirty acres of beautiful West Highland countryside, the Park is home to the likes of Susie and Jimmy Wong, a married couple of Vietnamese pot-bellied pigs, Bruce, an Anglonubian goat, and Morag the Highland cow. You can explore the park at your leisure, taking in the various paddocks and enclosures with their fascinating and unusual occupants. The Woodland Walk follows a meanering path, crossing and re-crossing the stream by numerous bridges with bracken, rowan and birch trees, ferns and colourful wildflowers on all sides. Having enjoyed your stroll, the tea-room provides a welcome resting point where you can relax with a refreshing cup of tea, tasty homemade fare and for those warmer days an ice-cream.

Oban Harbour and McCaig's Folly

On the North Pier is **A World in Miniature**, and it is exactly what the name implies. A visit here will have the whole family enthralled.

A World in Miniature, North Pier, Oban   0852-6272 or 0631-66300
Map Ref: D2

There are over 60 displays incorporating the work of 250 quality British miniaturists, with various exquisite room sets carefully

401

designed down to the last minute detail creating an incredibly accurate and lifelike scene. Handmade to the most exacting standards, the quality of work here is astounding; from the tiny Baby's Layette, to the exquisitely engraved miniature Silver Tea-service, from The Dining Room, complete with beautifully laid out table, candelabra and china cabinet, to The Music Room with its perfectly formed musical instruments, including double bass, harpsichord and saxophone. The myriad of delights here will have visitors marvelling at the skill of the artists who have created this beautiful World in Miniature.

Enjoying a peaceful location in its own grounds on Dalriach Road, **The Old Manse** is an attractive detached Victorian house with wonderful views across the bay and the Island of Kerrera to Mull. Run by friendly couple David and Miranda Giles, a warm, homely atmosphere is immediately apparent and you can't help but relax. There are three lovely guest rooms, one twin and two doubles, each with en-suite shower/wc, colour TV and hot drinks facilities. In addition to a full Scottish breakfast, Miranda provides an excellent homecooked dinner, with emphasis on using only the finest fresh ingredients. With the swimming pool, tennis courts and bowling green nearby and of course regular island crossings from Oban pier, your holiday is complete.

The Old Manse, Dalriach Road, Oban. 0631-64886 Map Ref: D2

For us it is back to the harbour and aboard the ferry for Craignure and Mull. The **Island of Mull** may not be as dramatic as Skye or remote as Harris and Lewis but it has a peace and tranquility all its own. Perhaps that's why visitors find themselves drawn back here time and again. Many parts of the rugged coast are easily seen from the main roads, but to discover the islands 'Hidden Places' demands you are a little more adventurous.

Though the main ferry lands at **Craignure** services sail from Lochaline on the Kingairloch Peninsula to Fishnish and from Kilchoan on Ardnamurchan Peninsula to Tobermory. All carry vehicles but the Tobermory service doesn't run on Sundays.

Ferries are not the only departures from Craignure. **The Mull & West Highland Narrow Gauge Railway** run a scheduled service between Old Pier Station and Torosay Castle; the stream and diesel-hauled trains running a mile and half through a superb sea and mountain panorama. **Torosay Castle** whilst not strictly a castle is certainly a prime example of Victorian Scottish Baronial Architecture, and in a magnificent setting. The 12 acres of Italian terraced gardens that surround it are by Lorimer and contain a statue walk and water gardens. If you crossed from Oban you won't have failed to spot **Duart Castle**, stood on a spit of land overlooking the Sound of Mull. The original keep was built in the 13th century, a royal charter of 1390 confirming the lands, including Duart, to the Macleans. The clan supported the Stuarts and the castle, which had been extensively extended in 1633, was taken by the Earl of Argyll in 1674. During the 1745 rising Sir Hector Maclean was imprisoned in the Tower of London and his estate forfeited. Garrisoned for several years it was abandoned and over the next century and a half became a ruin. It was recovered by the family in 1911, when Sir Fitzroy Maclean had it restored as the home of the clan chief

From Duart we head north-east past the ferry pier at Fishnish and on to the small village of **Salen**. Here is the **Glenforsa Hotel** which enjoys an idyllic setting in six acres of secluded grounds overlooking the Sound of Mull.

The Glenforsa Hotel, Salen, Mull. 0680-300377 Map Ref: C1

It is an attractive Scandinavian log-chalet style building where guests are assured of a relaxing break away from it all. Jean and Paul Price are the welcoming proprietors who provided first class accommodation in 16 attractively furnished and well equipped en-suite guest rooms. The fresh Scandinavian feel pervades throughout, enhanced by pine panelled walls and furniture, apparently constructed without using a single nail! Dining is a real treat, as the hotel's inclusion in Taste of Scotland proves. The imaginative menu incorporates both traditional Scottish and international dishes, all prepared using fresh local produce, including a wide range of fresh fish and accompanied by a carefully selected wine list. One thing's for certain, a holiday here is sure to leave you revitalised and refreshed.

We travel on to the islands 'capital' **Tobermory**. The bay here forms perfect shelter for boats, something appreciated by the British Fisheries Society when they nominated Tobermory, together with Ullapool as fishing stations in 1786. The industry flourished for nearly two hundred years and though fish is still landed today most of the boats in the harbour are pleasure craft. The harbour is an ideal base for sailing the islands, and the Sound is the finishing point for the popular Tobermory Yacht Race.

Set high above the town, the **Western Isles Hotel** is an imposing establishment where sumptuous surroundings go hand in hand with friendly Scottish hospitality.

Western Isles Hotel, Tobermory, Mull. 0688-2012 Map Ref: B1

Originally built in 1883, complete refurbishment has provided every modern comfort without detracting in any way from the original charm and character of the building. The 26 en-suite guest rooms are all beautifully furnished and equipped to the highest standards and the restaurant which is open to non-residents offers the finest in fresh

Scottish cuisine accompanied by an excellent wine list. There are breathtaking panoramic views from almost every vantage point and the town itself invites exploration.

One delightful feature of the harbour is its colour-washed houses on the water front. One of these house the Mull Museum, which has a number of displays covering local history. Out in the bay lies the wreck of a ship of the Spanish Armada. The surviving members of her crew were imprisoned in Duart Castle.

Enjoying an enviable position overlooking Tobermory and the Sound of Mull, **Ulva House Hotel** is a splendid 19th century period house where guests can enjoy first class accommodation in a friendly, relaxed atmosphere. Joy and David Woodhouse are welcoming hosts who have built up a reputation for the superb cuisine they serve, with a menu which includes a wide variety of local produce including game and seafood. The six guest rooms are all very comfortably furnished, three with en-suite facilities and some with wonderful views over the bay. David also runs Land Rover Wildlife Expeditions to see eagles, otters, seals and porpoise etc. Guests are given priority, though the trips are open to anyone visiting Western Scotland.

Ulva House Hotel, Tobermory, Isle of Mull. 0688-2044 Map Ref: B1

One place well worth visiting is **Sgriob-ruadh**, a farm lying just outside the town,. Here, using old-fashioned traditional methods, Chris and Jeff Reade make the Isle of Mull cheese, a unique product which had the prestige of winning a Gold Medal at the Paris Cheese exhibition. Using a herd of mainly Fresian cows the milk used is whole and unpasteurised, without any additives or colourings. Using traditional curd knives and milling by hand, the cheese is then pressed into traditional clothbound cylinders using old Victorian cheese presses. The most crucial factor in creating what is without doubt an exceptional cheese, is the turning and ripening, which continues for between 6-12 months, the cheese being stored at the Tobermory Distillery. Fortunately, the Reades make a certain number of smaller 1lb pieces of the cheese, so that you can take home a tasty memento.

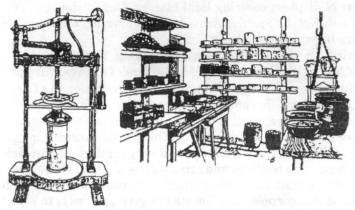

Sgriob-ruadh Farm, Tobermory, Isle of Mull. 0688-2235
Map Ref: B1

From Tobermory our journey turns inland across the Mishnish, though only briefly, as Mull's few roads mostly follow the coast. There are less than one hundred miles of roads on the island but once year in late autumn they are all closed for The Tour of Mull. This famous and very popular car rally sees the island reverberating to the roar of powerful rally cars for a weekend, before returning to peace and quiet. As a point of interest the rally is the only one in Britain to take place on public roads and needs an Act of Parliament, as well as the goodwill of the islanders to take place.

Dervaig is the venue of **Mull Little Theatre**, famous for 25 years as world's smallest professional theatre with just 43 seats housed in a converted cow byre (shed). Shows start at 20.30pm nightly, during the summer season and are a continuous repertory of four varied plays featuring two or more actors.

Nearby is the **Ardbeg House Hotel**, a delightful country hotel set in large gardens with plenty of car parking space. Built during the early 1800s, it was originally a girl's boarding school, but now is a charming hotel offering very comfortable accommodation in eight well equipped guest rooms, four with en-suite facilities and some with four poster beds. The hotel's spacious dining room is, rather appropriately, adorned with numerous items of theatrical memorabilia. The large picture windows overlook the extensive gardens and in these pleasant surroundings you can savour an excellent menu of freshly prepared local produce. Guests can also make use of the hotel's fishing licence on Loch Frisha and boat trips to the nearby islands can be readily arranged.

Ardbeg House Hotel, Dervaig. Mull. 0688-4254 Map Ref: B1

Crossing the Mornish brings you to **Calgary** and the **House of Treshnish**. Sat on a hillside above the village it offers extensive walks through rare and beautiful shrubberies with wonderful views over Calgary bay. Calgary gave its name to the Canadian city in Alberta via the city's founder, Colonel J.F. Macleod, who, it is presumed, was from around here.

Off the coast are the **Treshnish Isles**, which have large seal and seabird colonies. Nearby is **Staffa**. This romantic and uninhabited small island is famous for its basaltic formations and remarkable caves, the best of which is Fingal's Cave. Immortalised by Mendelssohn in his celebrated 'Hebrides' overture, its cluster of columns and man-made-looking symmetry gives the cave a cathedral-like majesty. Other famous visitors to the island have included Queen Victoria and Prince Albert, the artist Turner and poets and writers Keats, Wordsworth, Tennyson and Sir Walter Scott. To reach the Treshnish and Staffa you'll need to join one of the frequent cruises from Tobermory and Oban; bring your sea legs it can get choppy but is so worth taking.

Only a two minute ferry journey from Mull and yet definitely as its brochure says, 'a world apart', the **Isle of Ulva** is an unspoilt haven where you can enjoy nature at its best. As you land at Ulva Pier make sure you call in to The Boathouse, where you can learn the fascinating history of the island and then sample some of the excellent fare in the Tea Room and Oyster Bar. The quality of oysters served here is due to the pure and unpolluted waters surrounding the island in which they are reared. Having enjoyed some refreshment it is then time to discover the hidden secrets of this beautiful island, which although only small, has a wealth of bird, plant and animal life to delight the naturalist in you.

Isle of Ulva, Mull 0688-5243/264 Map Ref: B1

For those who prefer the independence of a self-catering holiday, **Killiechronan** (a mixed agricultural estate) situated just two miles from the village of Salen, provides excellent accommodation in several comfortably furnished cottages sleeping between two and six people. All carry a S.T.B. Four Crown Commended grading which gives you an idea of the facilities you can expect. The Steadings Cottages form a 'U' and offer breathtaking views down Loch Na Keal towards the hills beyond, while the other cottages enjoy individual and secluded locations surrounded by the lovely woodland of the estate.

Killiechronan, Isle of Mull. 0786-462519 Map Ref: C1

Much of the island's coast consists of cliffs and those overlooking the Isle of Inch Kenneth at Gribun are rather unstable. Below them the ruins of an 18th century cottage still lie, crushed under a boulder which killed a young couple on their wedding night. On the roadless shoreline south of Gribun is Mackinnon's Cave. Tradition has it that nobody has ever reached its far end and come out again. Legend also tells of the piper sent into the cave, in the days when people could interpret the music of the pipes, and was heard to play 'woe is me without three hands - two hands for the pipes and one for a sword'. No one knows what he wanted the sword for because no one ever saw him again! It is still possible to get trapped in the cave today as it is cut off at high tide.

There is much more to be discovered along the coast but to reach MacCulloch's Tree you'll need your walking boots. **The Burg** is a massive headland that can only be reached along a track that starts off B8035 on north shore of Loch Scridain near Kilfinichen Bay. It's around five miles to the MacCulloch's Tree, a forty foot high fossil imprint that is around 50 million years old and can only be reached at low tide. The track isn't suitable for cars and can get rough, so suitable footwear is highly recommended.

You'll need those boots again find **Carsaig Arches**. A three mile walk from Carsaig leads to these remarkable tunnels formed by the sea in the towering basaltic rock cliffs, which again are only accessible at low tide. On the way is Nun's Cave, with its curious carvings, said to be by that nuns driven from Iona at the time of the Reformation sheltering here. The path eventually leads right through to the village of **Bunessan** and its tearoom.

Assapol Country House Hotel, Bunessan, Mull. 0681-7258
Map Ref: B2

If it's real home from home comforts you are after, then you would be well advised to stay at **Assapol Country House Hotel**, a Three

Iona Abbey

Crowns Commended establishment in the village run by Harry and Mary Kay. Set in three and a half acres of grounds with wonderful views across Loch Assapol, the house is over 200 years old and was formerly a Manse. Today, after careful renovation, it is a charming hotel, full of character and warmth. Your every need is catered for here, from the seven fully equipped en-suite guest rooms, to the cosy lounge with its roaring log fires for those chilly evenings. Winner of The Taste of Scotland Award, dining is always a pleasure, with a fine homecooked dinner providing the perfect end to a day's activities. With Fionnphort just six miles away, providing access to the islands of Iona and Staffa, plus a wealth of fishing and birdwatching opportunities available, not to mention beautiful hidden beaches to discover, you have all you need for a perfect holiday.

At the end of the Ross of Mull lies the historic island of Iona, which is reached by the passenger only ferry from Fionnphort. In 563 St. Columba with twelve followers founded a monastery here. Often sacked by Norsemen it was replaced in 1203 but, along with the cathedral, fell into decay after first Dunkeld then St. Andrews became the religious capital. Restoration began earlier this century, and the monastery is now the home of the Iona Community (founded by Dr George Macleod in 1938). They have done much of the restoration to the Cathedral, which has a beautiful interior and interesting carvings. The oldest building is St. Oran's Chapel, built in 1080 and now restored. The remains of the 13th century nunnery can be seen and outside the Cathedral is 10th century St. Martin's Cross, 14ft high and elaborately carved. For centuries Iona was the burial place of Scottish kings and chiefs, no less than sixty lay around the abbey and swept by the laden salt spray and winds of the Atlantic it still holds a spiritual atmosphere.

The road through Glen More is traditionally haunted by a headless rider and driving in the darkness on the lonely roads of Mull can take the imagination back to a far different world. Part of that world stands at the head of Loch Buie. Moy Castle, or Lochbuie as it was once called, was the ancient seat of the Maclaines of Buie. Abandoned in 1752, when the nearby Georgian mansion was completed, today this simple oblong tower is wreathed in ivy but still retains a dignity all its own.

Rejoining the main road we have now just about completed our 'tour of Mull' and it is only a short drive back to Craignure and the ferry to Oban. As mentioned Oban is busy with ferries to many islands and you can sail to Tiree, Coll and Colonsay, as well as Barra and South Uist, which we have already visited. These islands are, like the Outer Hebrides, worlds apart, each with its own unique flavour.

For peace, tranquility and breathtaking countryside, **Lerags**

House in the small hamlet of Lerags, three miles south of Oban, is very hard to beat. This small late Georgian Mansion House is the charming home of Doug and Freda Macleod who enjoy sharing it with their many guests. First class accommodation is provided in six en-suite bedrooms and two suites, all tastefully furnished in keeping with the period character of the house. Freda is an excellent cook and in addition to a hearty breakfast, will happily provide an evening meal by arrangement, using only the finest fresh local produce. The grounds of Lerags House reach down to the shores of Loch Feochan, providing spectacular views that would inspire the most amateur artist or poet. This really is the place to come if you want to get away from it all.

Lerags House, Lerags, By Oban. 0631-63381 Map Ref: D2

Self-catering enthusiasts will find **Cologin Chalets** at Lerags provide a perfect base for a family holiday. They offer all the comforts of home in the peaceful surroundings of beautiful Highland countryside, yet are conveniently situated. Sleeping between three and six, each of the chalets is warm and comfortably furnished, providing you with a real 'home' to return to after a day's exploring. For those who enjoy walking, the surrounding countryside provides some spectacular scenery, whilst a short drive will take you to any of four unspoilt sandy beaches. At the end of the day, you can choose to relax quietly in your chalet or make your way to The Barn, Cologin's own inn where you can enjoy a friendly drink with fellow guests. Open all day, there is a wide selection of beer and ale available plus a menu of tasty bar snacks which can be taken back to your chalet if you prefer. For a real taste of Scotland though, make sure you don't miss the traditional ceilidhs and accordion evenings which are held in The Barn each week. With all this on your doorstep and many other leisure activities available within the Oban and Lorne area, a fun-filled holiday is assured.

Cologin Chalets, Lerags, By Oban 0631-64501 Map Ref: D2

We must away to the south, passing the ruin of Glyen Castle on Kerrera, in search of the bridge across the Atlantic. **Clachan Bridge** takes the B844 over the Sound of Seil and on to Seil Island and so crosses the Atlantic - by virtue of the fact that the sound runs into Firth of Lorne, which has some justification in claiming to be an arm of the great ocean. The bridge itself is single span, and was built in 1792, but isn't alone in claiming to span the Atlantic. Beyond the bridge is **Easdale Folk Museum** which chronicles the history of the slate mining industry in these islands.

Back on the A816, to the south is a delight for gardeners. **Arduaine Gardens** command great views of the Slate Islands scattered along Loch Lorn. Recently taken over by the National Trust this noted west coast garden, which shares its entrance with the Loch Melfort Hotel, will be of great interest to plantsmen and garden enthusiasts alike.

For a relaxing day out which the whole family will enjoy, it is worth making your way to **Ardfern** on the B8002. The Yacht Centre at the north end of Loch Craignish is the base of **Kingfisher Cruises**, a venture run by Peter and Christine Proudlove. Kingfisher is the name of their 27ft diesel-powered launch, which offers visitors a choice of cruises in the waters between Jura and Seil. The cruises range from an hour and a half to 4 hours, although longer trips can be arranged, and they give you the opportunity to see a variety of wildlife, seabirds and seals in their natural habitat or visit a nearby island. Kingfisher is fully equipped and meets all the DoT requirements and has a toilet and cooking facilities. The Proudloves also offer a bicycle hire service which can include the option of being ferried to an island and pedal off at your leisure.

Kingfisher Cruises, Hillview, Ardfern. 0852-5662 Map Ref: D3

Formerly a 16th century droving inn, **The Galley of Lorne Hotel** in Ardfern village is now a superb country hotel situated on the banks of Loch Craignish. Owned and personally run by Susana and David Garland, The Galley of Lorne provides guests with the perfect holiday base, surrounded by spectacular scenery and ideally situated for exploring this beautiful area of Mid Argyll. There are nine attractively furnished guest rooms, several with en-suite facilities and all equipped for maximum comfort. However, the highlight of staying here has to be the quality of the food, for which the hotel has a justified reputation. Locally caught seafood is a major feature of the extensive and varied menu, as is local game and other traditional Scottish fare. With a wealth of leisure activities readily available and a warm, welcoming atmosphere to return to each day, your relaxing break is complete.

The Galley of Lorne Hotel, Ardfern. 0852-5284 Map Ref: D3

The village also contains a hidden gem called **The Crafty Kitchen**. Here, in addition to a host of Scottish crafts, books, postcards and local guides, you will find an amazing range of Fairly Traded crafts from Self-Help Groups from across the globe. As well as being a craft centre, as its name suggests, this is also a café which serves excellent homecooked food all day and provides a 'carry out' service at very reasonable prices. The winter months feature occasional 'Special Evenings' when multicultural food is served and although the premises is unlicensed, customers are welcome to bring their own wine. The Crafty Kitchen is open from the week before Easter until the last week in October - Tues, Weds, Thurs, Sun 10.00am - 6.00pm, Fri, Sat 10.00am - 8.00pm (closed on Mondays). Open weekends only in November and December and closed from January 1st.

The Crafty Kitchen, Ardfern. 0852-5303 Map Ref: D3

Our route meanders southwards arriving at **Carnasserie Castle**. This rather imposing tower house was built by John Carsewell upon his appointment as first Protestant Superintendent of the Isles, which following the Reformation of 1650. Mary Queen of Scots later made him Bishop of the Isles, and though he was never consecrated he announced himself as Bishop from that day forth. He is perhaps best remember for publishing the first book in Gaelic, a translation of Knox's 'Liturgy' in 1567. He died in 1572 and the castle passed to Campbells of Auchinleck, later the castle was captured and partly blown up during Argyll's rebellion of 1685.

Almost opposite the castle is the B840, which takes you to the village of **Ford** at the head of Loch Awe. **Tigh an Lodan** (which means "House of the Wet Shoes") is situated in the village. Whilst the locality appears quite remote, it is in fact less than three miles from the main road and is therefore ideally placed for combining the tranquility of staying off the beaten track with exploring the attractions of Mid-Argyll.

A non-smoking establishment, this single storey house is built of red cedar and stands in half an acre of garden, with wonderful views to the fore over the Awe Burn and the hills beyond. Sheila and Donald Bannister are welcoming hosts who offer very comfortable accommodation in three attractively furnished en-suite guest rooms, with extra personal touches that make staying here a real pleasure. Sheila's culinary skill is apparent when you taste the delicious three course dinner she provides each evening. The accommodation is unsuitable for small children, but well behaved pets are welcome.

Tigh an Lodan, Ford. 0546-81287 Map Ref: D3

At **Ederline Estate** about a mile from the village you will find the perfect base for a self-catering country holiday.

Ederline Estate, Ford. 0546-81223 Map Ref: D3

The estate has three small stone-built cottages to let, sleeping between two and seven people. Each is simply furnished in traditional style and equipped with all the basic amenities you need, including firewood for a crackling log fire in the evenings. The estate is surrounded by beautiful countryside and is a haven for ramblers and birdwatchers, whilst for the fishing enthusiast, the gamekeeper at Keeper's Cottage can supply permits for various Lochs at very reasonable rates.

The B840 runs on up the side of the loch through the Eredine Forest emerging 20 miles later just below Dalmally, which we visited earlier. You'll meet few other vehicles on the single track road as it ducks and weaves between the trees and along the shore, passing through several tiny hamlets. An asides to our travels it is never the less a relaxing saunter on a fine day.

The small village **Kilmartin**, back on the A816, has the rather sorry remains of the castle that housed Rector Carsewell before he went up in the ecclesiastical world and move up the road. Rather more interesting is the churchyard which has a number of fascinating medieval carved grave slabs and large fragments of at least two 16th century crosses. The grave slabs commemorate Malcolm of Poltalloch and to this day there is a member of the family with the same name.

Visitors to Kilmartin will discover a lovely place to stay called **Cornaig**, a large country house built in 1867 and like so many large houses of that era, formerly a Manse. The home of Catriona and Jim McAuslan, Cornaig is open all year round and carries a Two Crowns Commended grading. There are five comfortable and well furnished guest rooms, two with en-suite facilities and a separate guest lounge to relax in. The atmosphere is warm and friendly and an added personal touch is that each evening at around 9pm, Catriona serves her guests tca and coffee with homemade cakes and biscuits.

Cornaig, Kilmartin. 0546-5224 Map Ref: D3

In the area to the south-west of the village towards the sea at Loch Crinan is the most concentrated site of prehistoric memorials in Scotland. Bronze Age burial cairns and standing stones are reached by the country roads around the Poltalloch estate. Further south, a footpath goes up to outstanding rock of Dunadd, where an Iron Age fort became the capitol of the sixth century kingdom of Dalriada. The path leads to a hilltop where the earliest kings of Scotland were crowned.

Also near Kilmartin, **Tibertich** provides a tranquil holiday base for visitors to this lovely part of Scotland. Set within a working sheep and cattle farm, Tibertich is the home of welcoming hosts Barbara and Chris Caulton who, between March and October, provide very comfortable accommodation in three attractively furnished guest rooms. In addition to a farmhouse style breakfast, they will readily provide packed lunches and homecooked evening meals by prior arrangement. Should you prefer, you can opt to stay in their lovely self-catering cottage, which is available all year round. For the fishing enthusiast they even have fishing rights on the local loch.

Tibertich, Kilmartin. 0546-81281 Map Ref: D3

Whether you prefer bed and breakfast or self-catering accommodation while on holiday, **Achnashelloch Farm** just 3 miles north of Lochgilphead village caters ideally for those seeking a quiet country break away from it all. Set within a 120 acre working beef cattle farm, this charming 200 year old farmhouse provides very comfortable accommodation in three beautifully furnished guest rooms. Breakfast is enjoyed in the pleasant dining room, with its attractive collection of blue and white china and in the evening you can relax in the comfort of the lounge. Self-catering guests can choose to stay in Shepherds Bothy Apartment which sleeps up to four or the

Byre Apartment which sleeps four to six. Both provide all essential amenities and the farm's location makes it ideal for day trips all over Argyll.

Achnashelloch Farm, by Lochgilphead. 0546-605273 Map Ref: D4

We continue down the A816 into **Lochgilphead**. A quiet resort, it stands on the Crinan Canal which links Loch Fyne with the Sound of Jura via a series of fifteen locks. Started in 1776 by James Watt, the canal was designed to facilitate travel for business people and locals who had previously had to sail the 130 miles around the Mull of Kintyre. The terrain proved to be difficult, skilled labour was scarce, and money ran out several times before the canal was finally opened in 1809, bringing the Western Isles and the west coast of Scotland to within easy reach of the Clyde and Glasgow.

Highbank Porcelain, Highbank Industrial Estate, Lochgilphead.
0546-602044 Map Ref: D4

It is also home to **Highbank Porcelain**, one of Scotland's most successful potteries. Originally established as a producer of hand decorated vases, today Highbank also creates exquisite porcelain animals, with over 100 different models available. A staff of 20 skilled craftsmen and women have developed a style and beauty within their work that is immediately recognisable, making Highbank sculptures popular the world over. Whilst here, visitors can enjoy a short guided tour of the pottery and watch the various stages of work in progress. Afterwards you can linger in the gift shop, which in addition to selling Highbank seconds, also stocks a wide range of quality Scottish crafts.

It's certainly worthwhile visiting the tiny village of **Crinan**, at the head of the canal, which still has a delightful character today. One of the grandest sights in Scottish sailing occurs early on the morning of Glasgow Fair Monday in July, when the second leg of the Tobermory Race starts from Crinan. On the turn of the tide, the whole fleet of around 200 yachts races away through the maze of islands towards the Sound of Mull.

Our Journey now take us down the longest dead end in the land, all sixty odd miles of it. Travellers have a choice of route down to Tarbert and on to Kintyre. If time is of the essence the A83 from Lochgliphead still provides great motoring but if you are content to meander and explore then the unclassified road south from Crinan or the B8024 make a delightful choices, with plenty to discover. At the southern end of Loch Sween stands its castle, high on a rock on the eastern shore. This is probably the oldest stone castle in mainland Scotland, built in the mid-12th century, and destroyed by Sir Alexander Macdonald in 1647. Around the promontory is St. Columba's Cave, traditionally associated with the Saint's arrival in Scotland. A mile north of Ellary on Loch Caolisport the cave contains a rock-shelf with an alter, above which are carved crosses, and a large basin, perhaps a stone age mortar, that may have been used as a font. The cave was occupied from the middle ages, and in front are traces of houses and the ruins of a chapel.

To the south on the B8024 at Kilberry is a fine collection of late medieval sculptured stones. Two miles north of our destination, on the A83, stands **Stonefield Castle Hotel Gardens**. The 60 acres of shrubs and woodlands surround a baronial house, designed by Sir William Playfair in 1837, on a dramatic site beside Loch Fyne. Some of the Himalayan rhododendrons are as much as 100 years old and there are also rare trees and shrubs from as far a field as South Africa and New Zealand.

Tarbert is the gateway to Kintyre, and the harbour to which a rather handy ferry arrives from the Cowal Peninsula, saving the long drive around Loch Fyne. Kintyre itself is all but an island it was here that in the 11th century Magnus Barefoot, having been granted any land he could take his ship around 'with rudder in place', dragged his ships across the narrow strip of land and claimed Kintyre. From nearby **Kennacraig** sail the ferries to Islay, Jura, and Colonsay. These islands are reputed to receive more sunshine than anywhere else in Britain. Of course it does rain but even in bad weather they retain a dramatic beauty. The waters are incredibly clean and there are deserted golden beaches everywhere. **Colonsay** should be explored on foot, there are few roads anyway and keep an eye out for the wild goats that were originally kept for milk. At low tide it is possible to walk across to Oronsay, of the south coast. It was once a sanctuary and there's the remains of a 14th century abbey. It is said that any criminal who could support himself here for a year and a day would be set free, which would be a feat today let alone centuries ago. On a clear day you may catch sight of Ireland, St. Columba did, which is why Iona is now famous and Oronsay isn't. **Jura** is as peaceful and quiet as they come, rugged and majestic and surprisingly free of castles. It is here that George Orwell wrote '1984', and on the very northern tip is the Gulf of Corryvreckan and its infamous whirlpool. This treacherous tide- race is very dangerous for small craft and the noise it makes can be heard from a considerable distance.

The largest of these islands, **Islay** is rightly famous for its fine malt whiskies, their distinctive flavour a result of the peaty water. There are several distilleries on the island and many single malts to choose from but most of this individual brew goes into blended whisky and few blends don't contain Islay malt. If you journey to the island be sure not to miss Kildalton Cross, carved in the 9th century by a mason from Iona, it is widely considered the finest in Scotland. At the village of Bowmore is the unusual Circular Church, built so as to give the devil no hiding place. Part of Daniel Campbell's planned village of 1769 and is believed to be a copy of an Italian design.

Back on Kintyre the traveller is offered the convenient choice of main road or back road to Campbeltown. The A83 follows the peninsula's Atlantic seaboard while the B8001 twists, dips and climbs along the coast above the Kilbrannan Sound, overlooking Arran. As they both achieve the same destination they make for a excellent round trip.

We are sticking to the A-road for now, heading for the village of **Tayinloan** and the ferry to **Gigha Island**. The island is noted for its ancient standing stones, for fine Celtic carvings, springy shell-sand turf and peaceful beaches. Views extend from the peaks of Jura to hills of the Irish coast, faint on the south-western horizon. But best of all on this island is the wooded gardens of **Achamore House**, where the collection of rhododendrons, azaleas and other exotic flowering shrubs has taken forty years to create and is now in the hands of the National Trust for Scotland.

Further down the coast at Glenbarr Abbey is the **Clan Macalister Museum**, full of artifacts telling the story of this Kintyre clan. The road turns inland above Machrihanish Bay, noted for its surfing, and into **Campbeltown**. The township once boasted thirty-four distilleries but nowadays gets by with just the two. In Campbeltown Loch there is a small island called Davaar. At low tide you can walk out to it along a single spit. There is a life-size painting of the crucifixion in a cave here, done in 1887 by one Archibald MacKinnon. He returned at the age of 80 to renovate the picture himself.

Nearing Campbeltown from the north along the A83, if you look for the 30mph sign and take the second left about 50 yards after this, you will find yourself on a farm road and about half a mile from the main road, driving through a farmyard, you will discover one of Kintyre's hidden gems - **Balegreggan House**. Built in 1861, this charming house stands in two acres of lovely grounds with wonderful views over Campbeltown Loch. Morag and Bruce Urquhart are super hosts who provide excellent accommodation in four attractively furnished, en-suite guest rooms. Bruce is a historian and will happily fill you in on some the local history. Morag prepares a substantial Scottish breakfast and will be delighted to serve an evening meal too if required, with guests invited to bring their own drinks if they wish. The Urquharts also have a luxury two-bedroomed self-catering apartment for guests preferring greater independence.

Balegreggan House, Balegreggan Road, Campbeltown.
0586-552062 Map Ref: D7

It's doubtful that many come only as far Campbeltown and don't take a run out to the end. The route passes through the village of **Southend**, who's beach is dominated by Dunaverty Rock. Know locally as 'Blood Rock' it was the site of a Macdonald stronghold and in 1647 saw about 300 people put to death by Covenanters under General Leslie, hence the name.

Knockstapplemore Farm can be found at Southend, and its self-catering cottages make super holiday bases. Phillip and Jackie Hazeldine are the friendly owners of this 100 acre beef and sheep farm and they have converted old stone barns to create four lovely cottages, all equipped with every modern convenience yet retaining an air of old world charm, with exposed beams and stone walls. Set on the hillside overlooking the Mull of Kintyre, the views from the farm are simply breathtaking and walking through this lovely scenery you will be rewarded with a rich variety of bird and wildlife. Guests are welcome to walk across the farm land and there is plenty of room for pets, even ponies! However if you haven't got your own with you, pony trekking along with fishing and various other activities can easily be arranged.

Knockstapplemore Farm Cottages, Southend. 0586-83208
Map Ref: D7

To the west in nearby Keil are Columba's Footsteps. Tradition has it that the Saint's first footstep on Scottish soil were near Southend. The footsteps are imprinted in a flat topped rock near the ruin of an old chapel. The Mull Of Kintyre (who can forget the song) itself is deserted save for its lighthouse and those who've come to admire its splendid views towards Ireland, just 12 miles distant.

Our journey back north on the B842 passes several places worth noting. At **Saddell**, nine miles north of Campbeltown, are the remains of an abbey built in the 12th century by the Lord of the Isles. Though only the walls are standing there are several carved tombstones of interest. A little further north are the gardens of **Carradale House**. This walled garden from around 1870 has a colourful shrubbery that thrives on Kintyres mild climate and a wild garden with laid out paths. The island south of **Carradale** harbour has the remains of a vitrified fort, one of several in Scotland, its stone walls fused together by great heat. You can walk across to the island except during high tide.

Set in its own extensive grounds in the village, with wonderful views towards the Isle of Arran, **Carradale Hotel** makes an excellent holiday base for visitors to this lovely part of Argyll. Built some 80 years ago, this delightful establishment is owned and personally run by Morag and Marcus Adams who put great emphasis on the warmth of welcome all their guests receive. The hotel is beautifully furnished throughout and very comfortable accommodation is provided in thirteen well equipped en-suite guest rooms. Dining is a pleasure, with a small, but imaginative menu offering mouthwatering dishes created using the finest local produce, particularly fresh fish. With various leisure activities available, ranging from squash, shooting, fishing and golf, on the adjacent 9 hole course, for the energetic and sauna and sunbed treatments for those wishing to relax, it seems your every need is catered for.

Carradale Hotel, Carradale. 0583-3223 Map Ref: D6

At the village of **Claonaig**, during the summer months, you can take the short ferry journey across the Sound to Arran, which we visited in Chapter Three. Along the coast lies **Skipness Castle**, which, despite an order to destroy it during the Argyll rising of 1685, stands looking out over the Isle of Arran. Built by the MacSween's in the late 1200's it ended its days as a farmstead before being taken into state care.

We must jump back north to Lochgilphead now to continue our saunters. On the outskirts of the town are **Kilmory Castle Gardens**, which were started in 1770 and include over one hundred varieties of rhododendrons, some of which were supplied to Kew Gardens. If you enjoy gardens a few miles further up the A83 you can indulge your passion further at Crarae Gardens.

Five miles from Inverary is the **Auchindrain Old Highland Township**. One of very few West Highland villages to survive almost completely unchanged it gives a fascinating insight into life on a joint tenancy farm in the late 18th century. The original longhouses and barns of the period are still standing and have most of their period furnishings and equipment. It really is an informative place and there is also a useful visitors' centre, shop and lovely picnic area. Not far north of Auchindrain the road passes close to the **Argyll Wildlife Park**. This 60 acre site has one of Europe's largest collections of wildfowl, with a large collection of owls and many rare native species. From here it is only a short drive into **Inverary**.

Situated just off the A83 Campbeltown Road at Inveraray, **Creag Dhubh** makes a lovely holiday and touring base for visitors to the area. Set in 2/3 acre of lovely gardens, this attractive 150 year old house was formerly a Manse of the Free Church of Scotland, but is now the charming home of Janice and Richard MacLugash, who between March and the end of November, enjoy sharing it with their many guests. There is a separate guest lounge to relax in and very comfortable accommodation is provided three spacious and attractively furnished bedrooms, one with en-suite bathroom and all with TV and hot drinks facilities.

Creag Dhubh, Inveraray. 0499-2430 Map Ref: E3

The wonder of the small town of Inverary is its magnificent Castle,

425

which is the home of the Duke of Argyll. The project of building a new castle was conceived by the third Duke in 1746. The castle is best known for its decor and interiors. The original building was by Roger Morris, with help from William Adam. Take a look around the interior as the relics, furniture and paintings are superb, including portraits by Gainsborough, Ramsay and Raeburn. Outside, the grounds are extensive, with many pretty walks, some by waterfalls on the River Aray. In the grounds you'll find the **Combined Operations Museum**, which portrays the lives and achievements of the hundreds of Commandos and assault troops that trained here during the Second World War. Inverary Bell Tower is 126ft high and houses Scotland's finest ring of bells and the world's second heaviest ring of ten bells.

Inveraray Jail is an innovative and award-winning museum, providing visitors with a vivid insight into prison life during the 1800s. Very much a 'Euro-museum', virtually all the information has been translated into French, German and Italian to help the overseas visitor. Sit and listen to trials in progress in the magnificent 1820 courtroom and then as you wander through the prisons taking in the atmosphere of 'life behind bars', you can talk to warders, prisoners and matron, all in period costume and watch the 'prisoners' performing traditional tasks such as picking oakum. The Torture, Death and Damnation exhibition is not for the fainthearted, with its gruesome details of mediaeval punishments. Having 'escaped' you can browse in the Jail shop which in addition to a fine range of Scottish crafts and books, has some unusual Jail souvenirs.

Inveraray Jail, Church Square, Inveraray. 0499-2381 Map Ref: E3

Dundarave Castle stands just a few miles north of the town on the shores of Loch Fyne. Nearly four hundred years old, and is the principle seat of the MacNachtan clan. Built in 1539 by the 12th chief of the clan MacNachtan, the castle itself is a grade A listed building its survival only ensured when it was restored from a roofless and ruinous state by Sir Andrew Noble in 1906, who set about making the castle habitable. He retained the original character of the old tower and added two further wings which enclosed a courtyard. Today it is possible to soak up the atmosphere and views in comfort as this magnificent castle is now a luxury hotel.

Our route rounds the head of Loch Fyne to the junction of the A83 and A815. The A83 takes you into Glen Croe and over to Loch Long but our travels turn south to explore the Cowal Peninsula. Close to the junction in the village of Cairndow you will find **Strone House** with its magnificent views and gardens. These contain the northernmost cork tree in Europe and the 188ft 'Grand Fir', the tallest tree in Britain.

Several roads criss-cross the peninsula and offer round tours full of Loch, forest sand Mountain scenery. We shall stick to the coast of Long Fyne, passing through Strachur and on down the B8000. Of note on the long but wonderful run around the coast is **Castle Lachlan**. It was first mentioned in a charter of 1314 and the ruins stand on a promontory overlooking Loch Fyne. It is the ancient home of the MacLachlan of MacLachlan. Today the clan Chief, Madam MacLachlan of MacLachlan lives in a nearby 18th century castle mansion, and if you happen to be a MacLachlan she welcomes family members by appointment.

At the end of the peninsula an unclassified road can take you down to **Portavadie** where the summer season ferry crosses to Kintyre. The nearby village of Kames was once a hive of industrial but now only the striking red-sandstone Ironworks Cottages and institute survive. Beyond the village a minor road peters out on the bleak moorland, in a hidden place that drivers should hold dear. Up here John McAdam had a tar-works, though he never thought to bind his famous gravel 'Macadam' road surface with it. A cairn was erected here in 1931 using the few stones that remained from the tar-kilns.

Our meanderings turn once again north through Tighnabruaich overlooking the Kyles and the Isle of Bute. This 16 mile stretch of water which presents a constantly changing view of great beauty and there are two special viewing points on the roadside with plenty of information on the wonderful vistas. The path we're taking briefly rejoins the A886 at Glendaruel. The name is an interesting one which has its origins in a battle fought in 1110 AD between Meckau, who was the son of Magnus Barefoot, the King of Norway, and the Scots. The Scots won and threw the bodies of their slaughtered enemies into the river, which flows through the Glen, turning the water red with their blood. The river became known as the Ruail, and the glen as Glen-da-ruail or glen of red blood'.

Again forsaking the A roads we take the pass through Glen Lean, on of the remotest and least inhabited areas of the peninsula. This emerges from the mountains and forests at **Holy Loch**, supposedly so named because a boat bringing consecrated soil from the Holy Land floundered in the loch. Until recently the loch contained a fleet of deadly American nuclear submarines but today the waters are only disturbed by pleasure craft and the fish.

At the mouth of the loch is **Dunoon**, a much favoured resort since the 18th century. The peace of the waterfront today is a far cry from the dark days of the 17th century, when the old castle was the scene of a bloody massacre. The Campbells of Argyll took advantage of a temporary truce to capture their enemies the Lamonts, and killed two hundred of them, throwing the bodies into a hastily dug pit. The grave was only discovered in the 19th century when a road was being built. There is now a memorial to those who died there. The lover of Robert Burns was from Dunoon and there is a statue to 'Highland' Mary Campbell at the foot of Castle Hill.

If you are looking for somewhere to stay the **Ardfillayne Hotel** will ideal. Offering the best of everything, from the idyllic location in 16 acres of natural woodland garden overlooking the Firth of Clyde to the first class cuisine in the intimate, candlelit ambience of Beverley's Restaurant, your relaxing break away from it all is complete.

Ardfillayne Hotel, West Bay, Dunoon 0369-2267 Map Ref: E4

The seven en-suite guest rooms are beautifully furnished and equipped for maximum comfort and the all-pervading atmosphere is one of bygone Victorian elegance and charm. With the finest in Scottish cuisine accompanied by one of Scotland's most exclusive wine cellars, you can be forgiven for feeling you have tasted heaven after staying here and one thing is sure, you will want to return time and again, a good base for a memorable holiday.

Not far awat from Dunoon is its near neighbour Kirn, and here too there is a good base from which to explore the area. The **Enmore Hotel** is situated on Marine Parade, with the most glorious views of the Clyde reaching out from its grand position. The hotel is the perfect place to stay if you wish to enjoy the many attractions of Dunoon, standing at the gateway to the Western Highlands with all its delights. From here you will be able to soak in the atmosphere of this genteel town, with the hotel's modern amenities catering for a wide range of interests and activities.

The fifteen rooms, all with finely tiled bathrooms en-suite, are everything one might expect from this fine hotel with views to the sea, mountains or to the gardens. They are individually furnished, comfortable and welcoming, and the perfect tonic to greet you after a long day's sightseeing.

Our hosts Angela and David Wilson were happy to give us guidance on what to see and to do during our stay. This was a great bonus, and helped to make our time here more pleasurable and interesting. It is their personal touch that ensures the hotel is such an inviting place in which to stay, and often guests will find fresh flowers, fruit and chocolates in their rooms upon arrival.

The Enmore Hotel, Marine Parade, Kirn, Dunoon. 0369-2230
Map Ref: E4

There are three attractive lounges in the hotel and an inviting cocktail bar, which is just the place to unwind and chat for a while before dinner. The food in the elegant restaurant is superb, and the hotel is justly praised for its five course 'Taste of Scotland' meals and excellent value. To complement our meal there was an extensive wine list which should cater for every palate. The hotel even has its own squash court, what better way to work up an appetite.

The Enmore Hotel really is a taste of the best of Scotland and you will enjoy your stay here, whether you come for a short break or make it your base for a longer holiday. The time of year is unimportant. The warmth of welcome from the Wilsons will more than make up for inclement weather.

Leaving Dunoon we go back around Holy Loch and up the shore of **Loch Eck**. In the loch is the rare Powan fish that is common only to this loch and to Loch Lomond. It is a species of fresh water herring that is believed to have been trapped here and left in the loch at the end of the last ice age. At the southern tip of the loch is the Younger Botanic Garden, which has a truly wonderful display of trees and shrubs. At the northern end of the loch are the **Lauder Memorials**. For a time Sir Harry Lauder lived at nearby Glenbranter House, which has now been demolished. During his stay his only son, John, was killed in the Great War and Sir Harry erected an obelisk on a knoll a short distance from the loch. In the same enclosure is a Celtic Cross, a memorial to Lady Lauder who died in 1927.

Passing through Struchar once again we turn right onto the B828 and into Hell's Glen. The narrow twisting road is hemmed in by thick forest on both sides as it wends its way down to the village of **Lochgoilhead**. You might like to take advantage of the renowned watersports facilities here, which include boating, fishing, sub-aqua, diving and water skiing. Lochgoilhead also possesses a golf course and at Drimsyne Leisure Centre between November and March you can have ago at the famous sport of 'curling'.

In this same arena during the months of April to October you can experience Europe's first indoor 'sheep show' the which pays testament to the hill farming that has been going on here for generations. There are a collection of nineteen breeds here on show, and if you though that sheep were too stupid to train the stage show will certainly change your mind. The accompanying talk is impressive, highlighting the differences between the breeds and their wool and meat. Visitors are also able to see a demonstration of sheep shearing and see the dog and sheep handling that is so essential to life here.

Lochgoilhead makes an ideal centre for enjoying the benefits of the **Argyll Forest Park**. The park was created in 1933 and covers some hundred square miles, much of which is open to exploration via Forestry Commission tracks. Some of the many activities that you can enjoy in the surrounds include hill walking, climbing and pony trekking. Along the loch from the village is **Carrick Castle** which stands right on the loch's edge. Built in the 14th century this great rectangular keep was originally a Lamont stronghold but ended up in the hands of the Campbells - a result of the Dunoon massacre? - and was used by the Scottish kings as a hunting lodge. During the Earl of Argyll's rebellion of 1685 the then owner Sir John Campbell of Carrick was called to book in Edinburgh over his small part in events. In 1715 he perhaps wisely came down firmly on the side of King George. Later in the century the castle passed on to the Murrays, Earls of Dunsmore and by 1800 had been abandoned. There are plans to have it restored as a residence, if it does happen someone will awake every morning to the most wonderful view.

We now climb up the B828 from Lochgoilhead to the summit of Glen Croe pass, the famous **'Rest and Be Thankful'**. It is the highest point on the road between **Loch Long** and Loch Fyne. Here the traveller is 803ft above sea level. There is a small car park at the summit at which can be found a stone marker inscribed with the summits name and the name of the regiment that built the military road over the pass in 1768. Still a laborious climb from Loch Long from the car park you get an excellent view of the original road, which takes a much less direct path up the glen.

Thankfully our journey decends through this rather dour glen to the banks of the loch and, passing the old Admiralty Torpedo testing station, round to **Arrochar**. From the village you get clear views of the curious rock formations at the summit of 2991ft Ben Arthur which give it its popular nickname The Cobbler.

We are again faced with a choice of routes at Arrochar. Both take us through to Dumbarton, our ultimate destination the easterly one along Loch Lomond and the westerly along Gare Loch. The route through to **Gare Loch** takes you along the A814, which barely deserves the classification. Narrow and twisting with numerous brows and glimpses of the waters of Loch Long through the trees it is a pleasant drive but hardly a route for heavy traffic. Climbing over a narrow neck of land affords wonderful views to the west of the mountainous and fjord like meeting of the two lochs. Along the banks of Gare Loch is the Naval submarine base of Faslane.

Beside the base is Faslane Cemetery and a memorial to a tragedy. In 1917 the unluckily numbered submarine K13 sank during acceptance trails. Trapped behind watertight doors 32 of the crew drowned, and it would be 55 hours before the rest of the crew were brought to safety from the bed of the loch. The memorial and the surrounding headstones form the outline of a submarine, a poignant reminder of the bravery of submariners.

At the mouth of the loch is the residential town and sailing centre of **Helensburgh**. This was the birthplace of John Logie Baird in 1888, a man who some hold has a lot to answer for by inventing television. An example of his 'televisor' is displayed in the Templeton Library. Another famous Scot left his mark on the town, Charles Rennie Mackintosh designing **Hill House** on Upper Colquhoun Street. Considered one of his finest works it stands overlooking the Clyde from the top level of this hillside town.

Another architectural curiosity are the red painted devils on the roof of a house on William Street, the pair appear to be glaring at the church across the road. From Helensburgh it is only a short drive to along the Clyde to Dumbarton.

Enjoying a peaceful, rural setting in **Cardross**, just five miles east of Helensburgh, **Kirkton House** makes an ideal base from which to explore The Trossachs, Loch Lomond and other popular places of interest. Awarded a Three Crowns Highly Commended grading and with a host of other credits to its name, this converted 18/19th century farm is the charming home of Stewart and Gillian Macdonald who offer their many guests first class accommodation and food, in an atmosphere of friendly hospitality. The large garden provides ample play space for younger family members and baby sitting can be arranged with prior notice. Dining here is a treat and as the premises are licensed you can accompany a superb dinner with the drink of your choice and what's more, your friends are welcome to join you.

Kirkton House, Cardross. 0389-841951 Map Ref: F4

We return briefly however to Arrochar taking the other route out of the village over to Tarbet, on the banks of **Loch Lomond**. The name of the town is said to come from the words tarrain bata' or portage which stems from the time when Haakon of Norway allegedly dragged

Mackintosh's Hill House, Helensburgh

his vessels over the land separating the two waters and to have sailed into Loch Lomond to carry on his raids of pillaging and looting.

The Loch is one of the largest expanses of water in Scotland, big enough to contain its own islands, some of which are inhabited. Many of the islands have legends or stories that surround them. Inchlonaig or 'Yew Island' was so named as it was supposed to have been planted with yew trees for the use of King Robert the Bruce's archers. On Inchcailloch the Fallow deer have been established since the 14th century and an ancient burial ground surrounds a ruined church, once the centre of a mainly landward parish. There is a ferry service to Inchcailloch from Balmaha on the eastern shore, which is also the base for the mailboat that visits the occupied islands on Monday, Thursday and Saturday mornings. Only a few people live on the islands, most of which are heavily wooded, but there are farms on some and the mailboat provides an important year-round link.

The A82 runs the full length of the west coast of the loch from Ardlui in the north, to Balloch in the south. If you are feeling a little more adventurous much of the east side of the loch is the sole preserve of the walker, enabling you to take full advantage of the beautiful scenery from the southern tip of the loch right up towards the towering form of Ben Lomond. There is certainly plenty of opportunity to get out onto the water as well with every kind of watersport catered for at centres up and down the loch. If there is a down side to Loch Lomond it must be its ease of access, at holiday times it can get very busy. Out of season though it can seem like you have the whole loch to yourself.

Loch Lomond is of course well known for that famous song about its 'Bonnie, Bonnie Banks', which has its base in an old celtic belief that when a man dies in a foreign land his spirit returns home by the 'Low Road'. The song itself is said to refer to the last moments together of two Scottish soldiers captured by the English during the '45 Rebellion. One was to be set free, whilst the other was to be taken to England and executed. His spirit would thus go home by the 'low road' while his friend returned by the 'high road'. Make the most of your time here as you will be in good company. Both Wordsworth, Coleridge and Sir Walter Scott were also visitors.

Alexandria, just south of the loch, holds a piece of motoring history. The Argyll was Scotland's first home-produced car, the first being built in 1899 and proving a great success. The magnificent neo-Baroque factory built on the company's early success still stands. Unfortunately it proved rather too magnificent. The Italian marble interior, 500 washbasins for the workforce and a resident Italian works choirmaster proved the companys undoing and it collapsed in 1908.

Our final call on this long journey is the town of **Dumbarton**, which lies above Glasgow and sits guarding the Clyde approaches. Like Stirling, it has its origins in its fortified rocks, from which it derives its name and was once the capital of the ancient kingdom of the North Britons who were a Pictish tribe. The name Dumbarton is derived from 'Dun-Briton' which literally means the fort of the Britons. There was a castle on the rock in medieval days, and William Wallace was reputedly imprisoned here for a short time and it was from here that Mary Queen of Scots set sail for France to marry the Dauphin. The castle was last used as a barracks during the First World War and is now a museum which makes an interesting visit.

Being situated on the river, the town developed an important position, controlling the pass into the Highlands and was formerly a port for Glasgow until the deepening of the river in the 19th century. There were famous shipyards in Dumbarton and one great ship that was launched from here was the famous clipper 'Cutty Sark'. The name incidentally was taken from an incident in Robert Burns' 'Tam O'Shanter', and means short shift or skirt. Another maritime gem in the town is the fascinating **Denny Ship Model Experiment Tank**. This was the first purpose-built experimental tank to be used commercially, and was built for the renowned Denny Shipbuilding Company in 1882. For over one hundred years it was used to test designs for hulls and propellers until it was taken over in 1984 by the Scottish Maritime Museum. The tank itself is over 300ft long with a depth of 10ft and there are many other interesting exhibits from this fascinating industry including workshops, model making processes and the drawing office.

It is in Dumbarton that our travels draw to a close, only a few miles from the Erskine toll bridge and the motorways back to Glasgow, Edinburgh and England. Scotland is a country all its own, independent of nature and full of great contrasts. A library of travel books would not do this nation justice, only finding out for yourselves could do that, and if our search for hidden places has whetted your appetite to explore, pointed you in the right direction or solved a puzzle then our book has succeeded. Safe journey.

TOURIST INFORMATION CENTRES

Centres in **bold** are open all year round.

ABERDEEN, St. Nicholas House, Broad Street. 0224-632727
ABERFELDY, The Square. 0887-820276
ABERFOYLE, Main Street. 0877-2352
ABINGTON, Welcome Break Service Area, Jct 13, M74. 0864-2436
ABOYNE, Ballater Road Car Park. 03398-86060
ADEN, Aden Country Park, Mintlaw. 0771-23037
ALFORD, Railway Museum Station Yard. 09755-62052
ANSTRUTHER, Scottish Fisheries Museum. 0333-311073
ARBROATH, Market Place. 0241-72609
ARDROSSAN, Ferry Terminal Building, The Harbour. 0294-601063
AUCHTERARDER, 90 High Street. 0764-663450
AVIEMORE, Grampian Road. 0479-810363
AYR, 39 Sandgate. 0292-284196

BALLACHULISH, Visitors Centre 0855-2296
BALLATER, Station Square. 0339-755306
BALLOCH, Balloch Road. 0389-53533
BANCHORY, Bellfield Car Park. 0330-22000
BANFF, Collie Lodge. 0261-812419
BETTYHILL, Clachan. 06412-342
BIGGAR, 155 High Street. 0899-21066
BLAIRGOWRIE, 26 Wellmeadow. 0250-872960
BONAR BRIDGE. 08632-333
BO'NESS, Hamilton's Cottage, Bo'ness Station. 0506-826626
BONNYRIGG, The Library, Polton Street. 031 660-6814
BOWMORE, Isle of Islay. 049 681-254
BRAEMAR, The Mews, Mar Road. 03397-41600
BRECHIN, St. Ninians Place. 0356-623050
BROADFORD, Isle of Skye. 0471822-361
BRODICK, The Pier, Isle of Arran. 0770-2140

BUCKIE, Cluny Square. 0542-34853
BURNTISLAND, 4 Kirkgate. 0592-872667

CALLANDER, Rob Roy & Trossachs Visitors Centre, Ancaster Square. 0877-30342
CAMPBELTOWN, MacKinnon House, The Pier. 0586-552056
CARNOUSTIE, The Library, The High Street. 0241-52258
CARRBRIDGE, Main Bridge. 0479-84630
CASTLEBAY, Main Street, Isle of Barra. 08714-336
CASTLE DOUGLAS, Markethill Car Park. 0556-2611
COATBRIDGE, The Time Capsule, Buchanan Street. 0236-21066
COLDSTREAM, Henderson Park. 0890-882607
CRAIGNURE, Isle of Mull. 06802-377
CRAIL, Museum & Heritage Centre, Marketgate. 0333-50869
CRATHIE, Car Park. 03397-42414
CRIEFF, Town Hall, High Street. 0764-652578
CULLEN, 20 Seafield Street. 0543-40757
CUPAR, Fluthers Car Park. 0334-52874

DALBEATTIE, Town Hall. 0556-610117
DALKEITH, The Library. 031 663-2083
DAVIOT WOOD, A9 by Inverness. 0463-772203
DORNOCH, The Square. 0862-810400
DRYMEN, Drymen Library, The Square. 0360-60068
DUFFTOWN, Clock Tower. 0340-20501
DUMBARTON, Milton, A82 Northbound. 0389-42306
DUMFRIES, Whitesands. 0387-53862
DUNBAR, 143 High Street. 0368-63353
DUNBLANE, Stirling Road. 0786-824428
DUNDEE, 4 City Square. 0382-27723
DUNFERMLINE, Maygate. 0383-720999
DUNKELD, The Cross. 0350-727688
DUNOON, 7 Alexandra Parade. 0369-3785
DURNESS, Sango. 0971-511259

EDINBURGH, Edinburgh and Scotland Information Centre, 3 Princes Street. 031 557-1700
EDINBURGH AIRPORT, Tourist Information Desk. 031 333-2167
ELGIN, 17 High Street. 0343 - 542666
ELLON, Market Street Car Park. 0358-20730
EYEMOUTH, Auld Kirk, Manse Road. 08907-50678

FALKIRK, The Steeple, High Street. 0324-20244
FORFAR, The Library, West High Street. 0307-467876
FORRES, Falconer Museum, Tolbooth Street. 0309-672938
FORT AUGUSTUS, Car Park. 0320-6367
FORT WILLIAM, Cameron Square. 0397-703781
FORTH ROAD BRIDGE, by North Queensferry. 0383-417759
FRASERBURGH, Saltoun Square. 0346-518315

GAIRLOCH, Auchtercairn. 0445-2130
GALASHIELS, Bank Street. 0896-55551
GATEHOUSE OF FLEET, Car Park. 0557-814212
GIRVAN, Bridge Street. 0465-4950
GLASGOW, 35 St, Vincent Place. 041 204-4400
GLASGOW AIRPORT, Tourist Information Desk. 041 848-4440
GLENROTHES, Kingdom Centre, Lyon Square. 0592-754954
GLENSHIEL. 059981-264
GOUROCK, Pierhead. 0475-39467
GRANTOWN ON SPEY, High Street. 0479-2773
GRETNA, Gateway to Scotland, M74 Service Area. 0461-38500
GRETNA GREEN, Old Blacksmith's Shop. 0461-37834

HAMILTON, Road Chef Services, M74 Northbound. 0698-285590
HAWICK, Common Haugh. 0450-72547
HELENSBURGH, The Clock Tower. 0436-72642
HELMSDALE, Coupar Park. 04312-640
HUNTLY, 7a The Square. 0466-792255

INVERARAY, Front Street. 0499-2063
INVERNESS, Castle Wynd. 0463-234353
INVERURIE, Town Hall, Market Place. 0467-20600

JEDBURGH, Murray's Green. 0835-863435
JOHN O'GROATS, County Road. 095581-373

KEITH, Church Road. 05422-2634
KELSO, Town House, The Square. 0573-223464
KILCHOAN. 09723-222
KILLIN, Main Street. 0567-820254
KILMARNOCK, 62 Bank Street. 0563-39090
KINCARDINE BRIDGE, Pine'n'Oak, Kincardine Bridge Road, Airth. 0324-417759
KINGUSSIE, King Street. 0540-661297
KINROSS, Kinross Service Area, Jct 6, M90. 0577-863680
b, 19 Whytecauseway. 0592-267775
KIRKUDBRIGHT, Harbour Square. 0557-30494
KIRKWALL, 6 Broad Street, Isle of Orkney. 0856-872856
KIRRIEMUIR, High Street. 0575-74097
KYLE OF LOCHALSH, Car Park. 0599-4276

LANARK, Horsemarket, Ladyacre Road. 0555-661661
LANGHOLM, High Street. 03873-80976
LARGS, Promenade. 0475-673765
LERWICK, The Market Cross, Isle of Shetland. 0595-3434
LEVEN, South Street. 0333-429464
LINLITHGOW, Burgh Halls, The Cross. 0506-844600
LOCHBOISDALE, Pier Road, Isle of South Uist. 08784-286
LOCHCARRON, Main Street. 05202-357
LOCHGILPHEAD, Lochnell Street. 0546-602344
LOCHINVER, Main Street. 05714-330
LOCHMADDY, Pier Road, Isle of North Uist. 08763-321
LOCHRANZA, Isle of Arran. 0770-83320
LOSSIEMOUTH, Station Park, Pitgaveny Street. 0343-814804

MALLAIG. 0687-2170

MAUCHLINE, National Burns Memorial Tower, Kilmarnock Road. 0290-51916

MELROSE, Priorwood Gardens. 089682-2555

MILLPORT, 28 Stuart Street. 0475-530753

MOFFAT, Churchgate. 0683-20620

MONTROSE, The Library, High Street. 0674-72000

MOTHERWELL, The Library, Hamilton Road. 0698-251311

MUSSELBURGH, Brunton Hall. 031 665-6597

NAIRN, 62 King Street. 0667-52753

NEWTON STEWART, Dashwood Square. 0671-2431

NORTH BERWICK, Quality Street. 0620-2197

NORTH KESSOCK, by Inverness. 0463-73505

OBAN, Argyll Square. 0631-63122

OLDCRAIGHALL, Granada Service Area, A1, Musselburgh. 031 653-6172

PAISLEY, Town Hall, Abbey Close. 041 889-0711

PEEBLES, High Street. 0721-720138

PENCRAIG, A1 by East Linton. 0620-86006

PENICUIK, The Library, 3 Bellman's Road. 0968-673286

PERTH, 45 High Street. 0738-38353

PERTH, Inveralmond, A9 Western city by-pass. 0738-38481

PETERHEAD, 54 Broad Street. 0779-71904

PITLOCHRY, 22 Athol Road. 0796-472215

PORTREE, Meall House, Isle of Skye. 0478-2137

PRESTWICK, Boydfield Gardens. 0292-79946

RALIA, A9 North, by Newtonmore.

ROTHESAY, 15 Victoria Street, Isle of Bute. 0700-502151

ST. ANDREWS, 78 South Street. 0334-72021

SANQUAR, Tolbooth, High Street. 0659-50185

SELKIRK, Halliwell's House. 0750-20054

SPEAN BRIDGE. 0397-81576

STIRLING, Dumbarton Road. 0786-475019

STIRLING, Broad Street. 0786-479901

STIRLING, Motorway Service Area, Jct 9, M9. 0786-814111

STONEHAVEN, 66 Allardice Street. 0569-62806

STORNAWAY, 4 South Beach Street, Isle of Lewis. 0851-703088

STRANRAER, 1 Bridge Street. 0776-2595

STRATHHAVEN, Town Mill Arts Centre, Stonehouse Road. 0357-29650

STRATHPEFFER, The Square. 0997-421415

STROMNESS, Ferry Terminal Bulding, The Pier Head, Isle of Orkney. 0856-850716

STRONTIAN. 0967-2131

TARBERT, Pier Road, Isle of Harris. 0859-2011

TARBERT, Harbour Street, Kintyre. 0880-820429

TARBET - LOCH LOMOND, Main Street. 03012-260

THURSO, Riverside. 0847-62371

TILLICOULTRY, Clock Mill. 0259-752176

TOBERMORY, Isle of Mull. 0688-2182

TOMINTOUL, The Square. 0807-580285

TROON, Municipal Buildings, South Beach. 0292-317696

TURRIF, High Street. 0888-63001

TYNDRUM, Main Street. 08384-246

ULLAPOOL, West Shore Street. 0854-612135

WICK, Whitechapel Road. 0955-2596

Index

A

Aberdeen	318
Aberdour	204
Aberfeldy	279
Aberfoyle	257
Aberlady	171
Aberlour	336
Abernethy	229
Aboyne	310
Achiltibuie	368
Airdrie	144
Alexandria	435
Alford	317
Alloa	253
Alloway	111
Altnaharra	365
Alyth	293
Annan	62
Anstruther	212
Arbigland	77
Arbroath	300
Archiestown	336
Ardencraig	127
Ardfern	413
Ardnamurchan	385
Ardrossan	115
Armadale,Lothians	192
Armadale,Skye	377
Arran	115
Arrochar	431
Athelstaneford	186
Auchindrain	425
Auchterarder	275
Auchtermuchty	229
Auckengill	359
Aviemore	348
Ayr	111
Ayton	9

B

Ballachulish	387
Ballantrae	103
Ballater	311
Balmoral Castle	314
Balquhidder	263
Banavie	380
Banchory	310
Banff	326
Barr	104
Barra	372
Bearsden	141
Benbecula	371
Berwick on Tweed	5
Bettyhill	364
Biggar	152
Birnam	286
Bishopston	131
Blackwaterfoot	122
Blair Atholl	280
Blairgowrie	290
Blantyre	146
Boat of Garten	348
Bolton	186
Bonar Bridge	356
BonchesterBridge	48
Bo'ness	244
Bonnybridge	245
Braemar	314
Brechin	302
Bridge of Allan	255
Bridge of Orchy	395
Brodick	115
Broughty Ferry	298
Bunessan	409
Burntisland	204

C

Cairnryan	98
Calgary	407
Callander	260
Campbeltown	422
Canonbie	63
Cape Wrath	365
Cardross	432
Carluke	149
Carnoustie	300
Carradale	424
Carrbridge	349
Castle Douglas	81
Catacol	124
Cellardyke	212
Chirnside	16
Coatbridge	144
Coldingham	9
Coldstream	19
Colmonell	104
Colonsay	421
Comrie	276
Connel	396
Corrie	124
Coupar Angus	290
Craignure	403
Crail	216
Cramond	195
Crathie	314
Creetown	89
Crianlarich	265
Crieff	276
Crinan	420
Cromarty	354
Crossford	149
Cullen	329
Culloden	349
Cumnock	110

Cupar	226	Elgin	338	Glendaruel	427
D		Elie	209	Glenfinnan	383
		Elvanfoot	152	Glenluce	94
Dailly	105	Errol	288	Glenrothes	233
Dalbeattie	80	Eskdalemuir	64	Glenshee	290
Dalkieth	191	Eyemouth	7	Golspie	357
Dalmally	395	**F**		Gourock	128
Dalmellington	109			Grangemouth	241
Dalry	124	Failford	110	Grant'n on Spey	348
Denholm	52	Fair Isle	361	Grantshouse	15
Dervaig	406	Fairlie	126	Great Cumbrae	126
Dingwall	354	Falkirk	244	Greenlaw	18
Dirleton	173	Falkland	230	Greenock	128
Dollar	255	Fettercairn	309	Gretna Green	61
Dornoch	356	Finavon	295	Guardbridge	222
Douglas	150	Findochty	330	Gullane	172
Doune	256	Fintry	245	**H**	
Drummore	95	Fochabers	332		
Drumnadrochit	352	Ford	415	Haddington	183
Duddingston	166	Fordyce	327	Hamilton	146
Dufftown	335	Forfar	295	Harris	371
Dumfries	68	Forres	339	Haugh Of Urr	81
Dunbar	176	Fort Augustus	352	Hawick	48
Dunbeath	358	Fort William	380	Helensburgh	432
Dundee	295	Fortingall	280	Helmsdale	357
Dundonald	113	Fortrose	354	Humbie	190
Dunfermline	203	Fraserburgh	325	Huntly	333
Dunkeld	285	Freuchie	231	**I**	
Dunoon	428	Fyvie	323		
Duns	17	**G**		Inchnadamph	368
Dunure	107			Innerleithen	33
Dunvegan	375	Gairloch	373	Inverary	425
Durness	365	Gairlochy	380	Inveresk	170
Dyce	321	Galashiels	32	Invergarry	378
Dysart	206	Gargunnock	246	Invergordon	356
E		Garlieston	93	Inverness	350
		G'house of Fleet	88	Inverurie	321
Earlsferry	209	Gattonside	31	Iona	411
East Calder	192	Gifford	188	Irvine	113
East Linton	179	Girvan	105	Islay	421
Eccles	18	Glamis	293	**J**	
Edinburgh	161	Glasgow	137		
Edzell	302	Glencoe	388	Jedburgh	43

John o'Groats	359	Langholm	63	Mauchline	110
Jura	421	Largs	125	Maybole	109
K		Lasswade	191	Meigle	293
		Lauder	26	Melrose	29
Keith	332	Laurieston	88	Melvich	364
Kelso	19	Leadhills	152	Menstrie	255
Kennacraig	421	Legerwood	28	Methlick	322
Keppel	126	Leith	169	Mey	359
Kilchoan	385	Lendalfoot	104	Millport	126
Kildonan	122	Lerwick	363	Milngavie	141
Kildrummy	317	Leswalt	97	Mintlaw	324
Killin	266	Letham	228	Moffat	66
Kilmarnock	113	Leuchars	223	Moniaive	71
Kilmartin	417	Leven	207	Montrose	301
Kilmuir	375	Lewis	371	Moonzie	225
Kilrenny	216	Lilliesleaf	42	Morebattle	24
Kilsyth	142	Linlithgow	194	Motherwell	145
Kilwinning	114	Lismore	398	Mull	402
Kingsbarns	219	Loch Awe	395	Musselburgh	169
Kingussie	349	Loch Ewe	373	Muthill	275
KinlochRannoch	280	Loch Fyne	427	**N**	
Kinlochbervie	366	Loch Katrine	258		
Kinlochewe	373	Loch Linnhe	397	Nairn	347
Kinlochleven	387	Loch Lomond	432	Nenthorn	21
Kinross	273	Loch Ness	352	New Abbey	74
Kippen	246	Lochcarron	374	New Cumnock	110
Kippford	79	Lochearnhead	264	New Galloway	89
Kirkbean	77	Lochgilphead	419	Newburgh	228
Kirkcaldy	206	Lochgoilhead	430	Newcastleton	54
Kirkcowan	92	Lochinver	368	N'mill-on-Teviot	52
Kirkcudbright	86	Lochmaben	66	Newton Stewart	91
Kirkoswald	108	Lochranza	124	Newtongrange	191
KirkpatrickFleming	63	Lochwinnoch	131	Newtonmore	349
Kirkwall	361	Lockerbie	65	Nisbet	42
Kirriemuir	294	Longniddry	171	Norham	19
KyleofLochalsh	374	Lossiemouth	339	North Berwick	173
Kyleakin	374	Lower Largo	208	North Uist	371
Kylesku	367	Lybster	358	**O**	
L		**M**			
				Oban	398
Lairg	356	Macduff	326	Old Dailly	105
Lamlash	120	Machrie Bay	122	Oldmeldrum	321
Lanark	148	Mallaig	383	Onich	385

Orkney	360	Sandhead	95	Town Yetholm	25

P

		Sanquhar	73	Troon	112
		Scapa Flow	361	Turnberry	107
Paisley	131	Scourie	366	Turriff	324
Peebles	36	Selkirk	40	Tyndrum	265
Penicuik	192	Shetland	363	
Pennan	326	Skye	374	**U**	
Penpont	70	SthQueensferry	196	Uddingston	146
Perth	286	South Uist	371	Uig	375
Peterhead	325	Southend	423	Ullapool	370
Pettycur	205	Southerness	78	Ulva	407
Pitlochry	282	Spean Bridge	378	**W**	
Pittenween	211	Spey Bay	332	
Plockton	374	St. Abbs	11	Wanlockhead	151
Port Appin	397	St. Andrews	221	Wemyss Bay	126
Port Glasgow	130	St. Boswells	25	West Barns	176
Port Logan	95	St. Kilda	372	Whitekirk	176
PortofMenteith	257	St. Monans	211	Whithorn	93
Port Seton	170	Staffa	407	Wick	358
Port William	94	Stair	110	Wigtown	92
Portavadie	427	Stirling	246	Woodside	292
Portknockie	330	Stonehaven	310	Wormit	224
Portnacroish	397	Stornoway	371	
Portobello	169	Stranraer	97	
Portpatrick	96	Strathaven	146	
Portree	375	Strathblane	245	
Portsoy	327	Strathdon	317	
Prestonpans	170	Strathpeffer	354	
		Stromness	360	

R

		Strontian	385	
Raasay	375	Swinton	17	
Reston	15	**T**		
Rhubodach	127			
Rosehearty	326	Tarbert,Harris	371	
Rosyth	203	Tarbert,Kintyre	420	
Rothesay	126	Tayinloan	421	
Rumblingbridge	273	Taynuilt	396	
Ruthwell	63, 70	Thorburn	71	
		Thurso	360	

S

		Tillicoultry	254	
Salen	403	Tobermory	404	
Saline	235	Tomintoul	317	
Saltcoats	114	Tongue	365	

THE HIDDEN PLACES

If you would like to have any of the titles currently available in
this series, please complete this coupon and send to:
M & M Publishing Ltd
Tryfan House, Warwick Drive,
Hale, Altrincham, Cheshire, WA15 9EA

	Each	Qty
Scotland	£ 5.90	......
Northumberland & Durham	£ 5.90	......
The Lake District & Cumbria	£ 5.90	......
Yorkshire and Humberside	£ 5.90	......
Lancashire & Cheshire	£ 5.90	......
North Wales	£ 5.90	......
South Wales	£ 5.90	......
The Welsh Borders (Salop, Here & Worcs)	£ 5.90	......
The Cotswolds (Gloucestershire & Wiltshire)	£ 5.90	......
Thames and Chilterns	£ 5.90	......
East Anglia (Norfolk & Suffolk)	£ 5.90	......
The South East (Surrey, Sussex and Kent)	£ 5.90	......
Dorset, Hampshire and the Isle of Wight	£ 5.90	......
Somerset, Avon and Dorset	£ 5.90	......
Heart of England	£ 5.90	......
Devon and Cornwall	£ 5.90	......
Set of any Five	£20.00	
Total	£	

Price includes Postage and Packing

NAME...

ADDRESS..

....

................................POST CODE..

Please make cheques payable to: M & M Publishing Ltd